Political Theory and Australian Multiculturalism

POLITICAL THEORY AND AUSTRALIAN MULTICULTURALISM

Edited by
Geoffrey Brahm Levey

Berghahn Books
New York • Oxford

Published in 2008 by

Berghahn Books

www.berghahnbooks.com

©2008, 2012 Geoffrey Brahm Levey

First paperback edition published in 2012.

Library of Congress Cataloging-in-Publication Data

Political theory and Australian multiculturalism / edited by Geoffrey Brahm
Levey.
  p. cm.
"In association with the Academy of the Social Sciences in Australia."
Includes bibliographical references and index.
ISBN 978-1-84545-492-0 (hbk.) – ISBN 978-0-85745-629-8 (pbk.)
  1. Multiculturalism–Political aspects–Australia–Congresses. 2. National
characteristics, Australian–Congresses. I. Levey, Geoffrey Brahm. II. Academy of
the Social Sciences in Australia.

HN850.Z9M846 2008
305.800994–dc22   2008019353

British Library Cataloguing in Publication Data
A catalogue record for this book is available from the British Library

ACADEMY OF THE SOCIAL
SCIENCES IN AUSTRALIA
Promoting the Social Sciences

This book is the product of a workshop sponsored by the Academy of
the Social Sciences in Australia and the Australian Government Department
of Immigration and Multicultural and Indigenous Affairs.

Printed in the United States on acid-free paper

ISBN 978-0-85745-629-8 (paperback)   ISBN 978-0-85745-630-4 (ebook)

Yet, Sir, there is one heroic achievement open to us, and that is
to confer upon this country that large measure of freedom, under
the protecting shade and influence of which an ennobling and exalted
patriotism may at last arise, which will enable the youth of this colony—
the youth of future ages—to emulate the ardour, the zeal, and the
patriotism of the glorious youth of Sparta and of Rome, and to teach
and make them feel that ennobling sentiment which is conveyed
in the line of the Roman lyric "Dulce et decorum est pro patriâ mori."

Sir, this is not our destiny, but I trust it will be the destiny of another
generation, who shall arise with larger feelings, and, it may be, purer aims.

*—William Charles Wentworth, Debate on the Second Reading of the New South
Wales Constitution Bill, Legislative Council of New South Wales, 6 December 1853*

Contents

Acknowledgments

On returning to Australia in late 1995 after many years studying, research-
ing, and teaching in the United States, Israel, and England, I was struck by
how little interest there appeared to be among Australian political theorists
in Australia's experiment with multiculturalism. This silence compounded
the more understandable—although no less regrettable—lack of attention accorded the Australian case in the debates over multiculturalism already then
raging in international political theory. In due course, I decided to do something about this. The opportunity came in July 2004 when the Academy of
the Social Sciences in Australia (ASSA) sponsored a two-day workshop I
organized on "Australian Multiculturalism and Political Theory: Balancing
Rights and Responsibilities in a Diverse Society," held at the University of
New South Wales in Sydney. This book is the outcome of that workshop.

I am grateful to all those who participated in the workshop. The intellectual exchange was enhanced by papers also from Larissa Behrendt, Susan
Dodds, and Laksiri Jayasuriya, and by several people who served as dis-
cussants: Adam Czarnota, Martin Krygier, Maria Markus, Garth Nettheim,
Paul Patton, and Aleksandar Pavkovic. The revised comments of Krygier
and Markus are included here. I am especially indebted to the contributors
to the book for their readiness to revise their papers in light of our discussions and more recent developments in Australian politics, and for their for-
bearance during the editorial process. These essays have been peer reviewed,
and though they cannot be named, the anonymous reviewers are also to be
thanked for their critical input.

The workshop was fortunate in having the substantial sponsorship also
of the Australian government's then Department of Immigration and Multicultural and Indigenous Affairs (DIMIA). The Faculty of Arts and Social
Sciences and the Faculty of Law at the University of New South Wales also
supported the event. I record my thanks to each of these bodies and to ASSA
for their support. It was a pleasure working on the organizational aspects of

the project with ASSA's Mark Pinoli, and with DIMIA senior officer Richard Manderson (who also attended the workshop). Peter Balint was a welcome and enthusiastic sounding board throughout the project, and his collegial input is much appreciated. A version of Duncan Ivison's chapter first appeared as "The Moralism of Multiculturalism" in the *Journal of Applied Philosophy* 22, no. 2 (2005): 171–84, and I thank Blackwell Publishing for permission to reprint that material here.

Finally, I am grateful to Marion Berghahn of Berghahn Books for seeing the international merit of this project, and to her team for their editorial and production finesse.

GBL
Sydney

List of Abbreviations

ATSIC   Aboriginal and Torres Strait Islander Commission

CEDAW   Convention on the Elimination of All Forms of Discrimination Against Women

CRE   Commission for Racial Equality

DIAC   Department of Immigration and Citizenship

DIMA   Department of Immigration and Multicultural Affairs

DIMIA   Department of Immigration and Multicultural and Indigenous Affairs

FECCA   Federation of Ethnic Communities' Councils of Australia

HREOC   Human Rights and Equal Opportunity Commission

ICCPR   International Covenant on Civil and Political Rights

NESB   non–English-speaking background

NTCCA   Northern Territory Court of Criminal Appeal

SBS   Special Broadcasting Service

SCNT   Supreme Court of the Northern Territory

Foreword to the Paperback Edition

Australian Multiculturalism Rides Again

Geoffrey Brahm Levey

When this book was first published in 2008, multiculturalism in Australia, as elsewhere, appeared to be in trouble. The conservative federal government of John Howard had unceremoniously abolished the term "multicultural-ism" from governmental use in its last year in office. In 2007, the Department of Immigration and Multicultural Affairs, for example, became instead the Department of Immigration and Citizenship, while a citizenship test was introduced for the first time that probed applicants' proficiency in English language and knowledge of Australian institutions and culture. This turn toward emphasizing citizenship, integration and social cohesion followed similar developments overseas—in Britain, the Netherlands, and elsewhere— such that talk of a "retreat" from multiculturalism in Australia was rife. The Labor government of Kevin Rudd, elected to office in November 2007, showed little interest in multiculturalism or matters of cultural diversity.

In 2008, I questioned the depth of this supposed retreat on various grounds. However, I accepted that the term "multiculturalism" as an official name for federal government policy might well be destined for the scrap-heap, even if the substantive policies for which it stood mostly remained. This impression of the direction in which Australia was headed was reaf-firmed when, in 2009, the government's Australian Multicultural Advisory Council (AMAC) solicited expert opinion in developing what it called a "new cultural diversity policy" for Australia (Demetriou 2009). Many, in-cluding myself, were thus surprised when things turned out otherwise. In its report to the government in April 2010, AMAC strongly recommended the retention of multiculturalism along with several measures to reinvigorate the policy. Then, in February 2011, the minority Labor government led by Julia Gillard suddenly and enthusiastically accepted AMAC's recommendations. During the 2010 election campaign, Gillard had rejected a "big Australia" based on high levels of immigration, stressed the preciousness of the "Australian way of life," and, on assuming office, removed "multicultural affairs" even from the title of the Parliamentary Secretary assisting the Minister for Immigration and Citizenship. Her government's switch to endorsing multiculturalism has been attributed to the Labor party's precipitous collapse of support in the 2010 election and the belief that, as one former Labor politician put it, "We abandoned multicultural Australia and they abandoned us" (Morris Iemma quoted in Kelly 2011). However, there is little doubt that the rethinking also had to do with the enduring commitment to multiculturalism of some government members, not least the new Minister for Immigration and Citizenship, Chris Bowen and the Parliamentary Secretary for Immigration and Multicultural Affairs, Senator Kate Lundy. In a ministerial reshuffle on 2 March 2012, Prime Minister Gillard announced that Australia would again have a federal Minister for Multicultural Affairs, appointing Lundy to the post. But whereas up until 2007 the ministry for Multicultural Affairs had been combined with Immigration, now, significantly, it would be a separate portfolio.

From an international perspective, the Australian government's reaffirmation of multiculturalism in February 2011 certainly seemed to buck a trend. Only months earlier, German Chancellor Angela Merkel had gained world headlines by declaring that Germany's effort to build a multicultural society had "utterly failed" (*BBC News* 2010). In early February 2011, British Prime Minister David Cameron followed suit by condemning multiculturalism as a failed state response to cultural diversity in Britain (*BBC News* 2011). Days later, French President Nicholas Sarkozy endorsed the negative assessments of his European colleagues (*Reuters* 2011). To be sure, neither Germany nor France had actually trialed multiculturalism policy. If anything had failed, it was these countries' policies on integration. Nevertheless, the international environment was clearly souring on the notion of multiculturalism. How, then, did the Australian government publicly justify its recommitment to multiculturalism at the very time it was being condemned elsewhere? And what should we make of this justification?

In his speech of 11 February, "The Genius of Australian Multiculturalism," the Immigration and Citizenship Minister directly responded to European criticisms of multiculturalism and sought to explain why they were of "limited value" to the Australian context (Bowen 2011). The success of Australian multiculturalism, Bowen suggested, lay principally in three factors.

First, Australian multicultural policy had always insisted on "respect for traditional Australian values," by which he meant mainly liberal democratic values, including the freedom of the individual, equality between the sexes, tolerance, the rule of law, and parliamentary democracy, but also English as the national language. Such values always prevail if ever there is a clash with minority cultural practices. The British Prime Minister had advocated "muscular liberalism" as the alternative to British-style multiculturalism, which he described as allowing communities to live largely "separate lives" and devoid of shared values. Bowen argued that "muscular liberalism" is precisely what Australian multiculturalism involves. Indeed, he suggested that Australia was more successful in this respect than even Canada, her fellow pioneer in state multiculturalism. In Australia there is a greater "national consensus on our values" and the "geographic integrity of our nation" is settled, whereas in Canada "debates about language and the ongoing make-up of the nation continue" (Bowen 2011).

Second, Australian multiculturalism has worked, Bowen argued, because it is a "citizenship-based model." Full rights and benefits are open to all those who take the pledge of commitment as a citizen, and migrants are generally encouraged to become citizens. This contrasts with the European experience of guest workers: "One could argue that the large Turkish guest worker populations have not properly integrated into German society because, frankly, they have not been invited to" (Bowen 2011). Segregation, separatism, resentment and ultimately alienation and violence are perpetuated among communities shut out from the mainstream. Australian multiculturalism, in contrast, promotes the integration of new arrivals and seeks to remove obstacles blocking their integration. Third, Bowen credited the success of Australian multiculturalism to its bipartisan support. Both Labor and Liberal governments had helped develop multiculturalism policy and guide it subsequently, so each party has seen itself as having ownership of the policy. The public debate over multiculturalism, while sometimes vigorous, largely transcends the usual political fray.

For the purposes of this book, each of these cited factors for the success of Australian multiculturalism warrants some comment. Several contributors to this volume explore the relationship of multiculturalism to liberalism and democracy, a relationship that is contested among liberals perhaps more so than democrats. However, Bowen is surely correct in suggesting that liberalism is integral to the Australian conception and practice of multiculturalism. Each of the three previous national multicultural policy statements made this much plain (OMA 1989; Commonwealth of Australia 1999, 2003). Bowen's speech and the new multicultural policy promulgated in 2011 are nevertheless notable in pressing the point that respecting liberal democratic values necessarily entails some multiculturalism. Bowen asserted this relationship pithily: "If Australia is to be free and equal, then it will be multicultural. But, if it is to be multicultural, Australia must remain free and equal." Multiculturalism, he said, is "a matter of liberalism" (Bowen 2011). Similarly, the new multiculturalism policy, *The People of Australia* (2011), states that the rights and liberties bestowed by citizenship "include Australians of all backgrounds being entitled to celebrate, practise and maintain their cultural heritage, traditions and language within the law and free from discrimination." The corollary, of course, is that Australian multiculturalism cannot be abolished holus-bolus without also circumscribing the liberty and equality of citizens. Judging by the Australian public debate over multiculturalism, with its frequent calls for abolition, this implication is still not well understood (or, perhaps, well regarded), even among the professional commentariat. A more intelligent debate would identify specific provisions and programs of multicultural policy—including the term by which the policies are known—and explain why they should be discontinued.

The suggestion that Australian multiculturalism works because it is a "citizenship-based model" also has some validity. There is little doubt that denying long-term residents a path to citizenship and its associated benefits, or, for that matter, leaving citizens from disadvantaged migrant communities fester in their disadvantage is a recipe for social and personal disaster. Still, a stress on integration comes with its own challenges. Bowen cited the Australian citizenship pledge as being the "most beautiful citizenship pledge in the world." Where others require new citizens to declare fealty to a monarch or president and "simply to abide the laws," the Australian pledge requires them to "share" democratic beliefs and to "uphold and obey" the laws. On this basis, migrants are "welcome to join us as full partners with equal rights" (Bowen 2011).

There is much to admire in the formulation of the current Australian citizenship pledge and how it connects to the Australian citizenship test (revised in 2009). However, the insistence on holding certain beliefs as against simply respecting the law has government involving itself with the interior life of its citizens which, for many liberals, is a mark of illiberalism (e.g., Mill 1972; Joppke 2010). In the United States, by way of contrast, attachment to the Constitution "is not addressed to the heart, demands no affection for or even approval of a democratic system of government, but merely an acceptance of the fundamental political habits and attitudes which here prevail, and a willingness to obey the laws which may result from them" (*United States v. Rossler* 1944 quoted in Orgad 2010, p. 55). Emphasizing integration into liberal democratic life can easily slide, then, into demanding a conformity that exceeds liberal democratic principles. The imperative of integration requires fine calibration.

Australian multiculturalism has benefitted from bipartisan support. In his speech, Bowen was realistic enough to wonder whether this would continue. I already have noted the Howard government's volte-face on multiculturalism in its last term, although, ironically, the Rudd Labor government in retaining Howard's reforms maintained bipartisanship. More importantly, the appearance of bipartisanship is belied by what Bowen did *not* mention in his speech, Australian national identity. There is general consensus (bar for some academic critics) that Australian multiculturalism should be tied to liberal democratic values. However, there is significant disagreement on the relationship of multiculturalism to Australian national identity, and, in particular, whether the Anglo-Australian majority culture should be recognized as foundational to that identity. Three views do most of the bidding.

One view rejects Anglo-Australian culture as having foundational status (and sometimes as even having content). On this "civic nationalist" view, shared civic values are glue enough for national cohesion, and insofar as Australia has a national identity multiculturalism itself is at its core. A second and subtler view is arguably the dominant perspective in Australian political life today and is recognizably "liberal nationalist." It accepts the foundational status of Anglo-Australian culture but also sees Australian national identity as inevitably changing over time with the changing composition of Australian society. In the meantime, on this view, government promotion of Anglo-Australian culture must be limited and the rights and inclusion of cultural minorities secured. The third or "cultural nationalist" view not only accepts the foundational status of Anglo-Australia but seeks to advance and protect this status in perpetuity. On this view, multiculturalism should be about the integration of migrants into the Anglo-Australian way of life. Cultural nationalists tend to be at best ambivalent about multiculturalism as it is deployed also by those wishing to challenge the foundational status of Anglo-Australian culture.

The main political battle concerning multiculturalism in Australia today is between the liberal nationalist and cultural nationalist positions. Civic nationalism is mainly confined to the intelligentsia and the universities. While liberal nationalist assumptions tend to predominate in both the mainstream left and right of Australian politics, cultural nationalist sentiment remains strong in the conservative parties. As Prime Minister, John Howard rarely missed a beat in promoting Anglo-Australia as the core of Australian national identity, and which migrants were expected to accept (Johnson 2007; Tate 2009; Tavan 2007). In a 1999 referendum, for example, he sought to have the legendary Australian tradition of "mateship" enshrined in the preamble to the Australian Constitution, while the first Australian citizenship test, introduced by his government in 2007, included questions on Australian cricket heroes and other cultural icons along with questions on Australian political institutions. While Howard has retired from politics, figures in the Liberal party continue to invoke Anglo-conformity as the measure of national belonging.

An example is the minor controversy caused by Shadow Parliamentary Secretary for Citizenship and Settlement Teresa Gambaro's remarks, in January 2012, that migrants should undergo "cultural awareness training." In particular, she nominated "wearing deodorant and not pushing in when lining up" as Australian cultural norms that needed to be taught to newcomers to facilitate their integration (*The Australian* 2012). Herself the daughter of Italian migrants, Gambaro quickly apologized. The thrust of her remarks, if not her chosen examples, doubtless resonated with many Australians; public opinion research consistently finds that a majority of Australians agrees with the proposition that migrants should adopt the way of life of the country rather than maintain their distinct customs and traditions (Markus 2011). Nevertheless, for the political class (and likely the educated, urban dwellers) Gambaro's remarks were considered unacceptable, overstepping, as they did, the bounds of the current liberal nationalist settlement. The civic nationalist, liberal nationalist, and cultural nationalist perspectives are each represented and explored in this volume.

Three further points should be borne in mind in assessing Australian multiculturalism and its broader significance. First, another probable factor in its success (if we credit Bowen's aforementioned points) is Australia's adoption of a skilled and selective migration policy (Jupp chap. 13; Hartwich 2011). The challenges of integration consequently have been less pronounced in Australia than in Europe. At the same time, some aspects of Australian migration law and policy raise concerns regarding public accountability and fairness (Glass chap. 11).

Second, while the enthusiasm of the Australian national government for multiculturalism has waxed and waned over the last decade or so, the story at the state level has been more positive and consistent. Most of the six states and two territories have enacted multiculturalism in law or in charters rather than simply in administrative policy, and have been proactive in the promotion and institutionalization of multicultural initiatives. This proactivity has been notably immune to the national debates and reservations about multiculturalism. In late 2011, Victoria's Liberal government even pressed the federal Labor government to introduce a national multiculturalism act along the lines of its own. Such a move, said the Victorian Minister for Multicultural Affairs and Citizenship, Nicholas Kotsiras, would help clarify the principles of multiculturalism at the national level, emphasize the Australian values of equality regardless of cultural background, and "recognise the valuable contribution that migrants have made to the life of our nation" (*The Australian* 2011). The opposition led by Tony Abbott dismissed the suggestion. The Gillard government responded cautiously, saying that while it did not intend to act on the proposal presently, it did not reject it either.

Third and finally, the place of Indigenous Australians in Australian multiculturalism continues to be anomalous. Official multicultural policy includes Indigenous Australians within its compass although Indigenous Affairs was removed, in 2006, from the Department of Immigration—which, until March 2012, oversaw multiculturalism—and added to the Department of Families, Housing, and Community Services. While many Aboriginal leaders have rejected the relevance of multiculturalism to the uniqueness of the Aboriginal experience and their distinctive claims for recognition, Aboriginal identity and government assistance programs for Indigenous people are often cited as part of the "multicultural industry" and questioned much like ethnic identification and benefits are for migrant groups.

The Andrew Bolt controversy is a case in point. In September 2010, nine mixed descent or so-called "fair-skinned" Aborigines sued Bolt, a prominent conservative columnist, under the Racial Discrimination Act for questioning their Aboriginality and implying that they so identified for material gain in two of his articles. A year later, the Federal Court found for the applicants. Like many commentators, Bolt framed the case as an attempt to restrict free speech in the service of multiculturalism. His ultimate concern, he said, was the unity of peoples. As he put it after learning of the Court's decision, "I argued then and I argue now that we should not insist on the differences between us but focus instead on what unites us as human beings" (*The Age* 2011). Such a stricture could, of course, also put a damper on expressions of Australian national identity, which was not his intention. Indeed, Bolt might have pondered Hannah Arendt's (1964: 268-9) observation that "human diversity as such" is integral to the "human status," and recalled what can happen when people want to erase that diversity. In any case, Australian multiculturalism does not "insist" that people assert their cultural difference; rather it merely allows and supports such assertions as another option open to all Australians expressing their freedom and equality within the law.

The first edition of this book sought to inject the Australian experience into the debates over multiculturalism then, as now, occurring in international political theory and to examine how these debates apply to the Australian case. International and local developments over the intervening four years have only added to the significance of Australia's experience with multiculturalism. I am pleased that this paperback edition will enable the book to reach a wider reading public.

Chapter 1

Multicultural Political Thought in Australian Perspective

Geoffrey Brahm Levey

The aim of this book is to explore how the Australian experience relates and contributes to political thinking about multiculturalism. Multiculturalism has been one of the dominant themes of research and reflection in political theory over the last fifteen or so years. Among other issues, attention has focused on how multiculturalism relates to liberal principles of individual autonomy, toleration, equality, and justice; where, and on what basis, the limits of liberal toleration should be drawn; and the implications of multiculturalism for current and emerging conceptions of citizenship. For the most part, these debates have been conducted at an abstract philosophical level or else have been informed by, or applied to, the Canadian, American, and, increasingly, the European contexts. Although Australia was, along with Canada, one of the first liberal democracies to commit to a national policy of multiculturalism, in the 1970s, political theory has devoted scant attention to Australia's experiment in multiculturalism. The considerable scholarly literature on Australian multiculturalism has tended rather to come from cultural studies and the empirical social sciences. Indeed, it is fair to say that aside from the recent attention on the rights of indigenous peoples, Australian political theorists and philosophers have mostly shied away from multiculturalism and cultural rights as areas of study in general.[1]

Just why this should be so when such issues are of central concern to political theorists in Canada, the United States, Britain, and continental Europe is worth pondering. But whatever the reasons, the lack of interest is doubly unfortunate. First, from an Australian perspective, the work of politi-

cal theorists addresses many of the issues that routinely figure in this country's public debate over multiculturalism as a set of ideas and policies for
managing cultural diversity. Multiculturalism in Australia has always had its
critics. However, since the World Trade Center attacks in September 2001
and with the rise of militant Islamism more generally, public anxieties over
the meaning, value, and implications of multiculturalism are today being
voiced in Australia, as elsewhere, with particular stridency. Sober analysis of
what multiculturalism is and may be in a liberal democracy like Australia,
of the various arguments offered to justify it, as well as of its theoretical and
practical problems, is needed now more than ever. Australian public policy
and debate can only benefit from having the Australian experience situated
and evaluated in light of more general arguments about multiculturalism,
liberal democratic values, national identity, and citizenship.

Second, from an academic perspective, multicultural political theory
can in turn benefit from considering the Australian case. Early multicultural
political theory was heavily influenced by the work of the Canadian political philosophers Will Kymlicka (e.g., 1989, 1995) and Charles Taylor (1994),
both of whom were self-consciously engaged in searching for a just solution to
minority claims as presented in the Canadian context, principally concerning the indigenous peoples and Quebecois. In terms of the sheer number of
scholars and output of work, however, the center of gravity in multicultural
political theory, as in so many other academic fields, is the United States. Yet
such work comes with something of a self-imposed caveat: while American
political theorists tend to generalize about liberalism and democracy based
on American institutions and conditions, Americans also tend to believe as
an article of national faith in "American exceptionalism"—the idea that the
United States is "uniquely unique" or fundamentally different from all other
polities and societies (Glazer 1999; Shafer 1991; Walzer 1992b).

Thus it is appropriate that recent years have witnessed a growing wariness of the "one model fits all" kind of liberal theorizing. Especially in the
case of multicultural political theory, there has been increased attention to
the importance of particular historical and cultural contexts in responding
to what may be the same or similar questions. A recent volume on multicultural citizenship, for example, attempts to chart what the editors call a
"European approach" (Modood, Triandafyllidou, and Zapata-Barreo 2006).
And Kymlicka himself has played a key role in regional inquiries into whether
and how Western models of multiculturalism may have application in Eastern Europe (Kymlicka and Opalski 2001) and in Asia (Kymlicka and He
2005). Similarly, in his contribution to this book, Philip Pettit argues that
there is "no such thing as the nature of citizenship in general, only the nature of citizenship under one or another civic structure." As Martin Krygier

notes in his comment on Pettit's chapter, the same can be said of the "nature of multiculturalism."

If comparison and contrast are essential to the quest for understanding, as they surely are, then it is appropriate that the Australian case also be included in our store of political thinking on multiculturalism. Australia has had a generally successful experience with creating and managing a culturally diverse society based on liberal democratic norms. It also occupies an intermediate position—politically, institutionally, and culturally—between the dominant Western spheres of "Old World" Europe and the "New World" of North America, and thus affords a unique vantage point for considering wider debates on multiculturalism.

This book, then, seeks to bring the Australian context into the discussion of multiculturalism in contemporary political theory. It critically examines the challenges, possibilities, and limits of multiculturalism as a governing idea in liberal democracies, with special attention to the Australian case. Some contributors draw on Australian examples to make or evaluate general arguments, some consider the implications of a particular philosophical argument for Australian democracy, while others evaluate official Australian multiculturalism directly. All, however, are concerned with the theoretical implications of Australia's attempt to manage an immigrant-rich, culturally diverse population and thus address some of the central questions of concern to political theorists and liberal democracies today.

In the remainder of this chapter, I will briefly profile Australia's multicultural society and move to adopt multiculturalism as official policy; identify some normative features of the Australian policy; consider the Howard government's apparent retreat from multiculturalism in its final year in office; and outline the contents of the book.

MULTICULTURALISM FOR A MULTICULTURAL SOCIETY

Australia was home to a culturally diverse population even before European settlement. Indigenous Australians comprised hundreds of distinct tribal groups and languages. The First Fleet of European settlement in 1788 also included a variety of ethnic backgrounds among its assortment of officers and convicts. The gold rushes of the nineteenth century along with the opportunities of a new society attracted Chinese, Afghanis, and Italians, among others, in search of better lives. Religious intolerance at home saw German Old Lutherans establish a significant presence—and one of Australia's renowned wine-growing regions—in South Australia from 1838. Nevertheless, multicultural*ism* as a political idea and public policy regime is a latter twentieth-century development. The term multiculturalism entered Australian parlance in 1973 following its introduction some years earlier in Canada.[2] Whereas Canadian thinking revolved principally around bilingualism and long-established cultural communities, multiculturalism in Australia developed as a response to post–World War II immigration.

From Federation of the Australian colonies in 1901 until World War II, Australia dealt with cultural diversity fundamentally through exclusion. The first act of the newly established Australian Commonwealth was the Immigration Restriction Act (1901) or "White Australia" policy, which defined the country as an outpost of the "British race." Under economic imperatives to "populate or perish," the policy's restrictive provisions were progressively loosened in the postwar period. The end of the White Australia policy was foreshadowed in 1966 when the Liberal coalition government admitted a small number of well-qualified people from Asia. However, the policy formally ended only in 1973, when the Whitlam Labor government removed all remaining vestiges of a racially discriminatory immigration policy.[3]

By any standard, the ensuing transformation of Australian society has been remarkable. In 1947, the Australian population stood at 7.6 million. This included some 87,000 Aboriginal and Torres Strait Islander people (compared to an estimated 314,000 prior to European settlement), with the rest mostly the descendants of people from Great Britain and Ireland. Almost 10 percent of the total population was born overseas, with three quarters of these coming from the British Isles. As of the 2001 census, the Australian population had grown to 18.8 million. Now 22 percent of the resident Australian population was born overseas, and 43 percent was either born overseas or had one parent born overseas. These figures have continued to increase since 2001. Thus, for many years now Australia has been even more immigrant rich than the other major "immigrant democracies" of Canada (19.3 percent circa 2000), the United States (12.3 percent), and New Zealand (19.5 percent), and it far exceeds, in this respect, the former imperial powers of Europe now coping with immigration, including Britain (8.3 percent), France (10 percent), and the Netherlands (10 percent) (ABS 2001; OECD 2006). Apart from Israel, no other country has virtually doubled its population through immigration in the space of half a century. James Jupp (2003, and this volume) rightly cautions against overstating the cultural diversity associated with some of these figures. Although immigrants to Australia hail from some two hundred countries, as of 2006, the two main source countries of Australia's overseas-born, for example, remain the United Kingdom (24 percent) and New Zealand (9 percent). By comparison, the main non–English-speaking source countries are Italy with 5 percent, and China and Vietnam each with 4 percent of the overseas-born (ABS 2004–5: 6).[4] Still, overall it is clear that Lord Campbell of Croy had a point in offering a personal recollection in the House of Lords: "My late wife once described [the United States] as the only country in the world where the majority of the population is homesick. They might dispute that in Australia."[5]

There have been significant changes also in religious affiliation. In 1947, 39 percent of the population identified themselves as Anglican, 21 percent considered themselves Catholic, and 28 percent aligned themselves with other Christian denominations and beliefs.[6] By the time of the 2001 census, those declaring a Christian faith had fallen from 88 to 68 percent (21 percent Anglican, 26 Catholic, 21 other Christian). Those identifying with a non-Christian religion had climbed from 0.5 to 5 percent, with Buddhism (2 percent), Islam (1.5 percent), Hinduism, and Judaism (each 0.5 percent) being the main minority faiths. While Christianity remains the most common religion among the overseas-born, growing numbers of immigrants from Asia and the Middle East have led to a stronger presence of non-Christian faiths. Indeed, between the 1996 and 2001 censuses alone, the number of persons affiliating with Buddhism increased by 79 percent, with Hinduism by 42 percent, and with Islam by 40 percent. Perhaps equally significant is the growing secularity of the population, with a fifty-fold increase since 1947 in those citing no religious affiliation or beliefs, from 0.3 percent to 15.5 percent in 2001.[7]

Officially, Australia is a monolingual country, recognizing English as the sole national language. However, in 2001, one in six Australians age 5 and above spoke another language at home. The majority of these (73 percent) were overseas-born, among whom the main languages spoken (in descending order) were Chinese, Italian, Greek, Vietnamese, and Arabic/Lebanese. Among the Australian-born (typically children of immigrants), the main languages spoken were Italian, Greek, Arabic/Lebanese, Aboriginal languages, and Chinese (ABS 2006: "Languages").

Like Canada and the United States, Australia explicitly managed its cultural diversity up until the mid-1960s through an assimilationist approach aimed at "Anglo-conformity." This approach had more to do with declaratory expectations and the *absence* of provisions for minorities than with formal legal sanctions. Arguably, much more powerful was the informal censuring that an overwhelmingly Anglo-Celtic society applied to new immigrants who exhibited their linguistic and cultural difference too conspicuously. By the 1950s, some sociologists were warning that assimilationist policies and norms were exacerbating rather than alleviating the problems of immigrant absorption (Lopez 2000: 54–55). Government documents claim that a new policy approach of "integration" replaced assimilationism from the mid-1960s, where the settling and servicing of large numbers of immigrants were emphasized, rather than the loss of their original language, culture, and identity (DIMA 2006b). Beginning in the 1970s, multicultural- ism developed as a series of tentative ideas and piecemeal reforms spon- sored by successive Labor and Liberal coalition federal governments. Unlike Canadian multiculturalism, which emphasized linguistic and cultural main- tenance from the start, Australian multiculturalism first took shape as a program of immigrant settlement and welfare support for people from non– English-speaking backgrounds or so-called NESBs (Jupp 1996; Lopez 2000). Some commentators nevertheless see in the multicultural approach during the Fraser government years (1975–83)–and, especially, in the Galbally Re- port (1978) that gave it direction–an emphasis on cultural pluralism, eth- nic groups as distinct and homogeneous cultures, and a neoconservative inclination to privatize welfare services (Castles 2001: 808; Kalantzis 2000: 104). Ethnic Communities' Councils were among the first nongovernmental institutions established to advance the multicultural agenda, beginning with the Victorian branch in 1974, followed by a New South Wales office in 1975. An overarching national association, Federation of Ethnic Communities' Councils of Australia (FECCA), was established in 1979. Publicly funded English-language instruction, translation services, immigrant resource cen- ters, grant-in-aid programs to community groups, facilities for recognizing overseas trade qualifications, and the establishment of ethnic television were among the main initiatives of this early period.

By the early 1980s, the ambit of multiculturalism had begun to be framed in terms of addressing "all Australians" rather than only immigrants and "ethnics," and had crystallized around the themes of social cohesion, cultural identity, and equality of opportunity and access. By the end of the 1980s, the first overarching national policy statement of Australian multi- culturalism–*National Agenda for a Multicultural Australia* (OMA 1989), inau- gurated by the Hawke Labor government–identified four main planks: the right of all Australians to maintain their cultural identities within the law; the right of all Australians to equal opportunities without fear of group- based discrimination; the economic and national benefits of a culturally diverse society; and respect for core Australian values and institutions–reci- procity, tolerance and equality (including of the sexes), freedom of speech and religion, the rule of law, the Constitution, parliamentary democracy, and English as the national language.

Subsequently, there have been two further national policy statements, *A New Agenda for Multicultural Australia* and *Multicultural Australia: United in Diversity* (Commonwealth of Australia 1999, 2003)–the latter a self-declared "update" of the former–both launched by the conservative Howard govern- ment.[8] These documents have further refined the policy's emphases and presentation of principles, although the 1989 provisions have essentially endured. If the Hawke government's *National Agenda* advanced a social justice-cum-citizenship model of multiculturalism, the *New Agenda* put greater stress on national identity, social cohesion, and community harmony. Thus, for example, the policy was henceforth to be called "Australian multicultur-alism" to better signal that "our implementation of multiculturalism has been uniquely Australian" (NMAC 1999: 3). There was increased emphasis on the obligations of Australians under the policy, as against their rights: what in the 1989 version were stated as "limits" after the cultural identity, access and equity, and economic efficiency provisions, were now positioned as the first plank of the policy. The *National Agenda*'s stress on the defining importance of Australia's British heritage also was replaced in favor of "our evolving national character and identity."[9]

The federal provisions on multiculturalism have their counterparts in each of the Australian states and territories and often in local governments as well. The states of New South Wales and Victoria and the Australian Capital Territory have each enshrined their multicultural principles and ap-proaches to cultural diversity in legislation, while the other states and the Northern Territory have followed the federal governmental model and opted for governmental policy statements or charters.[10] Indeed, in recent years, it has been state and local governments that have generally maintained the momentum behind Australian multiculturalism. The conservative Howard government (1996 to 2007) always had an ambivalent relationship to the policy (Kelly 1997). It is too early to say how multicultural affairs will be managed by the new Labor government under prime minister Kevin Rudd, elected on 24 November 2007. It is notable, however, that the new govern-ment has retained its predecessor's removal of "multicultural affairs" from ministerial responsibility (as described further below), although it has rein-stated the term and area at the parliamentary secretary level.

A word is in order about the place of indigenous Australians in this dis-cussion. Although official multiculturalism now applies to Aboriginal and Torres Strait Islander peoples, it also, to its credit, recognizes that "their dis-tinct needs and rights [should] be reaffirmed and accorded separate consid-eration" (OMA 1989: 5). Unfortunately, this commitment—repeated in the *New Agenda* but not in *Multicultural Australia*—has seen little efficacious policy. For their own part, many Aboriginal people have resisted their inclusion under the policy, believing that this ignores their distinctive historical ex-perience and undermines their claims and special status (Castles 2001: 809; Scott 2000). There now is a substantial literature on the political and legal recognition of indigenous Australians, examining such issues as land rights, self-government, treaties, political representation, customary law, and reconciliation (e.g., Behrendt 2003; Dodson 1995; Ivison, Patton, and Sanders 2000; Langton et al. 2004; Peterson and Sanders 1998; Povinelli 2002; Rowse 2002). For these reasons, this book focuses mainly on multiculturalism as it applies to *non*indigenous Australians. Nevertheless, several chapters devote some attention to the situation of indigenous Australians, and Moira Gatens examines the vexing problem of the clash between women's human rights and cultural group rights expressly in the context of Aboriginal customary law (chapter 9).

NORMATIVE FEATURES OF AUSTRALIAN MULTICULTURALISM

In recent years, political theorists have defended multiculturalism or, perhaps better, multiculturalism*s* on the basis of various principles and arguments, including identity and diversity; equality and justice; autonomy and liberty; democratic legitimacy; civil peace, inclusion, and the avoidance of harm; and economic and public goods (e.g., Benhabib 2002; Deveaux 2000; Gill 2001; Gutmann 2003; Habermas 1994; Galston 2002; Kymlicka 1995; Levy 2000a; Modood 2007; Parekh 2000; Reich 2002; Tamir 1993; Taylor 1994; Walzer 2004; Young 1990). The kinds of political recognition or cultural rights these arguments generate are similarly various, ranging over exemptions from standing law, public subsidization of minority cultures, symbolic recognition, special political representation, dual and multiple citizenships, intellectual-cum-cultural property rights, cultural defense in criminal proceedings, cultural and political autonomy, and even national self-determination (Levy 1997; Shweder, Minow, and Markus 2002). Other theorists have advanced expansive notions of cultural toleration, cultural autonomy, or minority self-government rather than cultural rights, as such (Kukathas 1997c, 2001, 2003; Nimni 2005; Shachar 2001; Swaine 2006; Tully 1995). The extent of the rights, toleration, and autonomy canvassed in these arguments in recent political theory far exceeds the "cautious" and "pragmatic" approach—as James Jupp aptly puts it in this book—of Australian multiculturalism.

This much is evident from some attempts to distinguish multiculturalism from previous liberal approaches to cultural diversity. Joseph Raz, for example, has charted three sequential liberal responses to cultural diversity: toleration, which largely leaves minorities to live as they please as long as they do not interfere with the dominant culture; nondiscrimination, which protects the individual rights and liberties of all citizens by outlawing discrimination on the basis of race, religion, ethnicity, and other group characteristics, and in so doing seeks to ensure that the common citizenship rights of liberalism are truly common; and finally, affirmative multiculturalism, which, Raz says, "rejects the individualistic bias" of the nondiscrimination model, recognizes the value of cultural diversity, and actively assists groups in maintaining their distinct cultures within the larger society (Raz 1994: 157–59).

Raz's synoptic account fails to capture key aspects of the Australian case. First, and perhaps most obviously, the longstanding White Australia policy suggests that, even beyond assimilation and Anglo-conformity, *intolerance* was in fact the initial dominant response in Australia (Kane 1997a: 542). Of more moment, Raz's distinction between nondiscrimination and affirmative multiculturalism, although helpful, needs to be recast in locating the Australian case. As we will see, Australian multiculturalism:

(1) centrally incorporates the traditional principle of nondiscrimination;
(2) extends this principle and the individualistic bias of liberalism more generally to embrace cultural identity; and
(3) affirms the value of cultural diversity, but again only on the basis of individualism.

The *National Agenda*—the first national multicultural policy—will serve to make these points, but they apply equally to the two subsequent national multicultural policy blueprints.

The *National Agenda* (OMA 1989: vii) identifies the following three dimensions of multicultural policy:

- *cultural identity*—the right of all Australians, within carefully defined limits, to express and share their individual cultural heritage, including their language and religion;
- *social justice*—the right of all Australians to equality of treatment and opportunity, and the removal of barriers of race, ethnicity, culture, religion, language, gender, or place of birth; and
- *economic efficiency*—the need to maintain, develop, and utilize effectively the skills and talents of all Australians, regardless of background.

The first point to make is that the right to cultural identity constitutes an important departure from both assimilationism and "mere" nondiscrimination. People are free to express their distinct cultural identities in public as well as in private, without hindrance and with substantial help from the government. Of course, the policy goes on to stress that the right is subject to "carefully defined limits."

Another crucial limitation is that the right to cultural identity is ascribed to and exercised by *individuals*. The phrasing used throughout the *National Agenda* is deliberate: it is "all Australians"—that is, each individual

Australian—who hold this right. Lest there be any ambiguity, the *National Agenda* states that "Fundamentally, multiculturalism is about the rights of the individual" (OMA 1989: 15). Cultural minorities *qua* groups as corporate entities have no entitlement. This qualification is of the utmost importance. It means that Australian multiculturalism remains committed to the liberal idea that the ultimate unit of moral worth is the individual, and it avoids one of the traditional liberal concerns about cultural and group-differentiated rights, namely, that the interests and rights of the individual are jeopardized in the interests of the group. In this respect, Australian multiculturalism follows closely the terms and reasoning of article 27 of the *International Covenant on Civil and Political Rights*—to which Australia is a signatory—which states, in part, that *"persons* belonging to [ethnic, religious, or linguistic] minorities shall not be denied the right ... to enjoy their own culture."[11]

One way of understanding the Australian right to cultural identity, then, is as an individual right to the free exercise of culture on the older liberal model of the free exercise of religion or freedom of worship, albeit one that has claims on public accommodation. So, for example, an individual may be entitled to wear his or her traditional garb or headgear even where standard uniforms are required, as in Sikhs who work for state railway services wearing their turban with the official badge in place of the conventional railway cap. Or individuals might exercise the right by observing certain rituals, such as securing time off from work to observe their festive holidays. Virtually all levels of Australian government, as well as many firms and businesses in private enterprise, now abide by codes encompassing these kinds of entitlements in their work practices.[12]

There is, however, a certain kind of *group* right that is also compatible with the individualistic terms and practice of Australian multiculturalism. Group rights may be conceptualized in a "collective" as well as in a "corporate" sense (Jones 1999a, 1999b). The corporate conception of group rights ascribes a moral status to the group in its own right, and is akin to the "solidaristic" image of the "citizenry" that Philip Pettit discusses in this book. The corporate conception is often what people have in mind in objecting to "group rights." As Peter Jones describes this conception, the "right is held not jointly by the several individuals that make up the group, but by the group as a unitary entity: the right is 'its' right rather than 'their' right" (Jones 1999a: 86). Australian multiculturalism clearly rules out such group rights. The concern is that granting powers, privileges, and immunities to cultural groups on this basis would both jeopardize their members' common citizenship rights and compromise Australian sovereignty and political integration. These concerns also figure in the reluctance of Australian governments, to date, to consider Aboriginal self-government.

Collective rights operate differently from corporate group rights. Here, the individuals comprising the group hold the right jointly, while the moral standing that grounds the right still belongs to each of the individuals. Unlike conventional individual rights, the interest of no single member of the group is sufficient by itself to justify the right and hence impose a duty on others (Jones 1999a: 85; Raz 1986: 208). Rather, a collective right arises where the accumulated interests of the several individuals comprising the group are necessary to put others under an obligation. In practice, we see such a collective cultural right recognized in Australia in the provisions, for example, covering state-recognized customary marriage and for establishing religious or parochial schools. In each case, while it is the interests of individuals that are being served, a community of members is required to give effect to the practice and to impose a duty of recognition on others.

It is important to note that political autonomy or group self-determination may also be grounded in a collective rather than a corporate justification. This is, perhaps, most obviously the case with the kind of national self-determination that Australians themselves claim, namely, one justified in the name of all Australians, which is jointly held by them, and which respects, at least presumptively, their liberal democratic rights. The same collective conception underscores the considerable legal and political autonomy of the six states and two territories that, along with the Commonwealth government, constitute the Australian federal system. The states and territories enjoy their self-government rights, however, as historically developed, regional and administrative units. Again, what Australia has not entertained—bar for some modest self-management for the now-abolished Aboriginal and Torres Strait Islander Commission (ATSIC)—is a collective right of self-determination or self-government for ethnic and subnational groups in Australia.

While the Australian right to cultural identity represents a significant departure from earlier practices of liberal democracies (assimilationism, toleration, nondiscrimination), it conforms to the moral ontology of liberal individualism. It does not so much break from liberal democratic norms as reinterpret and extend them. We see this innovation also in the second policy dimension—social justice. A traditional reading of the "right to equality of treatment and opportunity" would understand it to mean that people should not be denied offices and opportunities on the basis of their group characteristics, which is to say, on the basis of direct and invidious discrimination. Such a principle of nondiscrimination simply affirms, of course, the traditional liberal rights of citizenship, and has nothing *per se* to do with cultural distinctiveness or maintenance.

Recognizing direct discrimination leads, however, almost ineluctably to recognition of *indirect* discrimination as well. According to the *National*

Agenda, this kind of discrimination is "unwitting" and "systemic" and "occurs when cultural assumptions become embodied in society's established institutions and processes" (OMA 1989: 15). Or as the Racial Discrimination Act 1975 (Cth) puts it, indirect discrimination occurs when a "practice or policy appears to be fair because it treats everyone the same, but it actually disadvantages more people from one racial or ethnic group."[13] The social justice dimension addresses this concern through the removal of various group barriers. Like the right to cultural identity, the right to social justice more fully realizes, rather than breaches, liberal democratic norms and common citizenship rights. Thus, one finds even the United States, which does not have an official government policy of multiculturalism, endorsing similar provisions. For example, Title VII of the Civil Rights Act of 1964, together with the "Guidelines on Discrimination Because of Religion" of the U.S. Equal Employment and Opportunity Commission, have been used as instruments for accommodating religious dress and time off for religious holidays.[14]

In his vigorous critique of multiculturalism, Bristish philosopher Brian Barry (2001) argues that liberal multiculturalists misunderstand liberal equality. In insisting on state neutrality and common citizenship rights, liberalism does not pretend to be equally neutral toward all group traditions; rather, the point is to deny those groups that want to enlist state authority to impose their values on others. From an egalitarian perspective, cultural groups are not entitled to special treatment because "all groups are free to deploy their energies and resources in pursuit of culturally derived objectives on the same terms" (Barry 2001: 318). In recognizing indirect discrimination, however, Australian multiculturalism—like its counterparts elsewhere—notices how state institutions already embody and impose cultural values, and thus that not all groups *are* free to pursue their cultural objectives on the same terms. Further, it recognizes that alleviating indirect discrimination through special assistance or exemptions does not involve the state imposing minority cultural values on anybody.

Like the right to cultural identity, the right to social justice can sustain a wide array of claims in which cultural attachments and convictions are at stake. Often the two kinds of rights will reinforce each other. However, it is important to see how they address and protect cultural liberty in very different ways. Some cultural rights theorists defend multiculturalism primarily in terms of a broadened conception of equality, parity, or fairness. Kymlicka (1995), for example, argues that immigrant groups are owed "polyethnic" rights, which are essentially remedial rights enabling access to the societal culture to which everyone is entitled. Similarly, Nancy Fraser (2002) defends cultural recognition on the basis of "parity of participation in social life."

A major limitation of these approaches is that they can entail the serious restriction of cultural liberty.

Consider, for example, Fraser's attempt to apply her parity argument to the French controversy over the *foulard*. "Here the issue," she says, "is whether policies forbidding Muslim girls to wear headscarves in state schools constitute unjust treatment of a religious minority." The test is whether "the ban on the scarf constitutes an unjust majority communitarianism, which denies educational parity to Muslim girls." Fraser believes that this discrimination can "be established without difficulty," since "no analogous prohibition bars the wearing of Christian crosses in state schools; thus the current policy denies equal standing to Muslim citizens" (Fraser 2002: 35). Fraser was writing here some years before the French law of February 2004, which banned *all* "ostentatious" religious symbols and garb from being worn at state schools. On her argument, Muslims in France now enjoy equal standing. The only trouble is they, like many others committed to their religious traditions, aren't very happy about what parity has bequeathed. In this case, equality or fairness was secured at the price of individuals' freedom of religious expression.

There is, then, considerable wisdom in the Australian policy's recognition of an individual right to cultural identity separate from, and independent of, the right to social justice (and protection from indirect discrimination). Barriers to cultural expression should be removed or redressed where they unfairly disadvantage some citizens, without compelling overriding justification. But a right to cultural expression stands regardless of whether everyone's freedom to exercise it is similarly hobbled.

In a useful distinction, Robert Goodin (2006) differentiates between "protective" multiculturalism, centered on securing cultural rights for minority groups, and "polyglot" multiculturalism, centered on expanding the range of options and benefits available for members of the *majority* culture. Thus far I have addressed the "protective" aspects of Australian multicultural policy—the rights to cultural identity and nondiscrimination. But another major dimension of the policy turns on the idea that cultural diversity is a public good that serves all Australians. This is not exactly Goodin's "polyglot" multiculturalism, since the stated interest is on behalf of "all Australians" rather than only those belonging to the majority culture. That is, the stated interest is one of a genuine *public* good, not a group advantage, however dominant the group may be. Nevertheless, architects of the policy acknowledge that they needed to find ways to "sell" multicultural policy to "mainstream" Australians (e.g., Shergold 1994/95), so the difference between "public" and "polyglot" goods may be less than what it seems.

Be this as it may, we see the public good idea implied, albeit clumsily, in the third policy dimension of economic efficiency. Thus, for example, the retention of foreign languages by immigrants is to be encouraged so as to assist Australians and Australia to compete in the global marketplace. The bald instrumentalist terms of the economic efficiency dimension might be taken to mean that the interests of individual citizens are ultimately subservient to the national project that is "Australia." The *National Agenda* states, for example, that "All Australians should be able to develop and make use of their potential *for Australia's economic and social development*" (OMA 1989: 1; emphasis added). However, the policy clarifies elsewhere that the ultimate value resides in the individual: "By seeking to improve the management and use of our human resources, and thereby to contribute to a sustained improvement in our standard of living, multicultural policies serve the interests of us all" (OMA 1989: 26). The immigration debate has particular relevance here. One of the earlier fears expressed about multiculturalism was that the large influx of immigrants would rob established Australians of their jobs and diminish Australia's prosperity. The economic efficiency and, in the later policies, "productive diversity" dimensions transparently seek to allay some of these concerns by stressing the entrepreneurial and socioeconomic advantages of a culturally diverse workforce and society.

Public subsidization of ethnic groups is another cultural right defended by many multiculturalists. Australian federal, state, territory, and local governments have engaged in extensive funding programs related to multiculturalism. Three broad areas of funding may be distinguished. First, Australian governments provide information to the public in many languages, either directly in government brochures or via interpreter and translator services. Multilingual explanations appear on electoral ballots, census forms, and so on. While these measures might help to sustain linguistic and cultural distinctiveness, they are best understood as attempts to integrate new Australians from non–English-speaking backgrounds and to fairly and effectively administer the business of government.

A second area of public funding relates to community welfare and absorption matters, where governments have found community organizations to be effective—or convenient—deliverers of services to their needy members. Such measures constitute "special delivery" of welfare benefits rather than special benefits. Even here, governmental reliance on church and other nongovernment organizations to supply welfare services has a long pedigree in Australia, dating back to the colonial administrations in the nineteenth century (Garton 1990). This service delivery dimension, together with the traditional immigrant absorption and social justice emphases of Australian multiculturalism, may help explain why the international debate over whether multicultural policies divert attention and resources away from genuine cases of social deprivation, welfare need, and equal opportunity—the so-called "recognition vs. redistribution" debate (Banting and Kymlicka 2003b, 2006a; Barry 2001; Goodhart 2004; Phillips 1999)–has had little resonance in Australia.[15] There has been something of this argument over Aboriginal policy, with the Howard government insisting that improving Aboriginal living conditions or "practical reconciliation" is more helpful than symbolic reconciliation, apologies for historical maltreatment, and the questions of treaties and self-government. There has been generalized criticism of the cost of multiculturalism, usually based on exaggerated figures (e.g., Rimmer 1988, 1991). And there has been some criticism—as put in this book by Brian Galligan and Winsome Roberts—to the effect that Australian multicultural-ism has wrongly gotten caught up in questions of national identity and citi-zenship and should return to its original mission of immigrant absorption. However, there has been no comparable "recognition vs. redistribution" de-bate regarding Australian multiculturalism, presumably because, whatever else it may involve, so much of the policy has been about welfare, social justice, and equal opportunity.

Finally, some multicultural public funding is culturally and community oriented. It includes funding of SBS (the multicultural television and radio broadcaster), ethnic festivals, community activities and centers, and the like. There is in the *National Agenda* perhaps the suggestion of a moral entitle-ment to such funding: "All Australians should enjoy equal life chances and have equitable access to and equitable share of the resources which govern-ments manage on behalf of the community" (OMA 1989: 1). Nevertheless, the general rationale for this kind of public subsidization seems to be not that cultural minorities have a right to it, but rather that it serves the inter-ests of *all Australians* (or all residents in a state, territory, or municipality). This principle became even more pronounced under the Howard govern-ment's annual "Living in Harmony" grants program, where funds were al-located to community projects, on a competitive basis, that "aim to promote Australian values and mutual obligation, engage the whole community and address understanding and intolerance at the community level."[16] The un-derlying moral justification is the presumption that *everyone* benefits from the policy of state cultural subsidization—not only the minority members who happen to receive the assistance (as in minority rights arguments); not only the majority of a political community (as in some utilitarian justifica-tions and "polyglot" multiculturalism); and not only an abstract entity such as "the nation" (as with national corporatism).

Another notable feature of Australian multicultural policy is the *absence* of "inclusion" as a governing principle. This is unfortunate. As in the tri-colour values of *liberté, egalité,* and *fraternité,* valorisation of brotherhood and inclusion is deemed central to a democracy of equals. One might argue that the principle of inclusion is derivative of that of equality, and thus is implicitly recognized in the Australian policy's endorsement of social justice and equity. Some such assumption, for example, seems to inform the Rudd Labor government's "social inclusion" policy, which is framed entirely in terms of addressing socioeconomic harsdships.[17] However, seeing inclusion as simply derivative of equality overlooks the fact that one can enjoy equal citizenship rights and equal opportunities and still be socially alienated. It also fails to accord with Australian cultural norms. The latter famously include a strong tradition of egalitarianism and a "fair go," but they also mark out a separate and even mythic place for the value of "mateship," which is the quintessentially Australian sentiment of fraternity and inclusion. As Russel Ward (1958: 168) observed half a century ago, "[b]y the 1880's mateship had become such a powerful institution that often one could refuse an invitation to drink only at one's peril." However intimate their relationship, inclusion and equality stand as independent values.[18] While inclusion is surely served by stable employment, educational opportunities, access services, and support networks, it is also importantly facilitated through public rhetoric and symbolic measures (Levey 2008, 2007b).

Two cultural rights claims often discussed by political theorists and debated in various countries are the *symbolic recognition* of cultural minorities in official emblems, anthems, flags, public holidays, and the like, and *special political representation* in the legislature.

Australia has stopped short of the above forms of symbolically recognizing cultural minorities. Such cultural rights would presumably also apply to the dominant majority, and so some additional argument is required to explain why, in such circumstances, an established majority should not prevail at the symbolic level. Cultural rights theorists typically frame this additional argument in terms of respecting equality (e.g., Kymlicka 1995: 114–15; cf. Bader 2007). But, as a practical matter, it is not clear how one can include the images, stories, languages, and festivals of all or even most minority groups in the official paraphernalia of multicultural states. India offers a possible model in recognizing the festivals of all the major religions (Hindu, Muslim, Sikh, Christian, Jainist, and Buddhist) as official public holidays. As a proportion of the Indian population, the range in size of these faith communities is vast: from 82 percent in the case of Hindus to 0.4 percent in the case of Jains (National Commission for Minorities (India) n.d.). Cahill et al. (2004: 99) canvass a similar approach in relation to the prayers commencing and closing each Australian parliamentary day. They suggest that the current "Our Father" be replaced in the morning by a rotational series of prayers and readings selected by each faith group (including atheists and rationalists) having at least 0.333 percent of the total population, but be continued at the close of session in deference to the Christian majority. Symbolic recognition along these lines can certainly be considered. However, it is not clear whether such an approach is feasible where there is need to recognize considerably more than a handful of communities. Nor is it clear what consolation should be offered to those communities that do not meet the arbitrary numerical threshold for recognition. To include a few is tokenism, while to include some but not all is scarcely the fulfillment of equality, and may actually magnify the felt disadvantage.[19]

This does not mean that no symbolic adjustments should be made in response to the cultural diversity of citizens. It is appropriate and now customary for ethnic and religious bodies to be officially represented at national ceremonies and other significant public occasions. Similarly, some theorists have developed the idea of "acknowledgment" as a more congenial way of accommodating diversity than the strictures of "recognition" (Markell 2003; Tully 2000a). For example, in the case of the so-called December dilemma or Christmas wars, the choice need not be—as it is commonly presented— between abolishing the public celebration of the festival and its implied cultural hierarchy or publicly recognizing a festival of other ethnoreligious communities present in the population (e.g., Kymlicka 1995: n. 9, 222–23; 1998: 48–49; Markell 2003: 181). Rather, it might simply involve finding ways to acknowledge and make allowance for the fact that not all citizens observe Christmas (Levey 2006a).

Special minority representation, such as dedicated parliamentary seats, has limited relevance to Australian multiculturalism. Some scholars have made the case for such political representation in relation to a plethora of identity groups (e.g., Young 1990). However, in Australia it has been discussed mainly in relation to indigenous peoples (Anthony 2006; New South Wales Parliament 1998; Queensland Parliament 2003). Special political representation can take a number of forms. It might be arranged much in the manner of affirmative action policies, where virtually any individual member of the group is eligible for selection or, in this case, election to a reserved seat. The aim of this arrangement is to have the legislature better reflect the social composition of the population and encourage what Anne Phillips (1995) has called "the politics of presence." That is, the group is given a "voice" in the legislature only in the highly derivative and contingent sense that the minority members who are elected may be more sensitive to the concerns and interests of their group and may express, in their own way, those concerns. While this arrangement has been little discussed in Australia, a non–rights-based variation of it has been suggested. This involves encouraging political parties to run indigenous people in a certain number of winnable seats (e.g., New South Wales Parliament 1998). Because both these arrangements essentially entail a right and/or privilege held by individuals who happen to be members of a particular group, it theoretically conforms to the individualistic terms of Australian multiculturalism.

Alternatively, dedicated parliamentary seats might be filled by minority members who are authorized to represent the minority. This model is found in a number of liberal democracies that emerged out of the consolidation of various territorially concentrated ethnic and national groups (e.g., Belgium), or which entered into agreements with their indigenous peoples (e.g., New Zealand), and has been entertained by some Australian indigenous bodies (e.g., Council for Aboriginal Reconciliation 2000). Among other procedures, the minority's representatives might be nominated by the leadership of the minority whose names are then ratified (or rejected) by the legislature, or they might be elected directly by members of the minority. Whatever the procedure, the compatibility of this form of representation with the philosophy of Australian multiculturalism is an open question. The special status and needs of indigenous communities mean that, for them, the issue should be decided on grounds other than multicultural policy. Dedicated parliamentary representation for other ethnic and cultural communities has not been an issue in Australia.

RETREAT FROM MULTICULTURALISM?

The foregoing are some of the normative and institutional features of Australian multiculturalism. Their common and overwhelming attribute, both theoretically and practically, is one of liberal moderation. This has not prevented multiculturalism from being a focus of impassioned public criticism. Since the mid-1990s, there has been a discernible softening of support for, if not retreat from, multiculturalism or what some have called the "differentialist turn" in public policy in many liberal democracies (Brubaker 2001; Entzinger 2003; Joppke 2004). Australia is no exception to this trend. In late 2006, following reassessments of multiculturalism and general concerns about the integration of minorities in Britain and the Netherlands, the Howard government announced its intention to drop the word "multiculturalism" from government use (Robb 2006a). In January 2007, the Department of Immigration and Multicultural Affairs was renamed the Department of Immigration and Citizenship. The Rudd Labor government has retained this change.

In commenting on the apparent "return of assimilation" in France, Germany, and the United States, Rogers Brubaker (2001: 531) has observed that the return is not to the "old, analytically discredited and politically disreputable 'assimilationist' understanding of assimilation" but to a more complex notion. The same may be said of the policy changes flagged in Australia. The federal reforms include a new citizenship test that emphasizes English language proficiency and knowledge of Australian values and way of life (Robb 2006b); there is no suggestion, at least so far, that immigrants and their children should not speak foreign tongues *as well,* which was the case in the days of Australian assimilationism.[20] Similarly, the dropping of the word "multiculturalism" from federal governmental use appears to be symbolic or even semiotic. According to the government's announcement, the concern seems to be that talk of "multiculturalism" has sent the wrong signals to individuals and groups, that it has encouraged "separatism" and the idea that "anything goes." The hope is that the language of "citizenship" and "integration" and a renewed emphasis on "core Australian values" will arrest these perceived trends (Gambaro 2007; Robb 2006a). Indeed, it is striking how much of the criticism of multiculturalism focuses on the word and its perceived connotations, rather than on the various policies of minority inclusion and equal opportunity for which the word stands in the Australian context. Few of those calling for the abolition of "multiculturalism" specify which multicultural programs and measures they would terminate.

If we are witnessing a retreat from "multiculturalism," it appears to be a measured one. Although arguably the most culturally conservative government in postwar Australia, even what the Howard government promoted as "core Australian values" were fundamental civil rights and liberties such as individual freedom, equality between the sexes, respect for democratic institutions, toleration, and reciprocity. Otherwise, it emphasized, not unreasonably, the importance of having proficiency in the national language and some elementary knowledge of the country, its history, and its institutions—emphases that the Rudd Labor government has indicated it will maintain. The federal government also insists—as does multicultural policy—on an overriding commitment to Australia. Baldly stated, this last is somewhat problematic for a liberal democracy that values individual liberty and freedom of religion, let alone one that permits multiple citizenships. Treason and sedition are one thing, but as Kymlicka (2001a: 173) puts it, "An Australian who commits some of her time and resources to helping people in developing countries, or in her country of origin, or who pushes Australia to increase its foreign aid budget, may not be putting Australia's interests 'first and foremost,' but she is not doing anything wrong." Better that an "ennobling and exalted patriotism" may arise "under the protecting shade and influence" of freedom, as William Charles Wentworth (1853: 227) put it long ago.[21] Still, the proclaimed overriding commitment to Australia remains little more than exhortatory. No one has seriously suggested that integration requires supporting the national cricket team, as in Lord Tebbit's famous test of immigrant integration in Britain.

There are, to be sure, voices in the wider public debate over multiculturalism that give every impression of hankering after old-time Anglo-conformity and assimilationism, an aspect of the Australian story that I examine in chapter 15. Nor is it hard to find such sentiments expressed or implied, on occasion, by Australian political leaders, from John Howard during his long prime ministership to the now ousted maverick and xenophobic "anti-politician" Pauline Hanson. But precisely for this reason the Howard government's *formal* statements on integration, citizenship, and core values reveal how the debate over multiculturalism has fundamentally moved on from the question of "yea" or "nay." Almost all the things the last Howard government promoted in the guise of "integration" are key parts of the national multicultural policy statements. And the new emphasis on some knowledge of the Australian way of life is by no means inconsistent with those policy statements. Words are important, and perhaps "integration" better suits the times than does "multiculturalism" as an overarching rubric. But this should not be allowed to obscure the fact that liberal multiculturalism, in general, and Australian multiculturalism, in particular, are and always have been about integration. In this respect, it is unfortunate that the official historiography of Australia's move to multiculturalism—as outlined above—counterposes it to a preceding stage called "integration." The question is not whether immigrants should integrate into the general society, but rather what are the fair and prudent terms on which they should do so (Kymlicka 2001a: 36)? National chauvinism and exclusivity can spawn minority separatism no less than unbridled multiculturalism.

In short, it would be difficult to jettison what passes for multiculturalism in Australia, even if the federal government wanted to. The international and local landscapes have changed so profoundly. Migration patterns, international travel, instantaneous communications, and globalized markets and entertainment bear down on our ideas and expectations of citizenship, as Kim Rubenstein discusses in chapter 10. The cultural diversity of the Australian people will inevitably invite pragmatic adjustments to standing practices and institutions to better facilitate integration, as James Jupp stresses in chapter 13. There is the force of the elaborations and reinterpretations of liberal democratic principles, which locate and justify the policies of cultural recognition and accommodation in the terms of Australia's own proclaimed core values. Finally, multicultural programs and initiatives have been extensively institutionalized and are now woven into the practices of federal, state, and local government departments and services, as well as much of the private sector—which itself reflects the impact of these other factors.

None of this means that multiculturalism writ large or any particular interpretation or policy is beyond criticism. Quite the contrary, our contemporary condition and liberal democracy itself invite continued reflection and debate. Central to this debate, moreover, is the important issue of the place of national and Australian identity. Wentworth's Australia is long gone, but the question of how best to reconcile freedom and community is still very much with us. This book was conceived and the following essays are offered in the hope that they might carry the debate forward.

OUTLINE OF THE BOOK

The book is organized around four themes. Part I, *Liberalism and Diversity*, examines multiculturalism from the perspective of fundamental aspects of a liberal political order, including toleration, pluralism, nationalism, and the state.

In chapter 2, Chandran Kukathas presents a useful fivefold typology of responses to the problem of cultural diversity and notes how Australia has experimented with some of these approaches at various times while rejecting others. Kukathas defends the superiority of what he calls "minimalist" multiculturalism, since he sees this as being most consistent with classical liberalism and the idea of "pure" toleration. In this pure form, "any kind of cultural community or tradition must be accepted as part of the polity," even those that are intolerant toward other groups and the polity itself. While he acknowledges that such a position may be unrealistic in the world of practical politics, and is certainly rejected in Australia, tracing multiculturalism to its logical extension helps us see how we in fact limit multiculturalism in trying to realize other political and cultural values.

In chapter 3, George Crowder explores the implications of Isaiah Berlin's notion of value pluralism for multiculturalism. He argues that Berlinian pluralism provides only qualified support to multiculturalism in that it is subject to liberal democratic principles. Integral to these principles is a strong public commitment to the value of individual autonomy, and this overrides the kind of toleration of individual and group practices advanced by Kukathas. Crowder suggests that Australian multiculturalism basically conforms to these political implications of Berlinian value pluralism. However, he also notes the problems that a commitment to value pluralism raises for Aboriginal customary law and claims to self-government.

John Kane analyzes multiculturalism in relation to the unfolding tension between liberalism and nationalism (chap. 4). Once in ideological affinity, liberalism increasingly sought to distance itself from nationalism in the face of bellicose nation-states and vicious nationalist conflicts. Kane argues that ideological multiculturalism is liberalism's attempt to sideline nationalism completely by establishing a new order of liberal internationalism. However, as the Australian case demonstrates, the attempt is likely to fail because multiculturalism simply rechannels rather than disposes of nationalism. While official Australian multicultural policy has sought to posit Australian national identity in terms of a "civic nationalism" grounded in a commitment to liberal and democratic norms, Australians and their governments typically conduct their national affairs with a strong sense of *cultural* national identity.

The inadequate treatment of the state in discussions of multiculturalism is critically examined in chapter 5. Barry Hindess contrasts two influential approaches to the political problems that cultural diversity is taken to pose for modern states: "multiculturalism" (as found in the writings of Will Kymlicka, Bhikhu Parekh, Charles Taylor, and Australian multicultural policy) and the "politics of difference" (associated with Iris Marion Young). While the latter understands group disadvantage more broadly than the multicultural approach, Hindess argues that both approaches view the state too benignly as simply the context in which the problem of diversity is addressed, rather than as part of the problem itself. Citing recent cases of Australian government intervention, he concludes that greater attention needs to be paid to how states and their various agencies understand the problems involved in dealing with diversity in the populations under their control, and to the resources they have available for dealing with them.

Part II, *Democracy and Diversity,* explores the idea of citizenship and the possibilities of democratic inclusion in a multicultural society like Australia's.

In chapter 6, Philip Pettit examines three different pictures of the citizenry—"solidarist," "singularist," and "civicist"—that have each had a certain importance in political thought. He argues that the duties, virtues, rights, and benefits that are attached to citizenship will necessarily vary according to which of these "civic structures" is institutionalized or given prominence. While each model has some application in contemporary democracies such as Australia and the United States, it is the civicist conception, Pettit suggests, that "teaches the most arresting lessons." A civicist democracy will work best, for example, where there is a "division of civic labor," that is, where different people and groups assume different contestatory roles. Pettit's analysis suggests why, perhaps, cultural minorities in Australia should be taking a more proactive role in Australian democracy than they presently are, and than Australian multiculturalism tends to encourage. In commenting on Pettit's chapter, Martin Krygier in chapter 7 grants that the "civicist" conception of the citizenry illuminates many political conundrums, but wonders how civicist democracy can address disputes where the contending parties "do not share common argumentative traditions of presumption and evaluation," such as some Aboriginal communities.

In chapter 8, Duncan Ivison asks whether deliberative democracy might help build cross-cultural acceptance of multicultural policy itself. In Australia, as in other multicultural democracies, many people view multiculturalists as "moralists," that is, engaged in applying moral arguments to issues or areas where they are deemed to be inappropriate. Ivison examines this charge of moralism made against recent defenders of multicultural policies, and the social and political resentment that they generate. He argues that, despite prevailing tendencies toward moralism, there are ways of defending multiculturalism that avoid such political resentment. In particular, building cross-cultural acceptance of multiculturalism must be geared to showing how it serves both egalitarian justice *and* social solidarity. And the only way of securing this acceptance, he suggests, is through forms of democratic deliberation.

Part III, *Community, Culture, and Rights,* looks at three particular sites of competing memberships where rights and culture often conflict in Australia: women and girls who are at once citizens and "minorities within minorities"; individuals who are citizens of more than one political community; and immigrants and refugees seeking admission to the Australian community.

In chapter 9, Moira Gatens addresses the conventionally conceived clash between women's human rights and particular cultural norms as portrayed in Susan Moller Okin's (1999) provocative essay "Is Multiculturalism Bad for Women?" Gatens suggests that before this question can be answered, more attention needs to be paid to the background contexts in which such conflicts occur. Examining two recent cases of arranged marriage in Australian indigenous communities and the ensuing legal action, she argues that the notion of the "social imaginary" offers a constructive platform upon which rights claimants and the upholders of particular cultural norms that violate those rights may negotiate their differences. Such an approach also underscores the importance of women and girls from all cultural groups participating in the interpretation—and therefore reinterpretation—of social meaning and cultural identity.

The parallel significance of globalization for changing conceptions of Australian citizenship and multiculturalism is the subject of chapter 10. Kim Rubenstein suggests that the change to Australian citizenship law on 4 April 2002 (and more recently reaffirmed in the Australian Citizenship Act 2007) allowing Australian citizens to hold dual or multiple citizenship reflects a more profound change in our understanding of loyalty and allegiance to the nation-state. In the face of widespread international migration, travel, and population shifts, it was recognized that individuals could have "multiple connections" without this threatening their attachment to Australia. Similar factors and considerations, she argues, should underpin the endorsement of multiculturalism in Australia. However, if Australian citizenship is to express and realize "a progressive agenda of equality of membership," then multiculturalism must be further institutionalized in "administrative and legal frameworks."

In chapter 11, Arthur Glass probes the discriminatory aspects of migration law and the way in which administrative and legal frameworks—as recommended by Kim Rubenstein to entrench multiculturalism—can also powerfully *undermine* the principles of equal respect and public accountability. Glass argues that despite Australia's proclaimed liberal multicultural values, Australian migration law is compromised by an assortment of discriminatory selection processes and visa classes. Similarly, the case of refugee law vividly illustrates how indirect discrimination disadvantages particular cultural groups and challenges any presumed commitment to "equality as the proper acknowledgement of difference." A major problem is that the kinds of discrimination found in migration law are "buried in the detail of the admissions rules and not easily amenable to public discussion." Glass's analysis supports Barry Hindess's argument (chap. 5) that the bureaucratic machinery of state can be a daunting part of the problem.

Part IV, *Australian Multiculturalism: Success or Failure?* examines whether multiculturalism in Australia has worked as a policy for "managing cultural diversity" or lost its way.

In chapter 12, Brian Galligan and Winsome Roberts argue that in shifting focus from the integration of immigrants to the cultural maintenance of ethnic minorities and the redefinition of what it means to be an Australian, multicultural policy is at odds with the nature of Australian society. By and large immigrants are geographically dispersed, educate their children in English, and intermarry beyond their group, so it makes little sense, they contend, for policy to encourage the cultural differences that the immigrant generation may bring. In chapter 13, James Jupp argues that these criticisms are misplaced since Australian multicultural policy has always been less concerned with minority cultural maintenance than with social justice issues of access and equity. In Jupp's view, "ethnic closures" mainly occur as a result of access and equity being stymied. He also rejects the idea of there being a determinate Australian culture with which immigrants could be expected to identify. In chapter 14, Maria Markus offers a penetrating comment on the arguments in these two chapters and casts a cool eye on the suggestion that multiculturalism in Australia is now in a state of crisis.

Markus explicitly (and Jupp implicitly) appeals to the kind of postnational-ism or "constitutional patriotism" associated with Jürgen Habermas (and challenged by John Kane in chapter 4).

The book concludes with Geoffrey Brahm Levey discussing the problem of Australian national identity (chap. 15). He identifies the respective diffi-culties with the "postnationalist" and "liberal nationalist" arguments in the Australian debate, and he argues for a suitably revised account of the liberal nationalist position, in which the place of Australian culture and identity is acknowledged but politically delimited. Noting the enduring resistance to cultural difference in Australian culture and society, he suggests that a ques-tion of interest for political theory is how Australians negotiate the different domains of their national identity and the liberal democratic values that are asserted as central to the Australian way of life.

NOTES

1. Apart from some scattered essays, political philosophical work focusing on Australian multiculturalism only includes, to my knowledge, Kukathas 1993; Theophanous 1995; and Poole 1999. There are also a few normative inquiries into identity and citizenship in Australia, including Stokes 1997, and Hudson and Kane 2000.

2. Parts of the following discussion expand on points in Levey 2001a.

3. The measures included legislating to make all immigrants, of whatever origin, eligible to obtain citizenship after three years of permanent residence; policy instructions to overseas posts to totally disregard race as a factor in the selection of immigrants; and ratifying all international agreements relating to immigra-tion and race. See DIMA 2006a.

4. The New Zealand figure includes some Maoris and Pacific Islander peoples.

5. Lords Hansard, 14 May 2003.

6. These and the following figures in this paragraph are drawn from ABS 2006: "Religious Affiliation."

7. In 2001, a further 11.6 percent of respondents declined to answer, or inade-quately answered, the optional religious affiliation question; however, this fig-ure has remained steady at between 10 and 12 percent since the 1940s.

8. The *New Agenda,* a relatively brief document, constitutes the government's re-sponse to the more substantial commissioned report—*Australian Multiculturalism for a New Century: Towards Inclusiveness*–prepared by its National Multicultural Advisory Council. See NMAC 1999.

9. There is some irony in this, given that the more recent policies were prepared under the auspices of the socially conservative Howard governments and an arch-monarchist prime minister.

10. For example, the *Community Relations Commission and Principles of Multiculturalism Act 2000* (NSW); *Multicultural Queensland–Making a World of Difference* (2005), and the *WA Charter of Multiculturalism* (2004).

11. Emphasis added. *International Covenant on Civil and Political Rights*, opened for signature 16 December 1966, 999 UNTS 171 (entered into force 23 March 1976). See also *Declaration on the Rights of Persons Belonging to National or Ethnic, Religious and Linguistic Minorities* (adopted by the General Assembly on 18 December 1992).

12. See, for example, the "Ethnic Affairs Priorities Statement" of the New South Wales Government: www.crc.nsw.gov.au/eaps/what_eaps.htm [accessed 20 March 2006].

13. The parenthetical abbreviation—(Cth)—indicates that the act is a Commonwealth or federal parliamentary piece of legislation.

14. Title VII of the Civil Rights Act of 1964, 42 USC s 2000e; U.S. Commission on Civil Rights, *Religion in the Constitution: A Delicate Balance*, Clearinghouse Publication No. 80 (1983): 43.

15. Banting and Kymlicka's (2006a) cross-national collaborative study of the impact of multiculturalism policies on state welfare includes data on Australia, and found no systematic or clear-cut relationship between the two variables. There also has been some interesting research in Australia on the related, but quite distinct, question of whether cultural diversity erodes trust among people (e.g., Leigh 2006). As Banting and Kymlicka (2006b) note, there are conceptual as well as empirical difficulties in trying to link the findings on cultural diversity and trust to multiculturalism policies. A simplistic attempt to link them in relation to Australia is Wood 2007.

16. "Funded Community Projects": www.harmony.gov.au/grants/guides-apps.htm.

17. See www.alp.org.au/download/now/071122_social_inclusion.pdf

18. On the importance of differentiating equality and inclusion in responding to cultural diversity on campus, see Levey 2007a. On the place of fraternity and inclusion in the Danish cartoon affair, see Levey and Modood 2008.

19. I discuss equality arguments in support of symbolic recognition, public subsidization, and other cultural claims in detail in Levey 1997, 2001b, 2005, and 2006a.

20. Background on the test can be found at: www.citizenship.gov.au/test/background/index.htm

21. The classic test of patriotic sentiment is the readiness to "die for one's country," as Wentworth acknowledges in the passage that forms the epigraph to this book. Wentworth lamented the fact that his countrymen in the young colony hadn't been tested in this way; there had been no occasion to repress treason, repel invasion, or "seek glory" in foreign adventure. I examine the problem of individual freedom and "political dying" in Western and Jewish sources in Levey 2006b.

Part I

Liberalism and Diversity

Chapter 2

Anarcho-Multiculturalism
The Pure Theory of Liberalism

Chandran Kukathas

⟨◇⟩

THE PROBLEM OF MULTICULTURALISM

Most modern states today are, at least to some degree, culturally diverse. Trade, tourism, international dialogue among scholars, scientists, and artists, and the movement of skilled labor—as well as migration—have ensured that few countries do not contain within them significant numbers of people from alien cultures. The one cultural minority found almost everywhere is the international frequent flyer. Many societies today are multicultural because they are open to a diversity of peoples who come and go and, sometimes, stay.[1]

It is the fact that many seek to stay in the societies they have entered, however, that gives rise to the problem of multiculturalism.[2] For it gives rise to the question of the degree to which cultural diversity should be accepted or tolerated, as well as to the question of how cultural diversity should be accommodated. When people from diverse traditions have to coexist within a single society, a number of issues have to be settled so that the ground rules governing their common life are clear and generally accepted. There has to be some clear understanding not only of what kind of conduct is acceptable or required in public but also of what kinds of matters are matters of legitimate public concern. This means that it has to be clear, for example, what is the language of public discourse, what kinds of holidays are recognized, what customs are to be tolerated, what standards of public conduct and appearance may be expected, and what rights and obligations individuals and communities enjoy or owe.

The fact of cultural diversity has often given rise to conflicts because these issues are not always easily settled. People often have strong views about what is right and wrong, or about what is good and bad, and they are consequently unwilling readily to modify their behavior or change their thinking. Thus, for example, Muslim parents in France and (more recently) in Singapore have challenged the legality as well as the moral justifiability of state school regulations forbidding the wearing of headscarves favored by Muslim girls (or their parents). Defenders of animal rights in Britain have questioned exemptions given to religious minorities to allow them to disregard laws governing the humane slaughter of animals (to ensure that meat is kosher or halal). In many Western societies the practice of female genital mutilation insisted upon by some immigrant parents from East Africa has led to vigorous debate as authorities have struggled to find solutions that respect minority convictions without departing from more widely held social values. And in Australia, the cultural practices of some Aboriginal peoples, particularly in the Northern Territory, have brought into focus the issue of how far indigenous people ought to be able to live according to their own laws and enforce their own standards of justice.

In these circumstances, to seek the theoretical foundations of multiculturalism is to ask if there is any set of general principles that might guide our reflection on such issues as the ones raised above. What are the principles that govern a multicultural society?

In this essay, I shall argue that the best answer to this question is to be found within the theory of classical liberalism. The question of what is liberalism, however, is nothing if not controversial, so it ought to be made clear at the outset that what will be presented here is a particular understanding of classical liberalism, and a particular view of what it has to offer. There are others, however, who take a quite different view of what it is that liberalism requires or has to offer. In my own presentation I will therefore try to make clear where it is that I differ from other liberal views prominent today.

The essay is presented in several parts. In the next section I begin by considering five possible responses to the problem of cultural diversity. These are labeled isolationism, assimilationism, minimalist or pure multiculturalism, strong or eager multiculturalism, and apartheid. In the third section I suggest how these different positions are related and identify some of the theorists of multiculturalism and locate them in the schema described there. In the fourth section I argue that the third of the responses to the problem of diversity is most consistent with classical liberalism, and offer reasons why it is to be favored. The fifth section considers a number of arguments offered in defense of other versions of multiculturalism, and particularly other liberal versions, and explains why they should be rejected. I conclude with some general remarks about the nature of a multicultural society, the nature of political society, and the limits of the liberal theory of multiculturalism.

FIVE RESPONSES TO DIVERSITY

Societies may respond to the fact of cultural diversity in a variety of ways, not all of which involve an acceptance of the idea of a multicultural society. There are five responses that might usefully be distinguished.

Isolationism

The most obvious response a society might make would be to try to prevent any kind of cultural diversity from emerging by excluding outsiders from entering or making their homes within it—particularly if the outsiders are different. Both Japan and Australia have, at different times in their histories, adopted this particular approach. In Australia, the White Australia policy came into being with the first Act of the Commonwealth Parliament, the Immigration Act of 1901. The original aim of Australian immigration policy was to assimilate immigrants into the predominantly Anglo-Celtic population. Migrant selection was carefully controlled to ensure that the ethnic composition remained white and culturally British. Those most preferred were Britons, followed by Northern Europeans. Southern Europeans were considered less desirable, and Asian and other nonwhites were regarded as altogether undesirable. Migrants from the desired categories were thus offered financial inducements to move to Australia, while those from Asia were excluded (Lopez 2000: 43).[3] It was not until the 1960s that steps were taken to dismantle the policy, which was officially ended in 1973.

There are many reasons why a society or its rulers might choose the path of isolationism in a policy of excluding all outsiders but the select few. Sometimes it is because of a desire on the part of some to protect or preserve their established advantages or privileges. A predominantly Muslim elite, for example, might not want to see the growth of the substantial non-Muslim minority if this might reduce the size of its support base. Or the labor movement might be wary of immigration from poorer nations because it would threaten to lower wage levels by expanding the size of the market for unskilled labor. But a particularly important reason for isolationism in immigration policy is the fear of cultural transformation.

The problem with isolationism as a policy is that it is difficult to sustain, for the costs of the policy are greater than most people are willing to bear. If the aim of the policy is to preserve a kind of cultural homogeneity, the difficulty is that it will not be enough simply to try to maintain a restrictive immigration policy—one that keeps out people from particular cultural, ethnic, religious, or linguistic groups, or keeps out would-be immigrants altogether. There are many ways in which a society might come under the influence of foreign cultures besides through interaction with immigrants. Trade and tourism alone will bring the domestic society to awareness of other ways of life. And any kind of openness to foreign artistic and literary traditions will exert its own influence on the local population, encouraging imitation and cultural borrowing. The importing of foods will change dietary habits. Participation in international activities, from World Cup football to international science conventions, will also bring home ideas and attitudes from other parts of the globe. To preserve cultural homogeneity it would not be enough to restrict immigration. It would also be necessary to limit contact with the outside world by restricting the freedom of the domestic population to travel, trade, and generally communicate with outsiders. Thus far, no nation has been able or willing to do this, and so no nation has been able to escape the forces of cultural transformation.

Assimilationism

One alternative to isolationism is a policy of admitting outsiders but with a view to assimilating them into the existing society, thereby limiting the extent of domestic cultural transformation. This is a policy that seeks to acculturate newcomers, though it might also be adopted with respect to, say, a minority indigenous population. For much of the era of the White Australia policy, the Aboriginal population of the country was seen as one that needed to be assimilated into the mainstream of a predominantly Anglo-Celtic and European society. In this regard, Australian social policy for much of the twentieth century was marked by assimilationist aims on two fronts, looking to make both newcomers and the original inhabitants conform to a particular cultural standard.

   The problem with the policy of assimilation, however, is that, like isolationism, its chances of success are limited even if one is prepared to pay a very high price to pursue it. First, assimilation is a two-way street: even as newcomers are being assimilated, they will be exerting their own influence to modify the practices and attitudes of the host society.[4] This, coupled with the other sources of cultural influence to which the society is subject, makes it fairly likely that it is not only newcomers or minorities who will change. Second, not all cultural minorities want to assimilate to the degree sought by the makers of social policy. In Australia, the turning point came when it became clear that many immigrants who had lived for some time in their new country began in the 1960s to consider returning to Europe because they saw their own cultural traditions and beliefs as unwelcome. This was one of the factors that prompted a change in government policy away from assimilation toward a more pluralist outlook. But even if cultural minorities are not willing to go so far as to leave the country, many will resist attempts to assimilate them. At the extreme, this may generate separatist tendencies if resistance leads to a hardening of attitudes on all sides. Third, assimilation may be difficult policy to pursue in a society that has strong traditions of respect for individual freedom, since such a policy may require restrictions not only on newcomers but also on native-born citizens.

Minimalist or Pure Multiculturalism

While assimilation may be difficult to enforce, it is also difficult to avoid. In any society in which there is a reasonable degree of freedom, people will associate with and imitate one another. There is a tendency to conformity that is as difficult to eradicate as is the inclination of some individuals to go in a different direction. And for reasons of expediency or prudence, newcomers or minorities in any society will be inclined to follow the dominant norms simply because it makes life easier, less costly, or more enjoyable. It is easier to learn the language that most people speak than to wait for them to learn our own. It is easier to make friends with people with whom we share something in common. And it is better to have a wide range of people with whom to speak or form friendships than to be confined to the company of a few who are like-minded in every way.

The multiculturalist response to the fact of cultural diversity is neither to try to prevent diversity from emerging in society by isolating it from others, nor to try to prevent diversity from taking root by assimilating minorities into the whole. Early immigration policy in Australia was concerned—alarmed—by the prospect of non–Anglo-Celtic minorities making their homes in Australia. In 1971, the then minister for immigration, Phillip Lynch, while willing to continue the new policy of accepting European and Asian immigrants, expressed a concern that Australia would be home to a large number of "undigested minorities" (NMAC 1999: 22–23). The multicultural outlook, however, is both willing to accept a diversity of newcomers to a society and untroubled if they remain undigested. The doors should be open to anyone who wishes to enter society; and the extent to which anyone assimilates should be determined by the desire and capacity of each individual to do so.

Strong or Eager Multiculturalism

One characteristic of the minimalist multiculturalist view, however, is that it leaves open the possibility that some people will assimilate into a society less because they wish to do so than because they have little other option. It leaves such people, members of minority cultures within the wider society, either unable to enjoy their separate cultural identity because the costs of sustaining it are too high, or unable fully to participate in the society because of their particular cultural beliefs or traditions. The strong multiculturalist view is that society should take positive measures not only to enable such people to participate as full members of society but also better to enable them to maintain their separate identity and traditions. Diversity should not only be tolerated but also fostered or promoted, and supported—both financially (if necessary) and by special rights for minority cultures.

The difference between the strong and minimalist versions of multi-culturalism is a matter of degree. Both variants have their roots in liberal political theory, with strong multiculturalism characteristic of modern liberalism and minimalist multiculturalism characteristic of classical liberalism. In this essay I shall defend minimalist multiculturalism against strong multiculturalism by defending classical liberalism against its modern competitor.

Apartheid

There is a fifth response to the fact of diversity that ought to be mentioned for the sake of completeness: apartheid. This response does not seek to exclude cultural minorities (usually because it is not possible to do so) but forbids them to assimilate to any degree. South Africa under white minority rule supplies an example of such a regime, though in this particular case the groups denied the right to participate fully in the society themselves formed a majority of the total population.

The problem with this response to diversity is that is hard to sustain given people's propensities to associate. It suffers from the same difficulties that beset the isolationist response. In some ways, however, it confronts problems that are even more intractable since the people it seeks to keep apart coexist within the same national boundaries. It is difficult to maintain such a regime without creating a polity in which different citizens have different and unequal rights and duties. It may be impossible to sustain such a form of political order without resort to repression.

A MODEL OF RESPONSES TO DIVERSITY

This typology of responses to diversity might usefully be presented on a graph illustrating their relations to one another. Responses toward cultural diversity might be plotted on a graph whose vertical axis measures the polity's attitude to the *integration* of diverse peoples into society and whose horizontal axis measures the polity's attitude to the *membership* of different peoples in the polity. At one extreme, a polity might simply deny minority cultures or communities within it the right to become a part of the society, refusing to allow them to integrate into the society. Equally, it might deny outsiders the opportunity to join the society by forbidding them to enter or to become members; it might even expel minorities from the polity. At the other extreme, a polity might require that some groups of people integrate into the society even if they have no wish to do so. Equally, a polity might require that a group of people acquire or retain membership in the polity whether or not they wish to do so. But political societies do not have to take extreme positions. They might try either to deter or to promote integration, or they might simply tolerate those who wish to integrate without let or hindrance. And they might respond in similarly moderate fashion to those who seek membership in the polity. A number of political positions can be identified along these dimensions. These are noted on the graph in figure 1.

Figure 1: Responses to Diversity

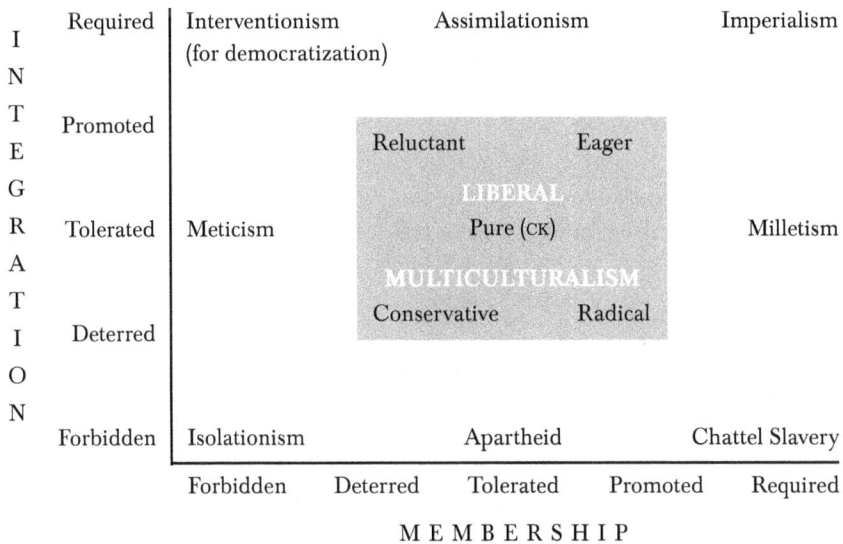

INTEGRATION		Forbidden	Deterred	Tolerated	Promoted	Required
	Required	Interventionism (for democratization)		Assimilationism		Imperialism
	Promoted			Reluctant Eager		
	Tolerated	Meticism		**LIBERAL** Pure (CK)		Milletism
	Deterred			**MULTICULTURALISM** Conservative Radical		
	Forbidden	Isolationism		Apartheid		Chattel Slavery

MEMBERSHIP

Societies that try to restrict membership by forbidding entry by outsiders, and also to enforce conformity within their boundaries by denying those who are different the opportunity to integrate, fall into the corner labeled "isolationism." Though it is difficult to find examples of societies that fall neatly into any category, Uganda under Idi Amin might fit here, since it not only restricted entry into the country but also expelled the Asian population rather than let it integrate or assimilate into the native population. Less extreme, in some ways, is the position labeled "apartheid." In such a society, the membership in the polity of diverse groups is accepted, but particular groups are forbidden to integrate into society. A more extreme position would be one that forced some into membership in a society while denying them any opportunity to integrate. Slavery in the United States falls into this category, since Africans were forcibly brought to America but, by virtue of being enslaved, were forbidden to integrate into society. (Historically, not all forms of slavery forbade the integration of slaves into society.)

Some societies are less hostile to others integrating into their way of life but remain unwilling to allow them fully to become members of the polity. A society might, for example, welcome guest workers and willingly allow them to live as a part of society but deny them full rights of membership. Germany's attitude toward Turkish residents and Malaysia's attitude toward Indonesian and Filipino workers supply possible examples here. To identify this position I use the term "meticism," after the metics or foreign residents of city-states of ancient Greece.[5]

Societies that want to see other peoples conform to their way of life but are unwilling to allow them to become a part of that society occupy the top left-hand corner of the graph. These are labeled "interventionist" societies. Crusading states would come into this category. They differ, however, from imperialist states, which are distinguished by a concern to incorporate other societies into a greater polity, expanding the membership of a highly integrated state. These states occupy the top right-hand corner of the graph. Not all imperialist states, however, seek full integration of subjugated peoples. The millet system of the Ottoman Empire required societies within the empire to remain members but tolerated a diversity of cultural practices and traditions.

States that tolerate or permit the admission of outsiders without seeking forcibly to enforce membership, but nonetheless require all members of society to integrate fully into the ways of the dominant culture, are "assimilationist" polities. These fall into the top center section of the graph. Modern France comes close to falling into this category, since it admits a diversity of peoples but strongly requires that they conform in various ways to French traditions; indeed, it requires that they become French.

Finally, those political societies that fall in the center of the graph are what might be called "liberal multicultural" societies. In general, they admit outsiders without either encouraging or deterring them from seeking membership, and tolerate their ways whether they seek to integrate into the new society or elect to hold on to their separate traditions and beliefs.

The various positions plotted in this scheme are highly stylized, and it would be hard to find any state that fell precisely into one of the corners or spaces identified. And the place a state occupies would be changeable to some degree depending on the policies pursued at any one time. This scheme is intended to be suggestive rather than indicative of any permanent or enduring set of relations among political societies. Nonetheless, this scheme is intended to make one claim clear: that the liberal attitude to cultural diversity seeks a medium among extremes. It is also intended to suggest that the differences among liberal multiculturalists reflect the way in which liberals are pulled in different directions. The position I wish to defend, however, is to be found squarely in the center of the conception of liberalism described by this construction.

CLASSICAL LIBERAL MULTICULTURALISM

Liberalism is a doctrine that is profoundly sympathetic to multiculturalism because it proclaims the importance of individual freedom to live a life of his or her own, even if the majority of society disapproves of the way that life is lived. According to liberalism's traditions, minority ways, or differences, are to be tolerated rather than suppressed. By implication, this means that minority cultures are accepted within a liberal society: people are not required to live by values they cannot abide, nor forbidden to live by values they cherish. The fundamental liberal concern, therefore, is to find some way in which those who hold to different values might live together without coming into conflict. This is a serious problem, since the potential for conflict is high in a society in which all seek, and in principle are granted the right, to live by values they cherish—or at least, not to live by values they cannot abide. Liberals have therefore argued vigorously among themselves about the basis upon which people's pursuit of their different, and potentially conflicting, purposes should be regulated. Perhaps the most famous liberal attempt to specify a basis for such regulation is John Stuart Mill's harm principle: only the prospect of *harm to others* can justify the restriction of individual freedom to pursue particular ends. As is well known, however, the principle is problematic because the definition of "harm" is itself dependent on one's understanding of what ends are desirable.

In spite of such difficulties, however, the virtue of the liberal view is that it takes seriously the idea that, when people disagree about what is good and what is right, the issue should not be settled by the exercise of power to enforce the dominant view.[6] In the face of disagreement or difference what should be sought is peaceful coexistence. This is why it is, in principle, sympathetic to the idea of a culturally diverse society, for in such a society people may associate freely with whomsoever they choose without being required to conform to standards they do not recognize or cannot abide. But this is only possible provided each respects a similar freedom for others. And it is the content of this proviso that liberalism tries to articulate.

What this requires, in the end, is a regime of toleration. And in the version of liberalism sometimes described as "classical liberalism," that toleration calls for what I have labeled "pure multiculturalism." In a society in which pure multiculturalism is the norm, people's freedom to associate produces an open society of which others may readily become members by associating with those who already belong to it. It neither forbids outsiders from entering nor forces them to join. Equally, those who are a part of the society are free to live by their own traditions, whether as part of a cosmopolitan whole or as members of minority cultures who associate with others to a minimal degree. The presence of different cultures or traditions is tolerated, even if those traditions do not themselves embrace or sympathize with liberalism or liberal values. A classical liberal multicultural society may contain within it many illiberal elements. Yet it will try neither to expel nor to assimilate them, but will simply tolerate them. What such a regime is most hostile to are isolationism, interventionism, imperialism, and slavery.

A classical liberal multicultural regime such as this could be described as a maximally tolerant regime. It is so tolerant it will even accept within its midst those who are opposed to it. At the same time, however, it will not give special protection or advantages to any particular group or community. It will not deter anyone from pursuing particular goals or from trying to sustain particular traditions; yet neither will it promote others or subsidize ones that are specially preferred. This is multiculturalism without fear or favor.

MODERN LIBERAL MULTICULTURALISM

To some liberal thinkers, however, this kind of multiculturalism is implausible, because it does not maintain a strong enough commitment to values that are central to liberalism. Some liberals are reluctant to embrace any form of multiculturalism and argue strongly that liberalism requires that all communities or cultures within the liberal state be liberal to some degree—perhaps even to a considerable degree.

Brian Barry (2001), for example, is highly critical of multiculturalism from a liberal point of view, arguing that the liberal state should not tolerate illiberal practices. This means that the state should, among other things, assume responsibility for the education of children to ensure that cultural or religious communities cannot inculcate implausible beliefs in the minds of the young. It should also ensure that the standards maintained within families properly recognize the rights of women and take steps to prevent cultural communities from disadvantaging those who withdraw or defect from such groups (cf. Kukathas 2002).

Other liberal theorists, however, defend a strong version of multiculturalism, arguing that a multicultural state should recognize group-differentiated rights and offer special protections to minority cultures. For Will Kymlicka (1989, 1995, 2001a), for example, the liberal state should take active steps to ensure that groups have the resources they need to sustain themselves.[7] This means not simply subsidizing their activities but also ensuring that legal and political arrangements do not discriminate against or disadvantage cultural minorities. Equally, however, the state should also make sure that cultural groups respect certain basic civil rights to which all individuals are entitled in a liberal order. For Kymlicka, the stance of "pure liberalism" offers a policy that amounts to little more than "benign neglect," and such a policy, he argues, ultimately fails properly to address the crucial questions that confront a multicultural polity.

Both of these thinkers resist the classical liberal call for the state to be less interventionist and more "neutral" on cultural issues, though Barry is inclined to push the state into greater efforts to liberalize cultural minorities, while Kymlicka prefers that the state take stronger measures to ensure that minorities can be secure in their effort to maintain their cultural independence. Other modern theorists, however, are resistant to classical liberal multiculturalism because they push away from it in quite different directions. For "cultural conservatives," what is needed for a sustainable polity is a society that is culturally homogeneous to a considerable degree. This means that the state, including the liberal state, has to be wary of admitting people who are culturally different and likely to dilute the cultural homogeneity of the society, so membership has to be deterred. Equally importantly, however, it is necessary that the state not be too quick to encourage those already within its boundaries to integrate into society because not everyone is suitable for citizenship. Those who are not culturally similar ought not to be encouraged to integrate, for the result will be a polity that is more heterogeneous. In this respect, it ought not to be easy for residents to become citizens—for diversity ought to be discouraged (Pickus 1998).

Other thinkers, who might be labeled postmodernists or radicals, push away from classical liberal multiculturalism for different reasons again. For them, the liberal vision is too individualistic and too homogenizing. A good polity ought to welcome diversity by admitting outsiders readily; but it ought positively to encourage them to preserve their own traditions. Far greater recognition needs to be given to the importance of cultural identity to minority groups struggling to maintain a worthwhile life in modern political society. Such groups need to be included as members of political society, but also helped to preserve their identities as independent cultural communities.[8]

The conservative and radical thinkers I have identified here might not be willing to regard themselves as part of the liberal camp. I place them there, nonetheless, because they do not resist or depart from liberal principles in many respects. In general, they are advocates of a constitutional order in which individuals enjoy a significant measure of freedom under the law, and which is, to a considerable degree, open to the outside world. What they share with the reluctant and the eager liberal multiculturalists is a rejection of the stance of classical liberalism. Where they differ, however, is in the level of their commitment to liberal values. Conservatives and radicals, in the end, are at best skeptical about liberalism and about the individualism they see at its heart. The theorists I have labeled "eager" and "reluctant" multiculturalists, however, are liberals who profess a serious commitment to liberal principles or liberal values. It is this commitment that is the source of their disagreement with the "pure" liberal position.

For thinkers such as Kymlicka and Barry, who differ quite significantly in their attitudes toward multiculturalism, a liberal society must be one whose communities or subgroups themselves respect liberal values—at least to some degree. For Barry (2001: chap. 4) they can only depart from liberal norms if they are associations that are fully voluntary associations of free adults. And such groups ought not to be given any particular encouragement to maintain their separate, illiberal, forms of association. For Kymlicka, on the other hand, it is important that minority cultural communities be helped partly because it is only if they receive assistance that their members will be able to enjoy a measure of the autonomy that, in his view, is a value liberalism particularly commends. If they are to be helped, this means that they must be given assistance in their efforts to not only integrate but also maintain their separateness. This means that they must be given legal and political dispensations that will better enable them to survive and prosper in society. This may mean giving them special political representation, recognizing their cultural beliefs (say, by incorporating them into the structure of national symbols or allowing the setting of public holidays to reflect minority as well as majority religious practices), and allowing some groups exemptions from certain legal requirements. But it also means, in the second instance, making laws that enable groups to protect themselves from outside influences. In the case of indigenous peoples in particular, Kymlicka advocates allowing and enabling groups to establish systems of self-government. In these respects, Kymlicka differs significantly from Barry; but they share a conviction that independent groups in a liberal polity should respect some basic liberal values. Groups may not be wholly illiberal.

The classical liberal position, as it is understood in this essay, is characterized by a far more significant degree of tolerance insofar as it is willing to tolerate illiberalism within its midst. Classical liberal multiculturalism is thus willing to accept that, in a multicultural society, there may be groups or communities of people whose basic traditions or beliefs or practices are not only disapproved of by the majority but are even hostile to liberal values. Modern liberals reject this position because it is too tolerant of illiberal values. Some radical critics of liberalism reject it because it offers nonliberal communities no more than toleration. And conservative critics reject it because it fails to embrace particular nonliberal values. But from a classical liberal point of view, these other perspectives should be rejected because they demand too much of a political regime, for they demand that the regime conform to particular substantive moral commitments. In the face of cultural diversity, this can only be a demand that a political society conform to the moral and cultural values of a particular—dominant—political group. The strength of the classical liberal view is that it resists such calls because, in the end, they can only amount to a demand that dissenting traditions be suppressed. If anything is characteristic of the liberal tradition, it is its wariness of the concentration of power and of the efforts of the powerful to suppress dissent. Liberal regimes have been notable for their commitment to the dispersal of power, and to the toleration of dissenting idea—be they conservative, socialist, fascist, theocratic, or simply antiliberal. If the liberal tradition accepts anything, it is that toleration is of fundamental importance, and that toleration requires a willingness to put up with what one dislikes.[9]

THE LIMITS OF CLASSICAL LIBERAL MULTICULTURALISM

The theoretical foundations of multiculturalism, from my perspective, lie in the political theory of classical liberalism. Yet the plausibility of this view will surely be questioned for at least one reason: that it presents what can only be an impossible standard for any regime to meet. In its purest form, a classical liberal multicultural regime seems at once to demand an impossibly high standard—a standard of complete tolerance—and, at the same time, no standard at all, since any kind of cultural community or tradition must be accepted as a part of the polity. Can such a position possibly be sustained, either theoretically or in practical political terms?

In theoretical terms, classical liberal multiculturalism is a perfectly coherent position. If the analysis in this essay is sound, it a position that is readily identifiable, and may be plotted quite precisely in relation to a number of other liberal multicultural views, and to other political positions more generally. But in practical terms, it is a position that is unlikely ever to be found in the real world of politics, for there cannot be such a thing as a political regime that is morally or culturally neutral. The world described by classical liberal multiculturalism is a world in which there is, literally, no political regime. And that is not only a highly improbable world but also very definitely not the kind of world in which we live.

In Australia, for example, it would be difficult to argue that not only Aboriginal peoples but also immigrants should be able to live by their own legal and ethical traditions, or for that matter, that borders should be open.

The obvious question this leads to is: what is the interest or relevance of this analysis of the theoretical foundations of multiculturalism, and of classical liberal multiculturalism more generally? The answer is that the idea of multiculturalism, insofar as the term identifies a philosophical stance rather than merely a political policy, and insofar as it bespeaks a commitment to accommodating rather than suppressing cultural diversity, is an idea that pushes away from the various other attitudes toward a conception of an open society. And the classical liberal conception of multiculturalism presented here describes the terminating point of multiculturalism. And while no actual regime may be willing, or able, to reach (let alone sustain) such a form of society, it may be useful to see exactly where the theory of multiculturalism leads. This may be useful because it makes clear that a decision to stop anywhere else along the road to multiculturalism will reflect the influence of certain cultural values that have great practical and political significance but, from a multicultural point of view, no particular theoretical warrant.

NOTES

1. One matter I do not address explicitly (for reasons of space) is the question of the nature of "culture." For an excellent discussion, however, see Parekh 2000: 142–78.

2. It is worth noting that many societies contain what are referred to as "indigenous" populations, and so are multicultural even without the inclusion of mi-

grants. Nonetheless, it remains true that the arrival of the first outsiders created the cultural diversity. Subsequent visitors have simply added to the complexity of the picture.

3. Of course, there already existed a certain amount of ethnic diversity in the Australian population. Apart from the indigenous peoples, there had been substantial Chinese migration to Australia in the nineteenth century (particularly during the gold rush period), and other Asian peoples had come into the country in small numbers.

4. This discussion of assimilation ignores many of the complexities that a more careful and thorough analysis would have to deal with. The classic discussion of assimilation is Gordon 1964. See also Kukathas 1997a.

5. Found in most city-states except Sparta, metics occupied an intermediate position between foreigners and citizens. They enjoyed the protection of the law but were subject to restrictions on marriage and had a limited right to own property. They did not enjoy any rights of political participation.

6. The dominant view need not be the majority view. It may simply be the view of the most powerful minority.

7. I have taken issue with Kymlicka's ideas in Kukathas 1997b, and more extensively in Kukathas 2003.

8. For an important defense of this view, see Deveaux 2000. The most important and influential advocate of a position such as this is Charles Taylor. See, for example, Taylor 1994.

9. I have argued this more fully in Kukathas 1999.

Chapter 3

Multiculturalism

A Value-Pluralist Approach

George Crowder

⬥

"Multiculturalism" means different things to different people. There is agreement on its general definition: public recognition of the value of multiple cultural identities within the same society. But when it comes to explaining what purpose is properly served by multiculturalism—and consequently the precise form that multicultural policy should take—opinions are divided. On the one hand there is the conservative view that multiculturalism should properly amount to no more than a pragmatic vehicle for integrating new migrants into the cultural mainstream (Galligan and Roberts 2004: chap. 4). Within this conservative position there are those, especially representing business interests, who see the principal purpose of immigration, and therefore of multiculturalism, as the promotion of economic growth; this view is prominent in the Australian federal government's principal policy declarations on multiculturalism (Commonwealth of Australia 1999, 2003). On this view, the chief value of cultural diversity is that it enhances the skilled labor pool, multiplies contacts for overseas trade, and expands domestic markets (Parkin and Hardcastle 1997: 494). On the other hand, some people conceive of multiculturalism in more radical terms, as a vehicle for the rejection of dominant norms that pretend to universality but that are in reality parochially Western (Parekh 2000; Tully 1995). This radical position is, in turn, condemned by its detractors as political correctness run riot, based on a romanticizing of indigenous and non-Western cultures, and implying a foolish abandonment of the standards of liberal democracy and even reason itself (Sandall 2001).

I propose a rationale for multiculturalism, in Australia and elsewhere, that is located between these conservative and radical poles. The view I defend is intended to avoid both the complacent acceptance of current norms (in particular, narrowly economic conceptions of well-being) and the radical relativizing of all standards. The ethical basis of my argument is the concept of "value pluralism." This is the idea, associated in particular with the work of Isaiah Berlin, that there are at least some generic universal values but that these (and other more local values) are irreducibly multiple, frequently conflicting, and sometimes "incommensurable" with one another. Pluralism in the Berlinian sense thus contains elements of moral universality and diversity. It also seems, immediately, to intersect with multiculturalism. If there are many distinct human goods, then one would expect that different combinations of these would constitute many genuinely valuable ways of life that are worthy of public recognition.

However, I shall also argue that the kind of multiculturalism that is supported by Berlinian pluralism is distinctly "moderate." By this I mean to identify a form of multiculturalism that is more than a mere instrument of integration but less than a demand for cultural sovereignty. In particular, I shall argue that pluralist multiculturalism is subject to liberal principles rather than a radical view in which liberal values represent only one legitimate cultural perspective on a moral par with others. Further, those liberal principles include a strong public commitment to an ideal of individual autonomy that will usually override toleration of individual and group practices. I thus take issue with much of the existing literature in which value pluralists have touched on multiculturalism. A dominant current within that literature has identified value pluralism with cultural pluralism in a strong sense, thus suggesting a link between pluralism and unrestricted multiculturalism—unrestricted, that is, by liberal principles. This tendency, I shall argue, rests on a misunderstanding of pluralism and its political implications.

My discussion is divided into three sections. First, I review the concept of value pluralism as it is found, in particular, in the work of Berlin. Second, I argue that Berlinian pluralism suggests a form of multiculturalism that is not unrestricted but subject to liberal principles. These principles include a public commitment to individual autonomy in contrast with alternative, toleration-based models of liberal multiculturalism. Finally, I offer some brief thoughts on how autonomy-based liberal-pluralist multiculturalism might bear on multicultural policy in Australia.

BERLINIAN PLURALISM

Value pluralism is a theory of morality that emphasizes the necessity of hard choices among conflicting goods. As Berlin (2002: 213–14) puts it, "the world that we encounter in ordinary experience is one in which we are faced with choices between ends equally ultimate, and claims equally absolute, the realization of some of which must inevitably involve the sacrifice of others."[1] Some goods are universal—that is, they contribute to the good life for any human being. As to the content of these universals, different pluralists give different accounts, although all agree that the universal goods must be highly generic. Berlin includes liberty, equality, and courage in this category; Martha Nussbaum and John Kekes provide more extensive and systematic lists (Berlin 1990: 12; Jahanbegloo 1992: 37; Kekes 1993: 39–42; Nussbaum 2000b: 78–80). Whatever the precise content of the universals, however, the more distinctive pluralist claim is that these and other goods are likely to come into conflict with one another, so that we must often choose between them. Liberty, for example, can sometimes be promoted only at the expense of equality. Further, and most distinctively of all, pluralists stress that these choices are sometimes difficult, because the values concerned may be "incommensurable" with one another. That is, fundamental goods possess their own "voice" or weight or logic, such that they cannot be made subject to a common measure or ranked in a single hierarchy. For example, when liberty and equality come into conflict in particular cases, there is no single, universal formula that will resolve all such collisions. Choices in such cases may be hard—both in the sense that they will inevitably involve real and uncompensated loss, and in the sense that they must be made without the guidance of any single, universally authoritative decision procedure.

In rejecting the authority of a single formula, value pluralism sets itself in opposition to moral "monism," the idea that a single rule or principle or ideal will answer all ethical questions. According to Berlin, moral monism (and monism more generally) is the dominant stream, the "perennial philosophy," of the Western tradition of thought (2000a: 5–7). Its manifestations include Plato's Form of the Good, Aristotle's ideal of the contemplative life, Hegel's notion of the rational state at the end of history, and Marx's goal of the emancipation of the proletariat. Some of these names suggest what it is that Berlin most fears in the monist outlook, namely, its potential for underwriting utopian ideals that turn into authoritarian nightmares. The single correct ethical formula suggests a single true way of life, hence a single legitimate political regime dedicated to enforcing that way of life and suppressing all alternatives.

Some pluralists would say that monism also harbors dangers that are more mundane than those of totalitarianism, but perhaps more pervasive in the twenty-first century. Examples include utilitarianism and cost-benefit analysis, the language of contemporary public policy (Crowder 2002a: 50–51; Nussbaum 2000a; Richardson 2000). Along similar lines, another critical target for pluralists is—or should be—what is known in Australia and New Zealand as "economic rationalism," the "neoliberal" assumption that economic prosperity and efficiency is the sole or overriding criterion for any question of public policy. Pluralists will allow that economic efficiency is a genuinely important value, but they will add that this should not blind us to the claims of other genuine goods: justice in distribution, equality of respect, and a sense of community, for example. As Michael Walzer (1983: 119–20) writes, "money is insidious, and market relations [tend to] transform every social good into a commodity." Pluralism, then, sets its face against one of the most powerful social tendencies of our time, the domination of public policy by the values of the market.

However, it is not only the narrowness of monism that pluralism opposes. At the opposite extreme, pluralists also reject another powerful current in contemporary thought and politics, namely the "anything goes" mentality promoted by cultural relativism. Cultural relativism is essentially the view that all cultures are morally equal, that each possesses its own sovereign and unassailable perspective on right and wrong. Berlin sometimes came close to such a position, but his more considered view was that pluralism and relativism are distinct and opposed.[2] For relativists, cultures are morally (and perhaps cognitively) incommensurable, each with its own incomparable ethical (and perhaps cognitive) perspective. For Berlin, it is values that are incommensurable, not cultures.

Cultures cannot be wholly incommensurable on Berlin's view, because if they were we would have no understanding of other cultures or periods. We would be imprisoned within the "impenetrable bubble" of our own unique mindset (Berlin 1990: 11). But we are capable of such understanding, however partial, and what makes this possible is a common "human horizon" of moral experience (Berlin 1990: 11, 80). Within the human horizon different cultures pursue many different goods, but these are often divergent interpretations of fundamental values that are common to all human societies. Cultures therefore overlap on the generic goods of universal experience, and if that is so then they cannot be wholly incommensurable. If they are not wholly incommensurable, then they are not morally sovereign. There are common standards according to which one can comprehend and appreciate the practices of other peoples. The same common standards also make it possible—although Berlin does not emphasize this corollary—to judge those practices critically. Aztec human sacrifice may express the same valuing of life and regeneration accepted by all cultures, but it does so in a way that is less defensible than alternative expressions of the same fundamental value.

Pluralism is therefore distinguished from cultural relativism by its acceptance of universals and, by implication, its rejection of "culture" as a decisive moral authority. In general, the emphasis in value pluralism is on the plurality and incommensurability of values rather than cultures. But the incommensurability of values might seem to leave pluralists with a problem not unlike that raised by relativism. When incommensurables collide, why should we privilege one set of values rather than another? For example, how can liberals such as Berlin justify their commitment to the values distinctive of liberalism?

There are three main responses to this problem in the work of Berlin and other pluralists. First, pluralists have sometimes embraced a "subjectivist" view, in which choices among conflicting incommensurables must be ultimately nonrational, or unguided by any reason that is decisive over others (Berlin 1997: 320; Gray 1993: 291, 295, 1995a: 61, 1995b: 69–70). When we have to choose among incommensurables, we just "plump" for one or another arbitrarily or according to personal preference. If this were true then neither liberalism nor any other political position would be rationally justifiable under pluralism. But the problem with this subjectivist view is that it fails to account for what seems to be a feature of our moral experience, namely, that even if deeply plural values cannot be ranked or commensurated in the abstract, we do seem capable of ranking them, for good reason, in particular cases. For example, equality may not outrank liberty in the abstract, or in every case, but there may be good reason to sacrifice a degree of liberty for taxpayers in exchange for greater equality for those unable to afford housing, health, or education (Berlin 2002: 172–73). Consequently, most pluralists have now distanced themselves from the subjectivist view of pluralist choice (Berlin and Williams 1994; Gray 1995a: 154–55, 2000a: 36).

The possibility of reasoned choice among incommensurable values in particular cases suggests a second, "contextualist," view of choice under pluralism. But although this view amounts to an improvement on the crude subjectivism of the first position, it still comes close to the cultural relativism that Berlin and other pluralists are supposed to reject. What sort of context should we look to for guidance? One obvious candidate is cultural context, and indeed Berlin sometimes speaks in just those terms, referring to the possibility of resolving hard choices by appeal to "the general pattern of life in which we believe," or "the forms of life of the society to which one belongs" (Berlin 1990: 18; 1997: 15; 2002: 47). In these passages cultural convention seems to be authoritative.

However, Berlin's texts contain hints of a third response to the problem of pluralist choice, and this is the possibility that interests me most. This may be called the "universalist" interpretation, because it appeals beyond particular contexts to principles of universal scope. These Berlin finds implicit in the concept of pluralism itself. His main argument along these lines turns on the idea and value of choice. If pluralism is true, then "the necessity of choosing between absolute claims is then an inescapable characteristic of the human condition. This gives its value to freedom" (Berlin 2002: 214). The pluralist outlook emphasizes moral plurality and conflict. On this view, choice moves to center stage in moral experience. If we must choose, Berlin argues, we must value freedom of choice, hence by implication a liberal order based on negative liberty. Unfortunately, this argument from choice, at least in the form in which Berlin presents it, contains a logical gap (Crowder 1994: 297–99, 2002a: 81–82; Gray 1995a: 160–61). To say that choice is unavoidable is not to say that choice, or freedom of choice, is desirable. Consistent with the fact that hard choices are often necessary, someone might respond that we should therefore avoid them as far as possible, perhaps passing the burden of making them to an authoritarian leader. The necessity of moral choice alone is compatible with authoritarian as well as with liberal politics.

It does not follow, however, that Berlin's argument from choice should be rejected entirely—shortly I shall argue that it can be resuscitated and improved. For the present, I note that the argument is important because it hints at the possibility that the idea of pluralism itself can generate principles to frame and guide our choices among conflicting incommensurables. Such principles cut across the claims of specific cultures, and qualify or condition the kind of multiculturalism that is acceptable from a pluralist point of view.

FROM PLURALISM TO LIBERAL MULTICULTURALISM

How does Berlinian pluralism bear on multiculturalism? My basic answer is that pluralism is supportive of multiculturalism in a moderate form—that is, a form that is neither narrowly conservative nor radically relativist. First, pluralist multiculturalism cannot be merely the conservative instrument of a monist outlook like economic rationalism. The multiculturalism commended from a pluralist point of view must be more than just a device for integrating new migrants into the workforce the better to maximize the overriding goal of economic efficiency. Rather, pluralism points to cultural diversity as possessing an intrinsic value linked to the many intrinsic goods that are likely to be promoted in a multicultural society. Under pluralism there are many legitimate human goods, and these can be legitimately combined in many different ways. Pluralism implies, therefore, that there are likely to be many valid cultures and cultural practices within a single political society. However, a second dimension of pluralist moderation places limits on the range of this legitimate cultural diversity. Pluralist multiculturalism values and promotes a substantial range of goods, but not all cultures equally and regardless of content. Rather, it values and promotes a range of cultures that is subject to, or contained within, the basic principles of liberalism.

This second point calls for more attention than the first, because it requires me to take issue with something of an orthodoxy among pluralist writers. The basic assumption in much of the literature is that Berlinian pluralism is virtually synonymous with radical cultural pluralism. Pluralist writers have tended to assume that the incommensurability of values is equivalent to the incommensurability of cultures, with the consequence that all cultures are, in effect, moral equals and cannot be subject to reasoned criticism except on their own terms. In other words, the tendency has been, in effect, to equate value pluralism with cultural relativism.

This tendency has been especially pronounced in the highly influential writings of John Gray, but it is present in other pluralist thinkers, too. For Gray (1995a: 143), pluralism implies "an irreducible diversity of worthwhile forms of life whose goodness is not commensurable by any universal standard." Consequently, liberalism is merely the political voice of one form of life among others, with no valid claim to superiority. Other pluralists, although allowing more substantial conceptions of universal standards than Gray does, similarly stress the moral authority of cultures and the limits of liberalism. Bhikhu Parekh, for example, holds that the legitimate cultural diversity implied by pluralism cannot be contained by liberalism. A fair framework for a multicultural society can be arrived at only through "an institutionalised dialogue" to which the liberal outlook is only one party among others (Parekh 2000: 14). William Galston (2002) argues that liberalism is universally valid as a political container for multiculturalism but adds that this must be a form of liberalism that tolerates nonliberal cultures and practices within its jurisdiction.

These views are mistaken because they tend to elide the distinction between pluralism and cultural relativism. To see cultures as indefeasible sources of value is to assume that they are morally incommensurable. But, as I have already argued, Berlinian pluralism refers primarily to the plurality and incommensurability of values or goods, not of whole cultures. This is not to say that there is no link at all between value pluralism and legitimate cultural pluralism. On the contrary, pluralism does imply valid cultural diversity, within a certain range, since if goods are plural and incommensurable, then (as Berlin suggested and Gray, Parekh, and Galston, for example, accept) there are many legitimate ways of ranking or combining them as general ideals or norms. In this sense, different rankings or combinations of goods yield different legitimate cultural patterns. The point I want to stress, however, is that this legitimate cultural diversity should be qualified by attention to the implications of value diversity.

What are those implications? The key line of thought here is one I raised earlier: the possibility that the concept of pluralism itself implies normative principles that apply across cultures. In that earlier discussion I rejected the particular argument proposed by Berlin, but I also promised to make some suggestions of my own. The principles I propose can be summarized under three main headings: value diversity, reasonable disagreement, and personal autonomy. My claim is that these are norms that are implicit in the concept of pluralism, that they qualify or condition the kind of multiculturalism that pluralism endorses, and that they do so in a broadly liberal direction.[3]

First, value pluralism implies a norm of value diversity. The general idea is sketched by Bernard Williams: "if there are many and competing values, then the greater the extent to which a society tends to be single-valued, the more genuine values it neglects or suppresses. More, to this extent, must mean better" (Williams 1978: xvii). Pluralism implies respect not simply for cultural diversity but also for cultural patterns that are themselves internally diverse. That imperative cuts across respect for cultures, which may themselves promote the plurality and diversity of human goods to varying degrees. The principle of value diversity gives pluralists critical leverage against existing cultures; it does not underwrite their authority.

This diversity argument is clearly in need of refinement and qualification. Pluralist diversity cannot simply be a matter of "more values rather than fewer" in the sense of maximizing units of value, since it is part of the core pluralist message that value does not come in measurable units. Further, pluralists know that to pursue some values, or packages of value, is necessarily to forego others—to seek a life of adventurous travel, for example, is unavoidably to miss out on the benefits of home and hearth. The diversity sought by pluralists raises questions not only of multiplicity but also of coherence among values (Crowder 2002a: 138–45). Still, it is clear enough that some societies can be richer than others in value diversity. This is true of liberal democracies in comparison with, say, communist societies of the Soviet era, with their prohibitions (de facto if not de jure) on freedom of speech and religion.

A second principle that is implicit in the concept of pluralism, and that provides a criterion by which pluralists can question the authority of cultures, is summed up in Charles Larmore's phrase "reasonable disagreement" (Larmore 1996: 122). This refers to the fact of widespread divergence among human beings concerning the content of the good life. Reasonable disagreement may be especially evident in modern societies, but on the pluralist view the problem is rooted in the moral experience of humanity at large: it is a permanent possibility in all human societies because of the deep structure of human value. Conceptions of the good life are essentially generalized rankings of values, including incommensurable values. Although pluralists should not accept that all such conceptions are automatically on a moral par, nevertheless the wide range of genuine human goods implies a wide range of legitimate permutations of those goods, that is, of reasonable rankings. Many such rankings will be reasonable, and concerning these there is consequently room for people to disagree on reasonable grounds. Where disagreements are reasonable in this sense they are likely to be permanent unless suppressed by overwhelming force. Since the use of force on a large scale is likely to lead to serious and unpredictable costs for all concerned, a realistic and prudent form of politics will, by and large, accept and accommodate reasonable disagreement rather than trying to overcome it. Liberalism, its defenders may fairly claim, is just such a realistic and prudent form. Here again, pluralists have reason to contain their multiculturalism within liberal bounds.

A third pluralist principle singles out the cross-cultural value of personal autonomy. If pluralism is true, then we are unavoidably faced with hard choices when incommensurable goods come into conflict. To choose well among conflicting incommensurables—that is, to choose for good reason—is to choose autonomously. This, in turn, points to a liberal framework for multiculturalism—indeed, to a particular kind of liberal framework, based on the promotion of personal autonomy as a goal of public policy. In the terminology developed by William Galston, this is liberalism in its "Enlightenment" form, in contrast with a "Reformation" liberalism based on toleration, including toleration of nonliberal practices (Galston 2002). In this debate, Galston supports Reformation liberalism, arguing that Enlightenment liberalism is too sectarian: modern societies include many conservative or tradition-based groups that do not accept personal autonomy as an ideal. In his recent work, Galston seeks to ground his position in value pluralism. But I believe that pluralism points to liberalism in its Enlightenment rather than Reformation version.[4] One way of supporting that claim is to revive Berlin's argument from choice. That argument failed in its attempt to pass directly from the necessity of choice under pluralism to the valuing of choice under liberalism. But the argument can be restated to emphasize not merely the inescapability of hard choices but the desirability of an autonomous response to those choices.

Why does choosing well among incommensurables require personal autonomy? First, it requires rational choice in the sense of practical reasoning. Arbitrary or nonrational choice is not an adequate response from a pluralist point of view, because it does not take the plurality of values seriously. Pluralists must acknowledge the full range of human goods as intrinsically valuable and worthy of implementation so far as possible. We cannot, of course, actually pursue all such goods simultaneously, and hard choices will have to be made. But in choosing which goods to pursue, pluralists cannot be merely indifferent to, or careless about, any genuine good. Consequently, they must think as carefully as they can about which goods they should pursue, and in which combinations. Taking the plurality of goods seriously means organizing one's choices, so far as possible, in a rational way. It involves, that is, a commitment to practical reasoning (Kekes 1993: 97–98; Nussbaum 2000b: 82).

Second, practical reasoning under pluralism involves autonomous judgment—that is, judgment made for reasons that are one's own in a strong sense. For one thing, conflicts among incommensurable goods cannot be decided for good reason merely by the mechanical application of a standard monist rule. Pluralists cannot rely on any ready-made monist procedure, such as utilitarianism, to resolve deep moral conflicts. Rather, they must go behind such perspectives to weigh for themselves the values those procedures embody. Nor can pluralists answer such questions merely by appealing to the authority of local tradition, since that would ignore the prevalence of reasonable disagreement.

Pluralism, in short, imposes on us choices that are demanding to a degree such that they can be made well only by autonomous agents. If pluralism is true, then the best lives will be characterized by personal autonomy. But one further step is required to complete the pluralist case for Enlightenment liberalism. Even if we accept that the best lives under pluralism are autonomous, it may still be asked why personal autonomy should be promoted as a goal of public policy. Why not leave it up to individuals or groups to pursue or promote personal autonomy in their own way? The answer is that without positive state intervention to promote its conditions, personal autonomy will be under threat from two main sources. The first is the market. A genuinely autonomous life requires material and other resources—income, education, health care, for example. The market is a powerful generator of these goods, but its distribution of them, unless corrected by state action, tends to be uneven and morally arbitrary (Dworkin 2000; Rawls 1971). Second, cultural traditions, as Galston observes, are not always, indeed they are relatively seldom, fully supportive of individual autonomy. Like economic laissez-faire, cultural laissez-faire can allow people to remain imprisoned within patterns of life that are not of their own making and that they would revise or repudiate if they could. Individual autonomy needs cultural as well as economic conditions in order to flourish, and these are no more likely to emerge automatically than are material resources. Their provision needs to be a goal of state policy.

I conclude, then, that pluralist multiculturalism will be framed by Enlightenment liberal principles that include a public commitment to the facilitation of personal autonomy among all citizens. This conclusion is similar to that reached by Will Kymlicka, who supports special rights for cultural minorities, but subject to the prior value of individual autonomy (Kymlicka 1989, 1995, 2001a, 2002). For Kymlicka, the chief value of cultural membership is that it provides a context within which people can make sense of their life choices. Consequently, there is a limit to the extent to which cultures or their characteristic practices should be protected: there should be no protection for those practices that actually undermine individual autonomy—for example, those that deny religious and other basic freedoms either to outsiders or to the group's own members. Indeed, Kymlicka sees his argument as justifying the liberalization of nonliberal cultures. Value pluralists, I suggest, should occupy a similar position, although they will arrive at it, as I have argued, by way of a number of different considerations in addition to the value of choice.

However, pluralists will also place several qualifications on this conclusion. First, "liberalization" cannot be understood by pluralists to mean the promotion of personal autonomy as an absolute or overriding goal. Under pluralism no value is absolute or overriding. There will be cases where the good of individual autonomy ought to yield to other important considerations, such as social unity or equality. Nevertheless, liberal pluralists can commend personal autonomy in general terms, to which there may be exceptions. As Galston argues, pluralism is compatible with strong commitments in the form of presumptions that can be rebutted in particular circumstances (Galston 2002: 69–78). Galston offers the notion of "rights" as an example. Similarly, the commitment to personal autonomy can be presented as just such a rebuttable presumption.

Second, individual autonomy need not be conceived as the central feature of a way of life, a substantial good in conflict with the goods distinctive of traditional cultures. In this connection Harry Brighouse draws a useful distinction between two kinds of liberal education: "autonomy-*promoting*" and "autonomy-*facilitating*" (Brighouse 1998: 733–34; 2000: chaps 4 and 5). Unlike autonomy-promoting education, autonomy-facilitating education "does not try to *ensure* that students employ autonomy in their lives, any more than Latin classes are aimed at ensuring that students employ Latin in their lives. Rather it aims to enable them to live autonomously should they wish to" (Brighouse 1998: 734). That is, the Enlightenment-liberal state need only facilitate autonomy, not promote it. Such a state need only ensure, principally through the education system, that its citizens have the capacity to live autonomously; it need not demand that its citizens' lives be comprehensively autonomous in content, like the energetically innovative lives celebrated by J. S. Mill (1972: 114–31). People may legitimately use their capacity for autonomy to opt for tradition-based ways of life in which individual self-direction is not highly valued, as in many religious traditions. I concede that even in this minimal sense, the introduction of the capacity for autonomous judgment can bring changes to a traditional society; conversely, the capacity for autonomy can atrophy if it is not exercised (Reich 2002: 102–3). My point is, however, that the relation between traditional practices and liberal facilitation of people's capacity for autonomy need not be understood as a simple relation of mutual exclusion. Rather, we should recognize the possibility that personal autonomy and adherence to group norms may be combined in varying degrees and ways, depending on the particular circumstances.

Third, state liberalization of nonliberal cultures need not be coercive or intrusive, since there is room for prudence and restraint in determining the means by which such an end is pursued (Kymlicka 1995: 167–71). This caveat is reinforced by the pluralist emphasis on the typically high costs, in terms of incommensurable goods foregone, of coercive action (Crowder 2002a: 172–74).

Finally, liberalizing policies can include a role for intercultural dialogue. Parekh is one among several recent writers who have argued that a genuinely multicultural society must be organized on terms acceptable to all its members, and that consequently minority cultures must have an active role in deciding those terms (see also Benhabib 2002; Ivison 2002; Shachar 2001). Pluralists should be sympathetic to this view. They will recognize that not all situations of conflict among incommensurable considerations yield decisive reasons for action, that some cases can be resolved only through compromise, and that compromise is best achieved through deliberative negotiation (Bellamy 1999).

Indeed, pluralism has its own contribution to make to discussions of multicultural dialogue. As Parekh points out, dialogue needs structure if it is to be useful (Parekh 2000: 267). Plausible candidates for structuring multicultural dialogue include the kind of dispositions of character, or "virtues," that are typical of the pluralist outlook (Crowder 2002a: chap. 8). First, pluralists must possess a degree of generosity or open-mindedness in order genuinely to appreciate the full range of human values and legitimate ways of life. Second, they should approach their task with what Berlin called "a sense of reality," or feeling for the real costs of moral and political decisions, conditioned in particular by the implications of incommensurability (Berlin 1978: 111, 207). Third, pluralists' rejection of neat abstract rules and insistence on the particularity of moral solutions should make them attentive to the relevant details of the choice situation, including the claims and circumstances of those people affected by the choice (Nussbaum 1992: 101). Finally, in the absence of authoritative rules or traditions, pluralists need to be flexible in tailoring their judgment closely to the situation to which they attend. These dispositions are similar to the conditions for fair deliberation listed by deliberative democrats such as Amy Gutmann and Dennis Thompson (1996; cf. Crowder 2002a: 253–54).

What of the scope or limits of dialogue on the pluralist view? Negotiation within the framework of Enlightenment liberalism is not a problem, but what happens when parties to the dialogue want to challenge the framework itself? If the challenge takes the form of reinterpretation, this too can be accommodated easily enough. If, on the other hand, a group wants to reject or seriously qualify fundamental principles like respect for individual autonomy, that is another matter. On the whole, pluralists should be prepared to resist such moves. Yet even here, they need not adopt a position of rigid resistance regardless of context. For one thing, flexibility and attention to context are among the pluralist virtues. And again, pluralists will see even the strongest principles as presumptions rather than rules that apply under all circumstances. It follows that pluralists cannot entirely curtail the reach of dialogue, even when it affects their own dearest principles. Nevertheless, they may fairly claim that presumptions like that in favor of personal autonomy are extremely strong, because held for good reasons. Such norms are rebuttable in principle, but only for better reasons still.

AUSTRALIAN APPLICATIONS

In this final section I consider briefly how the liberal-pluralist theory of multiculturalism that I have outlined might be applied in the Australian context. Multiculturalism has been official Australian policy since 1972, when the Whitlam government first declared Australia "a multicultural society." The general shape of the policy has three features that immediately seem sympathetic from the liberal-pluralist point of view I have presented.

First, the basic commitment to cultural diversity has obvious resonance with the pluralist principles of value diversity and accommodation of reasonable disagreement. The Howard government's policy document, *Multi-*

cultural Australia: United in Diversity, declares that "all Australians have the right to express their own culture and beliefs," and that this "productive diversity" generates "significant cultural, social and economic dividends" (Commonwealth of Australia 2003: 6).

Second, however, the policymakers have rightly acknowledged that cultural diversity is not the only social good. They have aimed to strike a balance between, on the one hand, recognizing the reality and value of multiple cultural identities within Australian society, and on the other hand, avoiding harmful divisiveness and maintaining an overarching Australian identity. This complex goal has been described as "ambivalent" (Jupp 1998: 139), but a pluralist perspective suggests that it could hardly be otherwise. Cultural belonging, social and economic equality, and political unity are all distinct (and perhaps incommensurable) goods that may come into conflict with one another. When they do, their rival claims should be taken seriously and weighed carefully against one another.

Third, Australian multiculturalism has been framed by liberal democratic assumptions, and in this respect too the general position is supported by liberal pluralism. "Despite conservative criticism, [Australian multiculturalism] does not endorse complete cultural relativity. From its origins in the early 1970s it has been a liberal democratic belief, which holds that all Australians should accept certain core values and forms of behaviour" (Jupp 1998: 145). This is in line with my argument that pluralism is not the same as cultural relativism, and that the kind of multiculturalism endorsed by pluralism will be qualified by a liberal political framework. In particular, I have argued, liberal pluralism emphasizes the central importance of the capacity for personal autonomy.

In short, Australian multiculturalism has been broadly in keeping with liberal-pluralist norms and constitutes a considerable achievement. Pluralists, however, should be wary of recent political developments that threaten the delicate balance between liberal universalism and cultural diversity that Australian multiculturalism has represented. On the one hand, the liberal ideal of autonomous, critical thinking is under assault from several quarters, including illiberal cultural groups such as Christian fundamentalists who regard "intelligent design" as a substitute for evolutionary science, and Islamic fundamentalists who preach a mindless *jihad.* Sadly, even some supposed defenders of liberal democracy have launched their own attacks on independent thought in overreaction to militant Islamism: the policies of the previous Howard government placed considerable pressure on civil liberties, including free speech. On the other hand, the goal of cultural diversity is also under pressure, in part through the same developments. The current fear of Islamist terrorism can only reinforce a trend of skepticism toward multicultural principles and policies that has been growing for the past decade (Jupp 1998: 146). Since the advent of the Liberal-National Coalition government in 1996, there has been "a marked reduction in multicultural migrant programs and services," amounting, in the view of one leading commentator, to a "consistent denigration and downgrading of multiculturalism over the past ten years" (Jupp 2000/2001: 31).

The most persistent and widespread reason for this gathering hostility has not been the fear of terrorism but a more general worry that multiculturalism is divisive, tending to undermine a shared Australian national identity. This view has been expressed most strongly by Pauline Hanson and her populist One Nation party, who urged the abolition of multiculturalism in order to "allow those from ethnic backgrounds to join mainstream Australia, paving the way to a strong, united country" (quoted by Jupp 2000/2001: 30). But similar views have been made public by Coalition leaders, including the former prime minister, John Howard, for whom "multiculturalism is in effect saying that it is impossible to have an Australian ethos, that it is impossible to have a common culture" (quoted by Jupp 1998: 147).

Pluralists, I believe, should defend multiculturalism against this kind of attack. One obvious response would draw on points already made: first, that multiculturalists need not deny that social unity is a significant value to set beside that of cultural identity; second, that adequate social unity is compatible with multiculturalism in the form of commitment to liberal democratic values—which, as I have argued, pluralists should accept as a framework for cultural diversity. To this it might be replied that such values provide merely a "civic" identity, and a correspondingly weakened sense of citizenship (Galligan and Roberts 2004: 95). Berlin might agree, since he emphasizes not merely political but also cultural belonging, and he argues that cultural belonging is understood better by nationalists than by liberal and other cosmopolitans (Berlin 1979: 351–55; 2002: 203). But Berlin's position here is incomplete. Not all cultural belonging is national belonging; and in situations where we *are* dealing with national belonging, nationalism suggests a case not only for nation-states but also for national groups within states (Crowder 2004b: 185–86). In other words, an emphasis on cultural identity (whether national or not) points to the need for political forms capacious enough to contain many cultural identities. This conclusion is reinforced by the pluralist principles of diversity and reasonable disagreement. Further, a shared civic identity is, in any case, compatible with some degree of shared cultural identity, as shown, for example, by generations of hyphenated Americans: Italian-Americans, Greek-Americans, and so forth. To be an American is a cultural as well as a civic identification, and one that can be hybridized with other identities.

Another objection to Australian multiculturalism might fix on this last observation as misleading. Yes, it might be replied, ethnic groups in the United States have maintained persistent distinct identities within an overarching Americanness, but the same cannot be said for ethnic groups in Australia. Thus, Brian Galligan and Winsome Roberts (2004: 75–76) have argued that Australia is not in fact a strongly multicultural society: "Migrants are for the most part geographically dispersed; their children are educated in English along with other Australian school children; and those children have a high propensity to marry out of their parents' ethnic group. Australia does not have distinct cultural groups that endure in any significant way." Multiculturalism has been, and remains, "a humane policy for accommodating migrants from non-English speaking backgrounds," but migrant families generally need no such special accommodation by the second and third generations. A somewhat similar point has been made by the former leader of the opposition, Mark Latham, who declared that Australians "do not necessarily see themselves as 'Chinese Australians' or 'Greek Australians' but rather, citizens with a range of interests and identities." For Latham, the multiculturalist "celebration of diversity for diversity's sake" is no longer necessary, since "our diversity speaks for itself." Rather, we should deemphasize ethnic identities and "recognise that multiculturalism lies, not so much between individuals but within them—the habit of living one's life through many cultural habits. This should be a unifying idea in Australia's national identity—a new and realistic way of thinking about multiculturalism" (Latham 2004: 4–5).

In short, the objection is that multiculturalism, understood as the public recognition of multiple cultural identities within the state, has only limited relevance in Australia, because Australian cultural diversity is limited. There is diversity in Australia, but this is not so much diversity among well-defined cultural groups as among individuals and groups whose interests and identities cut across ethnic and national cultures and are contained by a set of ideals and assumptions common to all Australians.

What view should pluralists take of this set of claims? To some extent they can be happy enough with it, since it amounts not to an outright rejection of multiculturalism but to the qualification of multicultural aspirations along lines not far removed from those I have argued for. Latham's idea that we should think of multiculturalism as lying "not so much between individuals as within them," and that we should think of ourselves as living not within a single culture but "through many cultural habits," is reminiscent of my argument that the primary emphasis in pluralism should be on a diversity of values or goods rather than of cultures. Similarly, Galligan and Roberts allow that multiculturalism still has a place as a policy for accommodating newly arrived migrants from linguistic and cultural backgrounds that are very different from those of Australia. This view is integrationist rather than assimilationist. That is, the immediate goal is not to push migrants to adopt an alien culture but to help them find a distinctive place for themselves—including a culturally distinctive place for themselves—within that overarching culture. As long as the overarching culture is conceived capaciously enough—closer to the civic than the ethnic model—pluralists can accept this as a reasonable attempt to strike a balance between competing considerations.

Two qualifications need to be added, however. First, pluralists should not accept integrationist policies that are merely instrumental for economic rationalism. Fitting people for the workforce is one reasonable goal of cultural integration, but not the only one. Pluralists should also be concerned with promoting other goods, including cultural belonging, civic unity, and personal autonomy, together with those values that are peculiar to particular ways of life. In this light, the language of the Howard government's *New Agenda for Multicultural Australia* (Commonwealth of Australia 1999), which spells out the economic benefits of multiculturalism while remaining vague about its social and cultural "dividends," seems unduly narrow.

Second, is it really true that ethnic identifications do not persist in Australia? Surely there is at least one major exception to this claim, namely indigenous identities. Indeed, the situation of the indigenous peoples remains the most contentious aspect of Australian multiculturalism. Compared with the 1960s there has been substantial progress in this field from a multiculturalist point of view. The previous near-invisibility of the indigenous peoples in Australian political life has been superseded by official recognition and support in various forms, including most notably the concession of a degree of self-determination with the creation of a national advocacy body, the Aboriginal and Torres Strait Islander Commission (ATSIC), and with the judicial recognition of qualified land rights in the landmark *Mabo* and *Wik* decisions. But these developments have met with a good deal of political and popular hostility, culminating in the abolition of ATSIC in 2004 and its replacement by a purely advisory and government-appointed National Indigenous Council. Self-determination has been linked to a raft of problems in Aboriginal communities, including chronic unemployment and low standards of health and education (Partington 2000). An alternative view is that the "severely dysfunctional" state of Aboriginal communities is due not to self-determination, since genuine self-determination has not been achieved, but to policies promoting "passive welfare" (Pearson 2000). Beyond these immediate questions is the deeper issue of the status of traditional Aboriginal law: should it be incorporated into the common law of

Australia, or respected as a parallel legal system? Indeed, should it be given official recognition at all (Levy 2000b; Shachar 2001)?

How should pluralists respond? In general, they should support the political recognition of indigenous claims, including self-determination, so far as these are consistent with the promotion of value diversity, respect for reasonable disagreement among different ways of life, and the facilitation of a capacity for personal autonomy. That is, pluralists should be sympathetic to such claims within the framework of autonomy-based liberalism. In light of the problems mentioned above, current arrangements do not seem to pass this test. Consequently, the abolition of ATSIC, although it might appear to be a backward step, may also open the way to improved institutions in the long run. A more troubling question is whether any form of indigenous self-determination is likely to pass the pluralist tests I have proposed. The problem is one noticed by Berlin (2002: 200–208): that collective self-government and individual liberty are two distinct and incommensurable forms of freedom, and that the former does not guarantee the latter. In the terms I used earlier, cultural diversity does not necessarily maximize value diversity. If indigenous Australian cultures were essentially hostile to diversity-creating values such as personal autonomy, then this would place a serious obstacle in the way of any pluralist justification of indigenous self-determination, except perhaps as a transitional expedient. But I have also suggested that the pluralist outlook is not averse to dialogue and negotiation, even where this challenges the liberal-pluralist framework itself. Consequently, it seems to me that pluralists should keep an open mind on indigenous self-determination, even while remaining alert to its problems.

ACKNOWLEDGMENT

I am grateful to the participants in the "Australian Multiculturalism and Political Theory" workshop (Sydney, 8–9 July 2004), and in particular to Susan Dodds, Chandran Kukathas, Geoff Levey, and Philip Pettit for their comments on an earlier draft of this essay.

NOTES

1. It should be conceded that Berlin's account of the truth of value pluralism, resting on our "ordinary experience" of moral conflict, is not conclusive. Monists could reply that our perception of these conflicts is superficial and compatible with there being an underlying monist order we have not yet understood. But

this logical possibility seems hollow given that the monist order is still undiscovered after many centuries of inquiry. On the case for value pluralism in general, see Chang 1997; Crowder 2002a; Hurka 1996; Kekes 1993; Lukes 1991; MacKenzie 1999; Nagel 1991; Nussbaum 1986, 1992; Raz 1986; and Stocker 1990.

2. For example, Berlin's account of pluralism in the work of Vico and Herder (Berlin 2000b) is hard to distinguish from relativism: see Momigliano 1976. But he insists on the distinction in "Alleged Relativism in Eighteenth-Century European Thought" (in Berlin 1990), and in "The Pursuit of the Ideal" (in Berlin 1990, 1997). For further discussion, see Crowder 2004b, chapters 5–6.

3. The arguments I present here summarize a case made in greater detail in Crowder 2002a, 2002b, 2004b.

4. For a more detailed critique of Galston, see Crowder 2004a, 2004b.

Chapter 4

Liberal Nationalism and the Multicultural State

John Kane

❦

Understanding the challenge of multiculturalism requires an appreciation of the ambiguous and altering relationship between liberalism and nationalism. The principle of political nationalism—each cultural nation to be self-governing within its own state—is quite distinct from the core principles of liberalism, and in fact liberalism offers no convincing basis for nationalism. Nevertheless, the development of an international system of modern states ensured that liberalism became firmly wedded to nationalism early in the nineteenth century, when the compatibility between their different principles of self-determination was simply assumed. In fact, the successful operation of a liberal polity was held to depend on the existence of a cultural nation. Hopes were high that a proliferation of liberal nations would lead to the kind of liberal internationalism envisaged by Immanuel Kant, producing a system of free states amicably federated on the basis of shared principles and mutual economic advantage.

These hopes were dashed with the rise of illiberal, conservative, and often bellicose nation-states whose very existence called into question the naturalness of the union of liberalism and nationalism. For liberal states in a hostile world, the relationship now seemed a mere marriage of convenience in which the partners contrived an effective division of ideological labor: liberalism worked to justify internal social and political arrangements, nationalism worked to mobilize populations when the state asserted itself in the external field of international relations. But in states that enclosed more than one nationality, the nationalistic principle worked, sometimes viciously, to provoke internal conflict aimed at domination and "ethnic cleansing." Interstate conflicts, on the other hand, unleashed alarming nationalistic passions even in liberal states. Scholars began to attack nationalism as inherently fallacious and dangerous. Liberalism thus found itself tied to a partner that seemed to have lost all intellectual and moral respectability. It began to distance itself from all forms of cultural nationalism and to emphasize more inclusive "civic" forms tied merely to political principles like toleration and equality. In the process, liberalism encountered the new challenge of multiculturalism. As formerly fairly homogeneous populations became more multiethnic through immigration, multiculturalists began to demand that liberal regimes extend rights to cultural groups for the sake of their protection and/or greater inclusion.

This essay argues that ideological multiculturalism should be seen as the next episode in the continuing story of liberalism and nationalism, and in fact constitutes an attempt to separate politics and culture by finally divorcing the pair. Multiculturalists argued for a downgrading or annihilation of the cultural nation-state even as they simultaneously argued for respect and protection of ethnocultural groups, or fragments of groups, within states, or within trans-state entities like the European Union. The old internal/external division of ideological labor can no longer be expected to work in such conditions. Liberalism would now have to contain *within* itself the ethnocultural principle of self-determination oriented toward a political state that had defined nationalism. As to the external realm, globalizing trends produced hopes that the gradual dissolution of state sovereignty would lead to a world where nonnational systems of peaceful political coordination would preserve and protect ethnocultural diversity. Multiculturalism was to be the reigning principle at home and abroad, creating a new order of liberal internationalism quite different from the one envisaged by Kant.

But debates, sometimes bitter, over multiculturalism and what could or could not be tolerated or encouraged, revealed that the doctrine had produced a variant of the old tension between liberalism and nationalism. Moreover, the endurance of the state form encouraged persistent tendencies to cultural nationalism, even if of a less exclusive variety than formerly. The denial of such nationalism, allegedly for the sake of maintaining "equality" among diverse ethnocultures, seemed an absurdity in practice and a contradiction in multicultural theory.

To try to understand the relationship of multiculturalism to nationalism, I will begin my inquiry by looking at what multiculturalist policy actually implies, and question the validity of the distinction that is usually made between multicultural states and multinational ones. I will observe the national exception that liberalism has traditionally made to its individualistic

premises and trace the long and difficult relationship that liberalism conducted with nationalism. I will then examine the nonnationalistic or post-
nationalistic hopes of ideological multiculturalism to argue that liberalism,
far from escaping its connection to an alien ideology, has in fact tried to
incorporate it within its own theoretical frame.

MULTICULTURALISM VERSUS MULTINATIONALISM

The debate over multiculturalism raised questions about the adequacy of
liberalism's account of human identity and belonging. Various "communitarian" critiques accused liberalism of maintaining an impoverished, trun-
cated view of the human personality. They argued that communities were
"constitutive" of people's very selves and therefore prior to individuality and
to individual liberty.[1] They diagnosed a pathological loss of psychic connection to others and a loss of mutuality in societies that promoted the liberal
ideal of individual autonomy. Real human relationships, they said, transcended the liberal's contractarian notion of mutual exchange for benefit
and formed an essential part of any coherent notion of the good life (Bellah
1996; MacIntyre 1984; Sandel 1982; Taylor 1977; 1994; Walzer 1983). The
communitarians argued that toleration and respect should therefore be extended from individuals to the particular cultures or communities to which
they belonged. Charles Taylor went so far as to recommend "that we all *recognize* the equal value of different cultures; that we not only let them survive,
but acknowledge their *worth*" (Taylor 1994: 64).

These communitarian critiques actually went under a variety of titles—
the politics of recognition, the politics of difference, and the politics of multiculturalism. Because each focused in some way on "identity," they were often
not clearly distinguished from one another in the literature. But, as Bhikhu
Parekh points out, subcultural pluralism (groups pursuing unconventional
lifestyles) and perspectival pluralism (people within the dominant culture
challenging it from diverse ideological perspectives) need to be set apart from
the kind of communal diversity to which the term "multicultural" properly
and historically applies (Parekh 1999: 27). Note that multiculturalism itself
denotes an ideological perspective, one that challenges monoculturalist presumptions by arguing that communal groups should be granted various
kinds of nonindividualistic, "group-differentiated" rights. It is hardly surprising that some liberals have responded with a defense of individual rights
and a rejection of multicultural rights that might permit illiberal cultural
practices (Barry 2001). Nevertheless, other liberal theorists (often keen to lay
old ghosts of national racism or to counter freshly induced bouts of xeno-

phobia) felt impelled to address the problem of resident ethnocultural groups that, on the one hand, may be the objects of unjust discrimination and, on the other, may resist assimilation to majority values. The liberal commitment to equality seems to be tested by the first condition, the liberal commitment to toleration and individual rights by the second.[2] Sympathetic theorists therefore identified different lists of possible group rights that an extended liberalism might contemplate: Will Kymlicka, one of the principal advocates of multicultural group rights, distinguished between self-government rights, polyethnic rights, and special representation rights; J. T. Levy found eight different categories of cultural rights claims: exemptions, assistance measures, self-government, external rules, internal rules, recognition/enforcement, representation, and symbolic claims (Kymlicka 1995; Levy 1997).

Close inspection of these reveals them all to serve one or both of two specific purposes: either they aim to preserve and protect a culture, cultural practice, or identity; or they seek the correction of unjust discrimination and exclusion from full democratic participation in the roles and benefits of a polity. Note that this is an analytical distinction, and that in practice particular claims may serve either or both purposes. For example, the right to have a minority language used in education, on ballot papers, or in courtrooms may be granted as a temporary inclusionary measure to permit immigrant communities time to adjust, or may be used as a means of preserving a linguistic culture. In the latter case, the right will serve both preservation and antidiscriminatory functions, permitting a group to maintain its own culture without being unduly excluded from participation in the rights enjoyed by the majority.

The fact that many different sorts of groups apart from "ethnocultural" ones lay claim to inclusionary rights sometimes confuses matters. The demand for special rights for gay people, women, the poor, and the disabled has little to do with multicultural recognition. Even "ethnicity" frequently turns out to be a mere euphemism for "race" applied to persons who, apart from certain obvious biological characteristics, are indistinguishable on cultural grounds from the majority population. The demand here is generally for an end to prejudice and victimization, and for greater substantive equality for all. Multiculturalism has certainly embraced this aim, but if it restricted itself to that it would hardly represent more than the kind of social justice–welfare policy that the Australian Labor Party used to champion. It is also more than a policy of tolerating cultural diversity so long as the majority culture is not disturbed. Genuine multiculturalism goes further and seeks some means of supporting the cultural integrity of different groups. The question is, which groups, and how far should a state go in pursuing multicultural rights and policies?

Any answer to this will no doubt mix political expediency and principle, and be crucially dependent on the context in which the question is asked. The Australian context is a very different one from, say, that of Sri Lanka, a unitary state dominated by Buddhist Sinhalese confronting a radically separatist Hindu Tamil group in the north; or a Turkish state wishing to join the European Union but dealing with a 30-percent population of Kurds whose language it outlawed years ago; or an Indonesian state encompassing several hundred language groups and with breakaway movements in Aceh and Irian Jaya. Of course in these latter examples, and in many others, multicultural and multiethnic diversity threatens the unity of the state itself, a problem that Australia does not face. Issues of nationalism and subnationalism grow, in these countries, from the fact that their politically defined territories happen to enclose preexisting cultural groups that are either numerous or large or both. Australia, by contrast, is generally labeled an "immigrant" nation because the major part of its population came originally from elsewhere. In fact, Australian territory also enclosed around five hundred preexisting, independent cultural-linguistic groups, but the indigenous population was so thoroughly subordinated, and so relatively small, that aboriginal subnationalism has presented no serious threat to national unity. If indigenous politics today raises significant challenges, the Australian state responds, insofar as it does, mainly because it is under moral pressure to do so, not because it is politically or militarily threatened. Nor is the Australian state threatened by the presence of immigrant groups from a variety of cultural backgrounds.

The fact of being predominantly immigrant does not necessarily exempt a country from problems of ethnocultural nationalism: think of Canada, or South Africa, or even that archetypal immigrant nation, the United States, whose nationalist question had to be settled by a civil war.[3] But when theorists distinguish immigrant nations from multinational ones, they mean to indicate that countries like Australia, which do not face pressing challenges from large subnational units, must nevertheless address multicultural questions of a different order. Actually, the distinction between multinational and immigrant countries has nothing to do with whether the majority of the population came from somewhere else. Practically all developed countries are now "immigrant" in the relevant sense, meaning that they have been significantly open to people from other, often poorer, countries, thus dramatically increasing their ethnocultural diversity. This is a consequence of general cultural and economic globalization and of the revolution in communications technology as well as of specific national policies. Today a country has to go to very extreme lengths to try to shut the world out—viz. the Taliban in Afghanistan—if it wants to preserve cultural purity and uniformity. As Parekh notes: "Contemporary multiculturality has an air of inexorability and irresistibility about it and poses challenges rarely faced by earlier societies" (Parekh 1999: 28).[4] It is generally supposed that the policies appropriate to these multicultural situations are different from those needed in cases of multinationalism. The question is to what degree multicultural immigrant groups should be required to assimilate to the norms of their adoptive country and how far they should be, not just permitted, but officially encouraged or enabled to retain the cultural norms and practices they brought with them.

And yet we must ask if the case for liberal democratic "immigrant" countries is really so different from that of multinational countries. If an immigrant state is dominated by one specific cultural group, then all other groups—presuming they do not wish to be, or are not permitted to be, wholly assimilated into the dominant culture—are surely in an analogous position to aggrieved subnationalities. They will need to struggle for recognition and protection of their own cultural practices and for access to the benefits of full citizenship, just as subordinate national groupings must. Indeed, it is sobering to find that Yael Tamir, defending a modern version of liberal nationalism, insists on using the terms multiculturalism and multinationalism interchangeably:

> This is not merely a semantic point; it emphasizes the similarities between issues confronting the multiethnic states like the United States, multinational states like Israel, multinational federations or confederations like Belgium or Canada, and regional organizations like the European community, all of which confront a similar issue: how to retain diversity on the one hand and unity on the other. (Tamir 1993: xvii)

As we will see later, some American multiculturalists have interpreted the multicultural question as exactly a problem of nationalism. This raises a significant and rather glaring exception that liberalism has always made to its individualistic premises. The exception was precisely the "nation" to which liberal individuals were presumed to belong. It is revealing in this regard to note that the primary aim of the group rights allowed by Kymlicka (at least in his early work) was to gain some measure of cultural protection for national minorities (such as indigenous "first nations" or Quebecois French) from the assimilative pressures of the dominant cultures within a state. Ethnic immigrant groups, according to Kymlicka (1995, 2001a), had less claim to cultural protection, and any public measures on their behalf should be a matter of policy, not rights (Kymlicka 1989, 1995, 2001a). Joseph Raz (1994) similarly made clear that his liberal multiculturalism was meant to apply only in states incorporating large subnational units.

The significance of such restrictions lies in the tacit recognition of liberal privileging of the community we call the nation. The legal and political authority of the liberal state has provided a secure environment in which individuals were accorded the status of equal citizenship in order to pursue their private ends, in particular their economic ends. Yet the liberal state was always something more than a contractual institutional device for the protection of natural rights to life and property. It faced the outside world in the guise of a cultural *nation,* something to which liberal individuals were presumed to *belong* in a particular way and to which they owed a special allegiance and special duties, even love. The nation was a community with rights that were not reducible to individual rights. It was also a community that could and did demand sacrifices from its members in the confidence that they would be made. Liberalism, in other words, prospered in the world by contracting a marriage with a different ideology, that known as nationalism.

From the point of view of some multiculturalists, the liberal state's historic connection to nationalism has been a disaster. They believe the connection must be effectively broken so that the promise of a pluralistic multicultural society can be realized. The liberal state must be truly "nonnational," which is to say neutral between cultures. I believe that the issue of nationalism is indeed important to the multicultural question, but will point out anomalies in any hopes for nonnational liberalism. To assess such a position properly, however, we must revisit the marriage of liberalism and nationalism, and look at how their alliance came into question as doubts over the powerful nationalist phenomenon grew.

LIBERALISM AND NATIONALISM

At the center of nationalist ideology lies the potent idea of the "nation." According to one of its early champions, Johann Gottfried Herder (an important German figure in the Romantic reaction to Enlightenment rationalism), the nation was an essentially "natural"[5] phenomenon. A nation was a product of historical growth and could be identified by the existence of common cultural factors such as customs, art, literature, and, above all, language. These, taken together, constituted a whole way of life. Herder believed the cultural nation was the proper basis for the political community and political identity and therefore rejected the liberal construct of a political community formed by rational, socially contracting individuals wishing to subject themselves to a common sovereign. Herder's ideal political community was antithetical to the modern conception of the sovereign, centralized state, which he argued impeded the natural growth of local communities and imposed undesirable uniformity. Each natural community had (or should have) the right to develop in its own way without imperialistic interference or domination by others (Herder 1968). Later German nationalists, including Hegel, took a much more positive view of the state (to the point of absurd glorification in the late nineteenth century). The nation remained a product of natural growth but one that required its own political state for its perfection or protection. It seemed to an age marked by both the ascendancy of the sovereign state and the romantic elevation of nature that each "natural" nation should be self-determining and self-governing within its own state.

There is good reason, however, for questioning the view of the nation as a "natural" (by implication, peaceful) growth. Did English people in the tenth century, or Italians in the fourteenth, or Germans in the eighteenth, regard themselves as nations lacking only a unified state? It is certain they did not. Whatever the linguistic or cultural commonalities that may have existed among a people in the past, it seems clear that the idea of constituting themselves as a nation required a distinctively modern political consciousness. Indeed, *pace* Herder, the nation is probably both a product of and parasitic upon the rise of the modern, territorially defined, centralized state with its "caged" population mobilizable for state purposes (Mann 1993: 61). Once the centralized state grew to dominance and became the most powerful modern form of political organization, there was an obvious, pressing incentive for other peoples to group themselves along similar lines. A freshly minted national state was no doubt easier to achieve if a certain level of homogeneity already existed among the population to be enclosed (though in truth coercion, usually considerable, was always required). We might properly define the nation, therefore, as an ethnocultural group that achieves political unity and self-consciousness by orienting its goals toward possession of a modern state.[6]

Of course, in the case of the first great modern states, France and England, the state undoubtedly created the nation rather than the other way around, indeed forged it in via a long history of conflict and accommodation out of a congeries of regional cultures and subcultures. By the time English liberal individualism held sway and the French revolution occurred, the existence of English or French state-created nations could simply be taken for granted. This was probably why English and French nationalism differed so much from the German in being relatively unselfconscious, and in proclaiming universalistic doctrines of liberalism and the rights of Man that apparently contradicted national particularism.

Yet, to be fair, many nineteenth-century liberals saw no necessary contradiction between liberalism and nationalism but rather accepted them as natural bedfellows—at least so long as nationalism was taken to *mean* liberal nationalism. The self-determination of individuals and the self-determination of nations seemed all-of-a-piece, the same ideal writ either small or large. The self-rule that nationalities attained in achieving their own state would, it was believed, naturally find expression in a liberal democratic polity.[7] Moreover, independent liberal nation-states, connected by bonds of mutually beneficial trade and amity, would coexist peacefully in an international order that would be an expanded version of the liberal national community. The natural extension of liberal nationalism, in other words, was liberal internationalism, an ideal that found its most famous expression in Kant's essay "Perpetual Peace."[8]

History would demonstrate, however, that the connection between nationalism and liberalism was contingent and fortuitous rather than logical (Meyer 1998: 63). Indeed, there seemed to be no principled reason why national states should not be antiliberal, as Otto von Bismarck proved in Germany, nor why illiberal nation-states should not reveal bellicose ambitions.[9] The liberation of peoples and cultures suffering the oppressive yoke of foreign domination, or their unification under a single political state, however laudable, rested on a presumption different from the individualistic and pacific premises of liberalism. Moreover, theoretical liberalism, though it had developed distinctive arguments about the state and the extent of the individual's obligations to it, had offered no explicit theories about the cultural nation.[10] The hero of French revolutionary mythology was the abstract individual "citizen," implying political participation in, and co-ownership of, the new republican state, but how did such a citizen connect with any particular cultural group or "people"? When liberal thinkers addressed this theoretical issue at all, their appeal was to expediency rather than to logic. In the mid-nineteenth century, John Stuart Mill, though he disbelieved the "natural" origin of nations, held essentially to the nation-state principle: "Where the sentiment of nationality exists in any force [and however it might have arisen], there is a *prima facie* case for uniting all members of the nationality under the same government, and a government to themselves apart." Moreover, Mill supposed that the successful operation even of liberal governments was dependent on this prior national principle. Free institutions, he said, were almost impossible in a state containing mixed nationalities that precluded "fellow-feeling" and sense of common identity (Mill 1972: 361). This was a doctrine that the new state of Australia took very seriously in 1901, for in an age of "scientific" racialism it lent itself readily, if not logically, to ethnocultural liberal nationalisms founded on race (Kane 1997b).

Those liberal-national states that exhibited, whether by fortune or design, a considerable degree of internal homogeneity in effect adopted a division of theoretical labor between liberalism and nationalism for internal and external purposes. Nationalism, because it does not differentiate between people of common nationality (or race), is useless for all arguments about justice and distribution within a relatively homogeneous state. It is invaluable, however, when there is a need to differentiate between a foreign "them" and a national "us," either on the sports field or the battlefield. Liberalism was therefore applied within the state to justify social, economic, and political relations; nationalism functioned externally in relation to other states. With the failure of liberal internationalism, liberal states often had recourse to an intense form of assertive nationalism whenever they found themselves under threat or challenge. This was why overt nationalism usually took the form of "outbreaks" during international crises or at times when the state wished to exert itself aggressively abroad. Nationalism, because founded in "the people" and their love of country, proved more effective in mobilizing a population on the state's behalf than did any other ideology.

Indeed, nationalism's general tendency was to strengthen the system of sovereign independent states and undermine all universalistic doctrines, not just the liberal one. Certainly it was a scandal for Marxists that the nation proved a more powerful cohesive force than international proletarian solidarity. Neither bourgeoisie nor workers showed any profound inclination to think or act as a "world class."[11] Worse, even avowedly Marxist regimes had to resort to arousing nationalist sentiment when defense of the Motherland was at stake. Nor did ideology long sustain fraternal solidarity among communist nations, who frequently pitted their enmity against one another as much as against the nations of the decadent West. The division of labor here tended to be between Marxism internally, nationalism internationally. Communism proved to be quite as amenable to, and perhaps as dependent upon, the formation of national varieties as had capitalism before it.[12]

If nationalism projected outward produced international conflict, it could be equally destructive projected inward in nonhomogeneous states. For the fact was that the ideal of one-nation-to-one-state, hardly even imaginable today, was seldom realized in historical practice.[13] The confusions of politics and history, the very multitudes of separate ethnocultures large and small around the world, produced actual states that were mostly "multinational" or "multiethnic." This meant either that distinct ethno-linguistic-cultural groupings found a way of sharing a single state (as in Switzerland, Belgium, or the Netherlands) or, more commonly, that a single culture claimed the state as their own and dominated or marginalized all others within its territory. One could see this process working throughout nineteenth-century Europe and just as clearly in twentieth-century nationalist movements in Africa and Asia. In the postcolonial period, "states" whose boundaries had been drawn quite arbitrarily across multiethnic groupings became the prize for which different tribal-cultural-religious groups inevitably competed, a struggle in which compromises were seldom contemplated or, when they were, seldom maintained. The problem of such warring nationalisms and subnationalisms remained undiminished at the start of the twenty-first century. Politicians continued to play the nationalist card at crucial moments, confident that people would respond with feelings of love and hate, loyalty and sacrifice. National groups continued to engage in bitter struggles to free themselves from domination or to gain hold of disputed territory in order to constitute themselves as independent nation-states. Nationalism's emphasis on belonging, loyalty, solidarity, and a readiness to kill or die for the nation often led to communal hatred and violence, and to obscenities like ethnic cleansing and genocide.

Nationalism now seemed merely a larger form of tribalism, no longer synonymous with liberation and peaceful self-determination, but instead with xenophobia and violence. The moral and intellectual respectability it had possessed in the nineteenth century dissolved under the scrutiny of twentieth-century scholars. For all its undeniable and indeed frightening power, nationalism no longer seemed to have any theoretical credibility. Political effectiveness was allegedly accompanied by "philosophical poverty." The principal problem was the allegedly "fictive" nature of the nation, which could always be shown to be a political creation rather than a primordial existent. Though nations were new things in history, they must appear to "loom out of an immemorial past" (Anderson 1983: 5, 11). The creation of nations involved the creation of myths (or downright falsehoods) about the nation's ancient origins—thus the ironic definition of a nation as "a society united by a common error about its origin and a common aversion to its neighbours" (Huxley and Haddon 1940: 16). If traditions were required to prove antiquity, then traditions would be invented, which was why Eric Hobsbawm claimed that no serious historian of nations and nationalism can also be a committed political nationalist: "Nationalism requires too much belief in what is patently not so" (Hobsbawm 1990: 12; see also Gellner 1971; Ginsberg 1963; Hobsbawm and Ranger 1983; Kellas 1991; and Anthony Smith 1986).

But if nationalism is no more, in the end, than a form of irrationalism, it can hardly provide a basis for serious political theory any more than for serious history. At best it may be the object of political analysis, amenable, like racism perhaps, to sociopsychological explanation. It surely cannot be deployed as a philosophical category with respectably normative force. As in Marx's view of religion, it can perhaps be explained only by being explained away.[14] It was no wonder that liberals began to assert antipathy to the nationalist phenomenon. The liberal state was a voluntaristic association of free individuals; the national state was a solidaristic "community of fate." Liberalism was individualistic, universalistic, and rational, nationalism was collectivistic, particularistic, and (apparently) irrational. According to Ernest Gellner, the conflict between liberalism and nationalism represented "a tug of war between reason and passion" (Gellner 1971: 149). Bad enough that liberalism should have made itself dependent on any collectivistic form at all, but worse to have hitched its fortunes to an "imagined community" that lacked either theoretical or historical justification.[15] Yet it was clear that, despite this fundamental deficiency, the liberal nation continued to conceive of itself as a community with a distinctive culture, history, and collective destiny.[16]

NATIONALISM AND MULTICULTURALISM

As nationalism's moral stock fell, liberal-democrats began to rethink their long-standing relationship to it. Some looked toward transnational forms of governance that might relegate the sovereign nation-state to a more subsidiary role. Some argued that increasing cultural and economic integration signaled the eventual decline of the nation-state, and others looked to the example of a European community struggling to come into existence as an alternative superarching political form that comprehended but did not discriminate against its regional ethnocultural entities. In Europe, a principle of "subsidiarity" was mooted as a basis for local autonomy within a framework of political coordination, a pattern that was to be preferred, too, *within* the old national states (de Schoutheete 2000; Martiniello 1995, 1998). Political unity and cultural autonomy were to be separated and *multiculturalism* was to be made general.

What was in effect being suggested was a new ideal to replace the outmoded Kantian one. Instead of an international community of genuine nation-states, there would be a series of political states or suprastates, not themselves nationally defined, within which many culturally autonomous nations or national fractions would be clustered. There were, of course, many questions about the practicability of such a vision, especially given the stubborn persistence of national-state entities. Europe over a half-century has gone furthest in attempting to transcend historical nation-states to establish some new order of political organization, but its success in economic coordination has hardly been matched by strides toward political unity. The crushingly low turnout for the 2004 elections to the European parliament, even in new states alleged to be eager joiners of the Union, showed that there is very little political identification with a "Europe" as such. On 19 June 2004, Tony Blair proclaimed a victory for the British version of the new European Constitution that, he said, preserved the nation-states (the primary sites of citizen allegiance) within a general structure of political and economic coordination. Blair's Europe, clearly, would remain a very weak confederation in political terms. The failure of the new European Constitution to gain electoral approval in France and Holland in mid-2005 seemed to halt the political unification project in its tracks. The divisions between the European states over the issue of Iraq had already shown how far Europe was from achieving what has always been regarded as the hallmark of sovereign power, the ability to speak univocally on matters of foreign relations. It was an issue that raised the general question about "inside-outside" that national states had already faced: even if the internal policy of a suprastate was egalitarian multiculturalism, this would hardly serve to orient it to a world of partly cooperative, partly competing sovereign entities.

Within established states the picture appeared hardly more promising. Nevertheless, it seemed to multiculturalists reasonable to ask whether liberal political states need be "national" at all. It was a question that Michael Walzer, one of the leading American theoreticians of cultural pluralism, answered with a resounding, "No!" Indeed, he defined America as a *multinational nation*. Distinguishing between liberal nationalism and *nonnational liberalism*, Walzer claimed that the latter is the official doctrine of immigrant societies like the United States (and therefore, by implication, Australia): "For the United States isn't, after all, a nation-state, but a nation of nationalities ... or a social union of social unions, in John Rawls's more recent formulation" (Walzer 1992a: 100–101). The different nationalities that allegedly compose American society have, since early in the twentieth century, been distinguished as "hyphenates"—Anglo-, Irish-, Italian-, Polish-, German-Americans and so on. Such nominations continue alongside a modern tendency to divide the population for both administrative and argumentative purposes into white, black or African-American, Hispanic or Latino, Asian-Pacific Islander, and Native American "nationalities." The American phenomenon of "black nationalism" was thus extended to other groups so that racial categories were converted into cultural-national ones. Jesse Jackson justified the substitution of "African-American" for "black" by arguing the greater cultural integrity and historical perspective provided by the former. It was a shift, as Michael Novak said approvingly, from "genetic appearance to cultural difference."[17]

Such differences, note, are not simply identified as factual by multiculturalists but are normatively encouraged as desirable. The hope is to preserve these differences in perpetuity, in which case any increase in intergroup marriage or any drift toward assimilation presents distinct dangers. Walzer, for his part, hoped to ameliorate such erosion, and to preserve the vitality of multiculturalism, by keeping the gates of immigration wide open.

"Whatever regulation is necessary," he wrote, "the flow of people, the material base of multiculturalism, should not be cut off." His wish was to prevent the development of a singular, generic American cultural identity, which he equated with the growth of an American nation-state and thus with the rise of an abhorrent American nationalism. Walzer *defined* America as an immigrant nation and argued that a radical program of Americanization would be un-American. Each hyphenate group may celebrate its own national heritage except, he argued, "the American-Americans, whose community, if it existed, would deny the Americanism of all the others" (Walzer 1992b: 17, 47, 74; Lind 1995: 234–45).

Walzer clearly believes that the old ideal of the nation-state is no ideal at all but rather a nightmare in which a dominant cultural group unjustly monopolizes the power and resources of the state to suppress all others. As his most recent collection of essays makes clear, his work is an attempt to combine multiculturalism with social-democratic redistributionist policies, and envisions state subsidization of underprivileged cultural groups to promote greater equality (Walzer 2004).[18] Subnationalisms are therefore permitted, indeed supported in their "cultural reproduction," but any overarching nationalism is forbidden, a stricture that defines Walzer's "nonnational liberalism." But this position is surely self-contradictory; the persistence of plural nationalisms in America must be parasitic upon the existence of nation-states from which the national fragments come, and some cultural allegiance to which they retain, but which are themselves morally condemnable.[19]

Walzer nevertheless pointed to a continuing tension within all liberal democratic states between nationalism and multiculturalism, one that has been equally evident in Australia. For example, the Australian Citizenship Council's 2000 report, *Australian Citizenship for a New Century,* recommended a commitment to an acceptance of cultural diversity by arguing that there was no need for a single Australian national identity.

> Why do we have to imagine we have an "identity" in any restricted sense which excludes many Australians? The Council considered it might be better to proclaim core civic values for all Australians to respect as the basis of our citizenship. In other words, it might be better to proclaim not a "national identity," but a national civic "compact." (Australian Citizenship Council 2000: 10; NMAC 1999)

This is Walzer's nonnational liberalism in an Australian context.

But far from transcending nationalism, liberal multiculturalism merely repeats the original nationalist project in a new form. It tries to orient plural nationalities or subnationalities toward a particular state upon which their welfare, protection, and preservation are held crucially to depend, only now the state itself must belong to no one group in particular but to all in general. This implies liberal neutrality taken to its utmost, so that the original marriage of liberty and nationalism is, at least in intention, consummated in a different and purer fashion. Habermas (1998: chaps. 4, 5) calls this arrangement of the liberal state one of "post-national" identity (see also Ingram 1996), but in reality it means that liberalism, rather than allying itself to nationalism, has tried to swallow it up, and to incorporate the national principle within its own theoretic form.

The tensions in this arrangement are likely to be just as profound as were those in the old marriage of liberalism and nationalism. Note, for example, Habermas's hope that postnational identity can be successfully founded simply on respect for rationally defensible principles and institutions. Clearly, principles that are rationally defensible in my estimation may be mere cultural prejudices in yours, in which case my desire to make you observe them will seem imperialistic. It is for this reason that no truly sovereign state can be genuinely "neutral" among cultures, for political culture is inevitably part of any culture. As Pye and Verba note, a political culture "assumes each individual must, in his own historical context, learn and incorporate into his own personality the knowledge and feelings about the politics of his people and his community" (Pye and Verba 1966: 4). It is this fact that has caused a conundrum for liberals, whose principled indifference to particular views of the good that individuals might pursue seems self-contradictory in light of it. Even liberal tolerance pushed to the unrealistic extreme of unconditional toleration of intolerant subcultures cannot evade this theoretical dilemma (since toleration itself would have to be enforced) (Kukathas 1992, 1997c).[20] Tamir argued that, though a culturally neutral state was an impossibility (because laws would always express particular values and therefore cultural-national differences would always have to be argued in the public sphere), a genuine liberal nationalism could nevertheless acknowledge the legitimate grievances of cultural minorities and formulate ways of alleviating them (Tamir 1993: 145). This seems unobjectionable, yet the sticky detail lies in defining what counts as a "legitimate" grievance and on what criteria such a judgment can be made.

Of course it is legitimate to ask whether liberal states might steadfastly maintain their political principles but dispense with the "thicker" ethnocultural barriers to full citizenship that existed in the past, especially insofar as these were largely reducible to matters of "race" (see Rogers Smith 1997; Wiebe 1975). The answer to this is that of course they can and should, as indeed Australia has done. The thorough discrediting of racialist theories of human superiority and inferiority leaves no plausible intellectual ground for doing otherwise. This is merely a matter, however, of ideological consistency:

liberalism affirms its doctrine of human equality by refusing to countenance morally indifferent characteristics as grounds for discrimination. It does not address the central desire of multiculturalism to *maintain* cultural diversity while preserving political unity. Unity, it seems, might require something more than acceptance (either grudging or sincere) of liberal political norms. Some theorists argue that it requires the kind of affective attachment to the polity that nationalism promotes, though they make concessions to multi-culturality by choosing "civic" or "republican" forms that defend thin bases of commonality such as language and "overlapping cultural values" (David Miller 1995, 1998; Barry 1999).

But how "thin" can such attachment be? The state can, and may at some point, demand that its citizens risk their very lives in its defense or on behalf of its international goals. In the process it will inevitably appeal to the citizen's love, honor, and loyalty—in other words, to his or her sense of *belongingness*, with all the moral and emotional implications that pertain to that concept. So long as states need to assert themselves in a world of other states whose interests and intentions may conflict with their own, they will need to call upon the loyalty and devotion of citizens who regard the state's demands as, at least provisionally, legitimate. Clifford Geertz argues that a state's claim to such legitimacy only makes sense if its acts are seen as "continuous with the selves of those whose state it pretends it is, its citizens—to be, in some steeped-up, amplified sense, *their* acts." It isn't even necessary to agree with the acts and policies of the present government of the state to make this identification (Geertz 1973: 316–7).[21] Whether we like it or not, we are identified with our affiliations, those we did not choose as much as those we did; family, firm, profession, partner, country—their pride is ours, as is their shame. It is for this reason that the recent "history wars" in Australia have assumed such significance. Whether on the question of white settlement and the Aborigines we belong in the "black armband" or the "denialist" camp (to give them their pejorative appellations), the fact is that insisting emotively on what we believe to be the "truth" about history only matters if we think it is, in some important sense, *our* history.

CONCLUSION

This leads to a concluding point about Australian national identity. As I have noted, the problem of loyalty and identification is much more acute where sizable multinational groups vie, sometimes violently, for political dominance or self-preservation, which is not the case in Australia. Moreover, it seems undeniable that there exists a strong Australian cultural-national identity that, though founded in a racially exclusive past, has maintained considerable continuity through adaptive change to altered values and increasing cultural and racial diversity. It is an identity that has, to a remarkable extent, accommodated continuing differences while effecting an acculturation of immigrant groups by means well short of ruthless "assimilation" (at least in recent times). It is, like many national identities, an *effect* of the existence of a political state as much as or more than its *cause,* and it is shared by many Australians, even indigenous ones, who feel unjustly excluded from full citizenship rights. To deny this de facto identity, or to wish to expunge it as Walzer does the equivalent American one,[22] would seem to be an absurdity for anyone whose general desire is the preservation of "cultures," however defined.

Of course, toleration of cultural difference within the limits of existing law should be the mark of the liberal Australian polity, and it is all to the good if the Australian national-political culture can extend itself even to welcoming or "celebrating" such difference. Such welcoming should certainly imply that existing law be interpreted and applied with more rather than less sensitivity to the needs of different cultures. The desirability of special rights in any particular case, however, must be debated in the usual democratic manner and gain the respect and acceptance of the majority if it is legislatively to succeed. My own view would be that, for any measures that will result in the greater inclusion and participation of groups within the activities and benefits of the polity, the burden of proof should be on those who would deny them; for any whose aim and tendency is to support and maintain groups in their cultural difference, the burden of proof should be on those who would affirm them.

The principle here should be one of caution, for there are certain perils associated with full-blown multiculturalism that are wider than the fear of ethnic "Balkanization." Multiculturalism in the British Empire was an exclusionary administrative technique to divide and rule different "autonomous" cultural-linguistic groups, forcing them to compete among themselves for central resources (Mamdani 1996). Multicultural policies within a liberal state, insofar as they require administrative definition of "a culture" and identification of the groups that qualify for whatever benefits or protections are on offer, may, whether intentionally or not, artificially freeze or privilege certain groupings and create tensions and rivalries among them. Also, it is obvious that the terms "culture" and "ethnicity" are widely used as mere euphemisms for "race" in liberal democratic nations. Rights and policies devised to support and sustain cultural diversity, therefore, may in time operate to sustain differences based merely on racial characteristics. The tendency for genuine ethnicity to decline over a couple of generations in liberal democratic-capitalist countries is well known, so that cultural pluralists wishing to support enduring communal subdivisions in society are liable to end up perpetuating the salience of racial identifications (Lind 1995: 243). This would be ironic in a country like Australia, whose multiculturalism, at its foundations, was a "bend-over-backwards" attempt to distance itself from its racialist past (Kane 1997; Lopez 2000).

NOTES

1. Most communitarians were less intent on destroying individualistic liberal values than in applying a corrective by pointing out that "the social fabric sustains, nourishes, and enables individuality rather than diminishes it" (Etzioni 1996: 14).
2. Raz (1994: 157–58) sees liberalism moving from a policy of mere toleration (leaving minorities alone as long as they do not interfere with the majority culture) to nondiscrimination (a country's public services, education, and so on are scrupulously open to individuals regardless of cultural identity) to affirmative multiculturalism (that transcends the individualist approach and asserts the value of groups maintaining their cultures).
3. A colleague, Haig Patapan, points out that one might argue that the only nations to escape serious multinational conflict are either those with one politically dominating culture, like Australia, or those with such a profusion of cultures, like India, that the accommodation of pluralism is the only option.
4. Parekh argued the need in this article for new political theory to properly accommodate the issue of multiculturalism, a need he later attempted to satisfy (Parekh 2000). There he argues for a genuinely pluralist view of human society that tries to walk a line between universal human naturalism and irreducible cultural relativism, and thus to draw lessons for creative compromises on cultural issues.
5. The two words have the same linguistic root in the Latin *nasci,* to be born.
6. Of course, not all self-identified nations have yet achieved statehood, and some may never do so.
7. The nation, being founded on a "people" rather than on divine right or natural social orders, seemed perfectly congruent with Rousseauean ideals of popular sovereignty and incipient democracy. For an account and explanation of Rousseau as one of the founts of modern nationalism, see Plattner 1997. Herder was a pupil of Kant and his thinking is clearly deeply influenced by Kantian liberal internationalism. I believe it is possible, in the theory of nationalism, to trace a line from the Abbé de Saint-Pierre to Montesquieu to Rousseau to Kant to Herder.
8. Liberal nationalism also received a huge boost from French revolutionary doctrine and French military success, which, through a combination of emulation

and reaction, inspired nationalist movements across Europe. European nationalisms were stimulated partly by enthusiasm for the French promulgation of the rights of Man and partly by resistance to French invasion during the Napoleonic era; see Roberts 1996: 362–64.

9. For the historical progress of conservative nationalisms, see Kohn 1966.

10. One could, of course, argue that a theory of community based on natural sociability and consent underpinned the Lockean liberalism of the *Second Treatise*. Locke's proscription of Catholics in his "Letter on Toleration," because of their allegiance to a foreign power (the papist church) and consequent liability to treachery, showed that patriotism of some kind was important to him—and indeed, Locke was a patriotic Englishman. However, his theory hardly formed the basis of an "ethnocultural" nationalism, even if religion can be taken as an important element of culture. That religious differences could bitterly divide a people of otherwise fairly common culture can be seen by the division of Germany in the seventeenth century into Lutheran and Catholic principalities.

11. Benedict Anderson's well-known book *Imagined Communities: Reflections on the Origin and Spread of Nationalism* (1983: 4) declared its aim to be to offer a more satisfactory interpretation of this "anomaly" than it had hitherto received.

12. Capitalism has always been an inherently "transnational" force, since trade and production tend to follow whatever pattern economics and entrepreneurial invention dictate. The productive power of capitalism ensured that emerging national states would seek to co-opt it for their own ends, or to form mutually beneficial relationships with business. Capitalism in the nineteenth and twentieth centuries typically took the form of a series of interconnected *national* capitalisms. See Kane 2004.

13. It still, however, defines the essence of nationalism. As Gellner (1983: 1) puts it, "Nationalism is primarily a political principle, which holds that the political and the national unit should be congruent."

14. Religion's real power over people's minds was, according to Marx, the result of the fantastical solace it afforded for present suffering, a solace bought at the price of obscuring the real forces preventing happiness here on earth. Nationalism could be regarded as a political illusion that is the secular extension of the religious illusion Marx sought to dispel, useful for binding people to political structures that, on deeper analysis, are inimical to their true happiness; see Cocks 2002: 26–30. For the religious impulse within nationalism, see Zamoyski 1999, who argues that worship and dedication originally channeled through the church was refocused on the cause of the people and the nation.

15. Anderson's formulation implies a contrast to "real" communities in which people deal with each other face to face. This is to suppose that face-to-face human communities are transparently existent and not themselves crucially the products of "imagination," which is arguable but, I believe, mistaken.

16. See Tamir (1993: 141): "But the liberal state has in practice continued to operate within the constitutive assumptions of the modern nation-state and to see itself as a community with a distinctive culture, history, and collective destiny. The

growing dissatisfaction of ethnic groups and national minorities living within liberal states lends persuasive support to this claim. Members of these minorities feel excluded from the public sphere because they realize that it achieves an appearance of disinterest in cultural issues by exclusion, namely, by rejecting all those who do not belong to the dominant culture."

17. Jackson quote from Ben Martin 1991: 98, and Novak 1993: 177, both cited in Lind 1995: 125. See Lind 1995: chap. 3 generally for the tendency of American multiculturalism to become racial-nationalism.

18. Walzer (2004: 60) does, however, have to confront the familiar liberal problem of tolerating and even, on his scheme, financially supporting highly illiberal "totalizing" groups, though in the final analysis he wants the government to "tilt" against such groups in the name of "decency." The state may, for example, coercively require the children of such groups to receive civic education for "democratic decision-making."

19. There is, admittedly, a peculiarly American strain of thought in evidence here; Walzer's view in fact represents another iteration of the tradition known as American exceptionalism. America is not Europe, he says, and must not become so. If this seems a curious argument in an era when Europe is, almost uniquely, striving to overcome the constraints of the historical nation-state, it nevertheless reflects the traditional, universalistic Jeffersonian-Republican hope that the American liberal democratic state would not be, must not be, parochially nationalist. Patriotism is laudable but should attach to the constitution, to the laws, to the very *idea* of liberal freedom, and not to any specific cultural group.

20. Note the rider in *Australian Multiculturalism for a New Century* after lauding multiculturalism: "While Australian multiculturalism values and celebrates diversity, it is not an 'anything goes' concept since it is built on core societal values of mutual respect, tolerance and harmony, the rule of law and our democratic principles and institutions. It is also based on an overriding commitment to Australia" (NMAC 1999: 36).

21. This is, of course, the test of legitimacy, and the explanation of citizen obligation, in political theories as disparate as those of Hobbes and Rousseau. The sovereign's decisions are held to be my own, either because I have consented to *have* a sovereign or *am* the sovereign (in concert with all my fellow citizens). In other words, it is my choice that legitimizes, thus confirming my freedom even as I admit my subjection. But the moral claim of Geertz is broader, in that it assumes we are obligated even when we have not chosen, and merely by virtue of the relationships we happen to acquire.

22. Lind (1995) makes a strong argument for the real existence of an American cultural identity that is the amalgamation and product of many cultures and conflicts. Lind (2000) also defends the now unfashionable view that shared "ethnicity" remains and will remain the real basis of nationalism in the twenty-first century. See also Anthony Smith 1986.

Chapter 5

"Something That Deserves Our Admiration and Respect"

Barry Hindess

In *Citizenship and Social Class* (1950) and a number of later works, T. H. Marshall takes up one of the central themes of late nineteenth-century social liberalism, arguing that the state has a responsibility to ensure that no one is excluded from the full enjoyment of their citizenship simply because they suffer from certain kinds of disadvantage. He describes citizenship as involving three sets of rights: *civil* rights to liberty and equality before the law; *political* rights to vote and to participate in the political process; *social* rights to participate fully in the way of life that is shared by the citizens as a whole. It is the role of social policy, in particular, to ensure that rights belonging to this last category are secured for otherwise disadvantaged citizens. Marshall goes on to argue that, at least in Britain and other Western democracies, his three sets of rights have largely been realized, and that the socially divisive effects of class inequalities have thereby been contained. The British people, he tells us, may find "the inequality of social class ... acceptable provided the equality of citizenship is recognised" (Marshall 1950: 8).

The most interesting feature of Marshall's argument, at least for our purposes, concerns his assumption that citizens participate in a single, over-arching culture and way of life, that they are members of a "civilization which is a common possession" (40). This assumption is one of the pillars of liberal constitutionalism's rule of uniformity, the view that a uniform set of laws and conventions for their interpretation should apply to all members of a state's population (Tully 1995). Moreover, as Will Kymlicka (1995: 2) points out, it is central to the liberal and democratic currents of modern political thought, which have "operated with an idealized model of the polis in which fellow-citizens share a common descent, language and culture." While, as we shall see, this ideal has also been disputed, governments and political movements have often made strenuous efforts to ensure a substantial degree of cultural homogeneity in the populations under their control. If the modern experience of cultural diversity poses a problem for democratic politics, an important part of the reason is that democracy itself has been understood in terms of this idealized model of the *polis*.

An influential body of literature on multiculturalism and the politics of difference suggests that indigenous peoples, ethnic minorities, and other groups might be oppressed by precisely the equality of citizenship that the rule of uniformity seems to require, that is, by the assumption that there is or should be a single overarching way of life among the citizens as a whole. Even if, the argument goes, civil, political, and social rights were to be effective in securing the equality of citizenship status that Marshall has in mind, those who inhabit minority or subordinated ways of life could still find themselves excluded from the full enjoyment of their citizenship. Multiculturalism insists that the aim of cultural homogeneity should be significantly weakened, if not abandoned all together. The National Multicultural Advisory Council (1997: 2) invoked this view when it suggested that multiculturalism had been adopted by Australian governments because the earlier "policy of assimilation was increasingly seen as outdated, ineffective and undesirable." Yet we shall see that Australian multiculturalism, like multiculturalism elsewhere, focuses on a restricted range of cultures, with the result that many disadvantaged minorities are not covered by its prescriptions. The politics of difference avoids this limitation, but its treatment of culture is problematic in other respects. We shall see also that the proposals advanced by multiculturalism and the politics of difference involve a significant shift away from the familiar and misleading image of democracy as a matter of government of *the* people, by *the* people, and for *the* people.

MULTICULTURALISM

We can begin our discussion here by noting that the assumption of a common culture or way of life raises a difficulty that Marshall's discussion of citizenship fails even to acknowledge. To the extent that they operate on this assumption and therefore seek to establish a certain uniformity of treatment for all citizens, contemporary democratic regimes leave themselves open to the charge that they may be discriminating against members of minority groups by effectively preventing them from operating according to their own preferred arrangements. According to this view, even if Marshall's civil, political, and social rights did in fact secure equality of citizenship for the bulk of the population, the presumption that citizens share a distinctive culture or way of life would still exclude indigenous and other cultural minorities from the full enjoyment of citizenship.

Multiculturalism has often been seen as addressing precisely this issue. It is concerned, Bhikhu Parekh (2000: 346) informs us, not so much "with the rights of immigrants or even minorities in general" as it is with "the place of culture in human life, its political significance, relations between cultures, and so on." In practice, as Gerd Baumann (1996, 1999) has shown, both the multicultural policies of governments and the multiculturalism of political theory draw on a very limited view of the place of culture in human affairs, and thus also of its political significance. Parekh's discussion is no exception, as we shall see below. While multiculturalism has been defined in various ways, the term refers most commonly either to a body of political theory or to an area of government policy, both of them responding to the fact of national and ethnic diversity among the citizens of contemporary states. *Multicultural Australia: United in Diversity,* a major policy statement issued in 2003 by the Australian government, begins by acknowledging the fact of diversity. It identifies Australia's multiculturalism with four principles: "responsibilities of all," "respect for each person," "fairness for each person," and "benefits for all." The first stresses the "basic structures and principles of Australian society" that enable diversity to flourish, while the last asserts the value of diversity for the community as a whole. The others focus on individuals, asserting the right of all Australians "to express their own culture and beliefs" and to freedom from discrimination, "including on the grounds of race, culture, religion, location, gender or place of birth" (Commonwealth of Australia 2003: 6).

While the mere presence of cultural diversity poses no great problem for the comparatively relaxed understanding of citizenship to be found in most modern democracies, the official recognition of cultural pluralism and its active promotion by public authorities is another matter entirely. It is a relatively recent development, dating from the early 1970s in Australia, and, as we shall see, it is also highly contentious, in part, precisely because it seems to conflict with the presumption that citizens participate in a common language, culture, and way of life.

Before we turn to the ramifications of this last issue, however, it should be noted that multiculturalism tends to treat *cultural, religious,* and *ethnic* diversity as if they were more or less equivalent. Kymlicka, one of the most influential academic writers on the politics of multiculturalism, has qualified the emphasis on these kinds of diversity, arguing that it may obscure

important differences in the ways in which minorities have been incorporated into political communities. Kymlicka is particularly concerned to distinguish between the situations, in Western societies, of *national* minorities
(e.g., Quebecois in Canada, Basques in France and Spain, Scots and Welsh
in Britain), *indigenous* communities (e.g., the indigenous peoples of Australia,
the United States, and Canada) and minorities resulting from voluntary or
involuntary *immigration*. Kymlicka (1995: 18) acknowledges that there may
well be significant cultural differences of other kinds, but he nevertheless
restricts his focus to cultural diversity arising "from national and ethnic differences." We might add that, along with the *Multicultural Australia* policy
statement, Kymlicka interprets ethnicity rather broadly to include identities
based on religion. The significance of this restriction to national and ethnic/
religious differences will become clear shortly.

The central argument of Kymlicka's *Multicultural Citizenship* (1995) is
simply that the fundamental liberal objective of equal liberty for all citizens does not necessarily rule out state promotion of group-differentiated,
or "collective," rights—for example, through special provision for minority
languages or religious practices. He makes this case by distinguishing between two kinds of collective rights, those that enable a group to restrict the
liberty of its own members and those that do not. As an example of the first,
Kymlicka cites the case of the Pueblo, a self-governing indigenous group in
the United States that has been accused of discriminating against those of its
members who converted to Protestantism by denying them access to housing and certain other benefits. In this example, it seems that the collective
rights that enabled the Pueblo to exercise a substantial degree of internal
self-government also enabled them "to limit the freedom of members to
question and revise traditional practices" (Kymlicka 1995: 40). Collective
rights of this kind, Kymlicka argues, should not be provided since they cannot be reconciled with the provision of equal liberty for all citizens.

On the other hand, he argues, there are collective rights—religious
schooling providing an obvious example—that serve rather to protect the distinctive culture of the group and to prevent it from being submerged in
the dominant culture within the larger society to which the group belongs.
Rights of the latter kind, in Kymlicka's view, need not conflict with individual liberty, and they may in fact be required for protection of the liberty
of members of many minority groups. Indeed, he argues, it is only through
participation in their own societal culture that individuals are enabled to
make meaningful choices for themselves. Thus, to the extent that majority
practices threaten the integrity of minority cultures, they can also be seen as
undermining the ability of members of these minorities to make meaningful
choices for themselves and therefore, in fact, as encroaching on their liberty.

Moreover, Kymlicka insists, group-specific rights (such as those regarding the use of minority languages) are often required to secure some approximation of equality of treatment by the state of minority and majority groups. In his view, then, there may be circumstances in which equal liberty for all citizens can be secured only through special public provision for cultural minorities.

This conclusion is one that many readers will find congenial, but the means by which it is reached give serious grounds for concern. We can begin by noting that Kymlicka's distinction between collective rights that are likely to be misused and those that are not is a difficult one to sustain. "All rights can be misused," Parekh (2000: 216) bluntly insists, "including individual rights." Few rights of any kind would remain if they were to be denied on the grounds that they might be open to abuse. We can hardly suppose, for example, that public support for religious schooling within minority communities could never be used, like the control over housing and other benefits that Kymlicka (1995: 40) describes in the Pueblo case, "to limit the freedom of members to question and revise traditional practices." Parekh goes on to observe that there is no good reason to privilege individual rights over collective ones, as Kymlicka's liberalism clearly does. "If collective rights can be used to oppress individuals, individual rights can be used to damage and destroy communities" (Parekh 2000: 216). We might think, for example, of disputes over access to the seashore or areas of great natural beauty. It is by no means clear in such cases that the rights of individual property holders should be allowed to prevail over those of the larger community.

However, the most important issues here relate to a crucial ambiguity in the connection Kymlicka draws between culture and individual liberty. It is only through participation in a societal culture, he argues, that people have a meaningful context for individual choice and thus for the exercise of individual liberty. This, the qualifier announces, is a culture of a very special kind, one that "provides its members with meaningful ways of life across the full range of human activities, including social, religious, recreational and economic life, encompassing both public and private spheres" (Kymlicka 1995: 76). There is more to a societal culture, he tells us, than "shared memories or values. ... It must also be institutionally embodied—in schools, media, economy, government, etc." At this point in his argument, as the institutions listed here suggest, Kymlicka associates societal cultures with what are often called "modern" societies. This interpretation is supported by his use of Ernest Gellner's (1983) work on nationalism to argue that the formation of societal cultures "is intimately linked with the process of modernization" in three important respects. First, a common culture is "a functional requirement of a modern economy." Second, it reflects the need for a "high level of solidarity with modern democratic states." Third, it is required by "the modern commitment to equality of opportunity" (Kymlicka 1995: 76–77). The clear implication of these claims is that societal cultures and the individual liberty that, in his view, they alone can sustain are essentially features of modern—that is, liberal democratic—states. Modernization theory, whether in Gellner's or some other form, strongly suggests that the features Kymlicka attributes to societal culture are simply not to be found either in premodern conditions or, indeed, in many contemporary cultures, including those of indigenous minorities in Australia and North America. These, the theory tells us, can provide their "members with meaningful ways of life" across only a limited range of human activities.

A few pages later, in a brief discussion of the situation of indigenous peoples in the United States, Kymlicka deploys the idea of societal culture in a very different sense. At the time of their forcible incorporation into American society, he insists, each of these indigenous groups already "constituted an ongoing societal culture. … Their language and historical narratives were already embodied in a full set of social practices and institutions, encompassing all aspects of social life" (Kymlicka 1995: 79). In this part of his discussion, Kymlicka simply abandons the crude evolutionism of modernization theory. Societal culture, it now seems, need not be linked to a modern economy, democratic state, or equality of opportunity. On the one hand, then, societal culture is essentially a product of "modernization." On the other, it is simply a culture that happens to be embodied in the institutions of some particular society. Kymlicka's own discussion of the Pueblo, which we noted above, suggests that there need be nothing particularly liberal about societal culture in this more general sense.

Kymlicka's claim to offer a *liberal* defense of collective rights for minority ethnic, national, and indigenous groups draws on both interpretations of societal culture. It is presented in some contexts as providing suitable cultural foundations for a distinctly liberal rule of uniformity and in others as underlying the way of life of a singular nation or ethnic group. The second understanding is more wide-ranging than the first, but it suggests that there is nothing distinctly liberal about societal cultures in general. It is this relaxed understanding of societal culture that allows Kymlicka to describe the ethnic, national, and indigenous minorities of contemporary Western states as having societal cultures of their own. Yet it is the first, restricted and judgmental, understanding—which he associates specifically with modernization and thus only with liberal democratic societies—that provides the link his argument requires between societal culture and what liberalism understands by individual liberty.

Charles Taylor makes a rather different case for multiculturalism in his contribution to *Multiculturalism: Examining the Politics of Recognition* (1994), a book that, as the subtitle suggests, treats the issue of multiculturalism as a problem of cultural recognition. Taylor notes that there are many different cultures and that they "have to live together more and more, both on a world scale and commingled in each individual society." Moreover, "cultures that have provided the horizon of meaning for large numbers of human beings … over a long period of time … are almost certain to have something that deserves our admiration and respect, even if it is accompanied by much that we have to abhor and reject" (Taylor 1994: 72–73). There is a sense in which Taylor's argument, like Kymlicka's, is a liberal one, but his case for cultural recognition does not rely on any supposed link between culture and individual liberty. As a result, his account of the cultures that are worthy of respect and admiration displays none of the ambiguity that we find in Kymlicka's discussion.

Nevertheless, there remains an important respect in which long-established and widely recognized cultures play a similar role in Taylor's argument to that of "societal cultures" in Kymlicka's. They are seen as cultures of a special kind and, in particular, as capable of providing the cultural foundations of social and political order within large-scale communities. Far from being concerned with "the place of culture in human life," as Parekh suggests, the multiculturalism of Kymlicka and Taylor is really concerned with the political significance of what they take to be an important, but nonetheless limited, range of cultures. In practice, Parekh himself takes a similar view. Thus, while acknowledging that there are many forms of cultural diversity, his discussion of multiculturalism is in fact restricted to what he calls "communal diversity." This, he tells us, "springs from and is sustained by a plurality of long-established communities, each with its own history and way of life which it wishes to preserve and transmit" (Parekh 2000: 4). He describes multiculturalism, in this sense, as appearing first in societies that, after "several centuries of the culturally homogenising nation-state," nevertheless "found themselves faced with distinct cultural groups" (Parekh 2000: 8, 4).

The problem that the multiculturalism of these authors seeks to address, then, concerns a difficulty that is thought to arise from the presence within an established polity of significant minority communities attached to cultures of the special kind just noted. It is the problem of how to maintain an underlying uniformity of treatment for all citizens while nevertheless allowing them, in the words of *Multicultural Australia* (Commonwealth of Australia 2003: 6), "to express their own culture and beliefs." Many commentators (e.g., Tully 1995) have noted the limitations of the view of culture as a self-contained unity, on which this multiculturalism seems to rely. Gerd Baumann's (1996) study of life in multicultural London shows that communities that live together also interact, often producing an unstable mix of identities and ways of life that do not fit neatly into such self-contained unities. There is no reason to suppose that the situation in multicultural Australia would be significantly different in this respect.

The focus of the political theorists considered here on discrete, "societal," or long-established cultures leaves no room for messy cultural realities of the kind revealed by Baumann's study. In many respects, indeed, their arguments seem to be in line with those of the long tradition of white Australian philanthropy described by Bain Attwood (2003), which invited us to admire and respect the traditional cultures of indigenous peoples in remote tribal communities while showing little concern for the way of life of the many who lived elsewhere. There is no presumption in this multiculturalism that equal value be attached "to recent cultures, cultures deemed deviant by whomsoever has the power to make such a judgement, and cultures that may arise tomorrow" (Baumann 1999: 109).

THE POLITICS OF DIFFERENCE

If multiculturalism leaves itself open to attack from those who fear that the needs of certain minorities are not being adequately addressed, it is also disputed by those who fear that its policies will undermine the fabric of uniformity. This is because the minorities with which multiculturalism is concerned appear to acknowledge foundations of social and political order that differ from those provided by the culture of the majority. Before turning to this second line of attack, however, we should also consider the political problem raised by Baumann's critique. There are disadvantaged groups in contemporary democracies whose difficulties do not arise simply from the coexistence of discrete and bounded cultures of the rather special kind that Kymlicka, Parekh, and Taylor have in mind. Following the appearance of Iris Marion Young's *Justice and the Politics of Difference* (1990), the last part of this title has served to identify an influential style of argument that aims to address this more general issue of disadvantage. The "politics of difference" moves beyond multiculturalism's focus on national, ethnic, and religious differences to insist that, important though some of these differences may be, the exclusive character of the dominant way of life in most Western societies also discriminates against many others: women in general, blacks, gay men, lesbian women, and those who are seen as having deviant lifestyles.

At first sight, it might seem that what is at issue in these cases is simply that policymakers, public service agencies, and mainstream political parties fail to acknowledge the concerns of certain minorities. This is the problem we noted at the beginning of the previous section: to the extent that they favor uniformity of treatment for all citizens, contemporary democratic states also discriminate against indigenous and other minorities. However, while many of Young's illustrations deal with the conduct of political and public service agencies, her analysis focuses on a rather different issue: namely, the culture of the majority and its tendency to discriminate against various minorities. I will return to this point in my concluding remarks.

Young's discussion also brings out the importance of a second issue, which is that the dominant way of life will sometimes treat various others as deviant or inferior. These two levels are brought together in her observation, in a later essay, that the norms of deliberation in the contemporary United States "are culturally specific and often operate as forms of power that *silence* or *devalue* the speech of some people" (Young 1996: 123, emphasis added; cf. Young 2000: esp. chap. 2). The problem in the first case is that people are discriminated against because their distinctive needs and concerns are not acknowledged, but in the second it is that, far from being ignored, their distinctive character is both acknowledged and stigmatized. The view that non-Western peoples are inferior has been a perpetual temptation of Western political thought, and it continues to play a part in the politics of all Western democracies. Indigenous minorities and many non-Western immigrant communities thus find that their difference is denied in some contexts and all too clearly asserted in others. They are subjected to a damaging rule of what Jim Tully calls "the empire of uniformity" while also being treated as inferior and not yet capable of properly managing their own affairs (Helliwell and Hindess 2002).

What is required to address these problems, in Young's view, is for the dominant groups to reform themselves, most especially by adopting a more open, less exclusive understanding of the citizens' way of life. This would enable them, she suggests, to recognize the concerns of various cultural minorities and the norms and values that those concerns represent. In fact, Young goes one step further, generalizing this last point to argue that such openness should be the responsibility of all members of contemporary democracies. Thus, adapting the multicultural prescription to encompass a much broader range of differences, she insists that all groups should "have a commitment to equal respect for one another, in the simple formal sense of a willingness to say that all have a right to express their opinions and points of view, and all ought to listen" (Young 1996: 126). Having adopted this prescription, Young suggests, all groups would eventually come to understand something of the perspectives and ways of life of other groups, thereby gaining "a wider picture of the social processes in which their own partial experience is embedded" (Young 1996: 128). The reference to "a wider picture,"

the perception of which could be shared, at least in principle, by all participants at some point in the future, invokes yet another version of the image
of an overarching culture or way of life—one that, in this case, is expected
to emerge from a multiplicity of suitably respectful interactions. A closely
related image of overarching unity is invoked by Parekh's (2000: 219) insistence that "a multicultural society needs a broadly shared culture to sustain
it. Since it involves several cultures, the shared culture can only grow out of
their interaction and should respect their diversity and unite them around
a common way of life."

As we might expect, defenders of the rule of uniformity take a different view of these matters. Far from promoting cultural pluralism among its
citizens, David Miller argues, governments should aim instead to establish
"*a common identity as citizens* that is stronger than their separate identities as
members of ethnic or other sectional minorities" (Miller 1995: 154, emphasis added; see also Barry 2001). We have just seen that Parekh's and Young's
rather different versions of cultural pluralism also suggest that there is a
need to promote a "common identity" among the citizens. However, while
the political theory of multiculturalism and the politics of difference see
this common identity as emerging out of dialogue between members of all
relevant groups, the defenders of the rule of uniformity see it more as a
matter of assimilating minorities to the existing dominant culture. According to this view, the fact that there are significant minorities in most democratic societies with members who are less than fluent in the language and
other practices of the majority invites a response of the kind suggested by
Marshall's view of social policy: namely, that the state has a responsibility
to ensure that no individuals are so disadvantaged that they are excluded
from the full enjoyment of their citizenship. It suggests, in other words, that
governments should deal with the impact of cultural pluralism on the civil,
political, and social rights of members of cultural minorities by integrating
them into the culture of the majority community.

Unlike the multiculturalism of political theory, the multiculturalism of
governments generally tends toward the latter view. *Multicultural Australia,*
the government policy statement, asserts that "all Australians have the right
to express their own culture and beliefs." Yet it also insists on their duty "to
support those basic structures and principles of Australian society which
guarantee us our freedom and equality and enable diversity in our society
to flourish" (Commonwealth of Australia 2003: 6). Far from emerging out
of dialogue between members of different cultures, the "structures and principles" that enable diversity to flourish are assumed to be already in place.

The discourse of uniformity implies that public support for minority
rights amounts to the promotion of sectional interest groups by the state.

The long-standing liberal concern with the effects of faction in public life suggests that attempts to ensure the representation of sectional interests outside of the electoral process will provide opportunities for the pursuit of those interests to the detriment of the interests of the community as a whole. This is the point of Glazer and Moynihan's (1963: 17) observation that the single most important fact about ethnic groups in New York City "is that they are also interest groups." Kymlicka's discussion of the Pueblo picks up on the consequences of interest group organization for minority communities themselves, arguing that it may well privilege particular groups or factions within these minorities. Australian governments have frequently taken this view, treating leaders of indigenous and many immigrant organizations as if they were not truly representative of their own communities.

PLURALIST DEMOCRACY?

Thus far, it seems that the multiculturalism of political theory, the more general politics of difference, and the objections to these positions that we have just noted are all predicated on similar ideals of uniformity. The argument, on the one side, is that a system of differentiated rights may be required to ensure uniformity of condition among the citizens and, on the other, that uniformity would be undermined by the provision of special rights for sectional minorities. However, there are elements within the politics of difference that tend, if not to undermine, then at least to relax the initial presumption in favor of uniformity.

Young (1996: 126), for example, suggests that what motivates politics within established states "is the facticity of people being thrown together, finding themselves in geographical proximity and economic interdependence. ... *A polity consists of people who live together, who are stuck with one another*" (emphasis added). This claim is far removed from Marshall's assumption that the citizens of a state participate in a common civilization or way of life. Young goes on to argue, as we have seen, that democracy requires something more than mere coexistence. In addition to the institutional arrangements of representative government, she argues, there should also be a practical commitment by all participants to a significant degree of "equal respect for one another" (Young 1996: 126). The problems posed by cultural and other forms of diversity are to be addressed by improving the conduct of all concerned.

In fact, neither "geographical proximity" nor "economic interdependence" need imply that people "are stuck with one another" in the same polity. To treat the integrity of the state as a given, as so much of the literature on multiculturalism and the politics of difference appears to do, is already to impose a significant limit on the views that are to be accorded "equal respect." This failure to put the state and its boundaries into question can be seen as an extreme case of a more general problem that I take up in my closing remarks.

I noted earlier that this invocation of equal respect as a means of dealing with the consequences of diversity nevertheless appeals to an image of overarching cultural unity. Yet it is a unity that is considerably less substantial than that suggested by most received understandings of democracy. The problem of how to accommodate difference is now seen as a matter less of ensuring some version of uniformity in face of the unsettling empirical fact of diversity than of enabling the members of a diverse population to live together in peace.

Before turning to the revised understanding of democracy that is suggested here, we should acknowledge an important tradition of political thought in the West that has long challenged the presumption of uniformity. Perhaps the most powerful recent statement of this challenge is to be found in James Tully's *Strange Multiplicity: Constitutionalism in an Age of Diversity* (1995). While Tully approaches the question of cultural diversity from a rather different direction than either Parekh or Young, he too argues in favor of collective rights for indigenous and other minorities, and for dialogue based on mutual respect, without any assumption that the dominant community provides the standard by which the others can be judged.

The key to the empire of uniformity in Tully's view is the assumption that the constitution of a modern state can be treated as if it had been established in a single foundational act of agreement—a social contract—between the citizens as a whole. The most important effect of this assumption is to rule out any possibility of recognizing prior agreement amongst the members of a minority group to operate according to their own separate and distinctive arrangements. Thus, while defenders of the rule of uniformity might well acknowledge, as a matter of brute historical fact, that the provenance of constitutional arrangements commonly has a complex, disordered, and even distinctly unsavory character, the regulative idea of a foundational social contract implies that a uniform set of laws and conventions for their interpretation should apply to all members of the population in question. From this perspective, Tully argues, lack of uniformity within the population and the territory of a state is likely to be seen as an unfortunate historical residue, a problem that has to be overcome by the harmonization of laws, the establishment of a single national language, and, of course, measures to combat resistance to such developments. There may still be room here, as Kymlicka tries to show, for special provision for minorities, but only within the limits set by the overarching rule of uniformity.

Tully begins his critique of the presumption of uniformity by acknowledging the difficulty of establishing a morally defensible framework in which we might examine the justice of claims emanating from culturally diverse groups. He observes that an inquiry into justice should first of all "investigate if the language in which the inquiry proceeds is itself just: that is, capable of rendering the speakers their due" (Tully 1995: 34). This simple point, frequently overlooked by liberal political theorists, directly challenges the bland assumption—which Kymlicka's discussion, for example, takes for granted—that the conduct of indigenous and other minorities can reasonably be judged according to the liberal standards already embedded in the institutions of the presumed majority.

In fact, Tully suggests, if we examine constitutionalism from the perspective of the struggles of Aboriginal peoples, then the empire of uniformity appears in a radically different light. First, it appears substantially less attractive than conventional accounts of the history of modern political thought would have us believe. Rather than working to secure the foundations of a just social order, we observe that the empire of uniformity exhibits a studied indifference toward many historical and continuing injustices. Second, Tully's examination brings to light the importance in modern political thought of a subordinated but nonetheless influential style of constitutional thinking that sees modern states as consisting precisely of peoples, cultures, and ways of life that are, in Young's words, "stuck with one another." He cites, for example, the works of Montesquieu, Matthew Hale, and Edmund Burke and again, more recently, the majority *Mabo* and *Wik* judgments of the Australian High Court.

We should add that, while his argument focuses primarily on the problems posed by the assumption of uniformity, Tully's discussion also brings out the importance of the issue of stigmatization noted above: the fact that far from being ignored, many kinds of difference have been treated as clear signs of inferiority (Helliwell and Hindess 2002). He notes, for example, that the cultures of indigenous minorities within modern states have frequently been located at "stages of historical development" below those of the majority, and again that many groups seek, often with only limited success, to participate "in ways that recognise and affirm, rather than exclude, assimilate and denigrate" (Tully 1995: 11, 4).

This pluralist challenge to the empire of uniformity has taken us a long way from the idealized image of the *polis* with which we began, a *polis* whose citizens "share a common descent, language and culture" (Kymlicka 1995: 2). Government of, by, and for the peoples, groups, and associations who happen to find themselves together in the territory of the one state has little of the appealing simplicity of government of, by, and for *the* people of that state.

It is complicated further by the fact that many of these peoples, groups, and associations have members who belong to other states. These points suggest that, while still retaining the sense of representative government, democracy should no longer be seen as an affair of a body of citizens who together constitute a singular people. Rather, it is an affair of citizens who belong to a diverse collection of peoples, groups, and associations.

In practice, notwithstanding the rhetorical power of the image of the *polis,* the institutional arrangements of modern democracy have often been tempered by arrangements of other kinds: a federal system of states, semi-autonomous regions, corporatist interest-group mediation, and more or less self-governing associations of various types (Lijphart 1999). Multicultural political theory and the politics of difference strongly imply that such institutional pluralism should be seen as an integral part of democracy itself. The politics of difference goes further to insist that this pluralism should always be open to the needs of new minorities. Once the presumption of uniformity has been relaxed in this way, there can be few general rules for determining what institutional arrangements might be required to complement those of representative government. It is clear, for example, that arrangements designed to accommodate the concerns of national and indigenous minorities will often have little to offer minorities of other kinds, and that established arrangements may have to adapt as new minorities emerge and older minorities change. Moreover, to say that one set of institutions should be tempered by another is also to say that they may sometimes come into conflict. Here the arguments of multicultural political theory and the politics of difference in favor of dialogue over constitutional arrangements suggest that the outcome will normally be some kind of mutually acceptable accommodation.

Yet such an accommodation may well be difficult to achieve—as it is, for example, in the North of Ireland—and it may, on occasion, prove to be impossible. I suggested earlier that, if we take the idea of mutual respect seriously, then the integrity of the state would have to be seen as potentially open to discussion. The image of the *polis* is an unsatisfactory instrument for addressing the issue of diversity, then, not simply because it suggests an ideal of linguistic, cultural, and ethnic uniformity. It also presents the state, not as part of the problem but rather as the unquestionable frame in which the problem has to be addressed. The image of the *polis* suggests, finally, that the state consists of, and is ultimately reducible to, its citizens. Young's observation that a polity "consists of *people* who live together" (1996: 126, emphasis added) reflects the continuing appeal of this last idea, at least to political theorists. So, too, does the rhetoric of recognition, admiration, and respect that we find in so much of the academic literature on multiculturalism and the politics of difference.

There is no place here for the modern idea of the state as "the coldest of all cold monsters" (Nietzsche 1969: 75), a substantial apparatus of government that is clearly separate both from the person of the ruler and from the subject population (cf. Skinner 1989). Australia and other Western states are usually said to be democratic, which is to say that the ruler and the subject population are in some sense identical, but they nevertheless have interests, concerns, and objectives that are not reducible to those of their citizens. To address the condition of disadvantaged groups within these states, we need to consider how states, and the different agencies within them, understand the problems involved in dealing with diversity within the populations under their control, the resources available for dealing with them, and so on (cf. Hindess 2000, 2001; Walters 2004).

The conduct of the Howard government's Department of Immigration, Multicultural and Indigenous Affairs (DIMIA) itself provides a textbook illustration of this last point. The Migration Act of 1958 requires authorized officers to detain any person they know or reasonably suspect of being an unlawful noncitizen—that is, of not holding a current visa. In February 2005, the family of Cornelia Rau, who lives in Australia and holds a visa that allows her permanent residence, discovered that she was being held under these powers in the Baxter Immigration Detention Facility. Before her move to Baxter, she had been held for six months in the Brisbane Women's Correctional Centre. Rau had suffered from psychotic episodes for some years and, throughout her detention, she claimed to be a visiting German tourist. The publicity surrounding this case forced the Australian government to establish an inquiry, which found that DIMIA officers had not seriously considered the possibility that her story might be the product of mental illness. Rather, their inquiries were concerned to establish "her identity for the purposes of enabling her removal from Australia" (Palmer 2005: 8). As for holding her on the suspicion that she was an unlawful noncitizen, the inquiry noted that

> DIMIA officers are authorised to exercise exceptional, even extra-ordinary, powers. That they should be permitted and expected to do so without adequate training ... and with no genuine quality assurance and constraints on the exercise of these powers is of concern. The fact that this situation has been allowed to continue ... for several years is difficult to understand. (Palmer 2005: 9)

The inquiry also revealed disturbing features of the internal culture of DIMIA, which it saw as "unwilling to challenge organisational norms or to engage in genuine self-criticism or analysis" (2005: 172). It found that these attitudes were "pervasive at senior executive management level" and insisted that the necessary change must come from the top (2005: 169, 172). While this inquiry was under way, it was discovered that an Australian citizen had been held by DIMIA and then deported to the Philippines, her country of birth. The public outcry over these two cases and over the more general treatment of detainees that they brought to light compelled the government to establish a broader inquiry. The Australian ombudsman is, at the time of writing, looking into many other cases of possible wrongful detention. Unfortunately, it is not within the terms of reference of these inquiries to consider to what extent the problematic culture of DIMIA may have been fostered by successive Australian governments.

For our purposes, however, the point to notice is that the culture and attitudes that determine how DIMIA exercises its "extra-ordinary" powers are those of DIMIA itself. It would be naïve to suppose that these were entirely independent of the majority Australian culture. Yet, as the public concern over these cases shows, they do have distinctive characteristics of their own. They cannot be seen simply as expressions of the broader culture in which they are immersed. The model of the *polis,* which dominates so much of multicultural political theory, suggests that we need hardly concern ourselves with such quibbles. It invites us to focus on the culture and the attitudes of the people themselves and thus to ignore what is distinctive about the armies of professional politicians, public servants, and other corporate functionaries, and the numerous state and nonstate agencies in which they serve, all of which play such a significant part in the life of all modern states, democratic or otherwise. The entirely commendable injunction that citizens should practice "equal respect for one another" (Young 1996: 126) does little in itself to address the problems that the practices and objectives of these agencies pose for disadvantaged groups within the subject population.

Part II

Democracy and Diversity

Chapter 6

Three Images of the Citizenry

Philip Pettit

⊰◈⊱

CITIZEN AND CITIZENRY

Despite the high level of attention paid in recent years to the notion of citizen and citizenship (Kymlicka and Norman 1994; Norman and Kymlicka 2003), I know of no treatment of the collective idea of the citizenry. Perhaps the reason is an assumption that "the citizenry" is just a collective way of designating the assemblage of citizens: that there is no collective entity that it names. What it is to be a citizen is defined in more or less independent terms, so the assumption would go, and the citizenry make an appearance as the natural effect of multiplication. "The citizenry" on this approach has no valid connotations over and beyond the connotations of the plural usage, "the citizens."

I reject this assumption. Citizenries may vary in nature, without this variation being just a reflection of differences in the characteristics of their members. And if we think of citizenship as membership in a citizenry then, depending on the nature of that citizenry, it can mean any of a range of quite different things. I hope to substantiate those claims in this chapter. Before attempting to do so, however, it may be useful to address what some will see as a questionable belief that citizenries are collective entities that can differ without the differences reflecting differences in the characteristics of their citizens. How could this be so?

Consider a parallel question. How could a molecule differ from a non-molecular set of its constituent atoms without the difference reflecting differences in the characteristics of its atoms? The answer is that of course no difference is possible without a difference in the individual parts but that the individual differences that make for differences in the whole may not be intrinsic differences in the parts themselves, but rather differences in the way in which the parts are organized in relation to one another. Organizational differences are what make the difference between a disjointed set of atoms, comprising a pair of hydrogen atoms and a single oxygen atom, and a molecule of water or H_2O. They are what give a water molecule its distinctive identity and enable us to individuate it as an entity distinct from its parts and reidentifiable across different times and different possible histories. They are what make it natural and useful to think of such a molecule—and molecules in general—as a unit in its own right, not just as a set composed of more basic atomic units.

In a parallel way organizational differences can make for a difference between a citizenry and an aggregate of individuals, or between different citizenries—different *populi* or peoples. One and the same set of individuals might constitute nothing but an aggregate of persons—a *multitudo* or multitude—or it might constitute a citizenry or people. And, depending on the mode in which those individuals are organized in relation to one another—depending on the civic structure they instantiate—they might constitute this or that type of citizenry. To the extent that citizenries are distinguished by their civic structures, we can think of them as units in their own right, not just as sets or collections of more basic individual units.

I believe it is ontologically misleading to think that citizenries can be treated as just numbers or pluralities of citizens. But it is not merely ontological bookkeeping that will suffer if we do not recognize the lesson I want to underline. Let citizenship be cast as membership in a given type of citizenry—a citizenry organized around a given type of civic structure—and two lessons follow. First, there is going to be no such thing as the nature of citizenship in general, only the nature of citizenship under one or another civic structure. And second, there is going to be no such thing as the normative content of citizenship in general; with variations in civic structure, there is liable to be a variation in the set of civic duties and virtues, rights and benefits that go with citizenship.

I try to provide support for these implications in the remainder of this chapter. I look at three rather different pictures of the people or the citizenry that have each had a certain importance in political thought. These are ideal types that abstract away from more detailed social structures. Then I argue that associated with these different pictures of the citizenry are different views of the nature and norms of citizenship. What picture applies in a contemporary society such as the United States or Australia? I suggest that each has a certain limited application and that many differences among theorists of citizenship turn on which picture is given prominence.

The chapter has four remaining sections. In the next three I look in turn at the three different sorts of citizenry mentioned and, very briefly, at their different implications for the nature and norms of citizenship. Then in a final section I try to show that while each has a certain application in contemporary democracies, the third image teaches the most arresting lessons.

THE SOLIDARIST CITIZENRY

I describe the first model of the citizenry as solidarist in character; it represents the citizenry as a corporate body. The best way of approaching this model is to imagine how any corporate body of individuals might form and what it would require of its members. With the abstract possibility sketched, we can then look at the history of thinking about the citizenry as a body of just that kind.

Suppose that a collection of people all agree to promote a certain set of purposes in common, implicitly fulfilling relevant conditions (see Bratman 1999; Gilbert 2001; Seumas Miller 2001; Tuomela 1995; Velleman 2000). They each intend that they together bring about those purposes; they each intend to do their individual bit in pursuit of the purposes, because they expect others to do their bit, too; and all of this is above board, as a matter of common awareness (Pettit and Schweikard 2006). Now suppose in addition that they agree, implicitly or explicitly, that the actions taken on behalf of the collectivity in support of those ends should be directed by one and the same set of canonical, collectively endorsed judgments—say, at a first approximation, the set of judgments supported by majority voting or by some such procedure (Hobbes 1994b: chap. 15, Ss 15–17). And suppose, finally, that when any of the members act on behalf of the collectivity—when they act in a representative role, in the group's name—they allow their actions to be guided not by their own particular beliefs but by the canonical judgments.

When conditions of this kind are fulfilled, it is perfectly reasonable to say that the collectivity constitutes a corporate agent (Pettit 2001, 2003). The collectivity will have a set of judgments and a set of purposes—something like a system of belief and desire—that is distinct from the systems of belief and desire that its members individually instantiate; if you like, it will have a single vision by which it operates (Rovane 1997). And when individual members act in its name, they will act on the basis of that system of judgment and purpose, not in expression of their own particular attitudes. The entity in question may be an ad hoc organization of activists, a parish council, the editorial board of a journal, or whatever. And of course it may be an organizationally complex entity, like a company or church or university; such an entity will be itself articulated out of many corporate subagents, each designed to have a province of action of its own.

A corporate group of the kind envisaged will not be capable of varying independently of how members at any time are related to one another and are disposed to behave in representation of it. But still it will constitute an agent that cannot be identified with any one agent amongst them, or even with any majority of those agents. It will have properties, in particular attitudes, that are discontinuous from those of its members. And it will even have the capacity to gain and lose members, while sustaining those attitudes and remaining the same collective body. It will have its own integrity and autonomy as an agent.

The claim about the discontinuity between corporate and individual attitudes is crucial and it may be worth pausing to emphasize why it is more or less inevitable. Recent work in social choice theory—strictly, social judgment theory—has shown that a corporate group may be quite rationally led or required to form judgments that differ from what the majority judge on those issues, or even from what all the members individually judge (Dietrich 2006; List and Pettit 2002, 2004; Pauly and Van Hees 2006). Suppose, to take a simple illustration, that there are three members in the group, A, B, and C, and that they have to make judgments on whether p, whether q, and, at the same or a later time, whether p and q. A and B may vote that p, C against; B and C that q, A against; and A and C that not p-and-q, with only B opposing. But the group cannot act on the single set of judgments that this voting would produce, for no agent or agency can act as if it is the case that p, as if it is the case that q, and as if it is the case that not p-and-q. Thus the group members will have to find a mode of judgment-making that allows the group to endorse judgments—and that requires members to act representatively on judgments—that the majority of them may individually reject. The agreement reached in our little group, for example, might be that the group will act as if it is the case that p, that q, and that p and q, though A and C both personally disbelieve that compound proposition.

The possibility of a corporate agent of roughly this kind came to be identified in medieval legal theory, as the idea of the corporation was developed in order to cope with the realities of guilds, universities, cities, and the like (Canning 1980; Coleman 1974). Thinkers in this tradition argued that a corporation was a *persona ficta*—an artificial person—that transcended its members. It survived changes of membership and had rights and responsibilities of its own, independent of those of its members. It was a unified entity that comprised any number of individuals and acted through representatives. The members or representatives would determine the *mens* of the corporation—its system of belief and desire—and the representatives would lend it their tongues and limbs when they spoke and acted in its name; it would speak and act through them.

With the idea of the corporation explicated, we can see how it might be applied in certain context to a political citizenry. And applied, it was. Fourteenth-century scholars such as Bartolus of Sassoferrato and Baldus de Ubaldis (Canning 1983) used it to characterize the citizenries of a number of Italian city-states in their own time. They argued that de facto if not strictly de jure—as a matter of conventional if not statutory law—these cities had the status of corporations in their relationships with their own residents, with outsiders, with bodies such as guilds and universities, and with the great powers represented by the pope and the Holy Roman Emperor. By casting them as corporate bodies that governed themselves, they could resist the thought that even through periods when he had done very little, the emperor—the *dominus mundi* or lord of the world—had remained their only governor; were the cities not to count as corporate bodies, then the absence of any other candidate would have reinforced the emperor's claims to be the sole authority in their lives and affairs.

The *populus* or people or citizenry in each of the cities that concerned Bartolus and Baldus—and of course the members were all propertied, mainstream males—was represented by a *concilum* or council, to which all had access, and it determined the *mens populi*. It acted representatively in pursuit of the purposes endorsed in that popular mind, according to judgments endorsed in the popular mind. Such a people or citizenry, so the thought went, was a *persona* in its own right; it was self-governing in the manner of an individual person, and it was capable within certain legal limits of determining its relationships with outside individuals and bodies.

This medieval tradition of representing the people was very influential, according to recent scholarship (Skinner 2002), in shaping the emergence of the notion of the people in early modern political theory. The radical monarchomachs of the sixteenth century took over the corporate notion of the people and gave it a contractual twist. They argued in the name of religious minorities such as the Huguenots in France that those minorities were citizenries in their own right, represented by their local magistrates; that as corporate entities of that kind they must be presumed to have made a contract with the monarch and his or her heirs to be governed according to certain terms; and that since the king had clearly violated those terms in persecuting them, they no longer had any duty to obey. Acting through its local magistrates or representatives, the people was entitled to rebel (Garnett 1994).[1]

With this brief historical reference we begin to see what the solidarist conception of the citizenry involves. Let the citizenry constitute a corporate agent in the sense involved—let the citizenry be roughly as theorists such as Baldus and Bartolus took the peoples of the small Italian city-states to be—and that conception materializes. The citizens will endorse common purposes; the citizens will validate a procedure, say one involving a representative council, for establishing relevant judgments to do with priorities, opportunities, means, and so on; and those who are authorized at any time to act in the name of the people will be constrained to act in pursuit only of such purposes, and in accord only with such judgments.

I describe this conception of the citizenry as solidarist because it depicts the citizens as constituting a corporate entity that is distinct from the individuals involved: an entity with its own power of purpose and judgment and action—in a word, with its own will. The conception was very effectively attacked by Thomas Hobbes (1994b), who was anxious to undermine the radical monarchomachian movement. He took over the medieval and monarchomachian view that the people could exist as a corporate agent in its own right but only so far as it was represented. And he then argued that the only effective representative or "personator" of the people—the only one who made them into a "civil person," as he said—was the sovereign. The upshot was that the people as a whole could not be thought of as having made a contract with the sovereign such that the sovereign might be in breach of its terms; the people would dissolve themselves into a multitude, as he put it, should they kill or reject the sovereign: regicide would amount to suicide.

Jean-Jacques Rousseau (1973) reinstated the conception of the solidarist citizenry in the eighteenth century but hardly with any lasting success. Rousseau adopted a democratic version of the Hobbesian view, according to which the one and only representative and sovereign possible is the body constituted by the citizens in assembly. Hobbes had admitted that the sovereign might be a democratic body of this kind but did not think that it would work as well as monarchy. What Hobbes had presented as a marginal possibility, Rousseau depicted as the one and only legitimate mode of government. He urged us to think that in the polity the individuals must come together to constitute a corporate entity with its own will—the general will—and that all legislation had to emanate directly from that assembly, all administrative action emerge on an indirect, delegated basis.

The solidarist conception of the citizenry is worth isolating, because it gives us a useful point of reference and because it may still have a certain influence on contemporary thought. It suggests that to be a citizen is to be a member of an entity with a *persona* of its own and that as a citizen one can legitimately speak of what we the people seek or want, hold or insist on, without that being cast as mere metaphor. It suggests that there is a perfectly literal sense in which not only do we citizens each embody our individual person—not only do we enact that *persona,* as it were—we also combine to embody the person of the community.

There are three striking implications that this image of the citizenry more or less loosely supports. The first is that if the citizenry is a corporate body then the obvious political ideal is autonomy and the natural way to think of democracy is as a collective analogue to individual autonomy: a way of ensuring that the collective is able to act according to its own will, not the will of others. As every individual is ideally his or her own master, so the citizenry or people or community should be its own master. And that, ideally, is what democracy provides in establishing routines whereby the purposes and the judgments of the solidarist people—and thereby its corporate will—are identified and regimented.

The second implication bears on the duties and virtues of citizenship. Those duties and virtues are going to derive from the need to keep solidarist democracy going. They will require of citizens a wholehearted commitment to the flourishing of the corporate entity to which they belong and which they constitute. There will always be a temptation on individuals to free ride, not playing their part in the sustenance of the public persona and looking only to their individual concerns. And that will be the great betrayal under this account of the citizenry. It will count, in Rousseau's terms, as furthering the particular will rather than the general will; and this, despite the fact that the general will is the will of a people that one helps to constitute—despite the fact that it is in a sense one's own will.

The third implication, finally, bears on the rights and benefits of citizenship. The core rights are obviously going to be rights of participation in the formation and enactment of the public persona rather than rights of private protection, or anything of the kind. And the benefits associated with citizenship on this approach are going to be those associated traditionally with the notion of membership and participation (Berlin 1969; Constant 1988).

Although the solidarist conception of the citizenry was hard to reconcile with the large nation-state, it came to be celebrated in the nineteenth century with the romantic fervor of nostalgia. It was projected back onto classical Athens and Rome, despite the medieval provenance of the idea; whether or not the conception applied in the ancient world, it appears to have been first articulated in the medieval. The Rousseauvian version of the solidarist approach held a particular prominence, of course, and while most rejected it as part of an older and dead set of possibilities (Constant 1988), many continued to support a vestige of it in the more romantic variants on the ideal of national self-determination.

The solidarist model has continued to haunt more recent thought and may even be part of the common sense of democracy as an ideal of popular sovereignty: an ideal of government in which the preformed will of the quasi-corporate people is imposed via referendum or representation. One school of thought that has particularly emphasized an understanding of politics and citizenship that harks back to the solidarist conception is the more communitarian strain of thinking—often misdescribed as "republican" (Pettit 1997)—that one finds in writers as diverse as Hannah Arendt (1958) and Michael Sandel (1996). Another related approach goes with the argument that the written constitution gives a people a solidarist aspect, representing a temporally inscribed voice, and that it supports a corresponding view of democracy and citizenship (Rubenfeld 2001).

THE SINGULARIST CITIZENRY

A well-known tradition of thinking asserts that it makes no sense to posit group agents proper. There are only agents of an individual kind and the idea of group attitudes or group actions, even the attitudes or actions of an organized corporate body, is mere metaphor. Anthony Quinton (1975/76: 17) writes: "We do, of course, speak freely of the mental properties and acts of a group in the way we do of individual people. Groups are said to have beliefs, emotions, and attitudes and to take decisions and make promises. But these ways of speaking are plainly metaphorical." Following at least the spirit of Margaret Gilbert's (1989: 12) usage of the term, I describe this view as a singularist image of group agency (Pettit 2003). Singularism denies that there are group agents in any literal sense of the term, arguing that when we describe groups as thinking and doing things, that is just a *façon de parler:* in truth, the only agents involved are individuals.

   Singularism of this kind had a powerful impact in the nineteenth century, partly in reaction to the romantic excesses to which those who hailed group agencies were prone. The line, expressed in the curt prose of the English utilitarian John Austin (1869: 364), was that groups count as agents "only by figment, and for the sake of brevity of discussion." That line survived into twentieth-century social and political thought, particularly in English-speaking countries. It was briefly interrupted by the enthusiasm for legal persons—akin to the corporate entities of medieval thought—that was sparked by translations of the German medieval historian Otto Gierke (Hager 1989; McLean 1999; Runciman 1997). This movement was deeply organicist in its imagery, and it led adherents to speak, for example, of "the pulsation of a common purpose which surges, as it were, from above, into the mind and behaviour of members of any true group" (Barker 1950: 61).

But its organicism helped ensure that it never really caught on, particularly as organicism came to be associated more and more strongly with totalitarianism (Popper 1960).

Leftist thought maintained some uncertain connections with the solidarist tradition in the mid-century, but singularism came to dominate more and more circles of political thought, popular and professional. The apogee may have come with the famous remark of Margaret Thatcher: "There is no such thing as society."

The rise of singularism, as might be expected, had an enormous influence on thinking about the citizenry. It naturally led political thought from the Rousseauvian, solidarist extreme to the very opposite end of the spectrum: to a view under which there are citizens but not in any distinct sense a citizenry; there are persons but not in any distinct sense a people. The citizenry were reduced, in traditional terms, from the status of a *populus* to that of a *multitudo*. They were nothing more than what Thomas Hobbes (1994a: 124) described as a "heap, or multitude": a mass of people, unable by his lights "to demand or have right to any thing."

Under the solidarist view, the individuals who constitute the citizenry have relationships with one another of such a kind that they constitute a group agent, establishing a single system of belief and desire. Under the singularist alternative, there are no particular relationships, or none of any particular importance, that individuals in the same citizenry have to bear to one another. There may be no particular natural relationships between them, of course, such as those that bind members of the same family or tribe. The only distinctive relationships they have with one another will be contractual liaisons together with those relationships—ideally if only imperfectly contractual (Buchanan and Tullock 1962)—that make them subjects of the same political system and the same government. For all that belonging to the same citizenry requires, people may relate to one another in just about any fashion; they may be as heterogeneous and disconnected as the set of individuals who live at the same latitude.

But won't the individuals represented by government be united in virtue of that representation, as Hobbes (1994a) indeed had envisaged? Not so far as they each think of government as representing them—representing them at the same time that it represents others—in their individual capacity. Given that they each think of government in this way, there will be no question of their jointly intending, as in the Hobbesian picture, that the government's judgments count as their judgments. They will see the government, as they might see an attorney they commission in a class action, as an independent entity that acts in representation of their individual purposes or interests according to its own judgments.

This is enough, I hope, by way of introducing the singularist view of the citizenry. It strongly supports three implications that contrast nicely with those associated with the solidarist alternative. The first bears on the nature of democracy, the second on the duties and virtues of citizenship, and the third on its rights and benefits.

Assume that citizens are as divided and disconnected as singularism suggests, and it will be impossible to think of the ideal of democracy as one of collective autonomy, with government being forced to enact the popular will; there won't be such a will available to enact. The only alternative will be to think of it as an ideal under which each citizen has an equal degree of influence—a vote—in the choice of who is in government and what those in government do (Christiano 1996). The system may not enact the will of all but at least it will be sensitive in a suitable measure to the will of each. It will involve a competitive market where different candidates and parties compete at regular intervals and on equal terms to attract the votes of citizens and win office. The spoils will invariably go to the victors, of course, which argues for a limitation on what democratically elected government can do and for constraints on how it does it: otherwise a tyranny of the majority looms; and so on this image of democracy the constitution plays an important limiting and constraining role.

The classic exposition of the singularist view of democracy is in Joseph Shumpeter's (1984) work from the 1930s and 1940s. The assumption in that approach, and in the public choice tradition that he influenced, is that there is no single good—for example, no agreed common good—by reference to which people will or should decide to vote; they are each generally taken to vote according to preference—usually but not necessarily self-interested preference.

Now for the second implication. The duties and virtues of citizenship under any account of democracy are going to derive from what is needed to keep the relevant system going. But in this case, by contrast with the solidarist one, what will be needed is really rather thin: a willingness to vote, to recognize the legitimacy of elected government, and to submit appropriately to the acts of that government. Is nothing else required or recommended? Nothing beyond fidelity to the duties and virtues, whatever those are, that we owe to human beings anywhere: duties of noninterference, perhaps, and virtues of benevolence. The idea of having special duties to fellow citizens, or of being called on to exercise special virtues, will smack of parochialism. Singularism sponsors a distinctively cosmopolitan attitude, not having resources enough to distinguish the good citizen from the good world-citizen.

What, finally, of the rights and benefits of citizenship? The implication here is that these are the rights and benefits that will be enjoyed by anyone who is treated by others generally, fellow citizens or not, as he or she ought to be treated. They will include rights not to be interfered with, except so far as one consents—as it is assumed one would ideally consent to a certain constitutional democracy (Buchanan and Tullock 1962). And they will include the benefits that are going to accrue to anyone who enjoys noninterference and perhaps benevolence at the hands of others.

THE CIVICIST ALTERNATIVE

In the history of political philosophy, solidarism and singularism have been very prominent doctrines, but they do not exhaust the possible ways in which a people or citizenry may be organized. There is also a third possibility and I associate this with what I describe below as a "civicity" (pronounced as in "velocity").

Suppose that the individuals involved in the citizenry have certain purposes in common and a representative agency in place to advance those purposes: say, an elected government. But imagine that they are unwilling to leave the judgments as to the interpretation and implementation of the purposes entirely in the hands of their representatives. They debate among themselves, in smaller or larger gatherings, about what exactly the purposes are, about what they require in this or that respect, about how they can be best served under such and such circumstances, and so on. They will not be able to agree on those questions, of course, and to require the representatives to take heed of the agreements reached; if they did, they would constitute a group agent of the solidarist kind. But they still expect the representatives to take their guidance from that public deliberation and debate, and they hold them to that expectation; the representatives can expect to be challenged and perhaps dismissed if they do not meet it.

What can it mean for representatives to take their guidance from a public debate that does not reach agreement on specific judgments? If members debate about common purposes and how to serve them, they will have to recognize one another as suitable addressees of argument and persuasion, putting in place some framing assumptions as to how it is proper for their members to be treated. And if the debate achieves a certain robustness and vitality, then equally the members will have to put in place some working assumptions about the sorts of considerations that count as relevant in discussion. Some of those considerations will not pass general muster; they will be dismissed as sectional or self-serving or clearly false. But, short of the debate going straight to the ground, many will command general acceptance (Elster 1986). They will emerge as considerations that are treated on all sides as relevant to interpreting and implementing the common purposes of the group, even if they are not weighted in the same way by all.

These framing and working assumptions will constitute presumptions and valuations shared within the group—a sort of social capital (Coleman 1990)—and they will generate a natural constraint on how the representatives are to form their judgments and decisions. The representatives will be held to the expectation that their judgments and decisions should be justifiable on the basis of such presumptions and valuations. Or, if the presumptions and valuations are not determinate enough to support any particular set of policies, the representatives will be held to the expectation that the judgments and decisions should be made under procedures that are supported by the presumptions and valuations.

A group that satisfies this sort of constraint may be described, for want of a better term, as a "civicity." As with a solidarist group agent, the members of a civicity will be committed to debating about the purposes they purportedly share. But as with a singularist aggregate, they will not aim at establishing a body of common judgments on which to act; they will inevitably be divided on such detailed matters. Unlike both the group agent and aggregate, however, the members of the grouping envisaged will debate with a view to imposing a constraint on the individual or body commissioned to act in their name. This is the constraint of being able and ready to justify the judgments and decisions taken, or at least the mode in which they are taken, on the basis of the shared presumptions and valuations that come to be authorized as a side effect of that debate.

The notion of the civicity that we have identified may apply in a variety of contexts, ranging from the small to the large, the informal to the formal. But clearly it may apply, at least in principle, to a citizenry. We find something close to the idea being applied to a contemporary citizenry in a variety of contemporary approaches, including that of Jürgen Habermas (1984, 1989, 1995), John Rawls (1999, 2001; see also Larmore 2003), and neorepublican political thought (Pettit 1997, 2000a).

Democratic citizens inevitably debate about how their government should be constituted, what sorts of things it should do, and the like; this debate will materialize in workplace, café, and home, at the hustings, on the television, and in a multitude of other sites. And in debating about these matters they will generate among themselves, again more or less inevitably, a fund of considerations that everyone is prepared to admit as relevant in the determination of public issues, even if individuals weight them differently in importance.

You and I may differ on whether there should be a public medical system, for example, or on whether our country should be involved in a certain war, or on how far the separation of powers should be enforced on the legislature and executive. But in debating about such questions, we will almost always agree in common on the relevance of certain presumptions and valuations, even if they do not lead us in the same direction. I may argue that a public health system is necessary to guard against severe deprivation among the poor, or that it should help reinforce our sense of community. And even while you disagree on the conclusion that I draw, you may well admit that those are indeed relevant considerations: that is it important to guard against deprivation and to promote a sense of community. You may admit their relevance, even if you think that they do not have the weight I attach to them or that they are outweighed by considerations on the other side.

So far as common considerations emerge and crystallize in the society, it will naturally be a matter of general assumption, however far it may be breached, that ideally government ought to justify its organization and operation on the basis of such commonly accepted presumptions and valuations. Those considerations will tend to support certain general arrangements and constraints of the kind that are typically registered in a constitution. While they provide the currency in which debate on other, more concrete matters is conducted, they will not often support a particular alternative unambiguously. But they will certainly serve to reduce the number of alternatives that are found defensible and thinkable there. And they will usually provide a base for determining acceptable ways for government to make a decision between the alternatives that remain. They may license the rule of a parliamentary majority in resolving such matters, for example. Or they may argue for referring certain matters to a more or less impartial body—say, a court or tribunal or commission—that operates at arm's length from Parliament.

To the extent that a polity and citizenry is organized in this way it will constitute a civicity. While not amounting to anything as solidarist as a group agent, it will certainly amount to something more unified and arresting than a singularist aggregate. Confronted with individuals who are joined in the relations required by such a civicity, it will be impossible to hold that really there is nothing more to this society than the individuals who make it up. It would be as silly to think that as it would be to say that there is nothing more to a cell than the molecules out of which it is composed, nothing more to a molecule than the atoms that make it up. The civicity is going to be composed at any time out of an aggregate of individuals, of course, but it will be unified across time by the civic structure—the constantly evolving structure, as it will be—that enables it to perform in its characteristic role. And that structure, like the structure whereby individuals become a group agent, will make it into something more than the individuals who compose it. Let the structure survive, for example, and, even as generation succeeds generation, it will be possible to think of the society or people remaining the same.

Just as the solidarist and singularist images have characteristic implications for how to think of democracy and democratic citizenship, so the same holds here. If the citizenry in a society constitutes a civicity, then that already determines much about how its public affairs ought to be ordered. They should be ordered, ideally, so that either the constraints and laws and decrees that prevail there are justifiable on the basis of presumptions and valuations authorized as a matter of common awareness among the citizenry; or they are selected on the basis of procedures that are justifiable on that basis. Things should be arranged, in other words, so that what we might call common concerns rule: common concerns as distinct from an imagined corporate will or the several wills of an aggregate of individuals.

I have argued elsewhere that the only institutional form that promises to give reality to a rule of common concerns or interests is a democracy that has both an electoral and a contestatory side (Pettit 2000a). The idea very simply is that there are two ways in which common concerns might fail to rule: either through the false negative associated with a failure to identify fully what they are or support, or through the false positive associated with sectional interests ruling, on this or that matter, instead of or as well as common concerns. Electoral democracy represents a plausible way of guarding against the first problem, prompting a competition for the identification of platforms and policies that will gain maximal acceptance. Contestatory democracy guards against the second, exposing every public constraint or law or decree to the possibility of effective contestation: in particular, contestation on the grounds of not being justifiable by reference to common concerns—that is, not being justifiable by direct or indirect reference to commonly authorized presumptions and valuations.

What of the implications, under this sort of story, for our understanding of democratic citizenship? Citizens will have to develop those duties and virtues required for keeping the system going. And these are highly distinctive. They will require of citizens that they engage in the sort of debate that forms common presumptions and valuations—a sense of common concern; that they invigilate the performance of government and the operation of the governmental system to guard against a neglect or violation of common concerns; and, where necessary, that they contest and join with others in contesting that performance or operation, whether in appellate, parliamentary, or popular forums.

What of the rights and benefits of citizenship under this image? They will derive from the fundamental right of being treated equally under government, where that means being treated only in a manner that is justifiable—as contestation should help establish—on the basis of shared presumptions and valuations. If such a regime were to prevail, then everyone would stand equal before the law and the state, conscious of enjoying this status as a public and effective matter. This would be to enjoy what was called in the seventeenth century the status of a free man: the status that goes with enjoying protection and empowerment against political abuse—and so, on this front, freedom as nondomination (Pettit 1997)—as a matter of common knowledge.

THE LESSONS

Which image of the citizenry applies in contemporary democracies? My view is that all three images have a certain application. Like almost any object of complexity, contemporary democracy is an ambiguous gestalt. It can be seen—and it is routinely seen—now as a solidarity of citizens bent like a corporate agent on a common cause; now as a singularist concatenation of individual citizens, each focused on their individual returns; and now, of course, as a civicity in which common concerns emerge and are mobilized in the regulation and control of government. And depending on how it is seen, different sets of duties and virtues, rights and benefits, are given prominence.

The solidarist image of a society like ours is often in operation when we think about how we, the citizens of this or that country, relate to our forebears or to the bodies of citizens in other countries (Rubenfeld 2001). In such contexts, it is easy to see government as if it were like the council of a Renaissance city-republic and to think of it as our spokesbody, acting and articulating aspirations and views that have a claim to be collectively ours, and ours over different generations. Let the society be imagined on this pattern, and the duties and rights of citizenship will quickly assume the shape that they receive in the traditional patriot's manual. We will each see ourselves as the beneficiary of the people to whom we belong and we will see that people as having certain claims upon us. Whether the patriotism be nationalist or constitutionalist in character, the key idea will be that of loyalty to the nation, love of the country (Viroli 1995).

If patriotic or loyalist citizenship goes with the solidarist picture of the citizenry, what we might call cosmopolitan citizenship goes with the singularist. As we can look on our society as a more or less corporate entity, with a character and identity over time, so we can also look on it as a loose congregation of voters, bound together by the relatively shallow fact that they must each acquiesce in rule by a common government. Under this image, the crucial right of a citizen is to achieve respect and concern at the hands of the elected government—this is a right shared equally with other human beings—and the most important duty of the citizen is to ensure, if serving in government, that such respect and concern is given to others. This is a cosmopolitan ideal because it holds out a species-wide vision of the duties and rights of citizenship. Being a good citizen will mean being a good world-citizen; if people owe more to their compatriots than to foreigners, that will only be because of special dependencies or contracts, not just because they are compatriots. As patriotism may have a nationalist or constitutionalist character, the cosmopolitanism in question here may be thinner or richer in moral content, depending on whether we are thought to owe only respect for basic rights to others (Nozick 1974) or a more demanding brand of justice (Beitz 1979; Pogge 1993).

But contemporary democracies can be seen in the colors of the civicist image, as well as in those of the solidarist and singularist pictures. The citizenry in contemporary democracy generally manages, however haltingly and uncertainly, to generate a fund of more or less commonly authorized presumptions and valuations; generally expects those in government to try to justify the institutions and initiatives they uphold in terms of those ideas; and sees nothing amiss, but much to be admired, in the actions of those who challenge and contest government on such matters. Such a citizenry is going to be reliably content only so far as contestations of this kind are given a good and fair chance of being heard and, if appropriate, accepted. This image of the citizenry holds out a third, activist profile for the citizen. It will not be enough to honor the cosmopolitan rights of one's compatriots, or to display loyalty to one's people as a whole. What will also be required is that citizens play an active contestatory role in relation to government; make room for others to play that role if serving in government; and thereby establish one another in the enjoyment of a distinctive, civic form of mutual standing and regard.

Where does all of this leave us? The main lesson I take away is that we should not fall into the trap of enunciating the norms of citizenship as if they merely encompassed those of one or another image. We should insist that citizenship requires the minimal duties and provides the minimal rights associated with cosmopolitanism. We should allow that equally it grounds the obligations and claims that different versions of patriotism highlight. But we should not stop there. Above all else, we should insist that citizens also owe duties, and can claim rights, on the basis of belonging to an ongoing civicity. The civicist image requires special emphasis, as it is probably on this front that citizenship is normatively most distinctive and most interesting.

I conclude with two questions bearing on the civicist image in particular. Does the image fit well with the multicultural character of many, perhaps even of all, advanced democracies? And does it point us toward an image of citizenship that we can all embrace, both as a challenge to action and as a status that we can celebrate?

There is a danger in any electoral regime that the views of the mainstream—the presumptions and valuations that go without saying in their ranks—can dominate public life and systematically exclude and disempower a variety of those out of the mainstream: those who identify with any of the many different groupings that can command a special allegiance and identification (Gutmann 2003). There is a very special danger of this, where the grouping that commands such allegiance is an aboriginal nation or nations with very different traditions and cultures from those in the mainstream.

But while a solidarist or singularist image of democracy would have obvious problems in making a special, welcoming place for minority groupings of the kind mentioned, I think that a civicist democracy—an electoral-cum-contestatory democracy—holds out a relatively attractive prospect. The ideas that will get established as common currency in such a society will have to pass muster, not just among the mainstream, but in the society at large; to the extent that they do not, they will presumably attract contestation. And the constraints and policies and decrees—and the procedures for determining such measures—that are justified by reference to those ideas will have to be justified, not merely by mainstream lights but by the lights of everyone involved. This is a very demanding set of requirements and suggests that so far as a democracy truly conforms to the image in question, it can make room for a rich multicultural presence.

The prospect of serving a rainbow citizenry in this way is not as utopian as it may at first seem. As I have argued elsewhere, it can make special provision for minorities, without suggesting that there are special normative grounds for the claims made on their behalf (Pettit 2000b). Commonly received ideas may ground arrangements under which some groups are given quite special provisions; think of how the same claims on access to standard utilities such as electricity may ground very different levels of expenditure as between urban and rural communities. In the same way, commonly received ideas on what is owed among fellow citizens may provide an argument for acknowledging the special position of certain minority groupings and of making special provision for their needs. Special provisions can come in any of an enormous variety of kinds, including provision in some instances for devolved forms of self-government (Levy 2000b). Once this possibility is recognized, I think that the feasibility of a contestatory but multicultural democracy becomes less questionable; certainly the infeasibility becomes less obvious.

Finally, to turn to the second of the two questions raised earlier, does the picture of a civicist citizenry suggest an image of citizenship that we can all embrace, both as a challenge to action and as a status that we can celebrate? The challenge to action that is raised under this approach is quite daunting, apparently requiring heroic levels of activism in debate, in research, and in contestation. But the challenge may appear daunting only so far as it is assumed that everyone has to be virtuous in the same way. That may be a reasonable assumption for the duties associated with the solidarist or the singularist image, but it has little plausibility here. A citizenry will do very much better in organizing a contestatory regime in which everyone can feel fairly assured that common concerns rule, if it allows a division of civic labor. This would be a division under which different people assume different contestatory roles, with one person being active in the environmental area, another in the domain of consumer rights, another in campaigning for the rights of prisoners, and of course others in urging the case for this or that minority grouping, ethnic or otherwise. Civic virtue under the civicist picture of the citizenry is going to require virtuous citizens not to replicate one another in burgherlike homogeneity but to complement one another by their efforts in different spheres of activity.

Is this image of the dutiful, virtuous citizen an attractive one? Does it represent a status that one can celebrate? I think it does. It makes room for the idea that one can affirm one's unity with the polity and the citizenry as a whole while acting out of a sense of identity with this or that particular cause, or this or that particular subgrouping. And so, unlike many received images of citizenship, it holds out a role that is complex enough to have a wide appeal in a rainbow world (Norman and Kymlicka 2003). It endorses the need for unity, without subscribing to an ideal of the monochromatic burgher. And it makes room for diversity, without threatening us with the specter of disorder and centrifuge. It may not be a brightly beckoning beacon. But among realistic ideals of political membership it is probably as good as it gets.[2]

NOTES

1. It is worth noting that the contractual twist also had an antecedent in Roman law. The *lex regia* was purportedly an arrangement whereby the Roman people had transferred its power to the emperor. See Canning 1996 for a discussion of the origin and development of this idea. My thanks to Paul Sigmund for reminding me of its relevance.
2. My thanks to Martin Krygier for his searching and helpful comments on an earlier draft.

Chapter 7

"Civicity" and Multiculturalism

A Comment on Pettit

Martin Krygier

Philip Pettit's chapter is primarily concerned with "the collective idea of the citizenry," what might be called the social ontology of citizenship. Most of the chapter is devoted to expounding three different conceptions of that ontology, and exploring their normative-political implications. They are pregnant with implications for multiculturalism, but as is the nature of pregnancy, not all that is contained within has yet been delivered, at least not here. I want to say something about the implications already evident in the chapter and try to induce reflection on some others, not because I imagine Pettit has not conceived of them, but to discover and examine what he has conceived. I will speak first about ontology, then the interrelationships between democratic "civicity" and multiculturalism.

ONTOLOGY

In terms that Durkheim would appreciate, Pettit insists that "citizenries may vary in nature, without this variation being just a reflection of differences in the characteristics of their members." That being the case, "there is going to be no such thing as the nature of citizenship in general, only the nature of citizenship under one or another civic structure. And ... there is going to be no such thing as the normative content of citizenship in general." This is a crucial point, often made in other contexts by Philip Selznick: philosophical explorations of "the nature of" or "the essence of" abstract concepts too often ignore variation and context.[1] Yet these are all-important for understanding the *kind* of thing we are dealing with. As with the normative content *and logic* of law, for example, one form of which might be intimately and fatefully associated with repressive power and another with the taming of it, so too with "citizenry." As I will point out later, the general point might be made equally about "multiculturalism." It is hard, often dangerous, and sometimes foolish, to generalize about the normative implications of that as well.

The chapter explores three different forms of citizenry, each of them dependent on a different "civic structure" of the collective rather than on any differences between the characteristics of their individual members. One form is "solidarist." The citizenry is conceived as a corporate body with common purposes and representatives whose actions in support of those ends are "directed by one and the same set of canonical, collectively endorsed judgments." When the representatives act, they act on behalf of the corporation as a whole, not its members as individuals, and what they do, when they do right, is to express *its* will. Applied to a collectivity thought of and organized in this way, not only will the political ideal of citizenship have a distinctive character, but so too will the duties and virtues that best serve it, and the rights and benefits that flow from it.

A second form is "singularist": "there is no such thing as society." A collective noun is just a shorthand for the individuals who make it up. Here democracy is reduced to the right of individual citizens to an equal degree of political influence over representatives, who cannot be guided by any common collective judgments, since these do not exist, but will use their own judgments about how to serve common interests of their sovereign individual electors. They will stay in power, and it is right that they do, if they satisfy more individual citizens than they disappoint. What else is there? These citizens, in turn, will only need to display a modest array of duties and virtues, and in turn they will *receive* rather than need to *participate in* only the "rights and benefits that will be enjoyed by anyone who is treated by others generally, fellow citizens or not, as he or she ought to be treated."

But then we have "civicity": a noisy and, in a literal and nonpejorative sense, "disagreeable" crew who expect their representatives to listen to them and take guidance from their "public deliberation and debate." But since they are perennially arguing, there is no guidance to be had from common specific judgments. Rather, there will emerge in their debates common "considerations that are treated on all sides as relevant to interpreting and implementing the common purposes of the group ... presumptions and valuations shared within the group—a sort of social capital." Representatives won't be constrained to follow detailed instructions from the citizenry as a corporate entity, but rather to justify "the judgments and decisions taken, or at least the mode in which they are taken, on the basis of the shared presumptions and valuations that come to be authorized as a side effect of that debate." These won't likely be able to *determine* particular judgments, but they "will certainly serve to reduce the number of alternatives that are found defensible and thinkable. ... And they will usually provide a base for determining acceptable ways for government to make a decision between the alternatives that remain."

Pettit observes that "like almost any object of complexity, contemporary democracy is an ambiguous gestalt" of all three conceptions. However, most of his money is on civicity, for it captures the key fact that "the citizenry in contemporary democracy generally manages, however haltingly and uncertainly, to generate a fund of more or less commonly authorized presumptions and valuations; generally expects those in government to try to justify the institutions and initiatives they uphold in terms of those ideas; and sees nothing amiss, but much to be admired, in the actions of those who challenge and contest government on such matters."

Let me follow Pettit and begin with his overarching conception, and move on to how he believes it caters for, and how I believe it might be challenged by (certain kinds of), multiculturalism. I begin with some diffidence, ontology probably being best avoided by nonphilosophers, or the prudent more generally. However, ontology is crucial to Pettit's argument, and his discussion is clarifying, I believe, in relation to many key collective social practices and concerns, whose ontological character is often confusing. Such confusion can then lead one to say nonsensical things, such as "there is no such thing as society," with an altogether misplaced air of philosophical assurance. I will mention one such practice, law, and one concern, collective shame, where neither a solidarist nor a singularist account is particularly helpful, and where Pettit's account of the ontology of civicity helps us capture what is at stake.

Civicity is an example of a noncorporate collectivity, which is greater than the sum of its parts but still not "an entity with a *persona* of its own." Participants in it think and act differently than they might in another civicity, because their thoughts and actions occur within "shared presumptions and valuations." This is a good way of characterizing cultures and traditions, including (but not limited to) many that are institutionalized in ways that make certain officials spokespeople for the culture or tradition. Liturgy and rituals apart, the traditions of Christianity and Judaism, for example, have allowed a good deal of wiggle room over ages, but these traditions are scarcely irrelevant to the acts and thoughts of their members. Members of particular cultures and traditions, among them but not only their officials, think "alike," though they have many different thoughts, the likeness deriving from the complex layers of assumptions and presumptions borne by the cultures and traditions to which they belong.

Well-established legal orders are of this sort, too, unified less by canonical rituals and texts (though they have those, too) than by a common culture of argument, principles, values, presumptions, ways of thought. This was a crucial insight of the common law tradition as it was most sophisticatedly developed in the seventeenth century. The common law is, after all, much more than the sum of its parts, and however much its orthodox votaries might protest, it is not an entity held together by what Pettit describes as "one and the same set of canonical, collectively endorsed judgments," though it purports to have more of those than many cultures and traditions. But much of the common law is not canonical, and even those parts that are supposed to be keep changing, and keep being reinterpreted. It is held together, however, by dense layers of "shared presumptions and valuations" that matter profoundly to participants and to what they do in and with the law, even though they are chronically indeterminate in the guidance they give. And, without going into the theory of these matters, neither the significance of those shared presumptions and evaluations nor their indeterminacy is accidental (see Krygier 1986).

That has often seemed a conundrum to those who seek to understand the combination of "commonness" with constant change in the law. One explanation, perhaps that of Sir Edward Coke as J. G. A. Pocock interprets him (1987), is that the common law is a corporate entity that preserves "canonical, collectively endorsed judgments" and passes them down to judges, whose job is simply to discover, learn, and declare what they mean in relation to a case, "guided," in Pettit's words, "not by their own particular beliefs but by the canonical judgments." A lot of people have said that about law. There is even a name for it: literalism. Trouble is, no one really believes it.

A natural and common, if somewhat vulgar, response to law's obvious and frequent indeterminacy and changefulness is to say that it is all window dressing. Judges do what they like, and then just say what they need to say. However, even when the guidance a strong legal tradition gives *is* indeterminate, it is silly to imagine, as some have pretended, that it is irrelevant to decisions made within the law. "Thinking like a lawyer" is not an empty phrase.

The picture that seems to me plausible (see Krygier 1986, 1998) is roughly parallel to Pettit's picture of the way in which the argumentative traditions of a civicity can constrain, even constitute a collective entity, even though its individual parts and the lawyers who deal with them come and go, and even where, as so often, it delivers no clear corporate pronouncement that participants could simply follow and apply. Indeed, when the best of the classical common lawyers sought to explicate how the law could maintain its identity notwithstanding the coming and going of individual parts, they invoked the metaphor of "the Argonauts Ship [that] was the same when it returned home, as it was when it went out, tho' in the long Voyage it had successive Amendments, and scarce came back with any of its former Materials" (Hale 1971 [1713]: 40).

In part, the source and ground of this continuity, the common lawyers claimed, was that it stemmed from the anchoring of the common law, developed by the courts, in English customs that had been "handed down by tradition, use, [and] experience" (Blackstone 1979 [1765]: 17) and had survived (indeed, could only survive by) constant transmission, reception, interpretation, refinement, transformation, and application, from "time whereof the memory of man runneth not to the contrary" (Blackstone 1979 [1765]: 67). These customs had developed over the life of the country and had indeed become constitutive of "the people, into whom their ancient laws and customs [sic] are twisted and woven as a part of their nature" (Hale 1982 [1787]: 255). As these customs displayed continuity through change, so too did the common law, whose officials continuously drew upon them, interpreted them, argued about their meaning and their bearing, rendered them explicit, and declared them.

Now of course the common law was not, for most of its life, the law of a democracy, and, even within a political democracy, its internal operations have *never* been democratic in themselves. And the common lawyers no doubt exaggerated its representativeness and the connections between written law and common customs. Yet there are insights there into the organic life of cultures, traditions, and institutions, and the ways in which they and the debates in and around them can generate and sustain "presumptions and valuations shared within the group," to quote Pettit again. He is right, then, to resist a forced choice between a more grandiose holism and a more threadbare particularism, corporate will and unanchored individual wills. In between these falsely exclusive choices, there is something valuable to explore.

Second, and closer to our theme, is another matter, a psychosocial observation, of which Pettit's ontology helps make sense. A much commented-upon spur to intercultural empathy in Australians' thinking about their national relationship with Aborigines has been the feeling that *we* (which includes foreign-sourced hybrids like many who have participated in these debates, among them me [2005: esp. part 1], Raimond Gaita [1999], and most prominently Robert Manne [2005]) have some real connection with what we often call *our* relations with Aborigines even though neither *we* individually nor, often, any of our biological forebears had ever done anything to an Aborigine, which for many includes meeting one. That feeling is strong among those who have emphasized that shame is an appropriate response of Australians (though not necessarily of our grandparents, who may well not have heard of Australia) to things done earlier by Australians, and it is equally so among deniers of shame, who say there is nothing to be ashamed of: we should, on the contrary, feel pride. The singularist account makes such feelings, whether of pride or shame, seem bogus or at least rationally inexplicable, yet the solidarist account is implausible in relation to all but the actions and reactions of public officials. The ontology of civicity makes sense of a response that many have felt but have not found easy to articulate. For it draws attention to the environing cultures and traditions that we share with our cultural forebears and in both a literal and metaphorical sense *inhabit*—indeed, more than inhabit, possess and are possessed by. In my view it is right, and whether or not it is right it makes sense, for members of a common culture, full as it is of shared "presumptions and valuations" (and many other things), *participants in* and *bearers of* that culture, to be concerned about such things (as both the proud and the shamed so volubly are), particularly when, as is common, that recognition is in some, often anguished part, self-recognition as well. We are, none of us, self-constituting monads. We are, all of us, *creatures,* in part creations, of the cultures in which we are raised. We are not just participants in those cultures; they are parts of us. "Civicity" makes sense of moral responses appropriate in such circumstances.

DEMOCRACY AND MULTICULTURALISM

Now whether or not I have properly understood Pettit's ontology, it is clear that it could work for many social collectivities that are not at all democratic. So I move now more specifically to democratic civicity. What is peculiar to that sort of noncorporate collectivity? According to Pettit, for a *democratic* civicity to be in good shape, "things should be arranged ... so that ... common concerns rule," and the only form that ensures that is one that combines "an electoral and a contestatory side," the former able to inform decisions *ex ante,* the latter to contest them *ex post.* And that gets us, quite late in the piece, to multiculturalism. Since minority views are always in danger of being drowned out by mainstreams, a civicity will take care to ensure that "the ideas that will get established as common currency ... pass muster, not just among the mainstream, but in the society at large ... justified, not merely by mainstream lights but by the lights of everyone involved. ... So far as a democracy truly conforms to the image in question, it can make room for a rich multicultural presence."

Now, whatever else it does, the common law of England doesn't help us too much either with contemporary multiculturalism. Does civicity? Here I am not sure, partly because we have less to go on. So let me just pose a couple of questions. These are genuine questions, not leading ones. That is, they're ones to which I do not have the answers, but I do not quite know what answers Pettit would give, nor civicity generate.

One has to do with potential tensions between different, even incompatible traditions, "presumptions and valuations ... shared within the group." In explicating civicity Pettit explains that democratic citizens debate and should debate a lot, but that "in debating about these matters they will generate among themselves, ... *more or less inevitably,* a fund of considerations that everyone is prepared to admit as relevant in the determination of public issues, even if individuals weight them differently in importance" (emphasis added). But in profoundly multicultural polities, is that necessarily so? What if, after diversity is encouraged, difference applauded, contestation facilitated, we find that there are not enough of those common presumptions and valuations to go around?

Of course, cultures themselves are not solidary things with unbreachable walls separating insiders and out. They are permeable, they overlap, become parts of each other's history, change over time and in contact with other things—among them, other cultures, but also events, economic changes, political structures, and opportunities. Their elements are subject to recombination, interpretation, and replacement, by the faithful and not only the faithless. That is why a kind of *a priori* pessimism about cultural adaptation is, *a priori,* to be rejected (see Krygier 1999). Australia has often heard apprehensions about new immigrants, or even old ones (Catholics, among others), and yet it seems to me to be a civicity in remarkably good shape. However, unless culture is thought to count for nothing, a question remains whether one has reason to believe, again *a priori,* that a civicity will be able to presume or necessarily will generate "more or less inevitably, a [common] fund of considerations." Maybe it will, maybe it won't. Sometimes it will, sometimes it won't. It is worth asking, however, what resources civicities have to deal with considerations that are *not* common, all the way down. It is not clear to me what Pettit's answer would be.

Pettit is aware of the problem, but he assures us that "the prospect of serving a rainbow citizenry in this way is not as utopian as it may at first seem." Why? Because "[c]ommonly received ideas may ground arrangements under which some groups are given quite special provisions ... [and this] may provide an argument for acknowledging the special position of certain minority groupings." It seems to me that this could refer to two sorts of arrangements, one of which does not speak to the present problem of incompatible argumentative traditions, the other which speaks to the problem but does not solve it. Pettit might be arguing, as, for example, Dworkin argued (1978), that a decision to treat, say, all applicants for university places with equal concern and respect is compatible with deciding to treat members of different groups differently, as in affirmative action. I agree, but that is not the problem faced at the stage of *deriving* the decision. The point is that a shared commitment to equal concern and respect does not necessarily enjoin equal treatment. There is, however, a potential problem one step earlier: in *coming* to decisions, are we arguing from within common argumentative traditions of presumption and evaluation? I think some multicultural combinations can raise that sort of problem, though others won't. It is what policies of *nation-building* are about, and I wonder what Pettit thinks about them. Should you have a policy to generate common presumptions and valuations, and if so, are there questions of compatibility with multiculturalism, of the sort that Kymlicka (1995) believes can readily be solved and Huntington (2004) believes cannot? If you do have such policies, how respectful can you be, how respectful should you be, of inconsistent presumptions and valuations, particularly those that seem to go all the way down? And how successful are you likely to be? These questions raised with more urgency since 9/11. That event and what has followed may or may not alter our answers, but it needs to be considered.

Perhaps, though, Pettit is saying that where there is such argumentative discordance, we should devolve decisions in some way, say, on some sort of federal basis or according to some conception of subsidiarity, so that wherever the decision is made the people whose "presumptions and values" are in play are the relevant fraction of the whole polity. That might work in some circumstances, such as Quebec, but not in others, such as what was once Yugoslavia—or, for that matter, where minorities are geographically dispersed. And it gives a different and less integrative framework and rules-of-the-game quality to the "presumptions and values" that we supposedly without much difficulty—indeed "more or less inevitably"—all share. That is the brunt of some of the apprehensions about multiculturalism expressed by people such as Brian Galligan and Winsome Roberts in this book. How does civicity deal with this? How well equipped is it to deal with it?

A second question has to do with how things would look if one followed Pettit's caution against generalizing about citizenship, and applied it, more than he does here, to multiculturalism itself, and for precisely the sorts of reasons he gives at the start of his chapter. Do all sorts of multicultural allegiances or designations interact in the same way with civicity? If citizens are not all "homogeneous" or "monochromatic" "burghers," are some multicultiburgers more digestible than others? And if so, which sorts? The vision of a civicist citizenry is of one that "will do very much better ... if it allows a division of civic labor ... under which different people assume different contestatory roles, with one person being active in the environmental area, another in the domain of consumer rights ... and of course others in urging the case for this or that minority grouping, ethnic or otherwise." But not every sort of group identity is equally hospitable to this sort of free choice. Here both the nature and the aims of the groups involved will bear on the feasibility of an attractive civicist citizenry.

Let us start with nature, for the questions of social ontology Pettit raises do not merely occur at the level of the *polis*. They can be asked, as he recognizes, all the way down. What sort of entity is a particular "ethnic or religious minority": solidarist, singularist, or civicist, and how does it matter for a democratic civicity? When we look for institutions to answer to the differing needs of the "many different groupings that can command a special allegiance and identification"whose view of these needs is likely to count? Are the views of *citizens* of a group being expressed, or those of what the Indian anthropologist Dipankar Gupta (1999) calls cultural virtuosos, who purport to speak for them? Does it make sense to say of an "encompassing social group," as Avishai Margalit does (1996), that it has needs over and above those of its individual members? What if those members want to disagree? What if a Capulet wants to become a Montague? What if they just want the names to matter less in their lives? The ways in which a civicity would want to register the "views" of groups and their members would be affected by the answer one gives at every level, and the self-conceptions often mandated in some groups might close off some possibilities more civicist than others. If that happens, what does a civicist democracy do about such groups? And is not this where the discussion about active support of multiculturalism, as distinct from liberal tolerance, begins?

Aims will matter, too. Violent Islamist protestors against cartoons portraying Muhammad in ways they find offensive are not merely coming to a different policy conclusion on the basis of values common to them and the cultures they have joined. They, or some of them, have different, and perhaps incompatible values—not just particular views but "presumptions and valuations"—on key matters of public controversy. So do members and supporters of Al Qaida. Perhaps the greatest contemporary challenge to civicities is how to defend the *polis* in ways that do not betray the values that justify the defense. That is a huge challenge. I would be delighted, genuinely, not merely argumentatively, to learn how a civicity might rise to it.

With the signal and tragic exception of its Aboriginal peoples, Australia has in general provided a fine example of a civicity that has managed to absorb waves of immigrants from many places, with many cultures, into its common public spaces, conversations, and deliberations. And as I have argued elsewhere, this has "contributed much to the variety of Australian identities.... This variety has enriched the country in many ways. I see little evidence that it has eroded the common attachments that every nation depends upon" (Krygier 2005: x). That is a genuine achievement, and I believe a great one: civicity in practice. But it is contingent, not inevitable. Whether it continues will depend centrally on how civicities treat their inhabitants, but it will also depend on how those inhabitants relate to it. Just as there is going to be "no such thing as the nature of citizenship in general, only the nature of citizenship under one or another civic structure," so, too, and not really discussed by Pettit, there is going to be no such thing as the nature of multiculturalism in general. We have a stake in preserving the civicity of our multicultural citizenry from challenges on every side.

NOTE

1. Selznick has frequently insisted on this point. Perhaps the most concentrated distillation of its implications is in Nonet and Selznick 2001.

Chapter 8

Multiculturalism
and Resentment

Duncan Ivison

There are two kinds of resentment relevant to the politics of multicultural-ism today.[1] The first, which is basically Nietzsche's conception of *ressentiment,* occurs under conditions in which people are subject to systematic and struc-tural deprivation of things they want (and need), combined with a sense of powerlessness about being able to do anything about it. It manifests itself in terms of a focused anger or hatred toward that group of people who seem to have everything they want, and yet also symbolize their powerlessness to get it. For Nietzsche, of course, it was out of this set of emotions and psychologi-cal state of mind that the "slave revolt" that gave birth to modern morality emerged, supplanting the aristocratic values oriented around good and bad with the reactive and slavish values of those oriented around good and evil (Nietzsche 1998: 36–39). The desire to lash out or take revenge against those whom you perceive as keeping you down, keeping you from enjoying all the benefits and advantages others enjoy and that you want or feel you deserve, for Nietzsche, is a basic emotional orientation that can—in combination with other complex forces—reshape an entire culture. A second form of resent-ment is of a more moralized kind, a reactive sentiment bound up with hold-ing another morally accountable for their actions. I resent your curtailment of my liberty, for example, just because I believe we share certain moral commitments—for example, a commitment to justify any such interference in an appropriate way, which you fail to satisfy, and so on (Wallace 2003: chap. 2; Williams 2005: 87–89).[2]

I say both of these forms of resentment, and other related emotions, are associated with multiculturalism because they can feature in explanations of how, in part, multiculturalism arose and how it works.[3] On the one hand, multiculturalism arose partly as a response to demands by or worries about the situation of ethnocultural groups in liberal democracies (especially as a result of mass migration) and their integration into the wider community. The disadvantages they faced flowed both from their minority status within a basically majority-rule system, and their location within the confines of a dominant culture that was often hostile toward them in various symbolic and concrete ways.[4] On the other hand, once multiculturalism is up and running, not only does resentment persist on the part of minority groups—especially when it is perceived to be simply a less obvious and more indirect continuation of the original hostility and discrimination by other means—but it can also be felt by those who resent the costs imposed by the new multiculturalist ethos. Resentment, in other words, along with other related emotions such as disappointment, frustration, and envy, is a permanent feature of politics. It is one of the remainders of democratic politics, a by-product of the fact that disagreement in politics means that there will always be political *losers* (Allen 2004; Williams 2005). Left unaddressed, the alienation or frustration out of which resentment (in either sense) can grow corrodes the structures of trust between citizens. Left to fester, it can erupt in socially and politically damaging ways, and is most likely to do so when enough of the same citizens or groups are always the ones who seem to be losing. Even when we coerce someone in terms that we think are justifiable, there can still be resentment, or at least frustration. Indeed, there might be forms of "reasonable resentment": the remainder of political conflict between citizens who accept the need for legitimate political order, and even the process through which political decisions are arrived at, but who nevertheless resent particular outcomes (Williams 2005: 88–89, 125–26). At some point there might be nothing left to do or say that could assuage such emotions, and rightly so. But democrats need to be concerned with not only the positive effects (and affects) of collective political action but also the distribution of negative ones. We need forms of public practical reason that can address these common features of political life, not sidestep them.

One potential source of resentment is moralism, something that defenders of multiculturalism can be as prone to as much as its critics. One danger for both sides is to overmoralize political disagreement and conflict. But first: What do I mean by moralism? And how is it related to the politics of multiculturalism?

MORALISM AND MULTICULTURALISM

To accuse someone of moralism, generally speaking, is to accuse them of applying moral judgments to activities or spheres where such judgments have no application. But since almost no one believes that morality is *never* relevant for political judgment or action, that charge is too vague. To be more precise, moral and political philosophers are often accused of what we might call *undue abstraction.* Here the point is not so much that abstraction itself is the problem—how could it be, since without abstraction there is no thought—but that we can be unduly moralistic about the capacities of the people to whom our moral arguments are addressed to live up to the idealizations of our theories.[5] Moreover, undue abstraction can be depoliticizing: abstracting too much from the context of political action can induce naïveté about the unintended consequences of actions taken with the best of intentions. And it can mask other kinds of motivations and beliefs highly relevant to politics, such as fear, greed, prejudice, and indeed resentment. Second, there is what I shall call *unjustified moralism.* This is to impose moral judgments on people through the exercise of state power or public policy, which are inadequately justified. The danger here is that moralism associated with the exercise of power becomes a form of domination, one that infringes on people's basic freedom and dignity and generates frustration and resentment. Finally, there is the inversion of this phenomenon: *impotent moralism.* Here moralism is essentially reactive, an effect of the unhinging of one's moral values from a world that will not yield to them, which generates a desire to strike back at the forces that have rendered you powerless.

Each of these kinds of moralism has featured in interesting ways in recent criticisms of the political theory and public policy of multiculturalism. Here the charge is not so much that moral judgments have no application in relation to the treatment of minorities, but that the moral claims of defenders of multiculturalism are: (a) appealed to without any sense of the practical realities on the ground (the undue abstraction charge); (b) asserted as if they were self-evidently true (the unjustified moralism charge); which often results in (c) a stifling of reasoned criticism of the orthodoxy surrounding multiculturalism, disconnecting them (so this argument goes) from the attitudes of the vast majority of their fellow citizens and thus from any hope of realizing the reforms being sought (which engenders impotent moralism).

Something like these arguments has become prominent in recent years, as debates over the consequences of multiculturalism for national unity and the provision of collective welfare have intensified. In Australia, for example, defenders of Aboriginal peoples' land rights, or the recent "Reconciliation" process, have been accused of engaging in a game of moral ascendancy intended to stifle public debate. Leftist intellectuals are accused of taking the high moral ground in order to impose their views of the past and the moral consequences for the present upon a general public that is barely allowed a word in edgewise, corralled into a false consensus by the "Politically Correct Thought Police" (Barry 2001: 271, 328).

The general tone of this critique is well captured in a recent editorial by Nicolas Rothwell in the opinion section of *The Australian* newspaper:

> This climate of exquisite purism ... has intriguing consequences. Perhaps the most striking is its effect on public debate which, despite the retreat of ideology, has filled with moral intensity in recent years. The logic of this is straightforward: if you are among the enlightened and see the truth, then those who disagree with you are not just wrong but wicked.... Intelligent difference of opinion becomes impossible on a range of questions as various, and serious, as native title, mandatory sentencing or immigration.... The most critical function of the new moralism is not merely to provide an identity but to differentiate—for purism has the particular charm of separating the moral elite from the vulgar, unenlightened crowd. There are worse things than a nation whose public conversation is dominated by high ideals. But ideals, indulged without any sense of realism, can obscure and do great damage. The most painful example of this is the reconciliation crusade, a cause that, until this month, effectively blinded the purists to the crisis of violence and sexual abuse unfolding across Aboriginal Australia. Purism though, is far more appealing, in its essence, than a cool pragmatic appraisal of the landscape. (Rothwell 2001: 24)

Similarly, although from a very different perspective, the Aboriginal lawyer and community activist Noel Pearson has argued that "progressivists" have the analysis of Aboriginal peoples' situation wrong because of a misplaced moral emphasis:

> If you ask the progressivists, they will provide a catalogue of disadvantage factors that includes unemployment, dispossession, racism, culturally insensitive service delivery, trans- and intergenerational trauma, alcoholism, violence, educational failure and so on, and the bottom line will be a request for further unprincipled spending. But it is irresponsible to state some obvious facts and then go on to devise programs intended to create jobs, improve health, reduce substance abuse and so on, without a convincing analysis of the factors that have made previous efforts futile. Analyses based on the convenient explanations of racism and trauma explain too much (everything, in fact) and cannot be used for formulating credible action strategies in the current crisis. (Pearson 2001)

Although a strong supporter of Aboriginal land rights and a sharp critic of many aspects of Australian government policy to do with Aboriginal affairs,

Pearson is particularly critical of what he calls "progressivist confusion" about substance abuse and a general overemphasis on symbolic moralism. A propos the heated debate over whether the government should offer an official apology over the "Stolen Generation," Pearson writes:

> What about an apology? There are many Indigenous Elders who would deserve an apology before they die. It would be excellent if the Australian State and Federal Governments put policies in place that had any prospect of helping us, policies that would attack passive welfare, addiction and substance abuse epidemics head on, like we are trying to do in Cape York Peninsula, and crowned that with a formal apology. I would want to see an apology as soon as possible.... But an apology at this stage of our national indigenous policy failure would only hide the present lack of insight and ideas among the Australian progressivist and liberalist middle class. It would be symbolic in [the] sense of "meaningless." It would be like a coat of seventies purple plastic paint on a house full of white ants. I would reject such an apology whether it came from Labor or a re-elected Coalition. (Pearson 2001)

A concern with the moralism of multiculturalism can also be found in Brian Barry's recent, pugnacious attack on the work of Will Kymlicka, James Tully, Charles Taylor, and Iris Marion Young (among others), where he argues that support for group-specific policies actually undermines the pursuit of justice for the very people multiculturalists claim they are defending. Barry claims that:

> Pursuit of the multiculturalist agenda makes the achievement of broadly based egalitarian policies more difficult in two ways. At the minimum, it diverts political effort away from universalistic goals. But a more serious problem is that [it] may very well destroy the conditions for putting together a coalition in favour of across-the-board equalization of opportunities and resources. (Barry 2001: 325)

Special preferences, special rights, quotas and other group-targeted measures end up "pitting against one another the potential constituency for universalistic policies aimed at benefiting all those below the median income.... Not only does [the politics of identity] do nothing to change the structure of unequal opportunities and outcomes, it actually entrenches it by embroiling those in the lower reaches of the distribution in internecine warfare" (Barry 2001: 326). At one point Barry says that the demand that *all* minority groups *everywhere* be recognized and granted equal respect and equal worth is impossible to fulfill, both logically and psychologically (Barry 2001: 270–71). But since none of the multiculturalists he discusses actually says that, or believes it, this is a red herring. His deeper and more plausible point is that the politicization of culture that multiculturalism entails can backfire. The consequences of allowing electoral majorities (and minorities) to give legal effect to their own particular "cultural revolutions," whether conservative or liberal, is dangerous. It jeopardizes hard-won gains in the areas of basic human rights and social welfare legislation by leaving open the possibility that the exercise of political power will be taken up by moral and cultural zealots (Barry 2001: 271–79). For Barry, the "whole thrust of the 'politics of difference'... is that it seeks to withdraw from individual members of minority groups the protections normally offered by the liberal states ... and [that these groups] should be able to discriminate with impunity against women or adherents of religions other than the majority."[6] Now this last charge is a gross distortion, I think, of the views of people he actually discusses—especially Will Kymlicka, Iris Young, and James Tully. But his broader point that defenders of multiculturalism often fail to show how they can hope to attract broad-based support for the policies they are defending, and not just preach to the converted, is well worth considering. I will return to it below.

Yet another set of criticisms of liberal multiculturalism also comes from the left, broadly speaking, but with a very different set of concerns than Barry's. These too I want to evaluate from the point of view of the accusation of moralism. For these critics, liberal multiculturalism is condemned not for violating an egalitarian theory of justice but rather for being essentially continuous with the racist and colonial policies it succeeded. Since power, not moral argument, shapes social and political interaction, moral argument without a transformation of the relations of power is a form of vacuous moralizing. This critique breaks down into two further variations. First, liberal attempts at recognizing cultural difference are argued to be simply more sophisticated ways of governing it. Elizabeth Povinelli argues, for example, that liberal respect for Aboriginal "traditional" or "customary" practices represents, in fact, "the political cunning and calculus of cultural recognition in settler modernity." In "postcolonial multicultural societies," she argues, a distinctive kind of liberal power is at work, whereby recognition is "at once a formal acknowledgement of a subaltern group's being and of its being worthy of national recognition and, at the same time, a formal moment of being inspected, examined and investigated" (Povinelli 1999: 223; 2002). The inevitable failure of the indigenous subject to match the liberal's preconceived notion of what constitutes a *valid* "traditional culture" or custom then justifies the legal curtailment of the expression of this alterity. Thus undue abstraction slips into something more sinister: domination. On the other hand, this fixation on identity has itself been interpreted as the product of a certain kind of moralism. Focusing too narrowly on identity above all risks confusing the effects of subordination with its causes (Brown 2003).

HOW TO DEFEND MULTICULTURALISM

These critiques of multiculturalism highlight at least two ways in which its defenders can become moralists in the ways outlined above: first, by applying moral judgments about the past or the present to justify accommodating various kinds of multiculturalist demands without any clear sense of how to build broad-based support for these policies on the ground; second, by missing the extent to which it is *power,* not moral argument, that shapes politics and thus how appeals to the "recognition of difference" can mask more insidious forms of domination.

What is the best way of responding to these criticisms? The disagreement between Barry and a defender of Aboriginal rights is mainly over a substantive theory of justice. But consider first the claim that the politics of difference "crowds out" social justice, which I take to be a conditional and partly empirical one. In a recent essay, Keith Banting and Will Kymlicka (2003a) point out that the "crowding out" argument presupposes that political action with regard to welfare or multicultural issues is a zero-sum game, such that focusing on one necessarily detracts from the other. But why should we believe that? If it were true, then does the pursuit of racial equality "crowd out" the pursuit of economic justice? Does the pursuit of gender equality "crowd out" the pursuit of social justice? Does the history of the women's movement or of the civil rights movement suggest that identity-related claims always undermine the pursuit of social justice? It seems just as plausible to assume the reverse, or at least until we have a more fine-grained account of how the "crowding out" thesis is supposed to work. My own sense is that since racism and sexism, for example, cannot be reduced entirely to the workings of capitalism, broad-based social movements are always going to be drawing on a range of different experiences of injustice in the course of building support for their goals. It would be self-defeating to exclude such claims from the beginning.

More seriously for Barry, however, is that the purported causal connection between the retrenchment of the welfare state and the rise of multiculturalist policies is inconclusive, to say the least. First of all, the welfare state has been undermined both in countries that are strong supporters of multiculturalist policies (Canada, Australia) and those that are not, or at least less so (France, United States). There is certainly evidence to suggest that the constitutionalization of rights in many countries since the 1980s has done little to slow the growth of economic inequality. Nor has it significantly improved access for historically disenfranchised groups to education, basic housing, health care, and employment (Hirschl 2004: 155–68). But the causal relations here and conclusions to be drawn from them are ambiguous. Does it show that the constitutional recognition of Aboriginal rights in 1981 in Canada, for example, made Aboriginal peoples worse off, or contributed to a deepening of inequality more generally (given the "crowding out" thesis)? It might. But at most it shows that the constitutionalization of rights—whether cultural or socioeconomic—is not a sufficient condition for achieving social justice. But this is a point about the relation between constitutions and rights, not about multiculturalism (since multiculturalist policies are compatible with both "constitutionalist" and "political" approaches to rights).

More specifically, Banting and Kymlicka (2003a: 31, 36) show that, at least in terms of the relationship between the presence of what they call "strong" or "weak" multiculturalist policies and the proportion of GDP dedicated to social spending (including the extent of redistribution shaped by these expenditures), "there is no evidence of a consistent relationship between the adoption of multiculturalist policies and the erosion of the welfare state."[7] This is not to say that cultural and linguistic diversity does not pose severe challenges to the solidarity required to support universal provision of social welfare—it does. But the empirical claim that multiculturalism can be blamed, wholly or in part, for the recent erosion of the welfare state is not sustainable.

Barry's more substantive charge is that a scheme of differential citizenship rights violates an egalitarian theory of justice. The liberal multiculturalist disagrees, thinking a commitment to equality is compatible with a commitment to some forms of differential rights. I cannot provide a full defense of this argument here, but the gist of it is to link an ideal of equality with the recognition of a heterogeneous public sphere in which identity-related differences are both recognized and challenged in various ways (Ivison 2002; Laden 2001). The problem with simply ignoring these differences, or ruling them inadmissible from the beginning, is that for some citizens—especially, in this case, Aboriginal ones—they are tied to their sense of the legitimacy of the basic structure of society. To turn the tables on Barry, if one wants to build broad-based support for an egalitarian program of social justice, then treating people equally will require taking their claims for the recognition and accommodation of their identity-related differences seriously. Egalitarianism is best understood as involving a cluster of ethical commitments (White 2000). It includes the resourcist egalitarianism that Barry champions, but not only that. There is also civic egalitarianism, which is connected to the promotion of mutuality and sociability between citizens, and though not entirely independent of questions of resources, operates in a different register with regard to them. Civic equality is tied to the way in which citizens perceive and regard each other, such as whether they are being treated with equal respect or contempt, and the degree to which people either identify with or feel alienated from the main institutions of society. Thus, it might be that it is Barry who is unduly optimistic that a common political identity can be forged in a context where the claims of cultural minorities are automatically discounted, merely for being "cultural." Norms of recognition and struggles over their interpretation are, more often than not, tied to the currency of egalitarian justice; that is, to interpreting and defining the rights, resources and opportunities that are supposed to be distributed equally. The two processes are internally related. It is not that multiculturalism is undermining the possibilities for social justice and political community so much as transforming them—and we need to understand how and what kinds of new common institutions can be constructed in light of them.

Thus, arguments defending multiculturalism should aim to do two things: first, show how they contribute to the achievement of egalitarian justice by linking rules or norms of recognition to a defensible ideal of equality; second, show how this process can contribute to the development, as opposed to corrosion, of social solidarity. This might seem counterintuitive, but I believe it is potentially one of the strongest arguments the defender of multiculturalism has. Citizens come to value their membership in the general community when they feel that their identity-related differences, among other things, no longer block or distort their access to the opportunities and resources of a liberal political order. This does not mean, as Barry suggests, that multicultural policies aim at *withdrawing* them from the protections of the liberal state, but rather *adding to* our conception of liberal citizenship the disposition to acknowledge the different ways in which cultural and associational-related identities may be linked to matters of fairness and equal treatment. The point is not that identity or "culture" trumps the application of general norms and laws in every instance, but that in some instances claims related to culture or identity deserve serious consideration and may indeed call for various modes of accommodation. A *liberal* and historically sensitive multiculturalism is distinguished from other kinds of multiculturalism precisely because it is committed to making these kinds of distinctions, and taking a long hard look at what work the appeal to "culture" is actually doing.[8]

DOES MULTICULTURALISM UNDERMINE ITSELF?

This last aspect of the multicultural project brings us back to the discussion of moralism with which we began. For it might seem deeply unrealistic to expect multiculturalism to actually work out this way. And it might be that given deep disagreement over the interpretation of important social and political values, any attempt to implement multiculturalist policies will inevitably run afoul of the "fact of reasonable pluralism" and risk tipping into unjustified moralism. Recognizing and encoding in law the various differences between groups, even on the basis of egalitarian concerns, can generate resentment, both on the part of minorities and majorities, which can undermine the social solidarity required to achieve justice. Does multi-culturalism undermine itself, as Barry suggests?

I think this conclusion is premature, for both conceptual and empirical reasons. But the challenge of building broad social acceptance and support for the kinds of policies multiculturalism underwrites—such as Aboriginal rights—is a difficult one, and something defenders of them have been slow to respond to. These policies are particularly susceptible to manipulation by political leaders operating in circumstances where people feel economi-cally and culturally vulnerable. If defenders of Aboriginal rights are to avoid the charge of moralism, then they must be careful not to engage in undue abstractions about the circumstances on the ground. And they must be prepared to justify their claims to others on terms they could accept. But this does not mean giving up on the moral claims underpinning Aboriginal rights. The only option is the democratic option—of openly engaging one's fellow citizens in debate and argument about the grounds for these poli-cies—in other words, of engaging in and remaining open to the processes of public reasoning, paying attention especially to the motivational dimension of public argument, that is, to the means through which people are moti-vated to live with ongoing disagreement (or more negatively: to the sources that block or sour these possibilities). This is the only antidote to impotent moralizing. All politics is moral in at least this sense: if power does not in itself justify, then there is always (at least potentially) a basic question of legitimation internal to the political (Williams 2005: 5–6; cf. Forst 1999). Power always seeks to legitimize itself in *some* way in politics, or at least to delegitimate those who oppose it, because there is always someone who questions it, and thus always leaves itself open (at least in principle) to the counterlegitimizing moves and arguments of others. Insofar as politics con-stantly involves problems of legitimation, morality is in some way intrinsic to it—where the moral is internal to politics, not prior to it or imposed from outside.[9] Of course, this ever-present demand for justification can be under-stood (and met) in different ways. Consider two ways of conceiving of the way the demand for legitimation works (or ought to work) in politics.

One model contrasts an ideal speech or choosing situation undistorted by illegitimate relations of power with actual deliberations, as a way of pick-ing out valid normative beliefs about the exercise of political power. The challenge is then to show how the impartial decision rules that emerge can be established politically. For procedural theories of justice, such as Rawls's or Habermas's, the aim is to discover a set of rules for living together that are capable of gaining the free assent of all who are subject to them. The rules and norms are justified, in the first instance, at a higher and more abstract level, and thus the connection between my assent and their legitimacy (their normative accessibility) is much looser. Citizens engage in public reason when they address their collective arrangements, when they reflect upon and contest reasons provided to justify the coercive power of the state and matters of basic justice (Rawls 1993: 212–47). A political decision is legitimate, then, when it is arrived at via the right procedures fairly conducted. This does not mean that at various lower levels, in the actual formulation of various policies or in the details of legislation, one cannot appeal to more concrete conceptions of the good. The asymmetry between impartiality at the level of general constitutional rules (or the "basic structure of society") and the "partiality" of specific political decisions is not a contradiction but is to be expected. There will be many issues in a liberal democracy that are not matters of basic justice and that will involve all manner of democratic contestation and compromise (Barry 1995: 205–7; Habermas 1996).

But now consider two other criticisms of proceduralism, tied more directly to our concern with moralism. The first is a concern that the model of an ideal speech (or choosing) situation presupposes a sharp distinction between "free and un-coerced communication" and the exercise of (illegitimate) power that cannot be sustained. The most radical version of this critique goes something like this: All political interaction is essentially strategic interaction, and therefore all appeals to principle or morality are essentially strategic appeals, and thus the persuasiveness of political argument is derivative of the strategic positions of the interlocutors, not the quality of moral deliberation between them. As Stanley Fish has argued, when it comes to political argument, "Who gets to say what is and is not a plausible premise?... The answers are obvious and embarrassing because they point to an act of power, of preemptory exclusion and dismissal, that cannot be acknowledged as such lest the liberal program of renouncing power and exclusion be exposed for the fiction it surely is" (Fish 1999: 96). There simply are no other "different or stronger reasons than policy reasons" in public reasoning.

Stated this way, however, the argument is far too strong. Note, for Fish, the problem is the "preemptory exclusion and dismissal" of those who do not accept liberal premises of mutual respect. For Elizabeth Povinelli, whom we discussed earlier, the problem is the liberal state's hypocrisy in celebrating difference whilst all the while governing and "scarring" indigenous alterity, hence justifying the material and social disadvantages of indigenous people at the hands of the "liberal common law" (Povinelli 1999: 3–6). The rhetorical appeal, at least, is thus to the *illegitimacy* of exclusion and the "scarring" of indigenous alterity. These are moral appeals, to do with the value of freedom, or of cultural and political difference. Why should we care if democratic practices and institutions are justified in this manner? Because if they aren't, then democracy—or at least our public deliberations about matters of basic justice—risks becoming merely coercion. If Fish wants to accuse contemporary democratic institutions of being merely that, and to get us to imagine how they might be otherwise, then he has a conception of the "reasonable" despite himself. For both, the hope must be that politics *can* actually generate the right conclusions about certain questions, or at least a morally appropriate way of handling our disagreements about them (Fish 1999: 98).[10]

This leads to a second set of criticisms of procedural public reason and the kind of politics it promotes. Here the concern is with the way this ideal of public argument is tied closely to convergence on a theory of justice. It forms too convenient a connection, so this argument goes, between what counts as an acceptable premise in political argument and the kind of values and outcomes that Rawlsian liberals, for example, support.[11] Now, the problem here is not necessarily with the values or outcomes in themselves, but with the way they are arrived at and justified. In short: how is it that the "fact of reasonable pluralism," as Rawls calls it, applies only to conceptions of the good and not to standards of right? The "circumstances of politics," Jeremy Waldron (1999a) argues, entails that the centrality of disagreement to our practices of public justification is much more extensive than many Rawlsians admit. This concern with disagreement is often combined with a pragmatic or contextualist emphasis against the alleged undue abstraction of Rawls and Habermas. In particular, these critics doubt the extent to which any firm distinction can be drawn between legitimate and illegitimate discourse or power in advance of actual engagements between diverse citizens, and thus act from the beginning as condition for them (and as to what counts as a genuinely public or nonpublic reason within them).[12]

Another way of conceiving of legitimation in politics, then, is to situate it much more closely to history and practice, but at the same time not give up on the commitment to mutual justification. James Tully (1995, 1999, 2000b, 2001, 2003, 2005), for example, has been developing this approach in a series of recent essays (cf. Williams 2002, 2005). For Tully, the norms that emerge from these confrontations and negotiations are not best thought of as structured by an *a priori* set of determinative principles grounded in a theory of justice, or a transcendental claim about the nature of rationality. What emerges instead are "norms that come into being and come to be accepted as authoritative in the course of constitutional practice, including criticism and contestation of that practice" (Tully 1995: 116, 181; 2005: 206–8). These norms or conventions can be grasped in a variety of ways, and thus being guided by a convention is conditioned not only by the context in which it is applied but also by it having emerged from and being continually subject to criticism and modification by others. Applying this distinctive (Wittgensteinian) perspective to various Canadian examples, but especially to the claims of Aboriginal peoples, Tully identifies three particularly salient conventions: mutual recognition, continuity, and consent (Tully 1995: 116ff). These emerge out of a "living practice" of negotiation and accommodation, and are immanent to these practices, rather than derived from intuitions or beliefs about fairness or impartiality extracted from an "original position" or "ideal speech situation" which are then applied to politics. And yet, Tully argues, they can still act as norms of justification, and crucially, they provide critical leverage against existing practices and norms (Tully 1995: 138–39). The idea is not one of participants at an imaginary constitutional convention forging consensus on general terms that are then applied to specifics, but rather of starting with the specifics and working from there. Thus a greater emphasis is placed on the process and practice of deliberation and dialogue, as opposed to establishing independent criteria for evaluating the practice itself. We do not need to approach dialogue across gaps of belief and experience by way of agreement on principles. Instead, we look for moments of agreement in practical judgment and work from there, whether it is an argument between citizens of the same city or state, or between Australians and Zimbabweans. Part of the concern, no doubt (although Tully does not discuss it in these terms) is a motivational one: can practical public reason, at least as it is conceived by Habermas and other neo-Kantians, motivate in light of the "fact of reasonable pluralism"?[13]

But the alternative model raises some difficult questions of its own. "Living practices" of negotiation and dialogue can be warped, partial, and shot through with inequality. Particular groups within these practices can suffer from exclusion and discrimination, and the outcomes of particular deliberations might affect outsiders in morally objectionable ways. So how do we judge if the conventions that emerge, or that constitute the practice, are genuinely acceptable to the parties involved? And even if they are, what if they are deeply unjust in other ways? Appealing to consent may be a necessary condition of acceptability, but it cannot be a sufficient one, since the conditions in which people consent to a set of norms or rules are themselves not something they can consent to, and yet they often exercise enormous influence over the range of opportunities and options actually available to them. But in a way, this is precisely Tully's point. Just because it is impossible to transcend partiality and relations of power in any human practice, and especially those we find in modern politics, the sense and reference of our basic concepts and regulative principles must always remain open to contestation. But why should grasping the ambiguity of rule following lead to mutual recognition and respect, rather than only to toleration, as Tully clearly thinks it can? What keeps the parties not merely talking, but talking *in the right way*—that is, with mutual respect and with a view to finding reasons they can share (at least about the exercise of political power)?

This touches on a deep and familiar debate about the relation between foundationalism and forms of ethical and political dialogue, and indeed democracy. Tully, and others seeking to defend a form of contextual rationalism, locates legitimation in the collective activity and practice of ongoing deliberation, rather than in moral principles or constitutional rules established prepolitically. He thinks we can find normativity immanent in "the reciprocal conditions of dialogue" itself, wherein lies at least one basic rule—"perhaps the only universalizable principle of democratic deliberation"—which is: "always listen to the other side" (Tully 2005: 208, 252).[14] So the practice of democratic dialogue is rule-governed after all, but the rules are supposed to emerge from the practice itself. One challenge this kind of argument faces, however, is that for someone like Wittgenstein at least, the primacy of practice means that we really should not be looking for any other grounding for our beliefs or attitudes other than what the practice commits us to: our way of going on just is the way we should go on. We cannot appeal to a description of the practice to "ground" our beliefs, since if practice is primary this would mean that we would need to refer to another practice upon which *those* descriptions and beliefs rested, *ad infinitum.* But then how do we get the critical leverage on our concepts that Tully (and others committed to this approach) so desires, as well as any kind of *theory* of liberalism or the political to guide us?

One thing Tully and others appeal to at this point is a normative interest in freedom that human beings share, albeit one rooted in the particular historical conditions of modernity, and at the same time, the common materials of politics: power, coercion, fear, interests, and yet also hope. Insofar as our ethical and political practices are oriented toward criticism in this sense (i.e., that critique is part of "our" practice, including a constant questioning of what our use of "our" and "we" refers to), and insofar as they have a history and diversity about which we are particularly self-conscious, then we have the resources for the kind of critical engagement Tully seeks.[15] Different aspects of the practice can be brought to bear on each other and reinterpreted in different ways. And, according to this view, we *need* other interlocutors who challenge and redescribe our views in order to help us see the sense in which our own perspectives are always partial and incomplete, something always in danger of being overlooked, and yet something that, in light of our interest in freedom (here thought of as always incomplete and "undefined"[16]), we need to guard against.

Does this vision of a historically informed, dialogical liberalism suffer from the kinds of moralism outlined above? On the one hand, it seems primed to various realities on the ground, since it avoids overly abstract assumptions about the kind of consensus that can be sought between different people. It presupposes reasonable disagreement as opposed to reasonable agreement. On the other hand, is it not also a very demanding ideal? Certainly the kind of "vigorous public discussion" Tully favors (Tully 2005: 254–55), and upon which the ideal of democratic legitimation depends, suggests an active and engaged citizenry, something modern political life often makes difficult to sustain. Moreover, the very practices of contestation he so eloquently champions—of diverse citizens deliberating freely together over their shared and contested rules of recognition, distribution, and coordination—if they are also to generate new critical forms of democratic solidarity, will require participants who possess (or develop) a particular set of skills or virtues. They will have to be capable of explaining their views to others, listening to others, empathizing with them, and synthesizing or accommodating alternative views to their own. And they will have to learn to live with ongoing disagreement and demands for revisiting previously settled disputes, as well as with the fact of political loss and the social and political passions this can generate. In other words, they will have to develop the virtues of deliberative rhetoric, in the classical sense of appealing to each other—through both *logos* and *pathos*—in ways that support ongoing, productive deliberation about "public things" rather than undermine it (Waldron 1999b: 114–15; Abizadeh 2002; Allen 2004). The gap between their support for the institutions and procedures that govern the processes of political legitimation, and their desire for particular outcomes, will have to be kept within a certain bound. All of this presents a deep challenge for modern democrats, given the conditions of contemporary public spheres—riven with inequality and asymmetrical relations of power as they are.

However, one thing this model of citizenship may help us see is that pluralism is not only a social fact, as Rawls emphasizes, but a resource (Young 2000). What do I mean? There might be certain kinds of political disagreements, and ways of handling them, that can help build political community rather than undermine it, by contributing to more robust and fine-grained processes of legitimation. In societies where citizens have at least some freedom of speech and association, and the disparities of wealth are not too great (far from empty conditions, to be sure) people learn, through a combination of bargaining and arguing, to manage the conflicts thrown up by the inequalities and asymmetries that inevitably accompany life in such societies.[17] Moreover, such conflicts are not "managed" in the sense of being pacified, but produce demands for corrective action and reform (based on both self-interest and a concern for the common good) that can generate new arrangements and potentially new self-understandings on the part of citizens.[18] The "positive residue" of disagreement left behind is the experience of living in a society that learns to cope with its conflicts peacefully and in which various experiences of injustice are able to be fed into the political process. Social cohesion becomes a by-product of certain kinds of conflict and disagreement, and of the ongoing processes of managing and dealing with these disagreements successfully. But to do so we need a clear-eyed sense of the role of not only interest and power in politics but also the passions. There will be limits to these possibilities, to be sure. Societal learning is rarely comprehensive or linear and not always resilient. The potential for any positive residue to emerge or be sustained might be overwhelmed by the persistence of historical and contemporary injustice. And it is important to understand how and in what ways injustice (and perceptions of injustice) persist in our political disagreements in order to have any hope of finding satisfactory ways of dealing with them. As I have been arguing, resentment, or at least frustration, can accompany the exercise of both illegitimate and legitimate power. We should aim to take these reactions seriously, not only because they can be manipulated in harmful ways but also because they remind us of the fact that the process of political legitimation is always ongoing, as it is imperfect. The recent riots in Sydney (in late 2005), which flared up after a series of racially charged incidents on Cronulla beach, demonstrate how the demands of living with diversity, in combination with other factors (such as a global "war on terrorism"), can generate public expressions of deep misunderstanding and frustration. Living with difference is demanding, both morally and politically, and defenders of multiculturalism need to be attuned to this fact.

One of the difficulties with the argument about the positive residue of disagreement is that it involves achieving insight that seems *post hoc* rather than *a priori*. How do we know which conflicts will produce these positive residues—effects the participants themselves are possibly not even aware of? And what if we're wrong? Are not some forms of conflict better left off the political agenda, lest they deepen social and cultural cleavages that end up leaving everyone worse off? This is one justification for liberal constitutionalism and the "gag rules" that aim to keep religious or ethnic conflict, for example, out of debates about constitutional essentials (Holmes 1995). More deliberation and contestation is a fine idea, so the argument goes, but it is not an unambiguous good; at times it can poison mutual relations as much as improve them. There are strategic and psychological versions of this objection, too. According to the latter, in some circumstances, incessant deliberation might lead citizens to *harden* their attitudes toward others, especially if there are prevailing incentives to deliberate mainly with people you already identify with. At the very least, if pluralism and disagreement are as pervasive as pluralists say they are, more deliberation does not necessarily entail a higher probability of resolution. According to the strategic objection, removing limits on the politicization of political and cultural differences not only makes political deliberation more difficult but also risks opening up the exercise of political power to capture by moral and cultural zealots (Barry 2001; Shapiro 2001).

These are powerful objections, and they return us to some of the original problems with abstract and excessive moralism with which we began. But they also reinforce the importance of the democratic antidote to moralism. First, why assume that underlying interests and identities remain static, or at least self-contained, when confronted with each other? Politics, and the arguing and bargaining that it entails, can help to reshape those interests, which is a necessary (though hardly sufficient) step in moving the parties to a different and possibly better equilibrium point. But there are no guarantees. As Cass Sunstein points out, deliberative enclaves made up of like-minded people will emerge in large heterogeneous societies, because of limited argument pools and parochial influences (Sunstein 2001: 407). And they can move in extreme directions. But they are even more likely to fester and do harm the less opportunity there is for cross-cutting and inclusive forms of political deliberation (by both legislators and citizens).

What about the most extreme challenges to the kind of values and practices appealed to by both the foundationalist and practice-oriented modes of democratic dialogue? Racism and terrorism remain serious threats to our polities, a platitude that hardly needs reemphasis in an age of the "war on terror." But it is not clear that a concern to combat the most egregious forms of racism or terrorism should lead necessarily to one kind of foundationalism—to the search for a transcendental moment of unconditionality, to an Archimedean view from nowhere, or to principles established beyond the pale of political argument. After all, there is only so much philosophy can do, and, as I've argued, there are clearly resources within *both* frameworks examined above to condemn the beliefs that fuel racism. As Bernard Williams has put it, since no political theory can determine by itself its own application (Williams 2005: 28), it is not as though foundationalist arguments, on their own, offer any greater guarantee against the distortion of our political practices of legitimation than other theories might. But there is a more positive argument, too. The value and effectiveness of basic rights, for example, depend on our ability to understand, apply, and recraft these rights to meet new circumstances and conditions as required, including meeting new demands for justification of to whom they apply and when. And this might indeed mean revisiting old debates previously thought closed (because already thought justified and agreed, etc.), if only because there is always a chance the injustices identified in those older debates are being extended in new ways that cannot immediately be seen or anticipated. These reformulations and applications can end up changing the meaning of rights in profound ways. Thus even basic rights are ultimately provisional in this sense.

Moralism is an inherent risk in politics generally, and the risk of moralism when arguing about the nature of multiculturalism is no different. But the risk cuts both ways. Defenders of the inclusive logic of struggles over multicultural rights risk overestimating the capacities and virtues of citizens called upon to live with the tumults and disagreement caused by these debates. And they risk underestimating the psychological, institutional, and social preconditions required for living with ongoing reasonable disagreement and the social and political emotions it generates. But equally, those who argue that a whole range of basic principles are not up for negotiation, because already settled, risk overlooking the recurring demand for legitimation that is at the heart of our conception of the political.

NOTES

1. By multiculturalism I mean very broadly the accommodation of immigrant and ethnic groups through a range of public policies that supplement the protection of basic individual civil and political rights. Multiculturalism as public policy was introduced in Canada and Australia in the 1970s as a response, by and large, to issues arising from mass immigration. It is often extended to include the accommodation of the claims of indigenous peoples (in Australia and Canada) and the Quebecois (in Canada). But their situation (as nonimmigrant national minorities) is very different, as are their claims. However, unfortunately, at least in the Australian context in which this essay was written, "multiculturalism" has become associated with a general approach to cultural diversity that includes trying to accommodate the needs and claims of *both* immigrant groups and indigenous peoples. In this chapter I use multiculturalism in this broad sense for the purposes of exploring some of the criticisms and worries expressed about it, but I do not mean to endorse this broad usage. In fact, I have argued elsewhere that the situation of indigenous people deserves careful separate consideration (Ivison 2002, 2005).

2. So the difference is between a more and less moralized account of resentment. On the Nietzschean account, *ressentiment* seems primary and fuels the emergence of new values, as opposed to presupposing the values supposedly repudiated in the "slave revolt." But does not a sense of deprivation imply a set of evaluative concerns out of which *ressentiment* develops? This raises a complex set of issues for interpreting Nietzsche's argument that I cannot discuss here; but see Leiter 2002: 202–8; and Bittner 1994: 127–38.

3. Needless to say, resentment is not the only political emotion relevant to an understanding of multiculturalism; one might equally focus on pride, compassion, or hope. A more complete taxonomy of the political emotions relevant to a theory of multicultural democracy will have to await another occasion.

4. In Nietzschean terms, then, multiculturalism might represent yet another example of the triumph of slave morality over the aristocratic values associated with the higher types of humanity he praises in the *Genealogy of Morality* (1998) and *Beyond Good and Evil* (1969). For an interesting application of the notion of *ressentiment* to identity politics in general, see Brown 1995.

5. On the difference between legitimate abstraction in moral argument and problematic "idealizations," see O'Neill 1996: chap. 2.

6. Barry 2001: 326; also 21: "the [politics of difference] rewards the group that can most effectively mobilize to make claims on the polity, or at any rate rewards ethnopolitical entrepreneurs who can exploit its potential for their own ends by mobilizing a constituency around a set of sectional demands."

7. For the criteria according to which multicultural policies are considered strong, weak, or modest, see Banting and Kymlicka 2003a: 19–23, 25–30. See also Banting and Kymlicka 2003b: 59–66. One example of a strong commitment to social welfare combined with only "modest" multiculturalism is the Netherlands (interesting to consider given recent troubles there with its Muslim immigrant population). At least when compared with the United States and Germany, the Netherlands performs best according to social-democratic criteria to do with maximizing equality and minimizing poverty (along with maximizing income growth and minimizing family breakdown); see Goodin et al. 1999. But it is hard to draw any strong conclusions from this correlation; see Banting and Kymlicka 2003a: 26–27. The historical legacy of slavery and the politics of race in general have played a central role in American attitudes to the welfare state and its reform. But the relationship between race and multicultural policies (which came long after race became relevant) is complex and deserves separate treatment. There is certainly no easy analogy between attitudes toward race and affirmative action and multiculturalist policies and the welfare state.

8. I have argued for a more chastened approach to cultural claims in politics in Ivison 2002: 33–39.

9. I would go so far as to say that the demand for legitimation is a human universal, just insofar as coercion and power are among the universal stuff of politics anywhere.

10. The last two paragraphs draw on Ivison 2002.

11. This criticism is less effective against Habermas and his followers, since he is explicit that, aside from certain very general preconditions, the outcome of moral and political discourse is supposed to be radically open-ended. Moreover, like Tully, he too sees moral norms as emerging out of dialogue itself, but on the basis of a very different theory of communicative reason. Cf. the discussion of Habermas in Tully 1999.

12. For a version of this critique see Williams 2002: 226ff.

13. The problem is not a feasibility issue: it is not whether or not Habermasian discourse, for example, is unrealizable in practice (he is well aware that it might not be), but rather the deeper charge that it might be incoherent if it cannot show how rational (moral) discourse can be motivationally efficient.

14. A principle that, of course, will require further elaboration, clarification, and testing in light of other possible principles or norms.

15. The mixing of themes from Wittgenstein and Foucault is not seamless and deserves more careful attention than I can give here; cf. Owen 2002; Tully 1999. Both are resistant to large-scale abstract theorizing, albeit for different reasons and to different extents. But note that precisely because the scope of the practice is always itself open to question, there is nothing inherently anti-universalistic about an approach that takes the primacy of practice seriously. See, for example, the point made by Foucault, in response to a criticism by Richard Rorty (Foucault 1984: 385): "But the problem is, precisely, to decide if it is suitable to place oneself within a 'we' in order to assert the principles one recognizes and the values one accepts; or if it is not, rather, necessary to make the future formation of a 'we' possible, by elaborating the question."

16. The allusion is to Foucault 1997: 315–16.

17. This is not the claim that only those societies that undergo some specific process of social modernization are capable of generating the appropriate "moral modernization" that enables social conflict to be handled in productive ways. This kind of claim is often associated with Habermas's moral anthropology. Different societies will generate different kinds of social conflicts and thus different processes of social learning. Still, something like a basic demand for legitimation is close to being a universal, at least in most of the world today, whether or not it is associated with a particular language of rights.

18. Arguments about the benefits of conflict have a long lineage in the history of political thought, but perhaps one of the best known can be found in Machiavelli, especially in the *History of Florence* and the *Discourses;* for more discussion see Ivison 1997: chap. 3; McCormick 2001: 301–3.

Part III

Community, Culture, and Rights

Chapter 9

Conflicting Imaginaries in Australian Multiculturalism

Women's Rights, Group Rights, and Aboriginal Customary Law

Moira Gatens

Women's human rights theorists frequently comment on the asymmetrical effects on women and men of globalized markets, international politics, and the worldwide movement of so-called modernization. In postcolonial societies, such as Australia, these asymmetrical effects multiply the already deeply gendered nature of the historical practices of colonization (Wohlan 2005: 17). The imposition of European norms of femininity and masculinity, along with the norm of separating family life from public life, have had a profound, sex-specific impact on traditional Aboriginal ways of life. Human rights principles were, from the beginning, more adapted to "public man" and "public life," and many theorists have noted the difficulty of applying such rights to the situation of women.[1] In multicultural societies, this problem is acute for women who belong to "minority" groups. Prominent voices in both Western and non-Western cultures tolerate, or even welcome, human rights for men, while drawing the line at women's rights.[2] The desire to protect cultural distinctiveness from the flattening tendencies of modernity often puts unbearable pressure on marriage, the family, and those culturally distinctive norms that govern relations between the sexes. This desire burdens "minority" women with an increasingly difficult task, namely, the preservation of their cultures within largely "nonpublic" contexts. "Minority" women who speak out in support of institutional change and women's rights sometimes are portrayed as undermining, even rejecting, their traditional cultures. All these factors act to constrain women's opportunities to contribute to, and benefit from, the ways in which all societies change across time.

By discussing two controversial cases of arranged marriage in Australian indigenous communities I aim to revisit the volatile debate ignited by Susan Moller Okin's (1999) essay "Is Multiculturalism Bad for Women?" Although these cases concern particular cultures, at particular times and places, I aim to discuss them in a way that will throw light on the broader issue of the relationship between group (or cultural, or minority) rights and the human rights of girls and women within multicultural polities. In other words, I aim to provide some theoretical tools that are generally relevant to the deployment of "cultural defense" arguments in contemporary multicultural societies (e.g., "honor killings," wife murder, the physical assault, kidnap, and rape of girls and women). The essay is in three parts. First, I consider two legal cases where the entitlements of girls to basic human rights were compromised by men's claims to their cultural rights. In the second part, I address the clash between basic human rights, endorsed by liberal governments, and particular cultural norms, by suggesting that more attention be paid to the complex background contexts in which such conflicts occur. I argue for the utility of the notion of the social imaginary, understood in terms of the ubiquitous and permanent backdrop to meaningful social action. The social imaginary is posited as a fruitful "middle ground" where negotiations may take place between the ("top-down") universal rights of women and the ("bottom-up") particular cultural norms and customs that are seen to contravene those rights. Finally, I conclude that if human rights are to accommodate the rights of women and girls, then women and girls from all cultural groups must be recognized as legitimate stakeholders in, and valuable contributors to, the ongoing task of the reinvention and recreation of social meaning and cultural identity over time.

TWO CASES OF ARRANGED MARRIAGE IN AUSTRALIAN INDIGENOUS COMMUNITIES

One way to respond to the flattening tendencies of human rights discourses is to endorse the idea of group or cultural rights, that is, to signal respect for cultural difference by recognizing diversity in traditions, beliefs, and practices. In the context of multicultural liberal polities, Will Kymlicka has offered a cogent argument for why group-differentiated rights that protect minority cultures are not only consistent with liberal values but actually promote them. The force of his argument depends on the strong link he posits between freedom and access to what he calls "societal culture." A societal culture "provides its members with meaningful ways of life across the full range of human activities, including social, educational, religious, recreational and economic life, encompassing both public and private spheres" (Kymlicka 1995: 76). It is "a shared vocabulary of tradition and convention" that grounds one's sense of belonging and self-worth and provides the necessary context for one's ability to reflect on, and act in, the world.

However, as Kymlicka is aware,[3] and as feminist theorists continue to remind him, granting group rights to minority cultures may support discriminatory treatment of individual girls and women within the relevant groups.[4] Insofar as group rights take the group as their focus, they risk overriding the rights of individuals. Group rights, in other words, may strengthen oppressive gender norms within minority cultures. However, by their very nature, group rights expose the potential for dissent that is present in every group and so may function to provoke reflection on and debate about intragroup norms. Reflection and debate need not be seen as destructive of a shared way of life. Rather, they may be seen as indicators of a dynamic, living culture. This view of dissent within groups is particularly pertinent to indigenous peoples who are too often taken to be preserving an all but dead or frozen-in-time culture that is destined to disappear under the burden of the "modernizing" forces of colonization and the increasing reach of international law. Disagreement and debate drive normative change, and normative change is necessary if a culture is to adapt to new circumstances and endure.

The indigenous challenge to European conceptions of property rights and the demand for recognition and rectification of the many and continuing injustices of colonization[5] opens a path of communication through which contemporary notions about the just treatment of women and girls also may travel: cross-cultural recognition of difference inevitably will include a bilateral (albeit unequally so) component. To portray indigenous women's struggles for change in their own communities as "selling out" to the colonists, or succumbing to "Westernization," amounts to denying indigenous agency and self-determination. Indigenous women, no more or less than indigenous men, desire to contribute to the re-creation, as well as preservation, of indigenous values and practices over time. Indeed, as I will show, the re-creation of tradition is one way of preserving culture. Controversial cases of traditional arranged marriages in Australian indigenous communities have shown the degree to which challenges to traditional gender norms provoke heated disagreement and debate both within—and without—indigenous communities. They also expose the illiberal treatment of indigenous girls and women by some powerful nonindigenous representatives of the Australian liberal state.

Case One

In May 1986, when Jackie Pascoe Jamilmira was about thirty-four years old, he entered an agreement with the parents of a newborn girl that when she came of age he would take her as his wife. Traditionally, the agreement between Jamilmira and the girl's parents would have involved him giving them dillybags, boomerangs, or spears. In this case, however, Jamilmira had been making cash payments to the parents from his government benefit. According to press reports, it was the girl's mother who decided that given her daughter's emerging interest in local boys, it was time for her to join her husband. At this time the girl was fifteen and Jamilmira was forty-nine years old. The girl was living in a town in the Northern Territory and Jamilmira was living on an outstation some 120 kilometers away.

The arranged marriage came to the attention of the law because when her family and friends went to visit the girl the day after she joined Jamilmira, she indicated that she wished to leave with them. At this point Jamilmira discharged a shotgun into the air to dissuade them from taking her. They reported this incident to the police who called at the outstation and charged Jamilmira with discharging a firearm. He was also charged with having had unlawful intercourse with a minor. At this time, the police allegedly took a statement from the girl in which she claimed that Jamilmira had physically assaulted and raped her. This statement was withdrawn by the time the case came to the local magistrate.

This case was adjudicated at a number of levels: first, by a magistrate in a local court, who sentenced Jamilmira to thirteen months imprisonment for unlawful sexual intercourse and two months for the discharging of a firearm (Jamilmira appealed the decision); second, by Justice Gallop in the Supreme Court of the Northern Territory (SCNT), who found that in sentencing the magistrate had "failed to give due weight to a number of matters," including "customary or traditional law as it applied to the circumstances of the case; and the attitude of his community to this offending."[6] Taking advice from an anthropologist—who reported that arranged marriages involving young women and older men are considered "morally correct conduct" among the relevant community—Justice Gallop concluded that Jamilmira was exercising his conjugal rights in having intercourse with the girl and that "she knew what was expected of her" (*The Australian,* 9 October 2002). He reduced the sentence for carnal knowledge to twenty-four hours and that for the firearm offense to fourteen days. This judgment ignited intense public debate and comment from both indigenous and nonindigenous communities in Australia. This furor led to a further appeal. The second appeal was adjudicated by Chief Justice Martin in the SCNT Court of Appeal, which resulted in

Jamilmira receiving a twelve-month sentence for carnal knowledge and fourteen days for the firearm offense (*The Australian*, 16 April 2003). In February 2004 an application for appeal to the High Court of Australia was rejected.

Case Two

The second case of arranged marriage is, in many respects, similar to the first. In 2004, Mr GJ, a fifty-five-year-old traditional Aboriginal man, was charged with assault and unlawful intercourse with a fourteen- or possibly fifteen-year-old girl who was his promised wife, according to customary law.[7] Her family promised the girl to GJ when she was four years old. Although the girl was attending school in the city of Darwin, in June 2004 she was on school holidays and visiting her grandmother in Yarralin (the place of her traditional community). The trigger for the assault and unlawful intercourse mirrors that in the Jamilmira case: rumors were circulating in the community that the young girl had a boyfriend and had become sexually active. GJ, accompanied by the girl's grandmother, went to the house where she had stayed the night. At that time GJ assaulted the girl across the shoulders and back with boomerangs. GJ and the grandmother then took the girl to the grandmother's house where she was again physically assaulted by both of them. This was clearly meant as punishment for the supposed sexual activity. The child was then forced into GJ's car and driven to GJ's house on an outstation. Also present in the house was GJ's first wife and their two small children.

On the first night GJ dragged the girl, who was resisting him, into a bedroom where they were alone. GJ asked the girl for sexual intercourse and was refused. He hit her again. Although they slept in the same bed, no intercourse took place that night. The next night GJ again attempted intercourse with the girl, who in spite of being threatened with a boomerang, again refused. She was lying on her stomach on the bed. GJ then anally raped the girl, causing a deep laceration at the edge of her anus. During this ordeal the girl kicked and screamed. After four days GJ returned the girl to Yarralin where the child sought assistance and went to the police. This led to GJ's arrest.

This case was heard in the SCNT in August 2005. According to the court transcript, the girl told the police "that she was 'at that old man's place for four days' and that she was crying 'from Saturday to Tuesday'." Justice Martin commented: "She knew that she was promised to you [GJ] in the Aboriginal traditional way, but she did not like you. In the words of the child, 'I told that old man I'm too young for sex, but he didn't listen'."[8] Although

Justice Martin was at pains to make clear that Northern Territory law does not permit sexual intercourse with children under the age of sixteen, and that Territory law is concerned with protecting women and children from physical and sexual assault, he nevertheless attempted to balance "white" law with Aboriginal traditional law by taking into account that GJ was "asserting [his] rights as [he] believed them to be" under traditional law. On the basis of the evidence presented to him he said: "I am satisfied that you [GJ] believed that having sexual intercourse with the child was acceptable because she had been promised to you and she had turned 14. The Crown also accepts that, based on your understanding and upbringing in your traditional law, notwithstanding the child's objections, you believed that the child was consenting to sexual intercourse."[9]

Aspects of Justice Martin's reasoning in this case are not difficult to follow. He judged that *mens rea* was absent from GJ's actions: GJ lacked the knowledge that what he did was against (Northern Territory) law, and GJ believed that his behavior was permissible under customary Aboriginal law. The justice also said: "Mr GJ, I have a great deal of sympathy for you and the difficulties attached to transition from Aboriginal culture and laws as you understood them to be, to obeying the Northern Territory Law." It is noteworthy that Justice Martin determined to hold the court proceedings at Yarralin, under a tree, in the presence of the Yarralin community. This conduct of the proceedings, along with the public passing of sentence, was intended, he said, "to get the message through to all members of the community that what you [GJ] did to the young child was wrong."[10] The sentence imposed was five months for assault and nineteen months for unlawful sexual intercourse. The total sentence of twenty-four months was to be suspended after GJ had served one month, subject to good behavior for a period of two years after release. In addition to the factors already mentioned, in his sentencing Justice Martin took into account the following: the level of support GJ enjoyed in his community, the court presence and support of his first wife, his previous good character and conduct, and his role as "an important person in the ceremonial life of the community" and in "teaching young men the traditional ways."[11]

Other aspects of Justice Martin's reasoning and conduct are perplexing. Although he made a point of holding court in the Yarralin community, there is no evidence to suggest that efforts were made to ascertain the beliefs about customary law held by female members of the community.[12] As in the Jamilmira case, the promised wife was not present in court and had no voice in the proceedings. As far as I can tell, expert advice from female anthropologists was not sought in either case. Gender relations within indigenous communities are complex, and when cases involving indigenous people come before Australian courts, this complexity is overlaid not only by cultural differences but also by an acknowledged history of the legal sanctioning of the unequal treatment of indigenous peoples. Many Western feminists have written about women's disadvantage in relation to the "masculinism" of law (e.g., MacKinnon 1987). Others have written about indigenous peoples' disadvantage in relation to the racism of law (e.g. Cunneen and Libesman 1995). Indigenous women are thus doubly burdened in their dealings with the courts.[13] In these cases there was another factor: the young age of the promised wives and their status as children compromised their access to the court. The complexity of these cases derives, in part, from the layers of social divisions involved: liberal culture–indigenous culture, human rights–group rights, "white" law–traditional law, female–male, "white–black," private–public, and young–old. Each layer, moreover, has its own particular normative constitution. The intersection of these different social layers can produce discordances as well as surprising concordances. For example, Justice Gallop's observation that the girl did not need the protection of "white" law and that "she knew what was expected of her" sits well with Jamilmira's defense of his actions. Given the age, gender, and cultural location of the girls, and taking into account the seriousness of the cases, the failure to consult a female anthropologist arguably skewed the outcomes. Minimally, such a person may have been able to consult with women and girls in the relevant communities and acted as intermediary between community women and the court.

In any event, the judgment was appealed and heard in the Northern Territory Court of Criminal Appeal (NTCCA). The Human Rights and Equal Opportunity Commission (HREOC) made a submission to the Appeal Court in which it argued that the SCNT had failed to reach the correct balance between traditional law and the rights of the child.[14] HREOC argued that "a sentence which leads to impermissible discrimination against a woman or a child under international human rights principles is an error of law both in the balancing exercise under the provisions of the Sentencing Act and under the common law."[15] The HREOC submission sought to remind the court that although the International Covenant on Civil and Political Rights[16] (ICCPR) establishes the rights of minority groups to enjoy their own culture and language, and to practice their own religion (Article 27), it does not "authorise any State, group or person to violate the right to the equal enjoyment by women of any Covenant rights, including the right to equal protection of the law." On the contrary, Article 24 of the ICCPR mentions the obligation to protect female children from "all cultural or religious practices which jeopardise [their] freedom and well-being."[17] The NTCCA found that the sentencing judge in the SCNT had failed to reach a correct balance between the rights of Aboriginal men under customary law and the rights of the child. The NTCCA sentenced GJ to serve eighteen months before release.

The intense debates these cases provoked in indigenous communities reflect the internally contested status of customary laws and traditions. The views of community leaders, from various indigenous communities, ranged from one who argued that women need protection from men who think that they have "rights over women and a woman's body" to another who said that it is inappropriate to condemn, without debate, traditional marriage laws that allow sex with minors.[18] They also expose disagreement about how best to reach a balance between cultural norms, enshrined in traditional law, on the one hand, and women's rights, enshrined in international human rights instruments, and endorsed by liberal governments, on the other. The latter issue returns us to Okin's essay and its critics. There is a marked difference between the shape of the debate *internal* to indigenous communities and the shape of the debate in the "majority" culture.

Often, the response of the "majority" culture to cases such as those described above is that women from "minority" cultures need to be rescued from their cultures, which are sometimes portrayed as "barbaric" or "primitive" and inherently violent toward women. This response often stems from ignorance about the relevant culture and blindness to the ways in which "minority" cultures—and the meanings of their norms—change because of their beleaguered position within multicultural societies. Okin's assertion that it is unjustifiable to defend group rights where such rights act to preserve a minority culture that is "more patriarchal" than the "majority" liberal culture particularly aggravated many of her interlocutors.[19] Women from ("more patriarchal") minority cultures, Okin argued, "*might* be better off if the culture into which they were born were either to become extinct (so that its members would become integrated into the less sexist surrounding culture) or, preferably, to be encouraged to alter itself so as to reinforce the equality of women" (Okin 1999: 22–23; emphasis original). Although the harsh criticism this assertion received often was based on misquotation, and so was undeserved, the assertion remains problematic. Where is the Archimedean point from which one confidently could rank cultures from the most to the least patriarchal? In contemporary multicultural societies, how many minority cultures could boast members who were not, to varying degrees, already integrated into the surrounding culture? Supposing it to have the number of living members requisite to compose "a culture," what could it mean for a culture to become extinct? Okin's assertion, in other words, contains several unconvincing assumptions. It assumes that Western liberal feminism is able to act as judge of all cultures, thus implying that feminism's norms are culturally "neutral." It supposes that cultural membership is discrete rather than multiple or overlapping. Okin also fails to note the ways in which *all* cultures change over time without thereby becoming extinct.

Furthermore, Okin's assertion appears to contradict Kymlicka's important insight (which she appears to endorse elsewhere) that membership in a viable "societal culture" is necessary if one is to become a social agent at all. As I will argue, it is implausible to set women's human rights *against* the particular norms of their cultures as if this were a zero-sum game.[20] Targeting a norm as unjust, in isolation from the relevant cultural context, prevents an adequate understanding of the meaning and value of that norm. This understanding can be reached only by examining the norm in context. Asking how norms function in actual cultural contexts also reveals the way in which they tend to cluster around specific identities, practices, and institutions. Hence, criticism of one norm will involve critical engagement with the norm cluster in which it is nested. The assumption that it is the contingent cultural norms governing sexual difference that prevent women from becoming bearers of human rights is grounded in a widespread but mistaken assumption about the relation between culture and agency. The inattention to contextual meaning assumes the existence of an ahistorical, acultural, "essential" individual, whose desires and "nature" may be distorted, or illegitimately constrained, by her "insertion" into a specific place and time. This posits "woman" as a "universal" whose freedom may be secured by replacing distorting and oppressive local cultural norms with universally appropriate human rights. But there is no universal "woman" and no "acultural" individual. This means that the spur for normative change is endemic to the places and times in which actually existing women fight for historically and culturally specific causes. The value of the particular norms that govern the lives of embodied historical women therefore cannot be judged in the absence of understanding how the meanings of such norms are linked together and sustained by the cultural contexts in which they obtain.

If "enculturation" is necessary for action and choice, then the line between the embodiment of one's cultural norms and one's capacity for agency is difficult, if not impossible, to draw. Kymlicka's account of the link between agency and access to one's societal culture does not adequately address this problem or its complex implications for those who inhabit more than one societal culture. The situation of many contemporary indigenous Australians means that it is likely that they will be members of overlapping communities, which frequently will have inconsistent normative commitments and will typically offer limited, even contradictory, opportunities for self-development. For them, belonging to a valued culture that could provide the basis for self-respect is an ongoing struggle, not a given. Indigenous peoples in Australia want to preserve their culture but how they do so is a complex and internally contested issue. If Western liberal feminism is to make a constructive contribution to the position of "minority" women in multicultural societies, then it will need to recognize the considerable diversity in cross-cultural gender norms and the resultant variety in the forms of agency exercised by women.[21] This puts the values of equality and autonomy, favored by liberal feminists, under considerable strain. Feminists who view these values as nonnegotiable are forced either to say that in some cultures women's defenses of their own particular ways of being are based on "false consciousness" or to concede that women's agency can take different cultural forms. If my argument about normative behavior is correct, then agency *must* take different cultural—and historical—forms. Thus, Robert Post's comment on Okin's essay remains apt: "The feminist challenge to liberal multiculturalism thus forces feminism to sharpen its own normative claims" (Post 1999: 66). Despite its problems, Post (1999: 68) suggests that the value of Okin's essay is that it shows us "that distinguishing between enabling and oppressive cultural norms is a fundamental challenge of liberal multiculturalism, a challenge that has yet to be successfully confronted." The next two sections of this chapter endeavor to take up Post's challenge to feminism, to multiculturalism, and to the troubled relation between them.

CULTURAL NORMS AND THE SOCIAL IMAGINARY

The deeply contextual nature of normative behavior means that an adequate theory of how cultural norms function must explain how they connect up with broader social and cultural meanings. Normative cultural practices involve more than the abstract endorsement of a set of values. They also involve affective and embodied commitments, including those of which members of a culture are not consciously aware. The very notion of judging behavior as "good" or "bad" assumes an actually existing community of embodied individuals who are affectively, as well as cognitively, invested in the preservation of their identities along with the related values of their community. Norms deeply engage our emotions and this is one reason why their transgression carries heavy costs. To act contrary to a rule may mean one has to bear a bad consequence; but to act contrary to a cultural norm that underwrites one's identity may result in loss of self-respect and the feared, or actual, loss of community respect. In rapidly changing societies, maintaining one's self-respect may cost one the respect of the community, and vice versa. Norms have the power to affect the whole person and to engage feelings of fear, guilt, and shame. Cultural norms link together emotions, imagination, and intellect, that is, they act on and through our embodied selves and facilitate our belonging to a particular culture. Part of what it means to belong to a particular culture, and to participate in a particular social imaginary, is to have access to the taken-for-granted "'repertory' of collective actions at the disposal of a given group of society" (Taylor 2004: 25). This "repertory" of normative ways of being will differ according to sex, age, and social status. For those who inhabit more than one "societal culture," access to different "repertories" complicates what will count as "permissible" or "impermissible" action for them.

The power of the human imagination, in both its individual and collective expressions, is too often dismissed or ignored by social, political, and legal theorists. Understanding social and cultural narratives, images, and myths as "false consciousness", or quaint folklore, obscures the importance of the affective and imaginative dimensions of human collective life and thus forfeits the opportunity to understand how cultural meanings and norms combine to motivate and drive social actors. Sociability itself depends on the power of the imagination to bind together individuals, both temporally and affectively.[22] Our day-to-day encounters are guided by both habitual and practical orientations toward the general business of living. All this takes place against culturally specific backgrounds that are taken for granted. Two of the most common ways of imagining "community" are through religious or political narratives; and these two story lines are never easily separated (Lefort 1988: 213–55). Such stories play a large role in the constitution of various (legal, political, sexual) "social imaginaries."[23] I understand this phrase to include those images, symbols, metaphors, and narratives that help structure forms of embodied identity and belonging, social meaning, and value, and which, because they appeal to the imaginative faculty, attract strong affective investments.[24] These diverse significations will, of course, vary from culture to culture, and even within a single culture, but they are essential and permanent elements in the creation, maintenance, and revision of the meanings through which cultures make sense of themselves and offer justification for the variable status and entitlements of their members.

This notion of the social imaginary is necessarily a broad-brush approach to understanding how human collectivities construct an interconnected web of meanings that constitute a "second nature." Normative behavior cannot be understood, perhaps not even judged, apart from the particular imaginary, or imaginaries, that give it meaning. When judged from an external perspective, certain cultural norms might appear absurd, disgusting, or reprehensible, but these same norms may at least be understood (if not condoned) when adequately described with reference to the meanings they convey in their cultural context. However, a more fine-grained analysis is required if we are to account for the ways in which particular norms function to express a collective way of life. It is clear that if a norm is to retain a particular meaning, then it will have to remain more or less consistent with the broader social meanings and narratives in which it is embedded. In contemporary multicultural contexts normative disagreement may function to disrupt the meanings of "minority" norms, and such disruption, in turn, might threaten the coherence of their cultural imaginaries. Dealing with contradictory normative demands and expectations is one of the burdens of minority groups in multicultural societies. For example, the meaning of an arranged marriage between a young girl and an older man will vary according to the specific imaginaries (social, political, legal, religious, and economic) in which such practices obtain. In contemporary liberal democracies the dominant legal and moral meaning of this practice is child sexual abuse. In other cultures, it may be seen as morally appropriate behavior that functions to consolidate kinship ties and promote community coherence and intercommunity cooperation. How such behavior should be understood in a liberal multicultural polity, such as Australia, is the contentious issue raised by the cases under consideration.

The norms surrounding sexuality, marriage, and family are closely related to norms of sexual difference. These norms bite deeply into the identity of the individual and her or his place and status within any given culture. Moreover, normative change in sexual practices and normative change in women's identities cannot but have an effect on men's identities, as well as on marital and familial norms. Both the norms that govern sexuality and those that govern sexual difference operate interdependently. Hence, a challenge to women's normative roles inevitably will be perceived as presenting a challenge to men's roles. Although every culture constructs specific social meanings upon the sexual difference, the connection between sexual difference and the norms through which that difference is made significant are not acultural or ahistorical. This is one reason why, in multicultural societies, Aboriginal women (and women from other ethnic minority groups) so often become the focus of intra- and intercultural tensions. It is because minority women's identities are constructed at the intersection of two of the most fundamental social and political divisions: sex and race (or ethnicity). In overlapping communities, such as Australia, contradictions between "majority" and "minority" gender norms are inevitable.

In multicultural societies, the racial (and, all too often, racist) dimension of intercultural relations makes it all too easy for dominant groups to imagine themselves in ideal terms, forgetting the many ways in which they too systemically maltreat some of their members. These same groups are not always so generous in their assessment of minority cultures and will tend to identify problems of sexual and physical violence against girls and women with the traditional practices of the relevant minority culture. Dominant liberal culture thereby evades responsibility for the ways in which its past and present practices might contribute to the occurrence of such violence. The tendency to depict "minority" cultures as intrinsically violent toward women sometimes is based on ignorance about what are the actual practices of those cultures and the ways in which those practices—and their contextual meanings—may change under pressure from surrounding influences.

CONFLICTING AUSTRALIAN IMAGINARIES?

The indigenous population in Australia occupies an ambivalent place in the broader Australian imaginary. The sensationalism attached to the arranged marriages considered here reflects the Australian media's fraught relation to the country's first peoples and the complex range of affect that characterizes "black-white" relations.[25] Indigenous people make up only 2.4 percent of Australia's population and the vast majority do not live traditional lifestyles (Davis and McGlade 2005: 6). Most "white" Australians have little or no contact with traditional Aboriginal peoples, and there is widespread ignorance about the various Aboriginal laws and customs that govern traditional societies. When these laws and customs come to the attention of the general public, it is usually because they have failed to function, or have been prevented from functioning, in their context. This results in a partial and so distorted view of Aboriginal customary law. As Catherine Wohlan (2005: 1) has argued, "family violence and Aboriginal law are consistently presented as interrelated phenomenon [*sic*], whereas they should be understood as separate issues." This is not to deny that Aboriginal women and girls often experience extreme levels of violence in their own communities. Rather, it is to say that the rape and beating of girls and women "is not part of Aboriginal law" (Wohlan 2005: 11). On the contrary, this treatment of women indicates the breakdown of traditional communities and law.

The tendency to identify violence against women with traditional practices encourages the misuse of customary law to excuse acts of physical and sexual violence against women. This tendency "is of growing concern in Aboriginal communities, particularly among Aboriginal women" (Davis and McGlade 2005: 37). There is disagreement between Aboriginal men, whose actions have brought them before Australian courts, and Aboriginal women concerning what is, and what is not, customary Aboriginal law. The tendency for Australian courts to accept Aboriginal men's accounts of law, without checking the views of women, can set dangerous legal precedents that are prejudicial to indigenous women and girls. When courts engage the services of anthropologists—usually also men—the Aboriginal men's accounts are verified; but male anthropologists, for cultural reasons, often have garnered their knowledge of customary law exclusively from indigenous men in the first place. The meeting of traditional law and "white" law in a court setting has, according to some indigenous women, resulted in grave distortions. The colloquial term for the resulting hybrid is "bullshit customary law." One indigenous female lawyer has observed that it is "ironic that the imposition of the white men's law on traditional law" has distorted traditional law to the degree that it can be "used as a justification for assault and rape of women" (Sharon Payne, quoted in Davis and McGlade 2005: 37).

Many traditional indigenous communities have become critically dysfunctional under the burdens of colonization and are plagued by unemployment, illness, and alcohol and drug abuse. This hampers the capacity of traditional indigenous imaginaries to provide the robust background context essential to the preservation of traditional laws, customs, and norms. This appears to be the situation in both cases discussed here. In the Jamilmira case, Justice Gallop made the comment that the promised wife "knew what was expected of her." Despite this appeal to culturally normative behavior, it is clear that the girls' normative commitments did not match those of their promised husbands. Neither girl was living in a traditional community; both were town- or city-dwellers. Both attended mainstream schools and so presumably were exposed to all the usual normative influences that go with this lifestyle: TV, media, and the typical pursuits, values, and norms of teenagers. In the case of GJ, it is significant that rather than seeing GJ as a revered, powerful leader in his community—marriage to whom would bring with it status and respect —the girl referred to him as "that old man."

This might encourage one to concede a point made by the prosecution in GJ's case, namely, that the case involves "not just a clash of laws or of culture. It involves a clash of generations."[26] But the situation is more complex than this. Understanding its full complexity requires that we take into account the social imaginary. If the meaning and force of any given cultural norm requires an operational imaginary, then if that imaginary becomes dysfunctional, so will the norms. Marriage, in robust traditional settings, is a complex affair that involves the entire community and generates a range of rights and obligations amongst members of the community and between communities. Although the specific traditional norms governing marriage vary from group to group, in many communities mothers-in-law would attend to the well-being of young wives; the wife's brother, her mother's brother, and her father's sister could be expected to speak out on her behalf and to "protect her interests" (Wohlan 2005: 22). Diane Bell, an anthropologist who has worked extensively with Australian indigenous women, notes that arranged marriages in traditional societies had their own built-in sanctions and safeguards: "young girls in arranged marriages to older men would be protected by over-seeing co-wives and a semi-public life in open-air camps."[27] These aspects of traditional marriage were absent in the cases of Jamilmira and GJ. In both cases the young girls were removed from traditional communities—to which they had only an intermittent attachment—and taken to isolated outstations. Thus, the paths for assistance or support that traditionally would have been available to these girls were closed. Perhaps more significantly, these young people were provided with no guidance for how to deal with their dual membership in communities that only partially overlap and whose values, norms, and imaginaries are in deep tension. The difficulty involved in the older generation transmitting their culture to the younger generation is one important consequence of the pressures on indigenous imaginaries. Some indigenous communities have responded to this pressure in constructive and creative ways (Wohlan 2005: 43–46).

As Post intimated, the complexities of contemporary multicultural societies present a formidable normative challenge to both liberalism and feminism. Okin's confidence in the universal scope of the normative commitments of Western feminism does not sit well with the account of norms and the imaginary I have sketched. I have argued that understanding how normative conflicts arise involves appreciating how norms cluster to support important social meanings and rituals that are embedded in culturally specific social imaginaries. Whether an individual norm of action is one that constrains or enables any given social actor will depend on the nature of the cluster to which the norm is attached and how that cluster figures in broader imaginaries. The question of the link between culture and agency, or "societal culture" and freedom, raised by Kymlicka, is an especially complex link for indigenous peoples who did not choose to share their land and resources with the colonizers. The struggles of indigenous women today arise out of very specific experiences of colonization and its aftermath, and these conditions are quite unlike those that produced Western feminism. Indigenous women's attempts to preserve and transmit their culture through norms and values that are culturally specific should be recognized as a valid expression of their agency. Whether such attempts are viewed as enabling or constraining for Aboriginal girls and women in the present will depend on how those values affect their capacities to negotiate their membership in overlapping communities. Indigenous cultural imaginaries have been seriously, probably irreparably, harmed by the aggression and ignorance that characterized past practices of colonization. But this harm was often sex-specific and continues to have sex-specific effects. Obviously, this makes for a complex relationship between indigenous and nonindigenous law. Historically, nonindigenous law was brutally imposed from above and without any attempt to negotiate with existing traditional law. It would be wise to avoid repeating this history in relation to feminist and human rights norms in the present. Recent attempts made by Australian courts to recognize indigenous beliefs, laws, and values in terms of "cultural rights" attempt to rectify Australia's shameful past and avoid the repetition of past mistakes. However, great care must be taken to ensure that women in indigenous communities are consulted about what is (and what is not) traditional or customary law. In the context of these cases, the fact that GJ was an important member of the community who was involved in "teaching young men the traditional ways" is cause for concern. For some indigenous women the concern is not that their culture, traditions, and practices are becoming, or will become, extinct. It is rather that traditions and laws are being passed on to the next generation in a distorted form that is deeply damaging to the interests of women and girls (Wohlan 2005: 33–36).

It is, of course, possible to put forth a "fundamentalist" defense of customary law. This kind of interpretation is the one offered by Jamilmira after he was sentenced. He said, "our law is like the ocean, it is vast and affects all parts of our lives; it never changes. Your law is like a puddle of water, it is ever changing. I am being punished for following my law" (quoted in Bryant 2003). This view of law is consistent with the statement he made to the arresting police officers: "she is my promised wife. I have rights to touch her body"; "its [*sic*] Aboriginal custom, my culture."[28] This view supposes that there is only one correct and unchanging interpretation of traditional law. For Aboriginal people, that law is not written in books but dwells in the landscape itself. But one can accept the premise that Aboriginal law "never changes" and still note that indigenous people themselves disagree about how to *interpret* the law under changed conditions. Access to knowledge about the law is not evenly spread within indigenous communities. Different rights and obligations devolve to specific groups; for example, some things are "women's business" and others "men's business." Decisions about how to apply law in changed circumstances and for different purposes will be an interpretative and dynamic practice that will involve both men and women.

The conditions under which traditions are perpetuated change and so the practices associated with their observance require constant reinvention and renegotiation (witness Jamilmira's payments to his promised wife's parents with cash from government benefits rather than traditional items). The point is not that if a tradition changes then it loses its claim to "authenticity" or legitimacy, or that if a traditional culture changes significantly, we should therefore judge it as "extinct." Every tradition that survives does so by changing and adapting to new circumstances. In these cases the pertinent question is: can one claim to be practicing a tradition—such as wife promising—in the absence of the compliance of the promised wife and in the absence of the traditional sanctions, checks, and balances essential to the way the practice functioned in the past? I do not think so. If a community is incapable of effectively embodying a traditional practice and its sanctions, it is not viable for individuals to attempt to carry that practice forward into the future by sheer force. The use of force by individuals is more likely to undermine tradition and divide communities. If the important cultural function of traditional wife promising is to be preserved, new forms of its practice will need to be invented by communities acting inclusively and cooperatively.

The imaginaries of indigenous communities have been seriously breached. If they are to be repaired and rendered capable of sustaining distinctly Aboriginal ways of life, within a multicultural society, then all members of these fragile communities—and especially women and girls—must be consulted and allowed to contribute to the preservation and recreation of their culture over time.[29] Human rights, women's rights, and the rights of the child—endorsed and enforced by contemporary liberal democracies—need not be seen to contradict the right to practice one's culture. Rather, such rights, indeed feminism itself, might be realized in culturally distinct ways that preserve norms and traditions through their reinterpretation and reinvention in the present. This may or may not be possible, or desirable, with the practice of wife promising: that is not for me say. However, it has been shown that traditions that constrained or harmed women in the past can be reinvented in ways that enable women in the present.[30] Through the reinvention of traditional practices that aim to improve their conditions of life, women can express their agency without thereby abandoning the cultural distinctiveness of their norms and traditions.

ACKNOWLEDGMENTS

Research for this essay was supported by an Australian Research Council Discovery grant. I am also grateful to my coinvestigators, Paul Patton and Duncan Ivison, for their incisive comments on this essay. Danielle Celermajer, Chandran Kukathas, and participants at the Australian Multiculturalism and Political Theory workshop also provided me with invaluable criticisms and suggestions. Finally, Geoffrey Levey must be thanked for providing the occasion to offer this essay and for his comments on the revised version. Some sections of this essay draw on Gatens 2004.

NOTES

1. Hilary Charlesworth (1997) argues that women's confinement to the domestic sphere calls for a redefinition of human rights so that they are able to reach into the home and family life.
2. The Convention on the Elimination of All Forms of Discrimination Against Women (CEDAW) has the greatest number of reservations of any human rights instrument. See www.un.org/womenwatch/daw/cedaw/reservations.htm.
3. Kymlicka (1995) makes an important distinction between two types of group rights. Rights that constrain the choices and actions of persons within any given group he terms "internal restrictions" and argues against them on the grounds that liberal theory and practice should not endorse any right that inhibits the freedom of individuals or results in injustice. To this kind of right he contrasts those rights that provide "external protections" against the broader community, such as the right to native language use, land claims, political representation, and so on. The latter rights should be endorsed by liberal societies because they protect the "societal culture" of minority groups that, in turn, enables their members to express their social agency. See also Kymlicka's response to Okin's essay in Okin 1999. Kymlicka's distinction between what might constrain and what might enable agency is very difficult to maintain in practice. The distinction is a very complex one, as I hope to show in what follows.
4. Both Okin (1999, 2002) and Ayelet Shachar (1998, 2001) offer strong arguments to this effect.
5. In Australia, the *Mabo vs Queensland* (1992) judgment represents a crucial shift in the ability of Australian law to recognize European-based notions of property as only one, historically specific, way of relating to land. Larissa Behrendt (2003: 33) reports that her father explained her place in the world to her in the following terms: "Ownership for the white people is something on a piece of paper. We have a different system. You can no more sell our land than sell the sky." See Behrendt 2003: 31–55 for an extended account of the differences between "European" and indigenous conceptions of land and property. See also Ivison 2002: esp. 144–62.
6. Gallop A/J Transcript of Proceedings at Darwin on Tuesday 8 October, 2002, JA 49 of 2002 (20112873).
7. Martin CJ Transcript of Proceedings at Yarralin on Thursday 11 August 2005, SCC 20418849.
8. Ibid.
9. Ibid.
10. Ibid.
11. Ibid.
12. However, it is clear from the court transcript that the girl's grandmother endorsed GJ's "right" to the girl. But what does this "right" involve? The transcript is not helpful in determining the grandmother's attitude toward GJ's actions at the outstation. The role of older women in traditional cultural practices is complex. See Okin's (1999) views, especially her reply at 117–31.

13. I do not mean to suggest that the girls in this case are treated first as women (actually, girls), then as indigenous. Obviously they are treated as indigenous girls. Arguably, this means that they do not enjoy the privileges of men (black or white) or of (white) women or girls. "Double burden" does not capture the true complexities of their situations.

14. For complex legal reasons that need not concern us here, the NTCCA did not formally recognize the HREOC submission. See Mildren, Riley & Soutwood JJ, The Queen v GJ [2005] NTCCA 20, especially ¶42–73.

15. Submission of HREOC in Court of Criminal Appeal of the Northern Territory, No. CA 19 of 2005, ¶27.

16. The ICCPR was fully ratified by Australia in 1983.

17. Submission of HREOC in Court of Criminal Appeal of the Northern Territory, No. CA 19 of 2005, ¶37–40.

18. The first comment was made by Lowitja O'Donoghue (former chair of ATSIC), the second by Geoff Clark (ATSIC chair at the time of the offense). Their comments were reported in the *Guardian*, 30 December 2002, and *The Australian*, 16 October 2002, respectively. ATSIC is the acronym for the Aboriginal and Torres Strait Islanders Commission, a now defunct government-supported body that was intended to increase indigenous peoples' involvement in issues that particularly affect them. See www.atsic.gov.au. Views of other prominent indigenous people include John Ah Kit (NT Minister for Indigenous Affairs), who said in Parliament that the judgment of Justice Gallop had "failed in its humanitarian responsibility for the protection of children" (*The Australian*, 17 October 2002). Marion Scrymgour (indigenous member of NT Parliament) said that Gallop's comments were "misogynist in nature" (*The Australian*, 17 October 2002). Aden Ridgeway (then Democrat spokesperson for indigenous affairs) said that the girl in the case "has rights just like a young white girl in a city location, she shouldn't be treated differently or afforded any less protection" (*The Australian*, 15 October 2002). Finally, two female commissioners of ATSIC offered apparently contrary views, one claiming that "tribal law must be respected," the other that indigenous women were entitled to the protection of "white" law (*The Australian*, 15 October 2002).

19. For example, see the responses of Azizah Y. al-Hibri and Martha Nussbaum in Okin 1999. Other critics have accepted the thrust of Okin's arguments for the harms women may suffer in multicultural societies but disagree with her conclusions. For example, Chandran Kukathas (2001), in his provocatively titled article "Is Feminism Bad for Multiculturalism?", argues that Okin is right to pose the tensions between feminism and liberal multiculturalism as a zero-sum game. However, where Okin had argued that feminist claims should trump multiculturalism, Kukathas puts the reverse case. On his view, Okin's argument shows a misplaced confidence in the ability of liberal institutions to ameliorate the situation of women in minority cultures. It is important to note that his version of multiculturalism does *not* endorse group or cultural rights.

20. In this respect, Kukathas and Okin agree. Both view the relation between feminism and multiculturalism as one of irresolvable tension, where the claims

of one or the other must give way. Their disagreement is about which should give way: feminism or multiculturalism?

21. In her excellent and disturbing study of Islamic women's piety movements in Egypt, Saba Mahmood (2005) has begun the daunting task of rethinking feminist attitudes to women's agency in non-Western contexts.

22. As Benedict Anderson (1983: 6), in much-quoted lines, holds: "all communities larger than primordial villages (and perhaps even these) are imagined. Communities are to be distinguished, not by their falsity/genuineness, but by the style in which they are imagined."

23. For an excellent account of the role of the "imaginary" in contemporary social and political theory, see James 2002. See also Stoetzler and Yuval-Davis (2002) for a compelling account of the "situated imagination" and its role in social and political life.

24. I have made extensive use of this notion in earlier works. See especially Gatens (1996) and Gatens and Lloyd (1999).

25. For example, the journalist Paul Toohey (2005) begins his story about the case of GJ with the following words: "There can be genuine charm to Aboriginal culture. Two weeks ago, the Garma festival in Arnhem Land attracted hundreds of white outsiders to celebrate the non-secret parts of Aboriginal culture. They loved it: they always do. But they only stayed a week and then went home." By beginning his story in this way he encourages the belief that GJ's actions are a (hidden) part of Aboriginal culture.

26. Martin CJ Transcript of Proceedings at Yarralin on Thursday 11 August 2005, SCC 20418849.

27. Sonia Shah, Women's e-News, 29 November 2002: www.womensnews.org [accessed 29 March 2006].

28. From Jamilmira's statement at Maningrida Police Station (quoted in Davis and McGlade 2005: 37).

29. This is also what Okin (1999) recommends—though for different reasons than the ones offered here.

30. For example, a Kenyan national women's group (Maendeleo ya Wanawake Organization), working with rural communities in Kenya, have introduced an alternative to female genital cutting (or FGM), where girls are "circumcised" through words. The rite of passage is known as "Ntanira na Mugambo" or "cutting through words." According to Fredrick Nzwili: "The rite brings willing young girls together for a week in seclusion where they get traditional lessons about their future roles as women, parents and adults in the community. They are also taught about their personal health, reproduction, hygiene, communications skills, self-esteem and dealing with peer pressure. It is just like the traditional ritual, except that there is no cutting of their genitals." See Women's e-News, 8 April 2003: www.womensnews.org [accessed 29 March 2006].

Chapter 10

Loyalty and Membership

Globalization and Its Impact on Citizenship, Multiculturalism, and the Australian Community

Kim Rubenstein

A major change in Australian citizenship law occurred on 4 April 2002.[1] On that day, the governor-general of Australia assented to the passage of the Australian Citizenship Amendment Act 2002 (Cth).[2] Before that date, Australian citizens who took up a new citizenship (like Rupert Murdoch taking up U.S. citizenship) automatically lost their Australian citizenship. After that date, any Australian citizen taking up a new citizenship was entitled to keep their Australian citizenship. Underpinning the former provision and its repeal are differing views of loyalty and allegiance to the nation-state.

This chapter argues that the differing views underpinning the debate about dual citizenship are mirrored in policy discourse about the place of multiculturalism in Australia. Globalization has and continues to have a substantial impact upon legal status and membership and identity in both the nation-state and in the international legal system. These legal changes reflect the shifting notions of membership both in the Australian domestic framework and in the international framework. Moreover, these changes must be taken into account in balancing rights and responsibilities in a diverse society, so that multiculturalism and cultural diversity continue to be affirmed within the legal framework and public policy in the same way dual citizenship has been accepted.

THE PLACE OF LAW IN OUR UNDERSTANDING OF MEMBERSHIP

The power of law and its role in regulating identity underpins this inquiry into the meaning of membership in a diverse society. In a slightly different context, Madhavi Sunder argues that "law's conception of culture matters." She shows how "law has always been in the business of defining cultures and choosing sides in internal cultural debates" (Sunder 2001: 509, 552). In a similar fashion, Mahmood Mamdani (2001) argues in an analysis of the Rwandan genocide:

> When it comes to the modern state, political identities are inscribed in law. In the first instance they are legally enforced. If the law recognizes you as a member of that ethnicity, then you become an ethnic being legally and institutionally. In contrast, if the law recognizes you as a member of a racial group, then your relationship to the state, and to other legally defined groups, is mediated through the law and the state. It is a consequence of your legally inscribed identity. If your inclusion or exclusion from a regime of rights or entitlements is based on your race or ethnicity as defined by law, then this becomes a central defining fact for you the individual and your group. (Mamdani 2001: 22)

Mamdani's analysis also shows how law can control and influence identity and, as such, we must be mindful of law's power when considering policy underlying it.

While Australian identity issues are contested (as is shown, indeed, by the differing views on Australian multiculturalism expressed in many of the chapters in this volume) and are naturally going to be different from those of other nations, there is no disputing the broader principle that law and legal status profoundly affects Australian identity and membership.

This view of law and legal status has been central to the various promotions run by the now Department of Immigration and Citizenship over the years encouraging Australian permanent residents to become formal legal citizens.[3] This view of the role of law also underpins the Victorian government's Multicultural Victoria Act (Vic) of 2005, which this chapter later examines.

Finally, the legal meaning of citizenship impacts upon normative understandings of citizenship. As Karen Slawner (1998: 83) reminds us, the "legal definitions of citizenship always incorporate what is considered to be desirable activity." Moreover, the normative notion of citizenship, a progressive notion imbued with a belief in the importance of equality of membership and a commitment to civic participation, is fundamental to understanding the relationship between multiculturalism and membership of the Australian community.[4]

CITIZENSHIP AND LOYALTY AND ALLEGIANCE

Citizenship and multiculturalism are useful contexts for exploring questions of loyalty and allegiance. This first section examines the place of loyalty and allegiance to citizenship and nationality. Historically, there has been a very strong link between notions of allegiance and citizenship. Citizenship is also referred to as nationality—it is the term used in law to reflect the formal legal status of an individual in a nation-state.[5]

From a historical perspective, nationality is linked to the bond of allegiance between the individual and the state. Traditionally this bond was viewed as insoluble or at least exclusive.[6] It dates from the European state system in the Middle Ages when the relationship between individual and state was derived from the inherent and permanent bond between subject and sovereign.[7] The Common Law recognized this bond and expressed it in the doctrine *nemo potest exuere patriam* (no man may abjure his country). According to Blackstone (1787: 357), an individual's obligations to the sovereign represented "a debt of gratitude which cannot be forfeited, cancelled or altered by any change of time, place or circumstance" (see also Spiro 1997: 1420).

Similarly, Hale (1971 [1736]), writing on the problems of dual allegiance in 1730, stated:

> Hence it is, that the natural born subject of any prince cannot by swearing allegiance to another prince put off or discharge him from that natural allegiance; for this natural allegiance was intrinsic and primitive and antecedent to the other, and cannot be divested without the concurrent act of the prince to whom it was first due. (Hale 1971 [1736]: 68)

While the concept of insoluble allegiance was defensible in times of limited individual mobility, it became difficult to maintain in the face of large-scale international migration. Nonetheless, in the eighteenth and nineteenth centuries, characterized by aggressive nationalism and territorial competition between states, the concept of dual nationality was generally seen as undesirable, incompatible with individual loyalties, and destabilizing of the international order. Accordingly, insoluble allegiance was gradually replaced by exclusive but transmutable allegiance as the basis of nationality.

Just as the doctrine of insoluble allegiance was a product of medieval Europe, the development of exclusive allegiance as the basis for nationality reflects the state of international relations in the second half of the nineteenth century. This was the high-water mark of classical international relations and of state sovereignty as the organizing principle of international relations. In this context dual nationality was an intolerable affront to the absolute authority of the state with regard to its territory and its nationals.[8] Spiro (1997) captures it this way:

> Dual nationals represented on the one hand a constant source of international tension where one state attempted to protect its citizen from mistreatment at the hands of another state claiming the same individual as its own. On the other hand, the presumptively divided loyalties of dual nationals represented a potential threat from within the polity in times of international conflict. (Spiro 1997: 1414ff)

Throughout the first half of the twentieth century and well into the 1960s, there continued to be "a widely held opinion that dual nationality [was] an undesirable phenomenon detrimental to both the friendly relations between nations and the well-being of the individuals concerned" (Bar-Yaacov 1961: 4). Not surprisingly, then, this period saw a number of attempts to root out the occurrence of dual nationality by means of multilateral codification of the law on the subject. Among these are the *Harvard Research Draft* (1929), *The Hague Convention* (1930), *The Report of the ILC on Multiple Nationality* (1954), and *The European Convention on the Reduction of Cases of Multiple Nationality* (1963), each of which shared the premise that multiple national allegiances were undesirable and to be eradicated where possible. One example of this: *The Hague Convention* provided in its preamble that "it is in the general interest of the international community to secure that all its members should recognize that every person should have a nationality and should have one nationality."

Yet this resistance to dual nationality has undergone considerable change in the later years of the twentieth century and the move into the twenty-first century. "In today's world, dual citizenship is increasingly common, despite a global legal order nominally hostile to such a status" (Aleinikoff and Klusemeyer 2002: 22). The reality of dual citizenship is the result of various factors, but it is most commonly understood as a result of globalization. Aleinikoff and Klusemeyer (2002: 22) further argue, in their major citizenship research project looking at citizenship policies in an age of migration, that the old stance against dual nationality is no longer appropriate and that dual nationality should be accepted when it is a product of individual choice.

This historical outline shows that while loyalty and allegiance were central to legal understandings of citizenship, highlighted most poignantly in discussions on dual citizenship, the development in international law of nationality has been from more rigid to more flexible forms; and this development has occurred in response to the changing structure of the international political economy.

GLOBALIZATION AND ITS IMPACT ON MEMBERSHIP

Thomas Franck (1996) has written:

> We have entered an era of freely imagined identities, one in which personal choice is no longer circumscribed by accidents or manipulations of genetics, class, place or history.... Increasingly, by national law and international usage, [people] are being freed to design their own identities. (Franck 1996: 383)

Franck proclaims the freedom of individuals to determine their own identities in law. His views are situated in a world in which globalization is a strong force. While the state is still central to international law, it is not the only site of practical importance or meaning when it comes to identity and membership. There are, in fact, and arguably have always been, multiple and shifting forms of identity and membership.[9]

Globalization is a contested term.[10] By globalization I am essentially referring to the continued effect of the internationalization of the world framework. I am not discussing a world without states, but rather states fundamentally altered by the growth and interconnection of relationships between states and individuals around the world. This is not to say that the state is obsolete or that globalization is an entirely new phenomenon. The rapidity of the assault upon the state by the quickening turns of globalization is new, however, and states have sought to steady their state craft. Sovereignty has necessarily been altered without being abolished.[11] States hold their place as key planks in the world system, though they are no longer the only important actors.[12]

This chapter argues that globalization does alter the centrality and significance of national membership (which then has an impact on membership within the nation-state). Indeed, Scholte (2002), in discussing globalization, recognizes:

> Supraterritorial networks have given many people loyalties (for example, along lines of class, gender and transborder ethnicity) that supplement and in some cases override state-centered nationalism. In addition, many people in the contemporary globalizing world have become increasingly ready to give "supraterritorial values" related to, say, human rights and ecological integrity a higher priority than state sovereignty and the associated norm of national self-determination over a territorial homeland. (Scholte 2002: 288)

While it may not be about the demise of the state itself, it is, as Scholte argues,

> the demise of stat*ism* as a mode of regulation. Governance—a collectivity's steering, co-ordination and control mechanisms—now clearly involves much more

than the state. Contemporary governance is multilayered. It includes important local, substate–regional, suprastate–regional, and transworld operations alongside and intertwined with national arrangements. Moreover, governance has in recent decades increasingly worked through private as well as public instruments. In this situation, regulatory authority has become considerably more decentralized and diffuse. (Scholte 2002: 288)

Scholte's approach highlights the newer forms of identity and membership in the international order. But the existence of multiple forms of identity and membership is not new. Individuals have always had and will continue to have a range of forms of identity, within and beyond the nation-state. Australia has a history of this, not just in its multicultural sense of diversity and connections to other nation-states but also in its layered forms of identity seen through the various forms of legal status held throughout Australian history.

LEGAL CITIZENSHIP IN AUSTRALIA

The formal legal status of citizenship in Australia is a recent creation. Until 1949, the formal status of full members of the Australian community was "British subject." The Australian Citizenship Act 1948 (Cth) came into effect on 26 January 1949 and from that moment on Australians were *both* Australian citizens and British subjects. It was not until 1987 that Australians became solely Australian citizens.

The use of the word "citizen" rather than "subject" indicates something about citizenship. "To be a subject is to be subjected to authority—subjected to particular rules, laws and obligations, imposed by the state" (Jayasuriya 1994: 94). In contrast, there is a more democratic foundation to the concept of citizenship—the individual no longer has to be subject to the state; sovereignty lies with the people. Notions of equality and ideas of participation infuse this difference.[13]

But Australians were *both* Australian citizens and British subjects. This dual status until 1987 reflects upon loyalty and allegiance in Australia and shows Australians' ability to cope with varying forms of identity and membership. Australians felt they could and *should* be loyal to both Australia and Britain. In fact, when the Australian Act was introduced and debated in Parliament, there was concern about how it would reflect on Australia's connections to Britain. Helen Irving (2000) notes that "it still comes as a surprise to learn that the Nationality and Citizenship Bill was roundly attacked when it went before the parliament in 1948."

In introducing the bill, Arthur Calwell desired that it be "clearly understood, and this is a point which I cannot too strongly emphasize, that creation of an Australian citizenship under this bill will in no way lessen the advantages and privileges which British subjects who may not be Australian citizens enjoy in Australia."[14] The acting leader of the opposition, Mr Harrison, proclaimed:

> We are essentially British. We take pride in the fact that 96 per cent of our people are of British stock. Why should we be forced, as an essentially British community to tail along with Canada? ... The Government has not obtained a mandate to introduce this new concept of dominion citizenship, and sever the crimson thread of kinship which formerly bound Australia to other parts of the British Empire.[15]

Mr Bowden, member for Gippsland, expressed similar sentiments: "This measure means the breaking up of the British Empire, step by step. I do not believe that Australians as a whole accept this legislation, or that honourable members should acquiesce meekly in it because the present British Government which is making Great Britain a home of socialism, has accepted it."[16]

But the act did much to retain a sense of the "crimson thread of kinship." British subject status, and Australia's connections with Britain, complicated the development of an independent Australian citizenship and an independent loyalty and allegiance to Australia. The legacy of this dual loyalty and commitment is reflected today in various ways—through High Court cases where British subjects have successfully sought to defend deportation,* and in legislation like the *Commonwealth Electoral Act 1918* (Cth), which enables British subjects on the electoral roll before 1984 to remain members of the political community. An ability to have a sense of commitment to more than one nation is therefore part of Australian history and is relevant to the discussion on dual citizenship below. It is also relevant to the development of multicultural policy in Australia—Australia has a precedent of valuing varying forms of connection and commitment.

DUAL CITIZENSHIP IN THE AUSTRALIAN CITIZENSHIP ACT 1948 (Cth)[17]

Since the inception of the *Australian Citizenship Act 1948* (Cth) until 4 April 2002, there was a provision mandating loss of Australian citizenship for a person who acquired a new citizenship. Section 17 of the act ("Loss of citi-

---

*In recent judgments in the High Court it has been determined that British subjects who are not Australian citizens are less likely to be able to defend deportation.

zenship on acquisition of another nationality") stated immediately prior to its repeal:

> (1) A person, being an Australian citizen who has attained the age of 18 years, who does any act or thing: (a) the sole or dominant purpose of which; and (b) the effect of which, is to acquire the nationality or citizenship of a foreign country, shall, upon that acquisition, cease to be an Australian citizen. Subsection (1) does not apply in relation to an act of marriage.[18]

This wording was adopted in 1984. Before that time, the section provided: "An Australian citizen of full capacity,[19] who whilst outside Australia and New Guinea, by some voluntary and formal act, other than marriage, acquires the nationality or citizenship of a country other than Australia, shall thereupon cease to be an Australian citizen."[20] People often lost their Australian citizenship without knowing it. One context where this may have become apparent was when the person applied for an Australian passport.[21]

This approach to dual citizenship in Australian law was consistent with the developments in international law as explained above regarding allegiance and citizenship. If a person had the intention of acquiring a new citizenship, then this represented a break of allegiance with the nation. However, while this may have been the historical basis for the section, it had been questioned in Australian public policy. Dual citizenship was the subject of a 1976 review by the Joint Committee on Foreign Affairs and Defence (1976: 8),[22] and it was also considered in the context of the national consultations on multiculturalism and citizenship conducted by the Department of Immigration and Ethnic Affairs (1982: 28). Then, just prior to the 2002 changes, two further reviews considered the worthiness of s 17,[23] and a related parliamentary review of s 44(i) disqualifying dual citizens from becoming members of Parliament also considered related policy matters (Standing Committee on Legal and Constitutional Affairs 1997).

The debate about the desirability of dual citizenship involved several arguments. At one level there was a basic inequality in the former Australian system. Those people who were born with another citizenship and who also had, or later acquired, Australian citizenship were entitled to dual citizenship. So, for instance, a person born in Switzerland and a citizen of that country, who came to Australia and satisfied the requirements for obtaining Australian citizenship, was not bound in Australian law to give up that Swiss citizenship. This is because, according to international law, it is up to each state to determine under its own law who are its nationals, and Swiss law allowed its citizens to take up new citizenship without giving up their Swiss citizenship.[24] However, once a person was an Australian citizen, he or she could not take up a new citizenship under Australian law. Thus, some people were able to be dual citizens and others were not entitled to this privilege; it depended upon the order of obtaining the citizenship.

The more contentious policy issue that led to resistance to repealing the section and maintaining the status quo revolved around issues of allegiance and loyalty. It was felt that one was necessarily disloyal to Australia in taking up another citizenship. However, both the Joint Standing Committee on Migration and the Australian Citizenship Council were swayed by arguments to the contrary. The Joint Standing Committee on Migration (1994) stated:

> The overwhelming view in submissions was that Australia's insistence on single citizenship for those born in Australia is outmoded and discriminatory. In a world of increasing mobility, it was considered anachronistic that one section of the Australian population should be disadvantaged by a prohibition on accessing more than one citizenship. (1994: 206)

Implicit with this approach is an acceptance of connection to more than one country without undermining a person's connection with Australia. Considering matters such as globalization, the Australian Citizenship Council (2000) stated:

> As we move into the twenty-first century, the prevalence of dual citizenship internationally will rapidly increase. The law and practice of most countries with which Australia likes to compare itself permits citizens of those countries to obtain another citizenship without losing their original citizenship.... These countries simply recognize that they have an internationally mobile population and *that they can retain connection* with this population even if another citizenship is acquired [original emphasis]. (2000: 65)

The terminology of connection to Australia is different from loyalty and commitment. One can have several connections—the question is whether any one connection undermines and detracts from any of the others. Much depends on how one views citizenship and links to the nation-state. If one views it like love in a monogamous marriage, for instance, as a matter of fidelity, then a person should only have one citizenship or one loyalty, as the taking up of another "love" undermines the former. However, if citizenship is like the love from a parent to a child, then there is more ease with the notion of dual or multiple citizenships—parents can have love for more than one child without detracting or undermining each of the children's love and support. The discussion in the Australian Citizenship Council's response to dual citizenship favors a view of multiple citizenships without undermining Australia's claims on its own citizens.

MULTICULTURALISM, LOYALTY, AND ALLEGIANCE

Questions of loyalty and allegiance to Australia also simmer beneath the discussions about multiculturalism. The discussion is framed in terms of a commitment to "Australian values" over "other values." These concerns have recently surfaced with the changes to the Australian Citizenship Act 2007 and with the introduction of formal citizenship testing about Australian values.[25]

In summarizing the Commonwealth government's approach to multicultural policy, the Victorian government's discussion paper on the Multicultural Victoria Act highlighted three aspects of its history. They are useful highlights for reviewing the changes in focus of this policy:

> In 1977, in its report *Australia as a Multicultural Society,* the Australian Ethnic Affairs Council first defined multiculturalism as resting on the principles of social cohesion, equality of opportunity and cultural identity.
>
> In 1989 the then federal government's *National Agenda for a Multicultural Australia* defined the fundamental principles of multiculturalism as based on the right to cultural identity counterbalanced by the obligation to have an overriding and unifying commitment to Australia.
>
> In 2003, the current federal government published *Multicultural Australia: United in Diversity,* which updated its 1999 *New Agenda for Multicultural Australia.* These documents place emphasis on civic duty and the economic benefits of diversity. The 2003 document sets out strategic directions under the headings of community harmony, access and equity and productive diversity. (VOMA 2004: 10)

Through this shorthand summary we see a progression to emphasizing unity over diversity. By 2003, loyalty and commitment should be first and foremost to Australian values. The idea being promoted is that diversity has always been (and should always have been) understood within the context of a primary commitment to Australia. The Australian Citizenship Council's report *Australian Citizenship for a New Century* (2000: 19) included a specific section of its review on "Core civic values and Australian multiculturalism," in which it stated: "Australian multiculturalism has always been based on an understanding that there are certain core values that unite Australians."

Moreover, the report endorsed the National Multicultural Advisory Council's recommendation that support for "core civic values" should be the first of four principles of Australian multiculturalism. This reinforces a belief in a commitment to Australia and Australian values first and foremost—and a loyalty to Australia—before one can accept diversity and the other principles of multiculturalism. This policy reflects a concern that multiculturalism in its fullest, unrestricted sense could mean an abandonment of democratic principles—because other nondemocratic cultures not adhering to the liberal, Western, democratic norms that Australians do could lead to an abandonment of loyalty to Australia as "we" know it.

While there is unquestionable value in a sense of commitment to basic principles for social cohesion, it is my argument that multiculturalism should continue to be embraced in law and policy in the same manner as dual citizenship has been accepted, and the emphasis on unity over diversity is inappropriate. While both are important, it is crucial that multiculturalism continue to accept the duality or multiplicity of individual values and practices. Individuals don't just have one identity. Mainstream Australia accepts this in other contexts. As Galligan and Roberts (2004: 2) note, individuals have a variety of associations—"family, churches, community associations, sporting clubs, pressure groups, trade unions and political parties." My identity, for instance, is influenced by my gender, age, religion, family, and nationality. But in different contexts those identities assume different importance, value, and priority. While Galligan and Roberts argue that citizenship and membership in the political association is different in that political association exercises power over all others, is this necessarily the case in light of globalization, discussed earlier? It depends entirely on context. Moreover, a sense of multiple loyalties has definitely been part of Australian history and sense of political membership, and multiculturalism as a policy has enhanced and promoted a distinctive Australian experience. Certainly, the law has been an important tool for achieving that end.

LEGISLATING MULTICULTURALISM[26]

To date the Australian government has chosen not to legislate a specific act about multiculturalism. That is not to say multicultural principles have been absent from policy underpinning other forms of legislation or absent from law itself. In fact, Laster and Taylor argue that Australian law has incorporated multicultural policy in a discrete and cohesive fashion. In 1995 they argued that "Australian law today reflects a growing acceptance that our society is multicultural and that part of the function of law and legal institutions is to make multicultural social policy work" (Laster and Taylor 1995: 211). They argue there has been a "mosaic of substantive, procedural and cultural changes that are distributed unevenly across the Australian legal system."

In the procedural context there have been advances regarding access and equity and equality before the law. This aspect of multiculturalism and the law was paid significant attention in the Australian Law Reform Commission Report, *Multiculturalism and the Law* (1992). Indeed, the report covered areas such as information and education, interpreters and the legal system, family law, criminal law, and consumer contracts. The results of the report included improvements in the availability of interpreter services and gender and cultural awareness programs for judges, tribunal members, and court staff.

In the administrative field, multicultural policies have been implemented in a range of contexts. For instance, the Department of Immigration and Multicultural Affairs issued *A Good Practice Guide for Culturally Responsive Government Services: Charter of Public Service in a Culturally Diverse Society* (1998). The seven charter principles include access, equity, communication, responsiveness, effectiveness, efficiency, and accountability. Its approach to the diversity of experience also recognizes the intersections of identity. It acknowledges within the group of cultural diversity further differences such as gender, age, disability, and class of which the public service needs to be mindful in its development and application of policy.

Beyond the procedural, administrative context, the influence of a multicultural society on law has also been seen in substantive contexts where the law has been influenced by inequalities in status and power in society in the development of legal principles.[27] Yet the Law Reform Commission, as in later policy statements regarding multiculturalism more generally, acknowledged limits on its practice. It reaffirmed, in order to maintain social cohesion, that certain principles be accepted by Australians. But the report acknowledged something not stressed in the same manner more recently:

> Under Australia's multiculturalism policy, social cohesion depends on common acceptance of principles ... and on the free choice of people to be joined under one government and one law under principles of parliamentary democracy. At the same time, the goal of cohesion should not be used to justify the imposition of values of a dominant group on a minority. Cohesion is better advanced when people have the greatest possible freedom to express individual cultural values in a way which is compatible with respect for the same freedom of others and for common social goals. (1992: [1.23])

Other examples Laster and Taylor use include the Equal Opportunity Legislation of the federal government. This legislation has been amended, however, since Laster and Taylor made their arguments in 1995, and the strength of that legislation may need to be reviewed. Moreover, the federal government's emphasis on the economic value in multiculturalism may have diluted the impact of its policies supporting social harmony. The prevalence of racism, particularly since 9/11, has been of concern for those bodies implementing multicultural policies. The Human Rights and Equal Opportunity Report *Isma–Listen: National Consultations on Eliminating Prejudice Against Arab and Muslim Australians* (2004)[28] highlights the ongoing importance of various strategies the Australian Multicultural Foundation, funded by DIMIA, has had in place since 9/11.[29] The overwhelming message delivered to the Human Rights and Equal Opportunity Commission during its consultations highlights the continued racism within the community.

The Victorian government recently passed the Multicultural Victoria Act 2004, which came into force on 1 January 2005.[30] The philosophy underpinning it is the consolidation of multiculturalism policy and practice in Victoria. Indeed, in the discussion paper distributed in anticipation of the act being introduced into Parliament, the following principles were articulated:

> The Multicultural Victoria Act (MVA) will be an Act of parliament, which will foster a common understanding of the importance of cultural diversity and how it enriches Victoria.
>
> The Act will enshrine a set of principles relating to multiculturalism and a set of clear areas on which the government will report.
>
> It will also bring together and formalise existing Government policies and legislation including the Victorian Multicultural Commission Act.
>
> The Act will not create new "rights" for any Victorian, neither will it create any offences or penalties. (VOMA 2004)

This statement tells us much about the use of law as a tool for promoting policy. Legislation is being used here as a tool for explaining principles the government is seeking to promote. It is an educative tool. Moreover, it is a framework of accountability—for it provides an avenue for government reporting back to the community. Interestingly, however, it is not being used in this instance as a creator of rights or using law as a form of punishment.[31]

Moreover, the report acknowledges cultural diversity as an "asset" of great importance to the future. It acknowledges and affirms that diversity is within a framework of existing core principles—the "Westminster model of responsible government and on English parliamentary traditions and language" (VOMA 2004: 5). Finally, in returning to the role of government, it recognizes that government must in its own thinking and service delivery take into account the diverse nature of its own community (VOMA 2004: 12).

In debating the bill in Parliament, questions about loyalty and allegiance were canvassed. The Member for Shepparton, Mrs Powell (member of the National Party of Australia), read from a letter she had received from one of her constituents who had attended one of the public consultation meetings, held around the state in anticipation of the introduction of the act. Mrs Powell stated:

> He said that 90 per cent of the 100 people at the meeting were ethnic people. He made an interesting point: "It would be interesting to know how many of these ethnic people in attendance were naturalised Australians or if they intend to be naturalised Australians or not, and why should they have a say in our country if they are not naturalised."

Mrs Powell continued: "Not everybody would agree with that, but a number of people did say that if you are not a naturalised person it is very difficult to have a say in the laws of the land because you cannot vote."[32]

The theme underpinning this statement is reflective of the philosophy an act like this is intended to overcome. The word "ethnic" is code for the "other," and the use of the word "naturalized" is expressive of the need for the "other" to become assimilated in order to be seen as part of "us." Multiculturalism, as the act states in the preamble, is about "the freedom and opportunity to preserve and express their [the diverse people of Victoria] cultural heritage." Indeed, those present at that meeting could all have been Australian citizens, and even if they had not been, they may have been living and contributing to the community of which they were a part for many years.

CONCLUSION

Questions of allegiance and loyalty stir profound emotions, and the subject of citizenship is often a passionate aspect of an individual's identity. The 2002 change in the Australian Citizenship Act 1948 (Cth) to allow for dual citizenship followed extensive public consultation and the compilation of several reports. With each cycle, personal responses and examples significantly influenced government policy. Ultimately, the government's decision on dual citizenship reflects shifting attitudes to questions of loyalty and allegiance. Individuals can have more than one connection to a country without undermining their connection to Australia. This is consistent with a globalized world where movements between countries and connections to more than one country are becoming the norm.

So, too, as a matter of recognition of the environment within which Australia exists, multiculturalism has been and should continue to be enshrined and affirmed. Moreover, it is not enough to simply assert that a society is multicultural—the administrative and legal frameworks are powerful tools for ensuring that the practical reality is supported and extended and affirmed in a range of contexts. When this happens, Australian citizenship as a normative notion, expressing a progressive agenda of equality of membership, will be enhanced to become an embedded part of the country's institutional framework.

NOTES

This essay draws from my earlier work, in particular from my book *Australian Citizenship Law in Context* (2002), which looks at the relationship between citizenship law and broader understandings of membership. Sections also draw from my jointly written article, Adler and Rubenstein 2000.

1. Since writing this essay the Australian Citizenship Act 2007 has been passed, repealing the former Australian Citizenship Act 1948, which the 2002 Amendment Act amended. The 2007 Act includes the changes that were made in the 2002 amendment Act regarding dual citizenship

2. The parenthetical abbreviation—(Cth)—is the standard Australian way of citing a Commonwealth or federal parliamentary piece of legislation. As cited later in this chapter, legislation enacted by the parliament of the state of Victoria is indicated by (Vic).

3. This goes back to the period in the 1950s written about by Jordens (1997: 171ff), and then more recently through the Australian Citizenship Council's (2000) work.

4. I discuss the normative notion of citizenship more extensively in Rubenstein 2002.

5. These terms are generally used interchangeably to describe that link, but the word "nationality" is used more in the international context and "citizenship" is the term used in the domestic context.

6. A comprehensive historical study of dual nationality and its legal consequences is found in Spiro 1997. Although his article is written from a North American perspective, it contains much useful material on the history of nationality law in the international context.

7. See *Calvins Case* (1608) 2 St. Trails 559 at 614 and 629, discussed also in Spiro 1997: 1420, and in Wishart 1986: 689.

8. Expressions of the undesirability of dual nationality abound in the United States from the 1850s to the 1950s. See, for example, Spiro 1997: n. 83 (e.g., Wong Kim Ark, 169 US at 729 per Fuller J "double allegiance in the sense of double nationality has no place in our law").

9. I discuss this further in Rubenstein 2006.

10. I have written more about this in Rubenstein 2003.

11. The area in which it clearly is not abolished is that of immigration control. International law reduces state sovereignty in this area in the area of refugee law; however, as Australia is currently showing, this is often resisted in its implemen-

tation by states. Yet this is still an age of migration, requiring us to think about issues such as multiculturalism, which are a consequence of migration.

12. In fact, Paul Kennedy (1994: 134) argues that even if the autonomy and functions of the state have been eroded by transnational trends, no adequate substitute has emerged to replace it as the key unit in responding to global change. See also Hirst and Thompson 1995: 408.

13. There is extensive discussion about the different ways of viewing the concept of citizenship. For a general overview, see Bosniak 2000. In the Australian context, see Thomas 1993.

14. Australia, House of Representatives, *Parliamentary Debates* (30 September 1948): 1062–63.

15. Ibid. (18 November 1948): 3232 (Mr Harrison).

16. Ibid. (25 November 1948): 3569 (Mr Bowden, Gippsland).

17. As stated above n 1, the Australian Citizenship Act 1948 was repealed with the introduction of the Australian Citizenship Act 2007.

18. This section was inserted by Act No 129 of 1984, s 13, commencing on 22 November 1984.

19. The definition of "full capacity" in s 5(3)(b) of the *Australian Citizenship Act 1948* (Cth) was amended in 1973 by Act No 99 to change the age from 21 to 18. This Act commenced on 1 June 1974.

20. This section was repealed by Act No 129 of 1984, s 13, commencing on 22 November 1984. Senator Gietzelt (New South Wales Minister for Veterans' Affairs) stated in *Hansard:* "Clause 13 repeals existing section 17 and substitutes new provisions to the effect a person, being an Australian citizen of 18 years of age, will cease to be an Australian citizen, where an act is committed—whether inside or outside Australia, but other than marriage—specifically for the purpose of acquiring a foreign nationality or citizenship. But where that act was done under duress or unwittingly, clause 17 provides the person may, at the discretion of the Minister, resume Australian citizenship lost under new section 17." See Australia, Senate, *Parliamentary Debates* (4 May 1984), Vol S103: 1571.

21. See Australian Citizenship Council (2000: 60), where it is reported that around six hundred cases of loss of Australian citizenship come to the department's attention each year, often in the context of an individual applying for an Australian passport. The current application for a passport does not have a question about possible loss of Australian citizenship, but in the past the form did have such a question. Given there is no formal procedure of notification between Australia and other countries when a person applies for another citizenship, there is no method for the department to determine that a person has lost their Australian citizenship unless the person informs the department. The Department of Immigration and Multicultural Affairs is currently in discussion with the Department of Foreign Affairs and Trade regarding this matter. See further, Australian Citizenship Council 2000: 65–66.

22. The committee supported the policy that every person should have one nationality only but recognized that the holding of dual nationality by some Aus-

tralian nationals was inevitable given the differences in domestic nationality laws.

23. See Joint Standing Committee on Migration 1994: chap. 6, where it is stated that the issue of dual citizenship attracted most attention throughout the inquiry. See also Australian Citizenship Council 2000: 60–66, where it is stated that nearly three-quarters of the submissions to the council addressed the issue of loss of Australian citizenship upon the acquisition of another. The council sets out in detail many personal comments received regarding the consequences of s 17 (2000: 62–63).

24. This was also consistent with the developing multicultural nature of Australian society.

25. See further http://www.citizenship.gov.au/test/index.htm

26. This chapter does not consider the Constitution and its place in the relationship between law and multiculturalism. Several of the participants in the workshop that preceded this volume (Pettit, Czarnota, Nettheim, Behrendt, Glass, and Levey) made valuable contributions on that topic in a special issue of the *University of New South Wales Law Journal* 24, no. 3 (2001).

27. The case Laster and Taylor use as an example is *Commercial Bank of Australia v Amadio* (1983) 151 CLR 447 (1995: 215–16).

28. The report is available online at: www.hreoc.gov.au/racial_discrimination/isma/index.html.

29. These include the Believing in Harmony Project, the Religion, Cultural Diversity and Social Cohesion in Contemporary Australia project, and action by the Australian Federal Police in better liaising with Muslim communities throughout Australia. For a full list of strategies see: www.hreoc.gov.au/racial_discrimination/isma/strategies/index.html.

30. The Multicultural Victoria Act 2004 was assented to on 14 December 2004 and came into operation on 1 January 2005: section 2.

31. The other pieces of legislation in Victoria that are referred to in the context of formalizing "existing Government policies and legislation" include the Racial and Religious Tolerance Act 2001 (Vic) providing protection against racial and religious vilification. That act uses law as a "creator of rights" and "as a form of punishment."

32. Parliament of Victoria, *Hansard*, Legislative Assembly, Tuesday 30 November 2004: 1834.

Chapter 11

Multiculturalism and Migration Law

Arthur Glass

The multiculturalism of the title of this chapter refers not to the interests and claims of all diverse cultural groups that presently see themselves as distinct from the dominant culture. Multiculturalism has its conventional usage, at least in the Australian context, as a means of identifying the interests and claims of newer immigrant groups, often from non–English-speaking parts of the world, as against older established immigrant groups (primarily from the United Kingdom and Ireland). If further justification is needed for my delimitation of the term, I point to the other part of my title. For migration law is intimately connected to the interests of immigrant groups but not directly to the concerns of other cultural groups.[1]

Just to spell out the more obvious aspects of this connection: Migration policy directly affects the size of different immigrant groups here and ultimately the degree of cultural diversity in Australia. Each year the government decides how many family visas to give along with skilled visas and humanitarian visas. It decides the extent to which local sponsorship (and thus the presence of existing groups here) should play into these other visa types. We are a multicultural society because of our migration policy, and future policy is unlikely to reverse this development, though it may well change our multicultural character by changing the numbers of different groups.

There is more to migration policy than rules about admission. Of significance are also the rules about citizenship. For example, if permanent residents can move from this status to citizenship within two years without facing onerous language tests, then multiculturalism is promoted. And if dual citizenship rules are relaxed, then more permanent residents of diverse backgrounds will take this additional step toward full membership in the political community. Multicultural policy values cultural diversity but also the integration of diverse groups within the larger community.

This integration side of multiculturalism has for many years been a major concern of migration policy. It has been said, "Australian multiculturalism is best understood as an aspect of immigration settlement policy" (Jupp 2002: 93). Language and education programs funded by the Department of Immigration are a central part of this policy.[2]

These links between multiculturalism and migration policy are worthy of discussion, but this is not my topic. For a start it is not migration policy that is my present subject matter but migration law. Of course, much of migration law is simply the legal expression of migration policy. If the government of the day decides to alter our immigrant intake in a particular way, then regulations will be drafted to give this change legal efficacy; but there is more to law, and thus to migration law, than this. I have in mind the legal norms that put limits upon how we should treat people. These norms may be found in the common law, statute law, constitutional law, or international law. Of relevance for this chapter is the norm of equality of treatment under the law—though in the scale of things the values associated with due process are of far more significance for migration law but not for multiculturalism. The advantage of focusing upon migration law rather than migration policy is that we can see just what it is to make a decision about these matters within a well-identified institutional structure.

As I read the philosophical literature on multiculturalism, there are among other matters two linked concerns. What account of multiculturalism properly structures our thinking about the topic? And as the "our" of the previous sentence conceals the very problem of multiculturalism, through what institutions can "we" reach agreement about these matters?[3] While the "we" of multiculturalism may not share the same interests or the same worldview, they share the same nation-state. And as political theorists with an interest in this topic usually write for a North American, European, or Australian audience, the larger questions are, how should multiculturalism be thought of within a liberal state? Can the received ideas of liberalism be rethought in ways that justly deal with multiculturalism?

Perhaps we are no longer all multiculturalists, and possibly some of us are happier to be described as liberals than others. But whatever we call the topic or however we describe our standpoint, we will soon be talking about such values as equality, discrimination, fairness, tolerance, autonomy, mutuality of respect, and cultural diversity.[4] In addition, we will be worrying about the problem of managing multiculturalism—the problem of stabilizing its centrifugal tendencies. This is a familiar way of describing the tensions within multiculturalism.[5] But these tensions should not be seen simply as the pull of values on the one hand and of social facts on the other. For we are not contemplating the value of introducing into Australia a multicultural society; we are in fact such a society. And we are not just dealing with the problem of lack of integration or "balkanization" as a social problem, to be managed along with road accidents. Social cohesiveness may come in different forms (solidarity, patriotism, belongingness) but, speaking generally, it stands for something to be valued in a way that social fragmentation does not.

With the literature on multiculturalism in mind I have picked out two topics from migration law. The first concerns equality of treatment. I ask if our migration law is free of discrimination on the basis of national, religious, or cultural difference, as claimed. The second topic also concerns equality, but equality as the proper acknowledgement of difference. The potentially burdensome nature of general laws upon particular cultural groups is a staple of the literature. The issue of evaluating burdens and respect for different social practices arises in a particular way in refugee law.

The discussion proceeds as follows. I begin by identifying five areas of our migration rules where it might be claimed that these have a discriminatory effect upon different national or cultural groups. In addition, I discuss examples of admissions rules from elsewhere that are designed to favor cultural diversity. The next section sets out the refugee law example. I then discuss some consequences of dealing with these two examples—discriminatory effect and refugee law—as legal problems, rather than problems of everyday politics. What all of this tells us about the politics of multiculturalism is addressed by way of conclusion.

A NONDISCRIMINATORY ADMISSIONS POLICY?

We would do well to remember that the law dealing with admissions is inherently discriminatory. With the national interest in mind, the healthy are favored over the sick, the wealthy over the poor, the more skilled over the less skilled.[5] At times, with no justification other than convenience, men are favored over women.[6] But this is not the kind of discrimination that directly bears upon multicultural interests.

With regard to national and cultural differences, our present admission regulations are proudly neutral (DIAC 2007). Migration law focuses upon individuals and family members, not upon national or ethnic groups.[7] Notoriously in the past it was otherwise. But that time has passed (formally in 1973). Present admission regulations treat each application upon its own merits; there are no quotas or caps based on nationality or other cultural differences. Intention, however, is one thing, effect another. Here follow five examples where arguably our migration law discriminates in ways relevant to different national or cultural groups.[8]

Processing Costs and Times

Nationals from countries in Asia, the Middle East, and South America will have to pay more (in relative terms) for visa processing and wait longer for processing to happen than immigrants from Europe. To take two examples, the application fee for a spouse visa is $1,210 and a typical skilled visa $1,795, amounts of more significance in some countries than others.[9] Further, it takes on average 99 weeks for a spouse visa to be processed in Hanoi compared to 68 weeks in Nairobi and 14 weeks in London. A typical skilled visa takes on average 140 weeks out of Beirut compared to 162 weeks from Hong Kong and 125 weeks from Auckland.[10]

I am told that visas are allocated to areas and posts within these areas in quotas. For administrative reasons each post will have a set number of spouse visas, say, to fill each year. After a post fills its quota, successful applicants must wait for next year's allocation.[11]

Risk Factors–Students and Visitors

Student visas were reorganized in 2001. Different assessment levels, from low risk to extremely high risk, apply to nationals of different countries. The minister specifies the assessment level for particular countries by gazette notice.[12] Most European countries are of low risk, while many Asian or African countries are of high risk. When specifying countries regard must be paid to statistical information based on overstay rates, visa cancellations, unsuccessful applications, the use of fraudulent documents, and change of status applications.[13] The assessment level is used in various ways during processing, most significantly in the evaluation of the financial capacity to meet course fees and living expenses during the time of study. The assessment level will determine whether the applicant must possess funds (prior to entry) for the full period of study and who may be an acceptable owner of the funds, the acceptable source of these funds, and the period of time the source must be in the owner's hands before the application.

A risk factor system has been in place much longer for visitor visas.[14] Applicants who belong to a class of people specified by Gazette notice (determined by nationality, age, and gender) will find it harder to obtain one of these visas. Gazetted class members will have the additional burden of establishing not just that they are genuine visitors but that there is very little likelihood that they will overstay the period of time granted to them in Australia.

There is nothing improper about a concern with compliance or with the bona fides of visa applicants. And any argument about the use of the statistical material would be about its crudity in application, rather than its use at all.[15] Of course this approach visits the sins of prior applicants upon present applicants. But the over- or underreach of legal categories is an everyday aspect of legal regulation.[16] The relevance of the "risk factor system" here concerns neither its fairness nor its efficacy in reducing fraud, but its overall effect upon multiculturalism.

Many people come to Australia each year as visitors or students. While these are temporary visas, there is a well-trodden path from holding these visas to permanent residence and citizenship. This is less the case with visitors where it is a matter of taking advantage of being here and making connections with locals. But for students the government now gives a distinct advantage to those trained here when applying for skilled visas.[17] If certain ethnic or national groups are disadvantaged in obtaining these temporary visas (particularly the student visa), then ultimately this will affect the presence of these groups within Australia. And we are not just thinking about individuals, for the persons who obtain permanent residence will be those soon making use of the family reunion program.

Language Testing

The "dictation test" was a notorious aspect of our immigration system from 1901 to 1958. Immigrants who failed the test were subject to mandatory deportation. The application of the test was a matter of administrative discretion. The type and difficulty of the test was in the hands of an executive officer.[18] Its effect overall was as a deterrent to coming here in the first place rather than as a means of removal (Jupp 2002: 8ff).

We no longer have in place such a blatant discriminatory mechanism, but proficiency in English has become (since 1992) an important part of the skilled migration program. Points are awarded according to different levels of ability, and in addition, having "vocational English" is now a criterion for the skilled visa. One can see the reasons for this, but it gives a distinct advantage to English-speaking groups.

Skills Assessment

With skilled visas the significant question is often whether the applicant meets Australian standards for the nominated occupation. With many professions it is the local association or guild that is delegated the task of establishing these standards.[19] Applicants who have been admitted to equivalent guilds in traditional Commonwealth countries have a decisive advantage with such occupations as accountants, architects, dentists, engineers, IT professionals, medical practitioners, optometrists, pharmacists, physiotherapists, quantity surveyors, and veterinarians.[20] Similar points could be made about the assessment of trade skills (Ireldale and Nivison-Smith 1995).[21]

Family Visas

Australia, along with other similarly placed countries, permits permanent residents to sponsor (or bring with them) family members. The visa criteria and the policy surrounding these are devised with our understanding of families in mind.[22] The family household envisaged by the regulations is a spouse and minor children.[23] And, in accordance with present cultural understandings, family visas (with restrictions) have been "liberalized" so to apply to de facto spouses, homosexual partners, and parents.[24] However, other family arrangements that do not fit into this understanding of family do not come within our regulations—for example, more than one wife,[25] older but still dependent children,[26] and foster children.[27] In addition, such terms of art of the family stream as the "balance of family test"[28] and the "last remaining relative test"[29] favor small families over large families.

These five examples show some degree of different treatment for different groups of people. However, the connection between different treatment and unjustifiable discrimination on the basis of cultural difference is not clear cut. There are at least three complicating matters. First, even if there is unjustifiable discrimination at work, there is no direct connection between this discrimination and processes favoring cultural homogeneity (favoring traditional well-represented immigrant states). For example, any advantages that follow from speaking English will assist not only applicants from the United Kingdom or New Zealand but also those from former colonies such as Hong Kong, Malaysia, Singapore, Sri Lanka, or India. And rules that work to the advantage of small families over large families will advantage Chinese applicants as a group even more than Europeans.

Second, it is not clear just how many people are affected by these discriminations. How many more applicants or particular groups would be successful if we put more resources into particular overseas posts? How many more would be successful if we assessed skill differently? I do not know. But if I had to choose one example that at present clearly has a significant effect upon our multicultural composition, it would be the changes to student visas (the introduction of assessment levels) coupled with the advantage given to persons with Australian tertiary qualifications when applying onshore for permanent residence. These changes affect many people; as of June 2003 there were some 170,000 overseas students in Australia. Whether by accident or design, the student program now favors passport holders from first-world countries. As noted above, this change will influence our migration program for years to come.

Third, it is a matter of argument as to whether these examples demonstrate discriminatory treatment "of a relevant kind." Discrimination, of course, is not simply unequal treatment but unequal treatment for which there is no justification. Each of the five examples will have some justification. The point of the processing system is to have the user pay for some of these costs and to deal with applications as efficiently as resources permit. There will always be delays. Some are caused by the need for more detailed investigation. Different application fees would be a divisive issue. The risk factor systems are said to guard against dishonesty and to be tailored as far as is possible to this task. Language testing and skills assessment are in place to help us select persons of more advantage to our economic or social life, persons who can more easily fit in and who can more quickly find employment here. The family visa rules are to meet the demand that persons given residence should be able to bring family members, within reason. Allowing more children or more wives is not reasonable, and if the rules accommodated these differences it would be difficult to prevent abuse.

So far we have considered admissions law within the framework of anti-discrimination. If the lawmaker is doing something (regulating entrance), it should be done in ways that do not improperly favor one cultural group over another. But if we take multiculturalism seriously—as an approach to social life to be encouraged in Australia—the next step is to ask, should the government take active steps to promote cultural diversity through migration law?

For example, Canadian migration law takes account of Quebec's interest in maintaining its (linguistically based) cultural identity. The national and the provincial government have an agreement under which the basic framework for the selection criteria is set at the national level, but Quebec decides both who among the pool of applicants will be permitted to reside there and, more interestingly, what weight in making this selection should be given to knowledge of French and commitment to residing in Quebec.[30]

More relevant for our purposes is the American experience with "diversity visas." These visas were intended to redress a perceived imbalance between high-admission and low-admission regions and states. This imbalance was said to have been the result of the 1965 changes made to the U.S. immigration policy when it moved from a system of national quotas to a family reunion program based upon nondiscriminatory selection criteria. An unintended effect of this change was that more persons applied after 1965 from Asia, Latin America, and the Caribbean than from Europe. In response to this Congress introduced various programs that were said to promote cultural diversity but in fact favored traditional immigration countries, in particular Ireland, Canada, the United Kingdom, and Poland.

Briefly, it approved an additional ten thousand visas over two years (decided by lottery) for nationals from countries "adversely affected" by the 1965 changes.[31] Basically, these were countries whose rate of immigration "take-up" for the period 1965 to 1985 was lower than for the period 1953 to 1965. Sixteen of the first seventeen countries were European.

In 1988 this program was extended to thirty thousand visas over the following two years, and a further program was introduced to authorize twenty thousand visas for "adversely affected" nationals, nationals from countries that in 1988 used less than 25 percent of the maximum number of visas available to them. In 1990, forty thousand diversity visas were made available to "adversely affected" nationals, and a permanent "diversity visa program" was introduced (commencing in 1994) providing for roughly fifty thousand diversity visas per year for persons from states whose application rate was found (by a complicated formula) to be below traditional admission rates. The program was amended in the late 1990s to make it less favorable toward European nationals. Its justification now rests on the promotion of "new seed" immigration rather than cultural diversity ("new seed" immigrants are persons with no personal connection to America other than an assumed drive to succeed).

In Schuck's (2003: 126) account of these programs, they were not about diversity at all but the "ethnic equivalent of pork barrel politics." Irish interests in particular were favored. For example, in the 1990 changes, 40 percent of the visas were set aside for natives of Ireland (known as "Donnely visas," after the sponsoring Congressman). Further, Northern Ireland was favored as a discrete sending nation, as it was treated separately from the United Kingdom.

Of course, "cultural diversity visas" do not have to be administered in this way, and in as much as the American visas favored established groups already present in large numbers, these visas would be more fittingly named "anti–cultural diversity visas." I recount this tawdry history to remind you of the risks of making cultural diversity an overt goal of an admissions program.

There are various ways in which we could make allowance for the promotion of cultural diversity—through our points system, or preference in processing, or caps on visas, or quotas, or possibly a return to assisted passage. But should we do this? I would take some convincing that groups here (outside of the individual claim to family reunion) have a right to maintain their cultural identity through immigration. But, as I note at the end of the chapter, how is this claim different from claims for subsidies for schools or newspapers or acknowledgment of the need for exemptions from the ordinary law (claims for which I have some sympathy)? And if we find the Quebec example reasonable (as I do), then what difference in principle follows from the diffusion of our cultural groups rather than their concentration within a particular territory?

I do not claim that there is anything obviously sinister for Australian multiculturalism in the present admission rules. But that is the point; discrimination if present is not obvious, and in as much as these matters are concealed within the regulations, Gazette notices, or departmental policy, we are in no position to publicly debate their possible multicultural dimension.

REFUGEE LAW AND EVALUATING
DIFFERENT CULTURAL PRACTICES

How should we judge the social practices of different cultural groups? When should a law of general application take account of these differences? This is a familiar problem for writings on multiculturalism. Examples arise in the areas of marriage and divorce, education, religious observance, employment, and criminal law. This issue also arises in refugee law.

Applicants for refugee visas have to come within the convention definition of refugee.[32] They must possess a well-founded fear of persecution for reasons of race, religion, nationality, membership in a particular social group, or political opinion. The obvious example of "convention-relevant persecution" is where a particular group is picked out because of a preexisting characteristic (race, religion) and denied basic rights. But when does a law or policy that applies to an entire population amount to persecution? What if in Iran the general law imposes severe punishment for adultery on everyone?[33] What if China seeks to promote economic efficiency through a "one-child policy" that takes the form of general laws and policies? What if the standard policy toward women in Pakistan is thought to subject all women there to domestic violence?[34] What were we to make of the conscription policies of the Taliban?[35] The High Court has developed our response to this type of problem over a number of cases. The approach is summarized in the recent case of *Applicant S v Minister* as follows:[36]

> The criteria for the determination of whether a law or policy that results in discriminatory treatment actually amounts to persecution were articulated by McHugh J in *Applicant A*. His Honour said that the question of whether the discriminatory treatment of persons of a particular race, religion, nationality or political persuasion or who are members of a particular social group constitutes persecution for that reason ultimately depends on whether that treatment is "appropriate and adapted to achieving some legitimate object of the country [concerned]."[37] These criteria were accepted in the joint judgment of Gleeson CJ, Gaudron, Gummow and Hayne JJ in *Chen*.[38] As a matter of law to be applied in Australia, they are to be taken as settled. This is what underlay the Court's decision in *Israelian*. Namely, that enforcement of the law of general application in that particular case was appropriate and adapted to achieving a legitimate national objective.

In *Applicant A*, McHugh J went on to say that a legitimate object will ordinarily be an object the pursuit of which is required in order to protect or promote the general welfare of the state and its citizens.[39] His Honor gave the examples that (i) enforcement of a generally applicable criminal law does not ordinarily constitute persecution; and (ii) nor is the enforcement of laws designed to protect the general welfare of the state ordinarily persecutory. Whilst the implementation of these laws may place additional burdens on the members of a particular race, religion or nationality, or social group, the legitimacy of the objects, and the apparent proportionality of the means employed to achieve those objects, are such that the implementation of these laws is not persecutory.

The joint judgment in *Chen* expanded on these criteria:[40]

> Whether the different treatment of different individuals or groups is appropriate and adapted to achieving some legitimate government object *depends* on the different treatment involved and, *ultimately, whether it offends the standards of civil societies which seek to meet the calls of common humanity*. Ordinarily, denial of access to food, shelter, medical treatment and, in the case of children, denial of an opportunity to obtain an education involve such a significant departure from the standards of the civilised world as to constitute persecution. And that is so even if the different treatment involved is undertaken for the purpose of achieving some legitimate national objective. (Emphasis added)

To take the facts of *Chen*, if the one-child policy is implemented through a general program that discriminates against the educational or medical

possibilities of second children ("hei haizi" or "black children"), then the
Australian approach is that these are illegitimate means and thus convention-
related persecution.

The political response to the earlier case of *Applicant A* was extraordinary (see Mathew 2000: 105). The granting of refugee status in the lower
courts to a woman possibly facing a compulsory abortion if she returned
to China was met with a bill that directed that the terms of the convention
would not here extend to a country's fertility control policy (Migration Legislation Amendment Bill [No. 4] 1995). This bill was allowed to lapse after
the High Court ruled against Applicant A.

LAW AS AN EXEMPLAR

When issues of equality and multiculturalism are considered within a legal
context, two matters stand out. First, what are the advantages and disadvantages of resolving these matters by way of courts?[41] Second, what follows from
framing these as legal questions rather than as more general questions?

Courts are potentially effective institutions for discussing and deciding
multicultural issues. They have power. They can provide a remedy denied
by the lawmaker. In addition, they are available at least in principle to all.
They provide a public space for recognizing others, for acknowledging ignorance, for questioning prejudices, and for extending our cultural imagination. Through their decisions in particular cases, courts play an important
role in helping shape our collective identity.[42]

But courts will operate in courtlike ways. As an illustration, let me revisit
the material of part 2 and ask, as things presently stand, *could* our migration
law overtly discriminate on the basis of nationality or ethnicity? Australian
antidiscrimination law operates at the statutory level rather than the constitutional level. This is not to say that there are no present constitutional
limits as to what can be put into migration law, but these apply, if at all, to
the onshore processing and removal of noncitizens—not to the criteria of
their selection.

A general admission policy that discriminated on the basis of nationality or ethnicity would be judged in the light of our Racial Discrimination
Act. Two points can be made about this. First, there is an easy way for the
lawmaker to avoid the force of the Racial Discrimination Act, namely, by
making it clear that the migration rules take precedence over other statute
law (e.g., ss 186, 507 MA).

Second, the lawmaker may avoid the force of the act by formulating its
visa criteria in a particular way. For example, in 1997 the government intro-

duced a limited amnesty by way of a "Resolution of Status" visa available to certain specified passport holders and added that some passport holders had to be here prior to 1991, others 1993.[43] This initiative clearly favored some groups over members of other groups not specified (Filipinos, for example, were not specified), or those with the earlier date (Sri Lankans, for instance). A class action was brought on behalf of these other groups but was unsuccessful. Basically, the Full Federal Court construed the prohibition in s 10 of the Racial Discrimination Act as limited in its terms to discrimination on the basis of national *origin,* as that is what it specifically says, national origin being conceptually distinct from the holding of passports (which indicates not origin but *present* nationality). As it was present nationality and not national origin that the visa criterion picked out, s 10 was not offended. In addition, and less convincingly, it was successfully argued that as understood by the "terms of sensible practical causation," the reason why the visa class favored some groups over others was their different nationality, not the visa provisions. Both of these arguments—the national origins argument and the causation argument—turned on the specific form of s10, as interpreted in previous case law.[44]

But what if we strengthened the protection against discrimination by providing in our Constitution for equal treatment or nondiscrimination on the basis of national and cultural difference? In a few words, this would be highly unlikely to allow a successful challenge against any of the discriminations referred to in the first part of my discussion. There are a number of reasons for this. First, offshore immigrants are not usually thought of as members of our legal community. They would have no remedies here. Second, the central issue for the application of the legal norm of equal treatment is often an argued justification for different treatment. Here the issue is one of proportionality. Has the lawmaker chosen reasonable means to pursue legitimate ends? Review courts do not consider it their role to directly exercise their judgment on these matters. They scrutinize the judgment of the lawmaker or executive. Numerous legal doctrines operate to promote judicial deference on this point—presumptions of validity, margins of appreciation, and so on. The drive against scrutiny is particularly strong in migration law (if North American experience is a guide), for prominence is given in this area to the notion of plenary power.[45] Migration (like state security) is a matter where the starting assumption (and often the conclusion) is that the lawmaker should have a free hand to do what it considers best in the national interest. In migration law in general, and clearly with admission rules, rights provisions are to be applied if at all with a light touch. This result is not simply the product of law's inability to throw off foolish or outdated approaches. Ideas of judicial restraint or plenary power are based upon the concern of an unrepresentative and uninformed institution in a modern democracy.[46]

The awkwardness of courts deciding migration matters where there are potentially large consequences is shown by the refugee example. When we are assessing as a legal issue whether a particular individual might suffer "persecution for convention reasons," then it makes perfect sense to think of the means/ends relationship in the light of Australia's standards of acceptable treatment, or international standards, and not the standards of the home country. But courts are concerned with the applicant before them and not (directly) with the larger context. Government, of course, is concerned with the larger context, in this case the numbers of potential immigrants (and the deterrence of onshore asylum seekers). When courts decide these kinds of issues, this will have consequences that this institution is not in a position to properly assess.[47]

IMPLICATIONS FOR MULTICULTURALISM

Assume, for the sake of argument, that the examples of discriminatory effect and the refugee example, discussed above, have significant consequences (in terms of numbers) for Australia's multicultural character. I have made one point about the discriminatory effect material already. Any discrimination, if present, is buried in the detail of the admissions rules and not easily amenable to public discussion. The government has little interest in raising these matters, and it is hard for a local cultural group to do so. To take the most prominent example, it is the groups of students from non-European countries not here that are affected, not the students already here.

With the examples of discriminatory effect, the appropriate norm— namely, equality of treatment—is not in dispute. What is of concern is whether the interests of an affected cultural group are being properly taken into account. Here a distinction should be drawn between a cultural group's interest in having more of its members admitted into Australia and its interest in being treated by our law with respect. Is it reasonable for a cultural group here to expect our immigration law to work to its advantage? I do not think so. In the interests of cultural diversity, no particular cultural group in Australia has the right to be joined by more of its members. Whatever support the state might give to ensure the continuance of the group here (support for its schools or newspapers or language instruction in its language, etc.), this should be thought of as well short of maintaining the vitality of the group through bringing in more of its members.

What is wrong with discriminatory migration regulations is not that they do not favor particular groups in this way but that they fail to properly "recognize" the worth of an affected group. This is a point of some significance, for without acceptance of the various cultural groups as equal participants in our political processes, we will not have a healthy democracy. The government may well be justified in rejecting a claim of a particular group, but what is important is not just its decision but how it rejects the claim. Does it inform? Does it listen? Does it respond with reasons that can be publicly discussed? I add that at present there is a far more powerful example of lack of recognition in the migration field than failure to openly address possible unfairness in the admission rules. I refer, of course, to the mandatory detention arrangements. These are neutral in design but, as the world has it, have affected different national/cultural groups at different times, Vietnamese (1976), Cambodians (1980), Afghanis (1991), and Iraqis (2001). When the government of the day defends its policy by way of attacking the asylum-seeking group (as terrorists, as health risks, as ungrateful queue jumpers, as inhumane), it has lost interest in any reasoned discussion of these issues.

The refugee example raises the more usual problem for writings on multiculturalism, namely, different cultural/national groups with different understandings as to ends or the appropriateness of the means to these ends. Cases like *Applicant A* or *Chen* pose the question of whether we are keeping two sets of books if we promote sensitivity to cultural difference when the cultural group is within Australia but adopt an approach that appeals to *our* standards when asylum here is sought. But I do not think that the refugee examples disclose the use of double standards, just as one can be sympathetic to claims about dress, holidays, rules about slaughtering animals, and so on, yet oppose the "cultural defense" in criminal law. What holds these various positions together is not a rule to always, or never, stand by our "traditional understandings" (for want of better words). Presumably it is a coherent position to stand for some values even if these emerge from a particular way of life (freedom from persecution, freedom from violence) along with a tolerance in other matters for other ways of life. And this remains a coherent position even if at times the position of just where to stand and when to be tolerant is a matter of argument.

Just as law structures our thinking about the problem, accounts of multiculturalism attempt to do this when these issues arise for philosophical or political debate. But when concrete matters are being discussed, the guidance from this discussion is rather insubstantial. Of course, there is always a gap between theory and practice, between general principles and concrete decisions. But, at least with the examples discussed in this chapter, it is difficult to see just what different accounts of multiculturalism have to offer. Perhaps in this context versions of multiculturalism are better seen as rhetorical exercises that have us treat the *cultural* significance of the problem with more or less weight. When making a judgment about multicultural issues, it is important from where you start. Different accounts of multiculturalism are attempts to have the participants enter the question in one way rather than another. They explain the significance of the issue, the competing values at stake, with more or less sympathy for the group affected.[48] This may help us identify the salient facts, but the material of any decision will be given by the richer social context.

At times debates about multiculturalism raise the issue of how cultural matters might be fairly discussed. Within which institutional arrangements can we reason together about these issues? Through what procedures might a just decision be reached about these matters? At present we have Parliament; and we have executive agencies (Human Rights and Equal Opportunities Commission, Ombudsman) and courts. Parliament is unrepresentative of minority interest, agencies have limited legal power, and, as we saw in part 4, courts have the power but a limited focus. A call is made for new institutions. What would these be like?

Cultural groups have a vital interest in migration law. But they cannot reasonably expect this law to reflect their interest in cultural preservation. However, in any allocation of visas, or decision-making about visas, they can expect to be treated with even-handedness and with respect (individually and as a group) by lawmakers, executive officers, and courts. Where the migration rules work against this, this should be a matter for reasoned public debate. Sadly, the public arena in contemporary Australia is at present not a place where this is likely to occur.

NOTES

1. This is not to say that other cultural groups have no legitimate interest in migration policy. Indigenous interests are not obviously or immediately served by a migration program that brings to Australia groups in large numbers who feel no responsibility for Australia's past dealings with them. And other cultural groups will oppose perceived discriminations within the rules.
2. The federal government's immigration department has changed rubrics and scope a number of times in recent years, including the Department of Immigration and Multicultural and Indigenous Affairs (DIMIA), the Department of Immigration and Multicultural Affairs (DIMA), and, as of early 2007, the Department of Immigration and Citizenship (DIAC). References to the department and its policies in this chapter refer to all these incarnations.

3. Or at least have confidence in the legitimacy of any decision.
4. Notably the vocabulary of liberalism; but, as is often pointed out, one has to start from somewhere.
5. Section 4 of the Migration Act reaffirms that the national interest is the primary goal.
6. See the definition of "usual occupation," reg. 2.26 in the Migration Regulations 1994 (MR). If you have not been in paid employment for at least six months in the two years prior to the visa application, then you are treated as having no occupation.
7. One qualification concerns the humanitarian program. Circumstances may dictate the creation of a particular visa class for a particular group: the Kosovar Safe Haven visa (subclass 448) or the Citizens of the Former Yugoslavia (Displaced Persons) visa (subclass 209), for instance. And settling the figures for the intake of refugees each year calls for decisions about which countries, or continents, the refugees should come from. Decisions about settlement—about how well groups from the past have been absorbed—may well disclose discriminatory attitudes. An example is immigration minister Kevin Andrews's recent reduction of places for African refugees, because, as he put it, of "their problems in adjusting to the Australian way of life". See: www.abc.net.au/news/stories/2007/10/03/2050091.htm.
8. The points are made in general terms, although some may feel that even this is more than they need to know.
9. And added to this will be the far greater costs of health assessment, assurance of support, and possibly skills assessment and English language assessment.
10. This is a comparison of the granting of the spouse visa (subclass 309) and the Independent Skilled visa (subclass 136) as set out in the Abridged Guide to Visa Grant Times issued by the department, March 2004.
11. Though there is some possibility of readjustment to the quota at the end of the year.
12. Presently IMMI 07/014 of 13 April 2007. There are five kinds of student visas, and the assessment level for different countries is not the same for each visa.
13. MR regs. 1.03, 1.40, 1.41, 1.42.
14. Clause 4011 of Schedule 4, MR. Classes are specified with regard to overstay rates. This system can also be triggered by the applicant's unsatisfactory immigration history.
15. For an unsuccessful challenge to the "proportionality" of the regulations (the relationship of means to ends), see *Rahman v Minister* [2001] FCA 1236 (6 September 2001). The regard paid to "unsuccessful applications" in the national statistics on student visas is specifically criticized. For what is measured is the number of ill-prepared applications per country, or the department's attitude toward the applications, rather than the behavior of the applicants themselves. There are, for example, many ill-prepared applications from Chinese students.
16. This is not to say it is simply to be accepted. Much of judicial review (both administrative review and constitutional review) is concerned with ruling upon these types of arguments.

17. There are a limited number of places in the skilled program, and preference is given to successful onshore students over offshore applicants. In recent years the onshore applications for certain types of skilled visas have exceeded the quota. Onshore applicants are also favored through the waiver of the requirement for work experience (of between twenty-four and thirty-six months) if they apply within six months of completing their studies.
18. But see *R v Wilson ex parte Kisch* (1934) 52 CLR 234.
19. Through the interaction of regulations and department policy.
20. See the Procedures Advice Manual relevant to Schedule 6 MR: skills assessment.
21. R Ireldale and Nivison-Smith, *Immigrant's Experiences of Qualifications and Employment* Canberra AGPS 1995. For the skilled visas in place at present, see the assessing authorities specified in IMMI 07/058 of 28 August 2007.
22. For some discussion of this issue, see Carens 2003: 95, 98.
23. It is a little more complicated as members of the family unit can in some circumstances include other dependent relatives.
24. Parent visas have had a sorry history over the last few years. At present there is a capped visa (at 1,500) with a queue some fifteen years long and a contributory parent visa (4,000 at $60,000 each), which to date has not proved popular.
25. Apparently once acknowledged in French immigration law, but no longer.
26. Basically excluded are children over age twenty-five, or over eighteen but engaged or married, not in full-time study, or not reliant on the parent for their basic needs. See MR 1.03.
27. Children who are not natural children, stepchildren or adopted though in the care of the sponsor.
28. An applicant for an aged parent visa needs to establish basically that the number of children resident in Australia is greater than or equal to the number of other children. See MR 1.05.
29. MR 1.15. Basically, applicants must be the last relative of the immediate family outside Australia.
30. For a summary of these arrangements within the context of multiculturalism policy, see Shachar 2001: 151ff.
31. This is drawn from Schuck 2003: chap. 4.
32. United Nations Convention relating to the Status of Refuges 1951, as amended by the Protocol relating to the Status of Refugees 1967.
33. *Z v Minister* (1998) 90 FCR 51.
34. *Minister v Khawar* (2002) 210 CLR 1.
35. The factual context of *Applicant S v Minister,* cited below.
36. 206 ALR 242 (2004). The extract is from the judgment of Gleeson CJ, Gummow and Kirby JJ, 253f.
37. *Applicant A* (1997) 190 CLR 225, 258.
38. (2000) 201 CLR 293, 303.
39. (1997) 190 CLR 225, 258.
40. (2000) 201 CLR 293, 303.

41. Of course, there are other legal institutions apart from courts that might deal with complaints about discrimination–Ombudsman, Human Rights Commissions, and so on. These have their own advantages and disadvantages. The main advantage of courts is that they can grant an immediate remedy.

42. For discussion of these possibilities, see, for example, the writings of James Boyd White.

43. Subclass 850, 851, MR.

44. *Macabenta v Minister* (1998) 154 ALR 591. See also *Sahak v Minister* (2002) FCAFC (18 July 2002).

45. That on this issue the people should be left free to rule themselves through their representatives.

46. Uninformed, that is, about matters other than law.

47. Insufficient democratic warrant, insufficient knowledge. For a much-used discussion of this problem, see Arthur 1991: 90.

48. Thus, it is important to show respect for the group for reasons of personal identity (Taylor 1992) or the eventual integration of cultural groups (Kymlicka 1995) or the health of public discourse (Benhabib 2002). Alternatively, there is also the importance of cultural diversity as a source of cultural or economic creativity.

Part IV

Australian Multiculturalism

Success or Failure?

Chapter 12

Multiculturalism, National Identity, and Pluralist Democracy

The Australian Variant

Brian Galligan and Winsome Roberts

Australia is commonly called a multicultural society, and this description has been endorsed in official statements of national identity and citizenship. But what sort of multiculturalism does Australia have? And how does this fit with its national identity and strong pluralist democracy? Answering these questions is important for self-understanding as well as comparative analysis, and is the focus of our chapter. Most of our attention is directed toward Australian multiculturalism, examining its character and responding to critics of our recent account in *Australian Citizenship* (Galligan and Roberts 2004). We begin by locating Australia within the current broader theoretical and comparative approach to multiculturalism.

Australia has shared in the multicultural wave that has swept Western liberal democracies in the last three decades. Our concern, however, is with only one of the four major trends identified by Will Kymlicka (2005) as making up the liberal multiculturalism agenda—that is, with the integration of immigrant groups. Kymlicka's other three categories of concern are minority nationalisms that are geographically concentrated, as in Britain, Canada, Spain, or Belgium; "metics" or permanent residents who have been denied citizenship, such as the Turks in Germany or Kosavars in Switzerland; and indigenous peoples. While Australia clearly has indigenous people and indigenous policies have changed markedly, in part recognizing and encouraging cultural difference that parallel changes in postimmigration policy for those from culturally different backgrounds, indigenous people are unique and indigenous policies are on a distinctive plane (Chesterman and Galligan 1997). Aboriginal people have been a dispossessed rather than an immigrant people, and they make legitimate claims to uniqueness as the original inhabitants of the land. Regarding the integration of immigrants, Australia, along with the United States, Canada, and New Zealand, is one of the traditional "countries of immigration" in the West that have encouraged large numbers of immigrants to settle and become citizens after satisfying minimal conditions. As Kymlicka (2005: 25–26) puts it, these countries have undergone "a dramatic change" from assimilation to multiculturalism, moving to race-neutral criteria for admission and adopting "a more 'multicultural' conception of integration" for immigrants. Understanding Australia's variant of this key part of the multicultural agenda is our purpose here.

MULTICULTURALISM CONTESTED

Multiculturalism is strongly defended by its proponents as ideological orthodoxy and a fair description of what we actually have in Australia. In this chapter we examine whether Australia is a multicultural society, and if so in what sense. We show that Australia's version of multiculturalism has worked reasonably well as a humane policy for softening the integration of immigrants from non–English-speaking backgrounds. It has a welfare purpose of assisting those who are disadvantaged by their cultural background, and a liberal pluralist purpose of respecting and encouraging cultural diversity. If that were all, it might be celebrated as a complement to large-scale immigration, and an improvement on the less sensitive assimilation thrust of Australia's policy in the immediate postwar years. Multiculturalism has been contentious, however, because of the larger claims that its proponents have made about what Australia is, or should become, as a nation and a people.

The national debate moved beyond multiculturalism, after the damning Fitzgerald report (Committee to Advise on Australia's Immigration Policies 1988) and the reassertions of rather different versions of Australian nationalism by prime ministers Keating and Hawke in the 1990s. But vestiges remain in formal discourse, often in awkward juxtaposition with nationalist and pluralist affirmations: for example, in the Howard government's policy *Multicultural Australia: United in Diversity* that affirms "The Government is committed to Multicultural Australia, with policies and programs that unite us as Australians working to advance Australia fair" (Commonwealth of Australia 2003: 5). Howard himself, who rejected multiculturalism in the past and balked at even using the word when he first came to office in 1996, adopted a more relaxed attitude. He endorsed the policy for "nurturing our inclusive society with its proud record of community harmony" and as a way of encouraging "[a]ll Australians, regardless of their ethnic, cultural or religious background ... to participate fully in the wider Australian community to show a commitment to our nation, its democratic institutions and its laws" (Commonwealth of Australia 2003: 1). While some of the key architects of the policy, such as Jerzy Zubrzycki (1995) and Sir James Gobbo (1995), think the term has served its purpose and should be dropped from public usage, others, like James Jupp in this volume, remain fierce proponents. Multiculturalism has been a prism through which Australians have tried to understand their changing postwar nation and society, and a language that some, mainly in high places, have used to encapsulate the Australia that they see or would like to see.

In evaluating Australian multiculturalism we need to take account of dual aspects: on the one hand, multiculturalism policy as a practical, humane, and sensitive way of accommodating immigrants from non–English-speaking backgrounds, and on the other hand, multiculturalism as a prescription for changing Australian identity and citizenship. Having the same name for these two quite different things has been part of the problem. One alternative is to stop calling the former multiculturalism at all and recognize it as a sensible set of policies to assist integration and pluralism. Alternatively, if people think that would negate public usage over the last couple of decades and overlook the elements of policy that support cultural pluralism, we might call it "transitional multiculturalism." Transitional multiculturalism means the set of policies, part welfare and part cultural sensitivity and tolerance for difference, that assist in the humane and gradual integration of immigrants from different cultural backgrounds into the mainstream national culture. The main purpose of such a policy is not to create lasting enclaves of ethnoculturally distinct peoples—literally many cultures—or to change national identity and aspirations for such a thing. This alternative strong form of multiculturalism—making a nation of many cultures—might best be termed "national multiculturalism." Despite the advocacy of some, Australia has eschewed such national multiculturalism, which, in any case, was never a real option given the strength of integrationist forces and popular distaste for such an unlikely alternative.

But the Australian story is not as simple as that: transitional multiculturalism winning, and national multiculturalism losing. Multiculturalism discourse permeated the elite political and bureaucratic echelons of the state and became the language of official discourse for a couple of decades from the mid-1970s to the mid-1990s. In doing so it filled a void that had been left from abandoning old forms, also inadequate, of representing Australians as homogeneous, transplanted Britons (Hancock 1961). In absorbing the large postwar migration from Continental European countries, and the growing migration of people from Asian countries beginning in the 1970s, Australia was becoming more diversified and pluralistic. While that was well recognized, even earlier on by the architects and proponents of the large postwar migration, there was no appropriate official language developed to encapsulate it. With revisionists loudly denouncing the leaders of diversified postwar migration, Calwell, Holt, and Menzies as assimilationist, racist, and Anglocentric—all of which were partly true—political leaders and state officials in the 1970s quietly abandoned traditional accounts of Australian identity, the good with the bad, or the good because it was tainted by the bad.

Instead, they turned to multiculturalism. Although it was being advocated by a tiny elite (Lopez 2000), the language of multiculturalism was picked up in the formal language of national identity and citizenship. Of course, multiculturalism had to be modified because it was contrary to the Australian tradition; it did not describe Australia's unique history and practice, and it was uncongenial to most of its people. The public face of this was an anodyne form of multiculturalism defined mainly in terms of tolerance for difference and basic liberal democratic values from which were spun thin forms of citizenship and national identity. Multiculturalism invaded the formal language of the Australian state, where residuals still survive, and hampered the development of a fuller account of nationality and citizenship. We need to untangle the conceptual muddle about Australian multiculturalism and be clear about what it is in order to give accurate accounts both of Australia's continuing integration of migrants from diverse cultural backgrounds and of Australian national identity and citizenship. This is necessary for self-understanding, and for informing those from other countries who are concerned with integrating diverse migrant peoples and accommodating those from different cultures.

INTEGRATION AND PLURALISM

The first point that needs emphasis is that integration and pluralism are the hallmarks of Australia's policy, both in intention and outcome. Except for special categories, such as refugees, immigrants are now chosen on the basis of their skills and the contribution they make to an advanced market economy. Such immigrants obviously have a high integration facility. Otherwise, the policy is "color blind" or unconcerned with cultural background. Typical, and chosen to highlight the fact, was Australia's six millionth postwar immigrant who arrived in 2002. She was Ms Christine Jurado, a qualified computer systems analyst who came from the Philippines with her husband Karla, a production engineer, and their two children. Both are fluent in English and were among the 45,000 skilled migrants who made up 42 percent of the national intake in that year. Such people bring not only productive skills but also cultural richness and language proficiency from their native countries. This does not create multiple cultures in Australia but contributes to national diversity and cultural pluralism. The Jurado children will be educated in English-speaking schools and, on recent trends, probably do better than average. There is a good chance that they will marry non-Filipinos, and even if they don't, there is an even stronger likelihood that their children will. In short, the Jurados and immigrants like them become well integrated, without pressure for them to do so, and enrich Australia culturally as well as economically.

The immediate postwar migration was different in composition, bringing in larger numbers of nonqualified Europeans, and in its purpose, which was to "populate or perish" after the scare of facing Japanese invasion in World War II with only seven million people scattered over a huge continent. There was a preference for British immigrants expressed in the slogan "Bring out a Briton," and in the provision of generous paid passages. The millionth postwar immigrant happened to be Mrs Barbara Porritt, who arrived with her husband from Yorkshire, England, in 1955. Her arrival was the occasion for publicizing the success of the program in bringing out a million people in ten years, half of whom were British, rather than for the skills she and her husband might have brought. The other half of the early postwar immigrants were Continental European, from Central Europe and often people displaced by Hitler's war, and southern Europe, especially from Italy, Greece, and Malta. Many were poor, with low skill levels and no English, and they provided much of the manpower for postwar reconstruction and expansion of infrastructure and manufacturing. It is this large non-British part of the postwar migration that is relevant in considering multiculturalism.

Government policy at the time strongly favored assimilation. According to notable critics Zappalà and Castles (2000: 189), "Until the 1960s, official policy was to base national identity on British heritage and to deal with diversity through assimilation." Such assimilation, according to them, meant that "immigrants are incorporated into society through a one-sided process of adaptation: immigrants are expected to give up their distinctive linguistic, cultural, or social characteristics and become indistinguishable from the majority population." The reason for pushing assimilation was quick incorporation into Australian society to ensure equality of treatment and citizenship for new Australians. No doubt cultural chauvinism played a part in this settler society, although it was often pompous British envoys such as

Governor-General Sir William Slim who, in 1955, insisted that "at least until a few years ago, Australians were a more purely British stock than the people of the United Kingdom" (quoted in Galligan and Roberts 2004: 62). The Australian leaders of the day were rather more sensitive and perceptive, insisting that Australian culture was distinctive despite its British origins. They also anticipated that Australian culture and identity would be changed, and for the better, by this infusion of peoples from diverse cultures. This has not been recognized by critics but is well documented in our book so needs only brief illustration here.

Addressing the 1951 Jubilee Citizenship Convention, Governor-General William McKell, previously a Labor premier of New South Wales, recognized that "a wise handling of assimilation" of immigrants would be "a two-way process" of "mutual enrichment." One would involve immigrants adapting to Australia's "distinctive culture and way of life" and conforming to "our standards of citizenship." The other would be immigrants adding "their own contribution" of cultural enrichment: "For the migrants are bringing to Australia not only the benefits of their knowledge and skills, but of their age-old cultures. The old and new should blend into a better and more varied community of people." Chairman of the Australian Broadcast Commission at the time, Richard Boyer attended the annual Citizenship Conventions and in 1954 urged migrants "to catch the spirit of this country" but "never lose the warm spot in your heart for the land of your origin and the people of your past." He insisted, "You can have many loyalties," and urged them to keep their original names even if they sounded strange to Australian ears—his was originally French. Liberal prime minister Menzies recognized and saluted the change in addressing the 1963 convention in a speech titled "We Are a Changing Community." "So year by year, decade by decade," he said, Australia "has become a remarkably new community." Identifying himself as one of the "old brigade," Menzies said: "We must realise that, although some of us as individuals may not have changed very much, Australia as a community is experiencing a sea change into something rich and strange." Speaking to the same conference, and now leader of the Opposition, Arthur Calwell was rather more blunt: this country "needed a biological infusion," he said, "we were becoming a little too inbred." This is hardly the one-sided assimilation that critics denounce, but rather early recognition of integration and pluralism that characterize Australia's postwar immigration program (from Galligan and Roberts 2004: 60, 61, 64).

Curiously, if we put aside the bluster sparked by our treatment of multiculturalism in *Australian Citizenship* (2004), Jupp's own account of Australian multiculturalism is one of integration and pluralism. In his chapter in this volume, Jupp notes that Australian multiculturalism is essentially "pragmatic"; that immigrants are "carefully chosen with a view to their effective integration into society"; that, compared to Canada, there is "much less emphasis on cultural and ethnic group maintenance"; that English teaching remains "the largest expenditure that might be termed 'multicultural'"; that a touching manifestation is a Parramatta choir singing "Waltzing Matilda" in Maltese; and that people are allowed "to assimilate at their own pace, or not at all if they choose to isolate themselves and damage their future and that of their children." Most of the elements of the Australian story on multiculturalism are here: the primary emphasis on integration in our immigration policy, teaching English to enable immigrants from non–English-speaking backgrounds to facilitate their integration into society and the job market, allowing people to *assimilate* at their own pace, and all of this capped by modest support for cultural maintenance manifest in a Parramatta choir singing a quintessentially Australian national song in Maltese. These are all accurate representations of what we have in Australia and are more or less the same as what we have said—perhaps without being quite so blunt about assimilation. If we must use the term at all, this is multiculturalism of the transitional kind: assisting integration and not promoting distinct immigrant cultures that endure beyond the immigrant generation, and not having government policies directed at fostering distinct cultures. Except for the multicultural name that Jupp insists upon, this is integration and pluralism at its most obvious.

NATIONAL IDENTITY AND PLURALIST DEMOCRACY

It seems that proponents of multiculturalism are not so much opposed to our account of multiculturalism as to our claim that Australia has a national identity that is not multicultural. We spent much of a longish book establishing the complex and rich character of Australian identity—its multilayered building up over generations from an Anglo-Celtic base but infused with many immigrants from diverse cultures, its diffuse elements of natural, built, and cultural environment, its unique history and literature, with its own stories, symbols, and politics, incorporating the indigenous heritage that is being revived in art forms. Rather than entering the arid debates about defining "Australianness" in terms of national peculiarities, we see national identity as a rich and complex entity in which individual and group histories have been melded into something larger and shared in a unique continent with its own distinctive character and style. A shared "community of experience," as David Malouf calls it, underpins the community of political association in the Australian nation state.

Australian national identity is best captured in Australian literature and art, and none more eloquently than in Malouf's "Identity as Lived Experience: Uniquely Australian" (1994):

> Our common response to place, to land and landscape in all its diverse forms over the continent, to the events we call history, to the institutions that determine our relations with one another and through which we try to make a good and just society, to all we have added, over the 200 years of our being here, to the local scene: towns and cities, forms of domestic architecture, which also vary across the country, the trees and plants and animals we have introduced, along with the problems they have created, and all we have made, artefacts, tools, playthings, including works of art, to embellish mere living with the amenities of life. The things too, some of them intangible, that we found here when we came; which come out of the lives of indigenous people of the place and enrich us with views of the lives of the world that we would not have access to if we lived elsewhere.

And all of this expressed through English or "our local variety of it—in which what we experience is given shape and communicated and whose peculiar habits not only give form to that experience but determine what it will be" (Malouf 1994: 148).

Australian national identity is complex but real, with many diverse but identifiable components. Formal accounts of who we are as a nation and as citizens should be based on positive affirmations of this national identity, not on hollow affirmations of being a "Multicultural Australia: United in Diversity," as the current government slogan would have it. What we have is far too strong and distinctive to be rebadged or made over as multiculturalism. Proponents of multiculturalism such as Jupp seem to choke on national identity, which they caricature as some sort of narrow and conservative nostalgia for a mythic outback. Jupp (in this volume) opines, "it is hard to see the heirs of Shakespeare, Dante, Plato, Buddha, Muhammad, or Confucius being very impressed by Steele Rudd or the dog on the tucker box." Quite so, but instead of discarding "dog on the tucker box" caricatures for a more mature account of our complex society and national character, critics such as Jupp plump for multiculturalism, which they define in mainly liberal pluralist values to give it some plausibility. This blurring of meaning—mixing up multiculturalism with pluralist democratic values—is evident in the official reworking of multicultural rhetoric, as we shall see in the next section, and most blatant in Jupp's own case. In the last paragraph of his chapter, he lists the attributes of Australia "as a pluralist democracy"—it "does not impose a national culture"; there is no established religion; citizens have freedom of movement; schools "teach a variety of beliefs and values." These are indeed notable features of Australia and of pluralist democracy, which is hardly surprising because Australia is a pluralist democracy. But then he concludes: "This is what a multicultural society looks like." This is the case only if we redefine multiculturalism as pluralist democracy, but that perpetuates confusion and divorces accounts of nationality and citizenship from their base in the reality and lived experience of Australians.

EMBRACING MULTICULTURALISM

The same sort of blurring of pluralist democracy with multiculturalism has been evident in official discourse about Australian identity and citizenship. In proclaiming multiculturalism as an official description of what Australia was, or should become, official bodies fell back upon basic institutions and values of pluralist democracy to give this new mantra some plausible content in the Australian context. This is evident from a brief sampling of the development of multiculturalism as state policy.[1]

Futuristic and prescriptive overstatement was evident from the beginning. When Al Grassby, the colorful minister for immigration in the Whitlam Labor government, launched the multiculturalism program to address social and economic disadvantage of immigrants from non–English-speaking backgrounds in 1973, he used the ambitious title "A Multi-Cultural Society for the Future." Grassby (1973) borrowed the notion from Canada, where Pierre Trudeau had used it in 1971 in responding to the recommendations of the Royal Commission on Bilingualism and Biculturalism for addressing the English-French division in Canada. Trudeau's strategy was a dual one: official bilingualism to give equal status to French as a national language in order to accommodate Francophone Quebec, while the same time diffusing this main division in Canadian politics by recognizing all the other immigrant groups—hence multiculturalism. Grassby picked up the latter part of Trudeau's strategy. Because Australia did not have to deal with two deeply entrenched different national cultures, however, multiculturalism would never have much the same traction here.

Nevertheless, recognizing different cultural identities became a central plank of Australian multiculturalism that was packaged with pluralist democratic values and welfare concerns. Professor Jerzy Zubrzycki, a Polish immigrant and sociologist at the Australian National University, became the intellectual guru of this blended variant in government advisory committees and councils. Reflecting back on the evolution of multiculturalism in Australia, Zubrzycki (1995) claimed that the reports and recommendations to government from these advisory bodies provided "a coherent philosophical basis for the management of ethnic diversity." As chair of the Australian Ethnic Affairs Council advising the minister for immigration, he provided a blueprint for *Australia as a Multicultural Society* in the 1977 report. This was "the first formal definition of multiculturalism" that was said to entail social cohesion and equality of opportunity as well as cultural identity. Zubrzycki's ideas were taken up in the 1978 Galbally report on *Migrant Services and Programs* (Galbally 1978) that was instrumental in transmitting multiculturalism into policy practice. It championed multiculturalism as cultural maintenance, along with equal opportunity and access to programs and services designed in consultation with clients.

These ideas were taken up by the Fraser Liberal coalition government that was more sensitive to immigration and the ethnic lobby than the Whitlam Labor government had been, and reconstituted a separate Department of Immigration to which it added Ethnic Affairs, and commissioned the Galbally review. Fraser himself embraced pragmatic multiculturalism not as "an abstract or alien notion" but "a set of guidelines for action" and set up the Institute of Multicultural Affairs in 1981. Zubrzycki was more ambitious in the 1982 Ethnic Affairs task force that proposed *Multiculturalism for All Australians* and purported to give "the philosophical foundation for multiculturalism as an ideology." Zubrzycki and his band of ideologues went whole hog in advocating multiculturalism both as a set of pragmatic social support programs and arrangements and "a culturally diverse society." This was "a model to be worked for—a vision for the future": "multiculturalism should not just mean majority group assistance for minority cultural groups, but rather should be a way of perceiving Australian society as a whole." The Department of Immigration and Ethnic Affairs followed suit in a 1982 report that embraced multiculturalism as a visionary model for, and a way of perceiving, Australian society and citizenship. According to the department: "*Multiculturalism for All Australians* is not a survey of current social arrangements, but a model to be worked towards—a vision for the future ... a way of perceiving Australian society as a whole" (Department of Immigration and Ethnic Affairs 1982: 2) This was the high point in multiculturalism as a model for Australian society and citizenship.

BEYOND MULTICULTURALISM

Politics and national identity are contested fields, and multiculturalism never commanded the heights for long. It had always been a top-down policy devised by a small group of elites and taken up by senior politicians and public servants and used typically in restrictive ethnic forums and official pronouncements. Nevertheless, this began to generate a backlash that was picked up and publicized by the 1988 report of the Fitzgerald committee appointed to advise on Australia's immigration policy (Committee to Advise on Australia's Immigration Policies 1988). Dr Stephen Fitzgerald was a leading Asian scholar, and the committee's terms of reference were to investigate the current state of and future directions for immigration policy. It reviewed multiculturalism because that had become the domestic face of immigration policy and, according to Fitzgerald, was so unpopular that it was in danger of derailing immigration policy.

Fitzgerald called for renewed commitment to immigration with a strongly nationalist philosophy in which "emphasis is given to Australia, the Australian identity and commitment to Australia." The committee traveled around Australia and found widespread popular opposition to multiculturalism, which had come to be seen as "something for immigrants and ethnic communities only, and not for the whole of Australia." Aboriginals did not want to identify with it, and many older generation Australians believed it had nothing to do with them. They found "community suspicion of multiculturalism" that was widespread across the political spectrum, "from traditional Labor voters to traditional Liberal and National voters, from trade unionists to business people, from blue collar workers to academics, and from older generation to newly arrived Australians." The term itself had become contentious with many definitions forced upon it by both exponents and opponents: its "laudable original intentions have become obscured" (Committee to Advise on Australia's Immigration Policies 1988: 10–11). Fitzgerald recognized that multiculturalism provided important support for immigrants but was not a concept with which many could identify. Moreover, it was becoming a negative factor with people taking some of the utterances about a model for Australian society to imply "an intention by government to use immigration as some form of social engineering to achieve racial diversification in Australia" (Committee to Advise on Australia's Immigration Policies 1988: 58). Fitzgerald called for dissociating multiculturalism from immigration and national identity.

The Fitzgerald report added substantially to the public debate over multiculturalism that had erupted in the federal Parliament earlier in the same year. Prominent Melbourne historian Geoffrey Blainey had been criticizing multiculturalism since the early 1980s, and his comments that it was a dangerous and misleading slogan sparked a Labor motion affirming Parliament's commitment "to the establishment of a multicultural society in Australia." This was carried without dissension but was rejected by Blainey as a mindless response and a sham by politicians playing to the ethnic lobbies. The issue remained a live one because John Howard, as leader of the

Liberal coalition opposition, took up the fight against multiculturalism that
he called "a confusing, even aimless concept" and a "divisive policy." Howard had multiculturalism jettisoned from Liberal Party policy statements in
favor of "One Australia—From Many Cultures and Many Nations." However, he lost the 1990 election, and the leadership of the Liberal Party, in
the view of some because his attack on multiculturalism had backfired and
he had gone too far the other way in advocating a traditional Australia. As
prime minister from 1996 until late 2007, however, Howard would have the
leading say in reshaping national discourse around traditional Australian
symbols and values to his liking. Prime Minister Howard was uneasy about
multiculturalism until its thorough reworking as pluralist democracy by the
National Multicultural Advisory Council in 1999. Howard launched this
report, which affirmed Australia as "a pluralist democracy." Australian multiculturalism was built on values of Australian democracy and citizenship, it
said. Its core values were diversity, valued as a cultural, social, and economic
resource, tolerance, and a commitment to freedom and equal opportunity—
even Howard's favorites, mateship and a fair go, were incorporated in the
revised version of the report (NMAC 1999: 41–412). All of this was within a
united and harmonious Australia built upon democratic foundations.

In the interim between Howard's unsuccessful bid for government in
1990 and his win in 1996, Labor prime minister Paul Keating (1995) also
professed a nationalistic vision of Australia that emphasized its distinctive
heritage. He emphasized the central place of "the dominant cultures of our
history, those of the British Isles and Ireland" that provided the democratic
institutions and ideas essential to a culturally diverse society and welcomed
the early contributions of painters, scientists, and explorers from other
countries. Keating defined multiculturalism in terms of Australian political
values: it was a policy that guaranteed rights and responsibilities. The rights
included those of freedom of cultural identity, language, and religion, the
right to social justice and to equality of treatment and opportunity, while
the responsibilities were strongly couched in terms of loyalty to Australia
and acceptance of the basic principles of Australian society and democracy.
There had to be a balance between the promotion of individual and collective cultural rights and expression, Keating said, and the promotion of common national interests and values. His account weighted the balance firmly
on the common national interest side that cultural diversity served.

Political leaders from both sides of politics have reinterpreted multiculturalism in mainly nationalistic and pluralist terms, and its leading architects have thought it time to move on. A 1995 Global Cultural Diversity
conference gave the public opportunity for its primary architect Zubrzycki
(1995) to question continued use of what he now described as an ambigu-

ous and pompous term. Its introduction to Australia by Grassby's "on-the-spot" decision had been "almost accidental" for the range of policies being introduced. Zubrzycki questioned whether we still needed the "the clumsy, pompous word 'multiculturalism'" in order "to celebrate the diversity of our cultural makeup." It had "outlived its purpose," he said, having become associated with "all kinds of negative attitudes and incidents of political separatism." Perhaps multiculturalism was still necessary to capture the diversity of Australia, he thought, but otherwise he plumped for "Many cultures. One Australia." Sir James Gobbo (1995), the chairman of the Australian Multicultural Foundation at the time, also thought that the term should be phased out because it had served its purpose and was no longer necessary. He also insisted that cultural diversity had not replaced Australia's core culture but rather had added to it.

THE POWER OF INTEGRATION

Three decades on from Grassby's launch of his program for "a multicultural society for the future," and despite the rhetorical and policy extensions and embellishments by committed advocates, bureaucrats, and successive governments, Australia remains strongly integrationist. The second and third generation, children and grandchildren of immigrants, have a high propensity to marry out of their ethnic ancestry group. Intermixture and intermarriage are extensive and increasing. Charles Price (2001: 84) estimated that in 1996 "over 8 million Australians have at least three ancestries, and over 3 million have four or more; of these at least 4 million and 2.2 million respectively have some non–Anglo-Celtic origin." From analyzing the 2001 census, Siew-Ean Khoo from the Monash Centre for Population and Urban Research shows that, although rates of marrying out vary sharply among the second generation between different ethnic groups, by the third generation they are high for all groups. For example, Greeks have only a 10 to 20 percent likelihood of having a spouse of different ancestry in the first or immigrant generation, increasing to 35–45 percent in the second generation, but then increasing to 80 percent in the third generation. While it is too early to tell whether this will be the case for some of the more recent ethnic migrations, Siew-Ean Khoo (2004: 42) concludes that this "points to a high degree of social integration with Australian society by the third generation." If intermarriage is one strong indicator of integration, education is another. Here children of immigrants from non–English-speaking background, and even those from lower socioeconomic backgrounds, achieve above-average participation in higher secondary and tertiary education (Khoo et al. 2002).

Moreover, children are educated in the English language in nonethnic state and nonstate—mainly Catholic, but also various other religious denominational and private—schools, which provides a shared experience.

CONCLUSION

We have been concerned with establishing the character of Australian multiculturalism, both historically and analytically, and separating out its dual components as a set of policies and as a prescription for Australian society and identity. Transitional multiculturalism, or the set of pragmatic policies for facilitating integration while encouraging some cultural diversity, has been broadly successful. The dominant forces in Australia are integrationist, however, and tend to overwhelm significant cultural differences despitethe modest support that is given to them. The confusion and contention in Australia has been due to proponents extending multiculturalism as a recipe for society and national identity, and this being picked up and promulgated in official discourse. Australia does not have this stronger form of multiculturalism either in practice or as an aspiration of most of its people. Hence those who want to use multiculturalism to describe and prescribe what Australian identity and citizenship are or should be have to fall back on the established values and institutions of pluralist democracy. Faced with the same dilemma, successive governments and political leaders from both sides of politics have redefined multiculturalism to be almost entirely an affirmation of Australian nationalist and pluralist democratic values. While some proponents still valiantly defend the term, others have called for its abandonment. If we are all multiculturalists now, as the American sociologist Nathan Glazer (1997) suggests more in resignation than approval, and its meaning is only the diluted sense of recognizing different lifestyles, then it would be best to abandon the term altogether. If we retain it we should be clear about what it means.

While professing multiculturalism, Australia has been essentially integrationist with multicultural policies assisting immigrants to bridge the transition from their original cultures to Australian culture. This has been a two-way process of Australian national culture being enriched and diversified—into something "rich and strange," with the old and new blending into "a better and more varied community of people." Australia has been able to achieve an orderly and peaceful incorporation of millions of immigrants, where France has ghettos of ethnic distinctiveness and disadvantage. Admittedly, as has been the case with Canada, Australia's success has been partly due to selection criteria that favor those who have skills and capacities that allow them to readily integrate. Immigrants have not lived in ethnic enclaves, at least not for long, but have interspersed in more affluent suburbs as they have prospered. Their children have been educated in English in both state and private schools that are not ethnically based, and they have an above-average rate of participation in higher secondary and tertiary schools. And by the third generation most have married out of their ancestral ethnic group.

Australia is not without its own set of problems and uncertainties. There are concerns by some that those from Islamic backgrounds will form religiously reinforced ethnic enclaves, and concerns by others that they will suffer discrimination in the current environment of the domestic war on terror. We are more optimistic, however, and trust that assisting such migrants with special programs to overcome disadvantage and support religious and cultural identity is the appropriate way to go. Islamic schools should also be encouraged and supported as Catholic ones are. There have been Islamic people in Australia for much of its history, although in small numbers and under greater pressure to assimilate. The test of Australia's "more 'multicultural' conception of integration," to borrow Kymlicka's phrase, will be precisely whether it can deal properly with a new wave of Islamic immigrants. In light of Australia's postwar immigrant experience, we can be optimistic but offer no guarantees, as the inhumane handling of illegal refugees, termed "queue-jumpers," has shown. Australia's otherwise fine humanitarian image has been marred by processing such people offshore, detaining them behind barbed wire in isolated detention centers and generally making their lives and those of their children intolerable. The irony is that they are relatively few in number, only several thousand, and many eventually establish their bona fide refugee status and settle in Australia.

Dealing adequately with its own indigenous people remains the major challenge facing Australia. While official discrimination that denied them citizenship rights in their own country for generations ended in the 1960s, and a more enlightened policy of recognition of their distinctive place and culture in Australia has been followed since the 1970s, economic disadvantage and social deprivation continue. If indigenous affairs is included in multiculturalism—we think it should not be because of its distinctive character—Australia has performed rather poorly. But that is another story.

Finally, as our analysis shows, Australians have been tardy in developing a discourse to capture and articulate its changing national identity and culture. Multiculturalism has been tried and found wanting. At the end of the day, there is something entirely inappropriate in trying to use the same term "multiculturalism" to deal with continuing minority nationalisms that are geographically based and the integration of immigrants. The alternative is not to return to old stereotypes but to devise a richer language of analysis and public discourse. We cannot afford to leave this to poets and artists.

NOTE

1. For a fuller account, see Galligan and Roberts 2004: chap. 4, whence the following instances and quotations are taken.

Chapter 13

A Pragmatic Response to a Novel Situation

Australian Multiculturalism

James Jupp

Australia was founded in 1901 as a white, British nation and part of the British Empire, at that time the largest and most multicultural political entity in the world. There was almost unanimous agreement in the debates leading up to Federation that this white, British basis was not contestable. It enjoyed the political support of the great majority of the population, expressed through manhood suffrage and the secret ballot. Thus it was not an artificial formulation, imposed on a reluctant population, as in the Russian or Austro-Hungarian empires. But neither did it emerge from warfare, as in the United States. It lacked a heroic dimension. Its theoretical basis, such as it was, reflected British experience as interpreted by English and Scottish Protestant liberals, whether Australian politicians or Colonial Office bureaucrats.

Australia inherited its political institutions from the United Kingdom and modified them in the light of American experience with federation. This was natural for a polity that was created from six British colonies, inhabited overwhelmingly by immigrants from the British Isles and their descendants and supervised by the Colonial Office in London. Thus such debates as took place about the nature of the new system were enclosed within a limited range of ideas and practices. There was none of the theorizing that inspired French and American democracy a century before. Nor has there been much since, despite the ending of the empire and the diminution of British influence. Australian political debate has tended to be pragmatic.

Solutions are sought for perceived problems. These solutions are shaped by political expediency. They emerge from parliamentary politics and electoral considerations. They are informed by current wisdom as understood by politicians, bureaucrats, and journalists and as measured by public opinion polls and elections. They are often novel and in advance of similar solutions sought in the United Kingdom. In recent years policy has been liberated from dependence on British example. But it has still tended to reflect the wisdom and experience of the English-speaking world. The closest bureaucratic links have often been with Canada, while the influence of the United States has been expressed through conservative critics of multiculturalism.

Multiculturalism falls squarely within these traditions (ACPEA 1982; Australia 1996; Galbally 1978; Gardiner-Garden 1993; NMAC 1999). Australia has been innovative but cautious. It has been less inhibited by complex theories of nationhood than have many European states, which has generally been advantageous. It has been less reliant on judicial decisions than is common in the United States. Its closest parallels have been with Canada but without the need to balance the claims of "two nations" and to adhere to treaties with the "First Nations." It has been accompanied by less violence recently than in the United Kingdom. Australian approaches have been sensible, limited, and practical. But that has not stopped them from being roundly denounced by critics who frequently refer to the experiences of other societies or to "worst-case scenarios." Nor have they been free from the temptation to appeal to majority xenophobia, which has proved such a potent electoral force in many other democracies.

THE MONOCULTURAL, MONORACIAL STATE

The basic assumption on which Australia federated was expressed by Sir Henry Parkes—an English immigrant—at the Federation conference in Melbourne in 1890 as "the crimson thread of kinship runs through us all." Originally a Chartist and long an opponent of Catholicism and Irish immigration, Sir Henry overlooked the political battles of his youth and the sectarian divide that was still so important in his own colony. This classic appeal to "all of us" has not lost its utility. It still excludes many Australians but embraces a democratic majority. In the 2001 census 35.9 percent claimed Australian ancestry, 33.9 percent English, 10.2 percent Irish, and 2.9 percent Scottish. This total of 15.5 million included some with dual ancestries but excluded some from New Zealand, South Africa, and elsewhere who were also of British origin. The Australian population in 2001 was 18.8 million. Of these 3.7 million normally spoke a language other than English, while

12.7 million declared themselves to be Christians. The "crimson thread" was perhaps not as imperially red as in 1890. But Australia was certainly not "the most multicultural country on earth" as politicians of all hues were declaring (Castles et al. 1992; Jupp 2002).

The reality, then, was that Australia was not ethnically uniform in 1890, nor was it exceptionally varied in 2001. What was still being argued, as in many other states, was that a high degree of ethnic uniformity was desirable as the basis for social harmony, national unity, and consensual democracy. Liberals such as John Stuart Mill had held this view in the 1860s as strongly as conservatives Margaret Thatcher or Enoch Powell in the 1960s. Official Australian multiculturalism could not logically hold this position. Instead, it argued that social harmony would be achieved if the various cultural fragments were contained within "strictly defined limits," which included acceptance of the British political inheritance and the English language—but no longer the Protestant religion. In other words, it adopted the two-faced position that while Australia might now be multicultural, it would be most effective as a stable society if cultural differences were muted. This ambivalent attitude has acted as a brake on dynamic changes comparable to those undertaken by government in Canada or the courts in the United States. As former Australian Labor Party leader Mark Latham argued, there was a "challenge ... to modernise our multicultural policies, to make them relevant to our multicultural identity" (Latham 2004). But at the same time it was politically expedient to be cautious, given that at least one million Australian adults voted for Pauline Hanson's One Nation Party in 1998 on a program rejecting multiculturalism altogether (Simms and Warhurst 2000).

MULTICULTURAL POLICIES

Australian multiculturalism rests on the assumption that immigrants have been carefully chosen with a view to their effective integration into society. This obviously does not apply to indigenous minorities, although they too have been expected to assimilate or even to disappear, until quite recently. British immigrants were given preference at least until the 1970s and were free from almost all restrictions, provided that they were "white." The assisted passage system, applying to almost all arriving in the 1950s and 1960s, ensured that there was selection nevertheless (Jupp 1998). Even the convicts had been selected to some extent to fill labor vacancies or to improve the balance of the sexes. For 150 years assisted passages were granted to three million immigrants with the object of attracting the British and Irish who might otherwise have gone to America, balancing the sexes, filling labor vacancies, and avoiding ethnic and religious conflict. The White Australia policy between 1901 and 1972 was particularly concerned with these latter issues. On its abolition it was soon replaced by a visa system that allowed Australian governments to choose who would enter the country and under what circumstances—as Prime Minister John Howard put it in 2001. This offshore visa system now applies to everyone except New Zealanders. Even they are now selected for permanent settlement on the same basis as anyone else. Australia is almost unique among developed societies by insisting on a universal visa system for all entrants, whether permanent or temporary (Vrachnas et al. 2005). Breaches of this principle are rigorously punished, as policy on unauthorized asylum seekers recently underlined. While opponents of multiculturalism often deride it as "social engineering," the immigration policies that have created it are outstanding examples in the modern world of deliberate social engineering.

All this has meant that Australia has largely avoided the absorption of a very varied intake, many of them from rural and traditional backgrounds, which makes them hard to accommodate within an affluent urban society. Uncontrolled entry was available for white British subjects until the 1970s, but they were generally regarded as unproblematic because they belonged to the dominant culture already. Thus the challenges that promoted the adoption of official multiculturalism were less acute than those faced by societies such as the United States, Britain, France, and other states that did not have such a rigorous system of selection. This also meant that except for a brief period between 1987 and 1996, multicultural policy at the national level has always been developed within the Department of Immigration. From 2001 to early 2006, this arrangement was extended to include indigenous affairs, which had previously been regarded as a quite distinct area. In theory multiculturalism has been assumed to embrace indigenous people since 1989. But this administrative change was in practice a major departure, the impact of which has yet to appear in the vacuum caused by the abolition of the Aboriginal and Torres Strait Islander Commission in 2004. Some other agencies have also developed multicultural policies, notably the arts funding body, The Australia Council.

Despite the policy of selecting immigrants for their adaptability to Australian society and the economy, it was becoming clear by 1970 that the British character of the major cities was already changing due to the priority given to recruiting factory workers for an expanding manufacturing economy. While there was a major intake of the English in the 1960s, a large part of this working-class intake was from Europe. The pragmatic choice of manual workers had overtaken the pragmatic choice of the assimilable. Experience with European Displaced Persons had already shown that rapid and total assimilation was unlikely to occur in the first generation. The need to develop appropriate attitudes and measures was recognized by politicians and bureaucrats alike, although there were at least two major concerns. One was the fear that an ethnically diverse society would be unstable and riven with conflict, as was believed to be the case in the United States and was starting to show up in England with the arrival of large numbers of Caribbean and South Asian Commonwealth immigrants. Unlike these two familiar societies, color was not yet an issue in White Australia. However, the abolition of racial exclusion and the advent of a large number of Vietnamese refugees after 1975 made the issue of "managing diversity" increasingly urgent in many eyes. That Australia has a very limited history of violent race relations in the twentieth century was often overlooked in this perspective. More recently the absence of terrorist activity within Australia has not alleviated alarm but has provoked calls to end multiculturalism altogether.

The other approach, which was not necessarily incompatible, was from the labor movement and social democracy. As the great majority of European immigrants were industrial workers, they were of concern to the trade unions. As they were less skilled and less proficient in English than the majority, they were liable to form an "underclass" as they did in some other industrial societies. This either would be unfair in an egalitarian society or would create social disharmony—which brought this fear into line with the more conservative approach fearing violence and disharmony. Thus it was quite feasible for multiculturalism to appeal both to Labor and Liberal politicians—as it did strongly both to Whitlam and to Fraser. At the same time Labor and the unions had a long-standing fear of immigrants undermining working standards, while the Liberals were still Anglophile admirers of the British inheritance. The leadership of Whitlam and Fraser was crucial in gaining acceptance for what proved to be a historic departure from traditional attitudes.

Differing approaches and concerns naturally produced different policy responses. Mark Lopez, in his exhaustive study of the origins of multiculturalism, distinguishes four of these; cultural pluralism, associated with Jerzy Zubrzycki and Walter Lippmann; ethnic rights, associated with Alan Matheson and Des Storer; welfare multiculturalism, defined by David Cox; and ethnic structural pluralism, defined by Jean Martin (Lopez 2000). These different approaches did not prevent their various advocates from working together. Nor does his typology account for other influential figures from outside Melbourne, such as Bill Jegorow, Laksiri Jayasuriya, Stephen Castles, George Smolicz, and Andrew Jakubowicz. However, it is a useful way of looking at the early debates in the 1970s before the Australian government formulated an overarching definition through the Galbally report of 1978.

The "structural and cultural" approaches were less appealing to the government than a "welfare and rights" approach, which corresponded to what the Department of Immigration had already been doing since the arrival of the Displaced Persons in the early 1950s. The notion that there were "hard" and "soft" multiculturalists was a fantasy developed by Lauchlan Chipman in the 1980s, the closest to this being the two "pluralist" versions (Chipman 1980).

As it turned out, Australian multiculturalism put much less emphasis on cultural and ethnic group maintenance than did its Canadian counterpart (Kymlicka 1995). In particular, and of increasing relevance, it avoided discussing the impact of religion on cultural diversity. Structures created or subsidized from Commonwealth and state budgets were "panethnic," bringing many different ethnic organizations and individuals together for consultation, service delivery, and advocacy. Most important of these have been Ethnic Communities' Councils (which had their origins in 1974) and their federation (FECCA in 1979) and Migrant Resource Centres in appropriate neighborhoods. Subsidies to ethnic organizations from the Commonwealth have been predominantly for service delivery, as is normal in the social welfare field. Such organizations were also very useful in the range of consultations that characterized the Hawke and Keating government in many policy areas. Subsidies from the states have been quite minor, to encourage festivals and support newsletters and incidental expenses. Again, similar payments on a much wider scale are made to a variety of "mainstream" community, sporting, and social clubs. Each state and territory developed an agency for the delivery of services such as interpreting and translation and for administering these grants. In recent years, with the diminished enthusiasm of the Howard government, much of the initiative in multicultural affairs has passed to the states.

Whatever the national government chooses to say and do, there is now a whole network of institutions and organizations operating within multicultural principles. Thus the "abolition" of multiculturalism—advocated by Pauline Hanson—is not possible in a democracy. To argue, as Brian Galligan and Winsome Roberts (2004) have done, that multiculturalism has been "gutted" at the national level may well be true. This is not an overwhelming reason for supposing that its days are over. To hold, as they and many others do, that Australians now accept ethnic variety is to ignore the impact of Hanson and the adoption of many of her policies as a way of winning back support to the Coalition. To suggest that the immediate postwar generation is either assimilated or passing away and that its offspring have become predominantly "Australian" may also be true. Europeans do not come any more in numbers sufficient to sustain their communities at previous levels.

But non-Europeans are coming and will continue to do so as long as we have an immigration program. Moreover, their ethnic variety is even greater than before. Their desire to assert their cultures, religions, and languages is no less than for their European predecessors. While many in the second and third European generations have certainly moved away from the culture of their parents, many remain active in ethnic and panethnic organizations. Assimilation undoubtedly takes place, especially for the many of mixed origins. But it can take a long time, as the experience of North America suggests, and is often only partial. It may well be slowed down by religious allegiance, which usually outlasts linguistic diversity.

There are many different individual interpretations of multiculturalism as of liberalism, socialism, democracy, justice, and any other abstract concept contested within the political arena. The only reliable guide to what actually happens at the policy and implementation level is what public bodies actually do and say. The Galbally report was the foundation document of multiculturalism, and its principles have been repeated in all subsequent official statements ever since, up to the 1999 agenda of the Howard government (Galbally 1978; OMA 1989; NMAC 1999). Briefly these were:

- all members of our society must have equal opportunity to realize their full potential and must have equal access to programs and services;
- every person should be able to maintain his or her culture without prejudice or disadvantage and should be encouraged to understand and embrace other cultures;
- needs of immigrants should, in general, be met by programs and services available to the whole community, but special programs and services are necessary at present to ensure equality of access and provision;
- services and programs should be designed and operated in full consultation with clients, and self-help should be encouraged as much as possible with a view to helping immigrants become self-reliant quickly. (Galbally 1978: para 1.7)

The first multicultural agenda of 1989 put social justice issues at the center, where they remained for the term of the Labor government over the next seven years: "Multiculturalism expresses and complements the government's broader social justice strategy which is designed to ensure that the benefits flowing from its economic policies are fairly distributed throughout the community" (OMA 1989: 19). This reflected criticism that the Galbally and Zubrzycki approach had unduly emphasized cultural maintenance. It was aimed at implementing the principles of access and equity developed since 1985 within the Department of Immigration and by the Labor governments of New South Wales and Victoria. Neither the Galbally report nor the 1989 agenda advocated cultural relativism or any kind of separatism. Nor have these ever been supported since, except by minorities in relation to traditional Aboriginal issues in northern Australia, outside the normal framework of multicultural policy and marginally by advocates of *sharia* law on the fringe of the Muslim communities.

A decade later and under a government initially hostile to multiculturalism and social justice, little had changed in the official formulation, which was sanctioned by John Howard in 1999. The government did, however, reject a recommendation for a replacement as a monitoring agency of the Office of Multicultural Affairs, which it had abolished in 1996. The National Multicultural Advisory Council, which developed this agenda, was "optimistic about Australia's future as a culturally diverse society and ... confident that Australian multiculturalism will continue to be a defining feature of our evolving national identity and contribute substantial benefits to all Australians" (NMAC 1999: para. 3.4). Unlike previous reports, no new institutions were established. Multiculturalism remained as a minor function of the Immigration Department, although with its own junior minister. The Special Broadcasting Service (SBS) remained as the most important survivor of the Galbally era. English teaching, now put out to competitive tendering, remains the largest expenditure that might be termed "multicultural."

SOCIAL JUSTICE, ACCESS, AND EQUITY

In a speech in 2004 that was seriously misrepresented in the Australian media, Trevor Phillips, chair of the British Commission for Racial Equality (CRE) and a Guyanese, argued that multiculturalism needed to be reconsidered in the light of developments since the CRE was established in 1976. These included the growth of a large "mixed race" population that was British-born and had a declining affinity to the land and culture of its parents. These were essentially the "Black British." Immigrants from South Asia and their children were still more attached to their religions and traditions. The previous emphasis on tolerance and equal treatment, on which the CRE had been based, needed reconsideration. More important was equality of life chances, especially as so many immigrants from the Third World were unemployed and so many "Black British" were not progressing through the education system. What provoked controversy, as it would in Australia, was the claim that many recently arrived Africans brought with them cultural practices, including homophobia and contempt for women, that were incompatible with the needs of British society and their own ability to benefit. In his concluding words:

> Our claim for equality in an integrated society is founded on the certainty of our citizenship. It is founded on what we have in common with others, not on our differences.... We can have the samosas and the saris and the steel bands. But settling for that would be a betrayal of all that we have fought for. I want more. I want to be truly British, with all the benefits and burdens that the label carries—and I want everyone to know that it is my right to be so. (CRE 2004)

Australia no longer has a national body strong and bold enough to enter into this kind of debate. This is mainly due to the concerted effort of the Howard government to repress discussion of these issues, but also to the reluctance of ethnic and indigenous leaders to raise them—the point that Phillips was making in the British context. Multiculturalism has become stuck with what he would term "samosas, saris, and steel bands" and what Mary Kalantzis once called "pasta and polka" (Castles et al. 1992; Cope and Kalantzis 2000). The celebration of difference remains important, and in both countries folk festivals have been a major means of gaining acceptance from the majority population. But as long as Aborigines and Vietnamese and African refugees have much higher levels of unemployment than the average, they cannot be said to enjoy all the benefits of Australian citizenship. In many ways Australian multiculturalism was already moving in the direction desired by Phillips in the 1990s. But progress was stopped and the momentum lost. In neither country have community leaders been willing to criticize some of the problems found in their own groups or to negotiate with government representatives to alleviate them. The structure of consultation and research that existed between 1986 and 1996 has been run down. The need for such critical interchanges is particularly urgent in dealing with the indigenous and the Muslim minorities, both liable to be disadvantaged and alienated. Alienation has probably increased since 9/11 by the scapegoating of Muslims and attacks on such harmless symbols of religious adherence as the *hijab*—which has nothing to do with terrorism.

PRINCIPLES, PHILOSOPHY, AND IDEOLOGY

The conservative onslaught against multiculturalism began with Chipman's articles in 1980, proceeded through Blainey's speeches and book from 1984, gained major party support with Howard's address to the Liberals at Esperance in 1988, and burst into full bloom with Hanson's election victory in

1996. Most of the attacks of the preceding decade, which obviously influenced Howard, were misleading and even dishonest. They drew on overseas
examples with only a limited reference to what was actually being done in
Australia. They referred to worst-case scenarios such as Yugoslavia or Fiji
and to racial violence in Britain, the United States, and Europe, in the absence of any compelling examples in Australia. When Australia was the reference point—as with influential articles by David Barnett (1986) or Stephen
Rimmer (1991)—statistics used were grossly inflated (Rimmer 1988). Their
notion that "billions" of dollars were being used to subsidize ethnic minorities was taken up with enthusiasm by Pauline Hanson. These initial attacks
were built upon by subsequent critics, using the time-honored practice of
only quoting those who agreed with them.

Debates about multiculturalism tended to be argumentative and hostile
and free of philosophical references. Most of the critics were conservative and
assimilationist in the sense of denying the need for any state intervention in
favor of ethnic minorities. Essentially, they believed that such minorities presented a threat to social cohesion and national identity until they were fully
assimilated and domesticated. This view was extended to indigenous affairs
by Pauline Hanson, but others were hesitant to do so. That most critics were
fully in favor of large public subsidies to religious denominational schools
seems never to have raised the question of why ethnic minorities are undesirable when religious minorities should be supported. This becomes especially
puzzling once non-Christian religious minorities are established and the boundaries between religion and ethnicity become blurred. The Australian constitution prohibits the establishment of a religion and religious tests (s 116), but
religious schools have enjoyed substantial and growing subsidies, and places
of worship are often built on land granted to them by state governments. Unlike some European practice, these benefits are not confined to Christians.

In practice, then, three different attitudes to diversity have been common: that ethnic diversity based on race, language, or nationality should be
limited and controlled and preferably allowed to wither; that indigenous
people should be treated as a distinct entity from immigrant groups; and
that religious denominations should receive more generous treatment than
either of these. These differing attitudes are largely based on pragmatic
considerations rather than on ideological or philosophical formulations. Assimilation was officially urged both on the indigenous and on immigrants
until it was found to be practically impossible and electorally unappealing.
Religions were treated generously because they were regarded as a private
matter and electorally damaging if interfered with. Toleration followed intolerance and restriction, mainly as a political response to changing situ-

ations, as it did with the White Australia policy and state aid to church schools. This creates a policy puzzle, with Muslims urged to become "more like us" while at the same time encouraging a relatively small minority to create their own school system.

A recent onslaught on multiculturalism comes from Galligan and Roberts in their book *Australian Citizenship* (2004). Their critique contains little that is new, although Galligan later claimed improbably that Labor leader Mark Latham had "plagiarised" his ideas (*The Weekend Australian* 2004). It rests heavily on other criticisms going back as far as 1989. In their view, "multiculturalism was always a conceptual muddle of prescription and description" (Galligan and Roberts 2004: 96). Quoting only critics of the concept, they ignore consistent attempts at the national level to distinguish between multiculturalism as a "fact" and as a "policy." Moreover, although Galligan is a professor of political science, he is strangely oblivious to the fact that many contentious areas of public policy are a "conceptual muddle" because they are subject to differing interpretations and political uses. Politicians have always had to steer between the enthusiasm of literally thousands of activists who support multiculturalism and the much greater numbers who are dubious and hostile, drawn from the majority culture. Latham himself was a good example of the ambivalence this produces in politicians, especially if they represent, as he did, an area that has seen considerable tension around ethnic change.

Like many other critics, Galligan and Roberts do not address the considerable literature from 1978 onward that has tried to clarify meanings and develop concrete programs. Quoting the exhaustive study of Mark Lopez (to which James Gobbo and I gave praise at its publication), they ignore the possibility that many new policies are initially developed by small groups working on bureaucrats and politicians (Lopez 2000). Apart from the fact that Lopez confines his analysis to Melbourne, the claim that multiculturalism was "top down" and the work of a small clique ignores the reality of considerable demand from within the immigrant communities for improved services and status. Many conservatives outside these communities have had very little contact with them and did not seriously study the relevant policy statements summarized in the agenda approved by the Howard government in 1999 (NMAC 1999). The fact that all nine governments in Australia subscribe to and try to implement multicultural policy suggests that it is hardly superfluous, as Galligan and Roberts claim. That public funding is predominantly for "panethnic" activities rather than for supporting specific ethnic cultures is also ignored. In practice the great bulk of minority cultural activity is self-funding, denominational schools being the major exception.

The myth that "billions" of dollars have been expended on sustaining dying minority cultures is an excellent example of the power of the big lie.

HARMONY, COHESION, AND THE CLASH OF CIVILIZATIONS

Samuel Huntington, in his influential study *The Clash of Civilizations and the Remaking of World Order,* refers to Australia as a "torn society" (Huntington 1996: 151–54). This rather extreme view he bases on the abortive attempts by Paul Keating to redefine Australia as "part of Asia." Huntington rightly argues that this was to put too much emphasis on economic links at the expense of cultural reality. Yet Keating was careful not to say that Australia was an Asian country. He, like Whitlam before him, was trying to reposition Australia away from the nonexistent British Empire without submerging its identity and national interests beneath the very real American empire.

The assumption that Australia was peaceful and harmonious because it was ethnically uniform was one of the settled myths of the years between finalizing White Australia in 1901 and its eventual abolition in 1972. It was further assumed that this harmony and cohesion was based on British values and institutions. Yet the United Kingdom was neither ethnically uniform nor particularly harmonious. In both countries there were quite bitter political divisions and much social inequality. Until the independence of the Irish Free State in 1921, it was quite absurd to talk about a common political inheritance at all. Yet many did so. In quite recent British textbooks on government the long-running civil war in Northern Ireland is simply ignored. It would damage the notion of "peace, order, and good government" on which the myth of a British identity has been based for more than a century. Similarly, those who mention White Australia, the dispossession of the indigenous people, industrial strife, the depressions of 1890 and 1930, and so on are denounced for wearing a "black armband" and slandering the national myths of harmony, equality, and mateship (Windschuttle 2002, 2004).

The importance of the "clash of civilizations" theory for Australian multiculturalism has yet to be faced in serious public debate. Essentially it has been reinterpreted to mean "how should we cope with the Muslim minority already in our midst?" But this was not what Huntington meant by the emotive term "a torn society." Rather, he was arguing that Keating's attempts to identify Australian interests with those of Asian neighbors ran counter to the reality of Australia as essentially a European society in the Protestant tradition. This is a valid point, if somewhat exaggerated. Culturally, there is no such place as Asia (and Huntington does not claim that there is). There is such a place as the Muslim world, varied though it may be but united in fear of Western "crusades." As conceived over the past thirty years, Australian multicultural theory and practice is ill-equipped to come to terms with the issues now being debated in Britain and Europe as they face larger Muslim populations than does Australia. The main umbrella body for local Muslims, the Australian Federation of Islamic Councils, takes the position that it wants Islam to be recognized as an "Australian religion." This is centrally in the multicultural tradition. An optimist should believe that having a range of multicultural policies and structures and a public adherence to multicultural principles will make this easier to achieve than in more rigid societies such as France. A pessimist might argue that downgrading the commitment to multiculturalism and playing the "terrorism card" makes this much more difficult.[1]

AN AUSTRALIAN IDENTITY?

An often-repeated theme of critics, including Galligan and Roberts, has been that multiculturalism denies Australian culture and national identity by emphasizing diversity rather than common interests. Underlying assumptions of this critique seem to be that there is an uncontested Australian culture and identity and that multicultural policy is so influential that it can challenge this and delay the assimilation process whereby immigrants will conform to the majority. All these propositions are very doubtful. They repeat similar accusations in the more bitter "cultural wars" in the United States. There is no evidence that the modest multicultural programs adopted by state and Commonwealth governments since 1975 have either hastened or delayed the process of assimilation. Indeed, some critics would argue that multiculturalism is simply a benign variant of assimilation because it does not create resentment among new arrivals. Certainly there is evidence from much more rigid approaches, as in France, that trying to force the pace of assimilation does not work. This was the conclusion reached as early as 1978 in the Galbally report, the founding document of multiculturalism at the national level. It had already been accepted within the bureaucracy in 1974 when the Immigration Department replaced its Assimilation branch with an Integration branch. (It still has a Citizenship and Multicultural Affairs division.)

The basic problem in expecting immigrants to conform to Australian culture and assume an Australian identity is that there is no agreement among the majority as to what these might look like (Theophanous 1995). John Howard, with his frequent references to "all Australians" or the "Australian people," presumably believed that the great majority do have a common culture. However, like generations of politicians before him, he was less forthcoming about the content of that culture or the nature of Australian identity. Like many others, he is reduced to puerile references to "larrikinism," a "fair go," and "mateship," none of which has a self-evident content. When a larrikin becomes a hoon is never clarified. Why a fair go needs to be denied to refugees from Iraq and the Taliban was never satisfactorily explained.

Why trade unionism, the epitome of mateship, needs curbing is a very vexed question. Other queries might include: do indigenous Australians share equitably in society? Why should people deny their ethnic heritage but retain their religious heritage? Are there not subcultures based on social class or educational levels? Are values developed in the rural society of a century ago still valid today? The notion that John Howard and his erstwhile North Shore cabinet colleagues are the heirs of Henry Lawson and the "legend of the nineties" is highly amusing. In summary—is there a "real Australia" at all?

When advocates of Australian identity and national culture attempt to define what they mean in concrete terms, the result is often more of a conceptual muddle than they claim for multiculturalism. Galligan and Roberts, like many others, want Australian citizens "to share" in its history and heritage (this volume). As Australians—immigrant or native—have only a limited knowledge of that heritage, this is an especially tall order for newcomers. As generations of nationalists have complained, most of what was taught as "history and heritage" in the past was about Britain, not Australia. This dual inheritance is important to understand but can mean little to those who are not of British origin—at least one in four of the population. A more serious objection is that most of what is described as "Australian heritage" focuses on the formative years between 1850 and 1900 and has very little relevance to the suburban Australia of today. A central claim of critics—with echoes in the arguments of Trevor Phillips—is that minority cultures are fading away. This is not entirely true. Jewish life has been sustained since the early 1800s, Greek Orthodoxy since 1890, and Chinese organizations since the 1850s. Many aspects of minority cultures will change and even disappear, especially if not sustained by further immigration. But it is equally the case that cultural inheritances from Australia's rural and pastoral past are not going to be sustained, either. The decline of support for White Australia is a case in point.

Three recent attempts to define this inheritance are Robert Birrell's *A Nation of Our Own* (1995), Miriam Dixson's *The Imaginary Australian* (1999), and Galligan and Roberts's *Australian Citizenship* (2004). All are highly critical of multiculturalism and define local culture in terms of a historic heritage that was predominantly British in origin. Birrell's viewpoint is that Deakinite liberalism in Melbourne a century ago created a national identity that was both progressive and unique. He bases his case heavily upon the Australian Natives Association, which confined its membership to those born in Australia. Essentially Deakin's view was that racial unity was the basis for political unity and that a reformist program was the basis for social harmony.[2]

Miriam Dixson draws heavily on theorists of nation formation such as Anthony Smith, Benedict Anderson, Jacques Lacan, and Tom Nairn, which is rare in such debates in Australia (Smith 1991). She argues that a "new class" was diminishing the previous power of an Anglo-Celtic core, a point made at length by Katharine Betts in her two influential attacks on multiculturalism, *Ideology and Immigration* (1988) and *The Great Divide* (1999). While Dixson wants a new "synthesis," this must be firmly based on the British past. We should "let the old identity do its essential work, to go on playing the cohesive role it has discharged since 1788" (Dixson 1999: 172). This brings her closer to Galligan and Roberts than to Birrell. Her own radical past allows her to call for at least a recognition of the dark side of Australia's convict and Aboriginal experiences.

Certainly all three positions need to be engaged with. Galligan and Roberts are the most nostalgic in wanting a reaffirmation of many century-old myths and legends based on a sparsely populated, remote, and pastoral society. As they rightly say, "Australians have emphasised the bush and the outback because of the uniqueness of the Australian landscape" (Galligan and Roberts 2004: 126). This may well be true, although it overlooks the fact that many urbanized modern societies also have a myth of rural origins. Galligan and Roberts also favor a reassertion of nationalism and patriotism, being critical of the Civic Experts Group report of 1994. Their conservatism is unexceptionable if one accepts that there is a clear and uncontested tradition of what it means to be an Australian and that this is shared by the majority. But that is very much what the debate is about. Some have argued that Australia is a "postmodern" state, just as it was among the first "modern" states by having no long feudal past. In a globalizing world, patriotism and nationalism might become old-fashioned and dysfunctional, especially if based on a world that has largely passed away.

The Deakinite inheritance has been declared dead by contemporary figures ranging from Paul Kelly to John Howard. The British inheritance has likewise been buried by Paul Keating, among many others. As for the "legend of the nineties," this has surely been done to death over the past fifty years. As an inspiration for present and future immigrants and the native born, it lacks modern relevance. Moreover, it is hard to see the heirs of

Shakespeare, Dante, Plato, Buddha, Muhammad, or Confucius being very impressed by Steele Rudd or the dog on the tucker box.[3] They are much more likely to look to the United States, a society that has created the most powerful culture in the world, if one that is a synthetic and commercialized amalgam of many others. Alas, the future of Australian popular culture is in the hands of News Corporation, Hollywood, and the Disney Corporation, rather than Australian intellectuals. This is despite the excellent creative work of film producers, painters, and writers over the past fifty years.

That "ethnic" Australians have been persuaded by multiculturalism to turn their back on Australian culture is an especially absurd claim. A touching (if irrelevant) example I witnessed in Parramatta some years ago was a choir singing "Waltzing Matilda" in Maltese. Individuals and even groups and organizations adapt at their own pace. All "panethnic" activity (Ethnic Communities Councils and Migrant Resource Centres, for example) is conducted in English. Many "ethnic" clubs, for example, the highly successful Hellenic Club in Canberra, open their membership to all while retaining ultimate control in the hands of the relevant community. The ethnic media, and of course SBS, often have an English-language content aimed at reaching the young. To assimilationists this suggests that multiculturalism is fading. But it is perfectly possible to maintain ethnic distinctiveness in the English language, as many Jewish, Irish, Scottish, German, Indian, and Sri Lankan organizations have done for years.

The nationalist and conservative critics are scornful of attempts to base common loyalties on values and institutions rather than on cultural inheritance. But what has held Australia together for at least the last 150 years is precisely a democratic way of doing things based on governments elected by the mass of the people and constrained both by law and by values and traditions. What the official formulations of multiculturalism—from 1978 to 1999—all repeat is that Australia is an egalitarian democracy, that all citizens should have equal civil rights regardless of race, ethnicity, religion, or gender; that English is the national language but that those unable to use it should have translating and interpreting services; that equality does not necessarily require uniformity; that primary loyalty should be to Australia but without denying other heritages; that equitable access to public funds and services should be a prime objective in public administration; and that all Australians should be protected from discrimination, racial prejudice, vilification, and violence. In pursuit of these objectives some public funds are expended on services that are not available to all because the majority does not need them. Modest support is given to a variety of cultural activities that do not derive from the British Isles. The "contract" implicit in multiculturalism is that in exchange for these benefits everyone will obey the law, become citizens, and seek to make themselves economically productive (for example, by learning English). This does not preclude being a Muslim, but it does preclude supporting terrorism for whatever ideological or religious reasons.

None of this would need repeating were it not for the often absurd claims made by opponents of multiculturalism since the early 1980s. The alternatives are never spelled out. In practice "benign neglect" has been practiced in recent years rather than a reversion to the assimilation policies of the past. Immigration policy has been shaped by selection, which will attract economically productive and well-educated immigrants who will not need the welfare services developed in the past for European refugees and factory workers. These services have increasingly and rightly been focused on the humanitarian intake, which numbers less than 10 percent of the total.

As a pluralist democracy Australia does not impose a national culture or religion. There is no prohibition on the use of any language in private, on social occasions, or through media outlets. There is no established religion and many Australians are not actively religious at all. Once citizenship has been achieved—after a revised period of four years—there is no restriction on moving within the country or between it and anywhere else. Subject only to public examinations, a variety of schools teach a variety of beliefs and values. This is what a multicultural society looks like (O'Neill and Austin 2000; Kukathas 1993). It allows people to assimilate at their own pace, or not at all if they choose to isolate themselves and damage their future and that of their children. Immigrants understand and respond to all this. What they will not respond to is being coerced or nagged into becoming "real Australians."

NOTES

1. On different aspects of social cohesion in Australia, see Jupp and Nieuwenhuysen (2007).
2. Alfred Deakin (b. 1856) was the second prime minister of Australia (1903–4), and he later held office two more times (1905–8, 1909–10) (ed.).
3. Steele Rudd was the pseudonym of Australian author and essayist Arthur Hoey Davis (b. 1868). A radio series titled "Dad and Dave," which ran from 1932 to 1952, brought his characters to life and turned them into cultural icons. The "dog on the tucker box" is a monument based on a theme in a nineteenth-century bush ballad, which was later turned into a popular poem. The monument, in inland New South Wales, was unveiled by Joe Lyons, prime minister of Australia in 1932 (ed.).

Chapter 14

Is Australian Multiculturalism in Crisis?

A Comment on Galligan and Roberts and on Jupp

Maria R. Markus

◁◇▷

Let me begin with a series of questions that, I think, can be posed on the basis of the two previous chapters and are perhaps worthwhile to pursue somewhat further.

(1) Is there a crisis of Australian multiculturalism?[1]
(2) If there is a crisis, what does it consist of?
(3) And finally, how did it emerge and how can it be overcome, if at all?

The contributors focus mainly on various ups and downs of Australian multi-culturalism, relating them to broader theoretical debates, some suggesting not just its inescapable "demise" but straightforwardly the irrelevance of the concept in the particular Australian context. So the question of a "crisis" of multiculturalism—even if the term itself is not used by all the authors—is worth investigating. The meaningful answer to this question, however, depends on how multi–culturalism is conceptualized, if not in the extensive literature on the topic, then at least in the essays we are dealing with here.

Before proceeding with such clarification, I would like to make some preliminary points, hoping that it may help to elaborate my further argument. Above all, I would like to make it clear what multiculturalism—in my view—is not. Multiculturalism ought not to be understood as a mode of a new homogenization, which is to include the elements from various ethnic-cultural components of a given society, blending them into a "common culture." The application of the concept in this context would not make much sense. Neither should it be, however, understood as a loose conglomerate of cultural groups, separate and insulated from each other. As Bhikhu Parekh and other writers remind us, culture is a complex, multilayered phenomenon, hardly ever internally monolithic or closed from external influences. "Cultures grow out of conscious and unconscious interaction with each other and are shaped by the wider economic, political and other forces" (Parekh 2000: 148–49, 337, 338). Their boundaries are "fluid, porous, and contested" (Benhabib 2002: 184). This is true about most cultures; it is even truer about the cultures within multicultural societies, where they at least partially share various institutional arrangements. Thus the understanding of multiculturalism should focus above all on those channels, mechanisms, and legal structures of liberal democratic societies, which enable people of various cultural backgrounds to relate to each other with mutual respect and tolerance and to negotiate publicly the aspects of their beliefs and customs that may conflict with the society's civic and legal norms.[2]

Another preliminary point that should be made here is that, while cultures are collective phenomena, they live mostly through their individual members, and thus "belonging to a cultural community admits of much variation" with respect to which of the collective norms are observed and to what extent (Parekh 2000: 148). These are the decisions that every individual faces in relation to his or her cultural background. In constructing their own (again, fluid and changing) identities, individuals make choices not just between various components of their ethnic cultures but also between various other affiliations, among which culture may be (and in some way usually is) dominant, but not a sole component. So there are many ways of being Muslim, Lebanese, woman, or, for that matter, Australian.

It would be misleading, however, to assume either that porousness of all cultures is of the same degree or that all communities are equally prepared to open up self-reflectively to confront their own internal divisions and interpretative disagreements, and even less to face the critical eye of the "other."[3] Furthermore, not all individuals are equally able to make autonomous choices, either. With respect to individuals, one could make a generalization that the easier the access of the members of particular ethnic or cultural groups to various societal resources, the less likely they are to seek a shelter in ethnic or other cultural closures of whatever kind. With respect to communities, it could be said that the less resourceful and the less confident in its future a group is, the more likely it is to close its ranks and impose rigid norms upon its members (Markus 1998).

Brian Galligan and Winsome Roberts (in this volume) distinguish three possible functions or purposes (and thus meanings, I suppose) of multiculturalism, which are, however, collapsed later into two basic types. These are first, "a welfare purpose," assisting those who are disadvantaged by their cultural background" and which the authors designate as the "transitional" or "soft" form of multiculturalism. Second, there is a "liberal, pluralist purpose" of respecting and encouraging cultural diversity, which at this point they also consider as a form of multiculturalism in its "soft" version. Lastly, they speak also about a strong version of multiculturalism, which they propose to call "national multiculturalism" and which—according to their definition—aims to "create lasting enclaves of ethnoculturally distinct peoples" and to serve "as a recipe for society and national identity."

While the authors have some serious reservations with respect to the concept of multiculturalism in general, and accept it only reluctantly as a concession to established political vocabulary, they endorse the "transitional multiculturalism" and "cultural diversity," noting, however, that this type of multiculturalism is of relatively short duration—hence "transitional"—as gradual assimilation of the old immigrants and the improved criteria of the selection of the new immigrants will render it obsolete in the future.

The impact of neither of these processes (assimilation and improved selection) is, however, self-evident or unambiguous, nor does either allow for the conclusion that Australia does not have distinct cultural groups that endure in any significant way, the only such group being indigenous people. While there is undoubtedly a gradual intermingling of further generations of immigrants' descendants, this affects the "dominant culture" as well and also often leads to various (collective and individual) forms of hybridization of cultures.[4] Whether this creates better conditions for democratic integration or, in certain cases, leads to the "closing of the ranks" in defense of the purity of self-understanding of the particular group depends on a number of internal and external conditions. In any case, the existence of some ethnically/culturally strongly differentiated areas in Sydney, for example, is a well-established fact. Such differentiation is often reinforced by various economic and other social inequalities. What concerns the selection of the new immigrants with a "high integration facility" is that there is no guarantee that their "professional skills" will automatically ensure their more efficient integration. It is also more likely that the new immigrants will increasingly come from the less "commensurable" cultural backgrounds. Also, various humanitarian considerations may prompt the opening of immigration possibilities for unskilled immigrants, especially from the Pacific region. The authors themselves mention possible problems with groups from Islamic backgrounds, which may "form religiously reinforced ethnic enclaves." In the present international atmosphere, the closure of these communities is indeed a possibility, despite the fact that the Australian Muslim population is ethnically quite diverse, with only two larger minorities of Lebanese and Turkish Muslims. Both of these groups also have their own internal conflicts among themselves and with their non-Muslim ex-compatriots. Yet such a closure may not only emerge from inside these groups but also be reinforced by suspicion and distrust directed at them in a totalizing way from other communities, especially by those members of other communities who are unable to distinguish cultural specificities of a group from the criminal activities of some of its members.

No doubt some forms or manifestations of multiculturalism, which attempt to impose the rigid identities upon their members, may challenge key assumptions of liberal democracies. If these tensions are not given a space in the public civil sphere where they can confront each other, rearticulate the common frameworks, and reflectively reexamine their own standpoints, they indeed can lead to cultural closures and a total fragmentation of social fabric. It is then up to the members of these groups as individuals to seek either an internal transformation or reinterpretation of the collective beliefs and norm, or to exit; and it is up to the political community to make such an exit not just possible but also not too painful or costly in the human terms.[5] This, however, makes multiculturalism, as opening and maintaining the channels of social participation of all people, even more, not less, relevant.

In any case, there is some inconsistency in the authors' argument with respect to the impact of multiculturalism, its features, and its future and in their understanding of its "crisis." Speaking earlier about the "liberal pluralist purpose of Australia's version of multiculturalism," which is defined as a core of "democratic pluralism," the authors repeatedly describe it as a "two-way process."[6] The further argument in support of this thesis is, however, less than transparent. Various statements endorsing understanding of multiculturalism as "mutual enrichment" can be found throughout their chapter, with perhaps the strongest formulation stating that, due to this two-way process, "Australian national culture [is] being enriched and diversified into something 'rich and strange,' with the old and new blending into 'a better and more varied community of people'."[7] So it is quite puzzling why this "respect for, and encouragement of, cultural diversity," or "a cultural policy for enhancing the richness and variety of Australian life," is then so emphatically contrasted with this diversity affecting the self-understanding of the nation as a whole. It is unclear how the "mutual enrichment" of Australian culture could be accomplished without some transformation of a self-understanding of the nation. Perhaps it is the emphasis on "blending" that allows the authors not to consider it as contradicting their rejection of multiculturalism affecting Australian identity. Yet there is a not very well hidden assumption that multiculturalism, of whichever sort, is really "for immigrants," not for Australia. The authors insist that, whatever else can be said about multiculturalism, "Australia has a national identity that is not multicultural." The meaning of this statement is obscured further by its successive elaboration, which, on the one hand, recognizes the rich and complex character of this identity, with "many diverse but identifiable components," but, on the other hand, emphasizes its basic homogeneity.

If identity, on its collective and individual levels alike, is—as I think it is—a mode of creating a connection between past, present, and future, it has to be recognized that the past of many Australians cannot be blended together. They have to appropriate the present experience and to build up the future hopes from quite different perspectives.

I think that at least part of the problem with Galligan and Roberts's argument here is the absence of an analytical distinction between civic and cultural/ethnic concepts of a nation and nationalism. Such a distinction, while sometimes difficult and never absolute, would allow the authors to identify better the common components of the "political culture" of Australia, without attempting to push the argument about "unified cultural identity." Michael Ignatieff (1994: 7) reminds us that "according to the civic nationalist creed, what holds a society together is not common roots but law." It is worthwhile to note that in this respect the English traditions of rule of law and other political and legal institutions are of lasting significance for Australia, but this does not mean either that they are static and unchanged, or that they do not need a reinterpretation in which all citizens can participate.

Defining the crux of the crisis or, at least, the inadequacies of Australian multiculturalism in the gradual extension of the concept from immigrants to the society as a whole, Galligan and Roberts see the way out of this crisis in either abandoning altogether the idea and the policies of multiculturalism or, at least, in reducing it to what—according to them—it was originally designed for: namely, addressing the settlement and adaptation needs of immigrants from non–English speaking-backgrounds. This, however, involves an unacceptable and also not very consistent narrowing of the concept of multiculturalism, which, after all, is overwhelmingly supported by the Australian population.[8]

I shall return to the discussion of some of these issues, but let us first see how the question of the "crisis" is addressed by James Jupp who, in his chapter in this book, also puts forward some strong criticisms of the Galligan/Roberts position.

Jupp emphasizes the largely pragmatic, nonideological ("free of philosophical references") character of Australian multiculturalism, which can partly account for its relative success, making it easier to adjust various policies to the changes in concrete political and social situations. Yet this also means that there has hardly ever been an open public debate on these questions, and the Australian public has not really been involved in most of these decisions. Even the former structure of consultations and "critical interchanges" with some of the most affected groups has been, according to Jupp, basically run down. In consequence, Australian multiculturalism is "ill-equipped" to come to terms with such complex issues as growing Muslim population and various other transformations in the composition of the immigrant intake, which are made only more difficult by the complexities of the international situation. This, however, according to his view, does not spell the end of multiculturalism in Australia, but it may halt or slow down its further development and necessary adjustments.

In fact, Jupp is speaking not so much about the crisis of multiculturalism but rather about the negative role of its critics, who—beginning in the 1980s—systematically obstructed the working of multicultural programs, especially in their dimension of social justice and equalization of the opportunities for all members of the society. According to Jupp, Australian multiculturalism has been always oriented less toward the cultural maintenance of ethnic groups than toward the issue of social justice. It is frustrations on the latter front that, in his view, contribute most to the reproduction of ethnic closures. The democratic character of Australian society ensures not only that the "natural demise" of multiculturalism is not a viable perspective here but also that the conscious abandonment or "abolition of multiculturalism" is now scarcely an option. The influx of new groups of immigrants, facing increased difficulties of settlement and adaptation, further reduces the feasibility of abolishment. In addition, it is this dimension of social equality and equal opportunity and not above all the maintenance of cultural distinctiveness that is—according to Jupp—primarily desired by immigrants and other cultural groups themselves. "As long as Aborigines and Vietnamese and African refugees have much higher levels of unemployment than the average, they cannot be said to enjoy all the benefits of Australian citizenship," he says.

This seems to me quite a convincing and consistent argument. What is perhaps less consistent (or at least unelaborated), and therefore perhaps less convincing, are his scattered thoughts on assimilation. As Jupp himself notes, assimilation implies the existence of some stable or, at least, relatively fixed background to which to assimilate. At the same time, he quite rightly rejects any assumption that there is such uncontested, unified, and monolithic Australian identity and culture to which immigrants could simply assimilate. So the basis for integration, social cohesiveness, and solidarity, traditionally provided by the "national culture," in multicultural societies has to be sought elsewhere. Jupp is arguing that "what has held Australia together for at least the last 150 years is precisely a democratic way of doing things based on governments elected by the mass of the people and constrained both by law and by values and traditions."

Australian democratic arrangements can be quite lasting, but—as formulated here—they are basically procedural and not substantive. This implies that the changing social and cultural composition of the political community can (and probably does) influence the concrete arrangements themselves. In this respect, Jupp's argument resembles somewhat Habermas's notion of "constitutional patriotism" as a shared political culture of a society, separate (although not independent) from the plurality of "lifeworld cultures" present in any given society (Habermas 1992a, 1992b, 1994).[9] Habermas defines the cohesion and integration of political community as grounded primarily in the democratic interpretation of the constitutional principles; as a cohesion that depends upon a common *political culture,* in which individuals of various origins and affiliations participate as citizens and not upon an ethical-cultural form of life as a whole (Habermas 1992b: 17). Bhikhu Parekh makes a similar point, saying that "the sense of belonging [in multicultural societies] cannot be ethnic or based on shared cultural, ethnic and other characteristics, for a multicultural society is too diverse for that, but political in nature and based on a shared commitment to the political community" (Parekh 2000: 341). Acceptance of the framework of the political culture so understood could be thus posited as a normative requirement for all citizens and is safeguarded by the legal structure of the country. Or, as Jupp puts it in his chapter, we should "base common loyalties on values and institutions rather than on cultural inheritance." Such "political acculturation" does not involve, according to this conception, the necessity of giving up the person's particular cultural identification. Yet "the same universalistic content must in each case be appropriated from out of one's own cultural form of life" (Habermas 1992a: 241). For citizens are not abstract beings moving only in the political sphere. They are socialized and live within different cultural traditions and continuously redefine their identities through identification with various collectivities or communities and/or with different cultural traditions. Personal identities are thus deeply interwoven with collective identities of various sorts, including different ethnic groups, which themselves are also in a process of gradual transformation. This, of course, means that on the one hand, political culture is also not static but continually evolving and that, on the other hand, it is not only dependent upon the constituency of the political community but itself also contributes to the process of cultural identity formation. The transformation of political culture is, however, not only a rather protracted process but, concerning mainly procedural matters (not "what" we do, but "how" we do it), does allow for reaching agreement between participants in the negotiations.

While such a heuristic differentiation of the two forms of culture does make the prospect of maintaining a certain minimum of social integration without culturally restrictive or assimilationist policies of immigration more promising, this division is, no doubt, beset by its own difficulties. On the one hand, it is a challenge to those who attempt to make their entry into the already established political culture of the country and, on the other hand, to the majority culture's self-understanding, which is reflected in this culture and has to be redefined according to the expanding and changing membership. This challenge "becomes all the greater, the more profound are the religious, racial, or ethnic differences or the historical-cultural disjunctions to be bridged" (Habermas 1994: 118), something Australia—and the world in general—increasingly faces today. No less crucial from this point of view is the ability and willingness of the bearers of different cultural identities to maintain the intersubjective aspect of the process of identity formation, keeping it both internally reflexive and open to external questioning. Something similar—according to my reading—is hinted at by Jupp when he refers to community leaders' unwillingness to be self-reflective and critical with respect to their own groups. My impression, however, is that we can observe some slow changes in this respect. It is perhaps most visible within the Aboriginal communities, where such issues as domestic violence, rape, petrol sniffing, and drugs of various sorts are debated today somewhat more openly than was possible less than a decade ago.

There seems to be also an opening dialogue with the Australian Muslim communities. Especially in the wake of the 2005 London bombings, it has been realized that the majority of young people involved in various forms of unrest and violent actions in Australia also are locally born and bred. They are not "they," they are "us." This recognition created an uneasiness on both sides of the fence and led to some initiatives from the government but also from the Muslim communities to open a dialogue and to search together for some practical ways, on the one hand, to come to a better mutual understanding, and on the other hand, to address the underlying causes of the young Muslims' alienation from a society of which they are a part. Here we can point to such governmental initiatives as the August 2005 meeting with some "moderate" leaders of the Islamic community and the consecutive setting up of the Muslim Reference Group and several subgroups to advise and collaborate with the government on various issues of concern both to the

Muslim community and to the wider community.[10] Similar initiatives also occasionally come from the Muslim communities themselves. One of the controversial aspects of all these initiatives has been the question of "representation." Who can represent a community of over three hundred thousand Muslims, when, as pointed out earlier, they are significantly divided along ethnic and even religious lines? The criticisms here come from Muslims as well as from the broader community,[11] yet these initiatives should not be underestimated.

It has to be recognized, however, that to realize the ideal of a reflective openness is a very difficult task since it requires an ability to engage in a dialogue with others, to relativize one's own way of life in comparison with other ways of life. I would agree with Jupp's contention that access to resources is an extremely important precondition here, but it is not the only necessary condition of "bridging" the gap from both sides. No group should feel vulnerable to the extent that they can see no future. But also, no individual should be so vulnerable as to feel unable to choose (or reject) the collective identities fashioned by the various groups to which they may belong. For, to be sure, it is not only "minority" cultures that are susceptible to essentialization of their own cultural identity and to closure, which endangers the potential inclusiveness of political culture as one of the main integrative mechanisms in modern society. In the case of majority cultures, it is usually not existential insecurity that can lead to such a closure. Rather, it is a fear of seeing oneself with the eye of the "other" and taking this reflected image seriously.

One can thus perhaps speak of a crisis of multiculturalism in three different senses. First, such a crisis may be present if the relative closure of some ethnic groups–in itself often an understandable defense mechanism in view of their position of disadvantage–becomes coupled with two other tendencies: (1) it may provide a shelter for the forms of antisocial behavior (based, perhaps, on a lack of solidarity with the ethnically/culturally others, which can be easily reinforced by the totalizing stereotyping of these groups by the rest of society); (2) ethnic closure may become critical where the cultures affirm some principles that are irreconcilable with the prevalent values and political or social practices of the broader Australian society. These might include such practices as female circumcision, arranged marriages, "honor killings," sexual abuse of young girls, and so on. Such practices not only are rejected by the majority culturally; they clash with the basic legal framework of political society. Australia has witnessed cases of both of these sorts of conflicts, but they scarcely amount to a crisis, nor are they perceived as such by the society at large. One of the most obvious examples of the first type of conflict is provided by the recent riots on

Sydney's southern beaches and the following confusion about the ways of dealing with them. It is still unclear whether these cases are more drastic or more common than similar phenomena in the early history of ethnic groups (Irish, Italians) in Australia. While I don't think that these denote an acute crisis of multiculturalism, they certainly could develop in such a direction and point to the necessity of a much more transparent application of law and a much more vigorous and open public debate. Regarding the "irreconcilable values" type of problem, it seems to me that multiculturalism, in general, has worked quite well in Australia, and such cases are rather rare. Where they have arisen, they mostly are dealt with as legal issues, rather than as issues of culturally specific behavior.

Second, there can be a political crisis of multiculturalism in the sense that a significant segment of Australian society feels threatened and thus rejects the cultural pluralism that the state's policies accept as a fact and, to some degree, foster. This is a point made by Galligan and Roberts's chapter but rather vigorously rejected by Jupp. Needless to say, Australian society is stratified in a number of ways, not just by the ethnic or cultural divisions. Some groups of the population are no doubt resentful of multicultural policies (sometimes these include even earlier immigrants). This resentment, however, relates more to the real or imagined (mostly the latter) costs of the multicultural policies than to the cultural "purity" of the nation. This is one of the issues still being debated but is largely discredited together with Hansonism. According to various surveys, the proportion of the population rejecting multiculturalism as such is mostly well below 20 percent. As both chapters—especially Jupp's—argue, the complexity of the task is, however, increasing rather than decreasing, and it depends on the (primarily political) decisions of Australian citizens whether the society will be able to maintain its basically benevolent and tolerant character and to work toward reducing the existing or emerging cultural closures.

There is, however, in my opinion, no crisis of multiculturalism in the third sense of an acute danger that its idea and policies are or will be necessarily undermining the consciousness of national loyalty and thus cohesion. We all as individuals have multiple identifications (I don't think that we have multiple identities). Retaining one's connection with, and interest in, the culture of one's ethnic origin (often through many generations), and even the feeling and attitude of a specific solidarity with others of the same ethnic origin, does not contradict the loyalty and solidaristic commitment to the values and norms of the Australian political community and thus the consciousness of one's identity as an Australian. No doubt, our multiple identifications only in an ideal constitute a truly coherent set. Temporary conflicts between its various constituents in particular situations are always possible. But there is no principled contradiction between the cultural plurality accepted by multiculturalism and the unity implied by our common citizenship.

It is perhaps worthwhile to consider Habermas's (Habermas and Derrida 2003: 294) suggestion that "the reciprocal acknowledgment of the Other in his otherness ... can also become a feature of common identity."

NOTES

1. While I am restricting this question here to Australian multiculturalism, it could be formulated much more broadly, in relation to Canada and the United States, for example. The historical coincidence of the emergence of multiculturalism in various countries and the similar coincidence of its critiques, despite having some separate indigenous reasons, would deserve some attention in its own right, but this would go beyond the purpose of these comments.

2. Following Habermas's proposition, tolerance is understood here not in a paternalistic way of "doing a favor" or as an "act of mercy": "[w]ithin a democratic community whose citizens reciprocally grant one another equal rights, no room is left for an authority allowed to *one-sidedly* determine the boundaries of what is to be tolerated." Rather the "threshold of tolerance" has to be negotiated by a democratic community with a common reference to the "principles of the constitution" (Habermas in Borradori 2003: 40–41).

3. It is worthwhile noting that this is true not just about the "minority cultures" but about the "cultures of majority" as well.

4. I discuss various forms of cultural hybridity, their potential, and their ambiguity in Markus 1998.

5. Seyla Benhabib (2002: esp. 131–32) provides an interesting discussion of these issues.

6. It is, therefore, puzzling why the authors consider the connection between multiculturalism and pluralist democracy, as proposed by Jupp, unacceptable, or why, in their view, this "divorces accounts of nationality and citizenship from their base in reality and lived experience of Australians."

7. I am deliberately omitting the prior statement, which again speaks only about the adjustments of immigrants to Australian culture, but it is unclear how it can be reconciled with the "two-way process of mutual enrichment."

8. According to a recent poll, for example, more than 80 percent of the Australian population "supports" or "strongly supports" the policy of multiculturalism in Australia (*Sydney Morning Herald* 2005a).

9. The following brief summary of Habermas's propositions is largely drawn from Markus 1998.

10. See "Reference Group and Sub-Group Members," Australian Government Department of Immigration and Multicultural Affairs: www.immi.gov.au/multicultural/mcrg/05.htm [accessed 24 March 2006].

11. Perhaps the most interesting of such reflections is that expressed by Saeed Khan, a councillor in the Sydney district of Marrickville and a vice chairman of the Ethnic Communities' Council of New South Wales, who pointed out that "the way Muslims are organized—around mosques which operate largely along ethnic lines—has presented an obvious trap for the Federal government, which has selected a reference group to advise it on Muslim affairs from these religious groupings." What young Muslims need, according to Khan, is a "moderate mainstream model, rather than the religious leadership" (*Sydney Morning Herald* 9 March 2006).

Chapter 15

Multiculturalism and Australian National Identity

Geoffrey Brahm Levey

Perhaps the most animated controversy surrounding multiculturalism in Australia concerns its implications for Australian national identity. This, of course, is not surprising given that people's identity and sense of place and belonging are involved. But the controversy is also fueled by a perception that multiculturalism threatens social cohesion and the political integrity of the state, challenges for which a robust national identity has long been believed the necessary answer.

Among liberal philosophers, John Stuart Mill forcefully put this case for the crucial importance of common national sentiment. "Free institutions," wrote Mill (1972: 361) in 1859, "are next to impossible in a country made up of different nationalities." Mill, however, was unusual in this respect. Early liberal thinkers were primarily concerned with sectarian conflict and religious association rather than nationality or other forms of cultural identity. Their answer was to imagine the state as standing above the fray of religious convictions and group life, governing instead solely on the basis of the consent and interests of its individual citizens. The twentieth century saw many liberal theorists, especially in the United States, working to extend the principle of neutrality implicit in the earlier idea of the secular state to cover other cultural attachments and identity as well. On this model, refined to its most illustrious point in the work of the late John Rawls (1971, 1993), the state is blind to people's group identities and attachments, recognizing them only in terms of their common citizenship.

The point of departure for much multicultural political theory is the realization that the ethnocultural neutrality of liberal democracies is a fiction. All liberal democracies, including the standard exemplar of state neutrality, the United States, privilege particular cultural practices and traditions. They insist on a particular language or languages as the *lingua franca* of state business and societal intercourse; organize their year in terms of a particular calendar; recognize certain public holidays; prescribe what narratives are taught as history; and draw on particular cultural motifs and stories for the official symbols, insignia, flags, and anthems of the state. Some have gone— and do go—much farther than this in mandating particular cultures. Many multiculturalists believe that this cultural privileging—typically, of a majority group—warrants some redress for cultural minorities who are also members of the political community, if only to smooth the integration process. This readjustment clearly has implications for national identity, although what these might and should be are disputed.

Where does Australian multiculturalism sit in relation to these arguments?

THE AUSTRALIAN CASE

According to Will Kymlicka, perhaps the most influential political philosopher of multiculturalism, the Australian case is significant because it refutes the claim that multiculturalism is impossible in the Old World, where societies are both much older than New World states and far more culturally homogeneous. Australia may be a new society, Kymlicka notes, but it originally sought to recreate an Old World one. However,

> in a relatively short period of time, it has completely redefined itself from a monocultural British country to a multicultural "Asian" country. It now accepts more immigrants per capita than any other country in the world, most of them non-white and non-Christian. Although Australia was founded on a myth of British colonial settlement, not a myth of multiethnic immigration, it now very closely follows the model of older immigrant countries like the United States. (Kymlicka 2001b: 71)

Now, it is true that Australia has redefined itself, although not as dramatically as this statement suggests. For a start, the formative Australian identity was not simply a reiteration of that in Old World Britain. While nineteenth- and early twentieth-century Australia imagined itself as an outpost of Britain, it did so in its own fashion. It could not but be inventive. It was remote geographically, the landscape was harsh, and the local conditions were novel. Moreover, at the time of Australia's founding, there was no "British identity," as such, in Britain (Kumar 2003; McGregor 2006). This identity could only be forged where English, Scots, Irish, Welsh, and Cornish, among other settlers and their descendants, had to live with and rely on each other in a new environment (Rickard 1996). Whatever else it was supposed to mean, the claim that Australians were then "more British than the British"—a phrase invoked by many other British colonies—was literally true. Perhaps the most succinct way of encapsulating the formative Australian identity is to say that it was an amalgam of "Britishness," whiteness, *and* Australianness (Cole 1971; Kane 1997b: 121). To this profile, one probably needs to add masculinity (Crotty 2001; Lake 1986, 1997) and Christianity.

As for the more recent period, Australia has never defined itself as an "Asian" country in cultural terms; nor is it the highest per capita immigrant country.[1] It is true that most immigrants are non-Christian, but only if one includes those who did not formally define their religion, were of no religion, or did not state a religion along with those of non-Christian faiths. Otherwise, Christianity continues to be by far the most common religion among immigrants to Australia.[2] The claim that most immigrants are non-white is unfounded for the simple reason—aside from the vagaries of defining whiteness—that Australia has not devised or recorded any such category for decades. Overstatements, however, do not diminish the profound changes that *have* occurred in Australia's social composition and policies (see chapter 1). These changes are dramatic enough. The question is: if Australia has changed from a "monocultural British country," in the qualified sense above, what exactly has it changed to? In particular, what does its commitment to multiculturalism—in policy if not in word—mean for its national identity?

THREE ACCOUNTS OF AUSTRALIAN NATIONAL IDENTITY

Political theorists tend to debate these sorts of questions about national identity in terms of three broad approaches.[3] One approach—*ethnic nationalism*—understands the nation in terms of a community of shared culture and common descent (e.g., Anthony Smith 1986). A second approach—*liberal nationalism*—posits the nation in terms of a community of shared culture and language grounded in a territorial homeland, but rejects the requirement of ethnic or common descent (e.g., Kymlicka 1995, Miller 1995). The third approach—*postnationalism*—rejects the need of a national culture altogether, but divides over what should replace it.[4] Civic republicans emphasize the importance of sharing a *political* territory, history, and institutions in forging and sustaining a particular community (e.g., Taylor 1989; Viroli 1995). Constitutional patriots contend that citizenship or political membership should be grounded in an acceptance of rationally defensible general principles (e.g., Habermas 1992b; 1994). Cosmopolitans believe that modern identities are perforce made up of a diverse range of cultural and national elements (e.g., Waldron 1995).

These three approaches—ethnic nationalism, liberal nationalism, and postnationalism—also frame the public and scholarly discourse on Australian national identity, although the ethnic nationalist model as exemplified by the "White Australia" policy is today rarely defended.[5] The three accounts of Australian national identity on which I wish to focus are thus a bit narrower in range, but still very much in contention: namely, a "thick" and a "thin" version of liberal nationalism, and the postnationalist arguments. Both the "thick" and the "thin" versions of liberal nationalism are forms of cultural nationalism; however, for convenience and to help distinguish them in the discussion, I shall refer to the "thick" version as "cultural nationalism," while using "liberal nationalism" to designate the "thin" variant. Of course, even describing versions as "thick" and "thin" is relative to the context being explored. What today is considered a "thick" Australian identity, for example, is likely to be considered a "thin" if not anorexic identity elsewhere.

On the "thick" conception or cultural nationalist model, multiculturalism is considered to be, at best, inapt for Australian circumstances (Galligan and Roberts 2004: chap. 4, and this volume) and, at worst, destructive of Australian national identity and cohesion (Blainey 1984; Knopfelmacher 1982; Windschuttle 2004: chap. 11). Australia is said to have a distinct Anglo-Australian character and identity, which has great capacity to integrate newcomers. Advocates point to the fact, for example, that intermarriage rates among ethnic and mainstream Australians are high, increasing with each generation (Galligan and Roberts, this volume; Hirst 2001; Windschuttle 2005). This welcoming of intermarriage in a post–"White Australia" era indicates how the prevailing "thick" conception of Australian identity has changed since the days of the White Australia policy. Today, "thickness" is claimed not so much in terms of a strict ethnic nationality or a bloodline of ancestry—the "crimson thread of kinship," in Sir Henry Parkes's immortal words of 1890—than as a cultural heritage open to all.

"Thick" conceptions of Australian national identity have the virtue of recognizing the deep and abiding influence of Anglo-Australian culture on the institutions and patterns of life in Australia. However, the accounts are problematic in that they tend to do what they accuse Australian multicultural policy of doing—namely, essentialize ethnic group identity and membership, rather than allowing for their internal diversity, dynamism, and hybridity.[6] As John Hirst (2001: 30), historian and chairman of the Commonwealth Government's Civics Education Group (responsible for designing the civics and citizenship program taught in schools), puts the accusation: "Multicultural policy envisaged a world of distinct ethnic groups. This was more and more make-believe."[7] There is, of course, some validity to this claim. Attempts to administer resources to cultural groups will perforce invite the problems of group definition and intragroup hierarchy and control (see Kukathas 1992). Indeed, Stephen Castles (2001: 808) goes so far as to suggest that Clifford Geertz's "primordialist notions of ethnicity" found their way into early Australian multicultural thinking: "Australian society could be seen as a collection of relatively homogeneous ethnic communities, each integrated by a distinct set of values and cultural practices, interpreted by 'natural leaders' who were usually male and middle-class."

This picture of Australian multiculturalism is, however, also misleading. First, even at its most primordial, Australian multiculturalism has never endorsed the kind of culturally autonomous, self-governing communities evidenced elsewhere around the world or imagined by various thinkers, from libertarians (e.g., Kukathas 2003) to Austro-Marxists (e.g., Bauer 2000). Nor does it resemble Horace Kallen's (1998) original idea of "cultural pluralism" for the United States as a "democracy of nationalities." Though sparse on detail, Kallen's idea was framed in terms of a "federation or commonwealth of nationalities" and modeled on Switzerland—"a nation of three nationalities"—and on Great Britain—"a nation of at least four nationalities" (Kallen 1998: 108, 113-14; Levey 2005: 160–62).[8] Even the structural pluralism unsuccessfully promoted by early Australism multiculturalists, such as Jean Martin (1981), was mild and integrationist compared to worldly conceptions of cultural pluralism (Lopez 2000: 54–56). Second, while multicultural policy did turn on some assumption of "distinct ethnic groups," neither the assumption nor the administration based on it were such as to lock people in or out of ethnic group membership. Third and relatedly, Australian multicultural policy is, as I noted in chapter 1, highly individualistic. The rights to cultural identity and to social justice apply to individual Australians, however they define and practice their cultural identities. So the "multi" in Australian multiculturalism stands not only for diversity among groups but also *within* groups.

In contrast, Hirst's analysis treats ethnic groups monolithically, yoking the fate of members of ethnic groups to the choices of their coethnics. He cites figures to highlight the increasing assimilation of immigrants across the second and third generations and thus the supposed pointlessness of multicultural policy. For example, among Greeks, "ninety per cent of the first generation were Orthodox, 82% of the second; 45% of the third" (Hirst 2001: 30). But these figures also show how large proportions of this community in each generation wish to observe their faith and traditions. They beg the question of why these people should not be entitled to cultural consideration where necessary and appropriate. Nor is it clear why the cultural interests of present generations should be answered on the basis of the (anticipated) cultural interests of (some among) future generations. Here and now, many immigrants do seek to observe and retain their ethnoreligious heritage.

Why does Hirst not see this? Why is he so concerned to dismiss multi-cultural policy as misguided even where it might serve the interests of many immigrant groups or their members? Perhaps the answer is that his thinking about multiculturalism—like that of many other advocates of a "thick" conception of Australian identity—is based on the assumption that it necessarily denies the reality or importance of Australian culture. As he puts it,

> The migrants were and are in no doubt that there is an Australian way of doing things, an Australian culture. This is the second way that the multicultural label for Australia is misleading. It suggests that there is simply diversity; that there is no dominant culture. Migrants who want to get on and be accepted know better. (Hirst 2001: 30)

It is the postnationalists who are most concerned with denying the reality or political importance of a distinct Australian culture and identity. In many ways they are the mirror image of the "thick" conceptions. Whereas the latter see multiculturalism as undermining Australian national identity, postnationalists believe that invocations of a national cultural identity are antithetical to Australia's cultural diversity, multiculturalism, and/or universal liberal democratic values. To this extent, they express, in the Australian context, the traditional tensions between liberalism and nationalism, as examined in this volume by John Kane. They believe that Australia's commitment to liberal democratic values together with its cultural diversity requires that the state be neutral with respect to ethnocultural matters, although they vary in what this means.

Some argue that Australians should simply dispense with the idea of a national identity altogether. For example, in their well-known book *Mistaken Identity: Multiculturalism and the Demise of Nationalism in Australia,* Stephen Castles and his associates concluded: "We do not need a new ideology of nationhood.... Our aim must be a community without a nation" (Castles et al. 1992: 148). Similarly, Mary Kalantzis (2000) argues for a postnationalist social contract that she calls "civic pluralism," where the emphasis is on the acceptable rules of engagement rather than on a shared identity. Others argue that Australian identity should be grounded only in political or civic values, such as tolerance, individual liberty, equality, reciprocity and a commitment to democratic institutions (e.g., Horne 1997; Kukathas 1993a, 1993b).[9] And still others in this camp suggest that Australian identity should be centered on the idea or practice of multiculturalism itself (Jayasuriya 2005; Theophanous 1995; *Sydney Morning Herald* 2006). Ironically, this last idea found expression in the National Multicultural Advisory Council report that prepared the ground for the Howard government's *New Agenda for a Multicultural Australia:* "Australian multiculturalism will continue to be a defining feature of our evolving national identity" (NMAC 1999: 13–14).[10] Former Labor Party leader Mark Latham also picked up on the idea in the 2004 election campaign, giving it a cosmopolitan twist: we "should recognise that multiculturalism lies, not so much between individuals, but within them, the habit of living one's life through many cultural habits.... This should be a unifying idea in Australia's national identity" (Latham 2004).

Postnationalist arguments have the virtue of seeking an inclusive definition of Australian identity and culture that acknowledges the cultural diversity of the Australian people. Yet these approaches are flawed and seem destined to fail. First, as Kymlicka (1995, 2001b), among others, has argued, postnationalist arguments ignore the many ways in which liberal democratic states already and inevitably endorse particular ethnocultural traditions, from the language spoken to state symbols. Moreover, as John Kane points out in this book, the putative "political" or "civic" values of democracy, toleration, equality, and so on have deep cultural imprints and a jagged, if not always a sharp, cultural edge. The reason that stipulated limits of liberal toleration are often so controversial, for example, is precisely because liberal democratic values are anything but culturally neutral: they are friendly to some cultural traditions, not so friendly to others. In short, postnationalism overlooks the cultural dimensions of public institutions in liberal democracies and of the stipulated civic values themselves.

Second, national identity can and does play an important role in generating and sustaining social cohesion, a sense of belonging, and a commitment to the commonweal. Liberal nationalists rightly argue that all these features are legitimate interests of democratic states (e.g., Canovan 1996; Kymlicka 2001b: 20; David Miller 1995; Tamir 1993). They are features, moreover, that would seem to be all the more imperative in culturally diverse democracies. In his book *Veil Politics in Liberal Democratic States,* Ajume Wingo (2003) makes the case that universal values and constitutional principles are far less important for motivating ordinary citizens to accept democratic practices than are the symbols—including stories, rituals, monuments, and memorials—that a polity draws on or develops (cf. Abizadeh 2002; Mason 1999). These symbols or "veils," as Wingo calls them, are typically the very stuff of nation-building and national consolidation. To reject national identity as obsolete, then, or to define it as if it could be ethnoculturally neutral, is to forsake or to ignore one of the most powerful political forces available for bringing people together as a community.

Attempts to fashion a new Australian identity on multiculturalism itself fare little better. On the face of it, this approach seems to be a category mistake: that is, it mistakes political and administrative measures that variously allow, accommodate, and integrate the realm of diverse identities for an identity itself. Yet all national identities are constructed and imagined (Anderson 1983), so why not an identity imagined around multiculturalism?[11] The difficulty is at once semantic and symbolic. The American metaphor of the "melting pot" helps illustrate what a national identity focused on multiculturalism is up against. The image of the melting pot misdescribes American society, according to Wingo (2003: 126), since "the U.S. population is increasingly a collection of distinct subpopulations, with more diversity *between* ethnic, linguistic, or cultural groups than *within* those same groups." Yet the fact that the "melting pot" is a myth is irrelevant, he says; what is important is that it offers a powerful symbol of unity that well serves the legitimate interests of American democracy in creating a *sense* of solidarity.

Compare the Australian case. Australian society and culture are highly integrative—or so we are told. Intermarriage rates are high; the title of "new Australians" is or was eagerly bestowed on immigrants; the nomenclature of hyphenated identities is still uncommon (Hirst 2001: 31). "Multiculturalism," the proposed symbol for Australian identity, is also mythic, on this account, in misdescribing Australian society. Yet, unlike the metaphor of the "melting pot" in the United States, the proposed national myth for Australia *semantically* conveys diversity and difference rather than unity and solidarity. "Multiculturalism" lacks the rhetorical resonance of the "melting pot" for nation-building purposes.

I stress that the difficulty here is more rhetorical than substantive. Multiculturalism is, indeed, concerned with integrating a diverse society based on liberal democratic notions of liberty, equality, and justice. Nevertheless, while polls have consistently shown that the overwhelming majority of Australians support multiculturalism (Dunn et al. 2004; Goot and Watson 2005; *Sydney Morning Herald* 2005a; *The Australian* 2005a), it is also the case that many Australians are unable to warm to the term.[12] As the National Multicultural Advisory Council (1999: 96) reported, pollster "[Irving] Saulwick's research identified a strong desire for unity in this country. He showed that the concept of multiculturalism raised in many minds an emphasis on separateness rather than togetherness." By the mid-1990s, even one of the architects of Australian multicultural policy was calling for the term to be dropped, although he continued to support the policies for which it stands (Zubrzycki 1996). In 2007, the Howard government finally expunged the word from governmental use (Robb 2006a; Gambaro 2007). The Rudd Labor government has reinstated "multicultural affairs" in the bureaucratic lexicon, albeit as a parliamentary secretarial rather than a ministerial responsibility. It remains to be seen whether the new government will commend "multiculturalism" as well. At any rate, for all of these reasons, it makes more sense to construe multiculturalism as a set of principles, policies, and programs in the service of an Australian national identity than as the locus of that identity itself.

This brings us to the intermediate position of "liberal nationalists." Their "thin" account of national identity acknowledges both the legitimate national interests of liberal democracies and the need to make room for cultural minorities. The debate at this level is largely about the precise calibration of the "thinness." The Israeli philosopher, and now politician, Yael Tamir (1993) includes in "national identity" virtually all the cultural aspects that "thick conceptions" and even ethnic nationalists do at the level of nation-states. However, unlike these other positions, she insists that national self-determination does not require or presuppose political sovereignty or statehood, cultural attachments are matters of individual choice, and members of cultural minorities are just as entitled to express their "national identity" as are the members of the majority culture (Levey 2001b). For Kymlicka, "nation-building" in liberal democracies is legitimate where it is limited to creating and maintaining what he calls a "societal culture":

> I call it a societal culture to emphasize that it involves a common language and social institutions, rather than common religious beliefs, family customs, or personal lifestyles.... Citizens of a modern liberal state do not share a common culture in such a thick, ethnographic sense.... If we want to understand the nature of modern state-building, we need a very different, and thinner, conception of culture, which focuses on a common language and societal institutions. (Kymlicka 2001b: 18–19)

Kymlicka allows that liberal democracies also engage in nation-building by forming a national media, developing national symbols and holidays, and memorializing majority group heroes and events. Another liberal nationalist, David Miller (1995, 2000), emphasizes the multiple dimensions of a national identity or "public culture," as he calls it, under which he includes political principles, social norms, and cultural and religious values.

To my mind, liberal nationalist approaches—for all their good sense—wrongly dismiss or ignore two important dimensions of national identity. First, liberal nationalists too quickly discount the place of "national character."[13] The inclination to do so is understandable enough given the obscene ways in which such notions have been politically exploited or socially expressed in modern history. However, as liberal nationalists know better than most, nationalism itself can serve both illiberal and liberal goals; the task is to distinguish its legitimate roles and uses. The concept of national character is often challenged on the grounds that the attributes highlighted are stereotypical and contradicted by competing images and stereotypes. Consider one of the most celebrated portraits of the Australian character, Russel Ward's *The Australian Legend* (1958: 1): "According to the myth, the 'typical Australian' is a practical man, rough and ready in his manners and quick to decry any appearance of affectation in others." Chandran Kukathas (1993b: 147–48) cites Ward's portrait and then Jonathan King's opposing assessment to the effect that Australians are "lazy, arrogant, racist, urban money-grabbers who have surrounded themselves with the myth that they are outback heroes." Joining many other commentators on the subject, Kukathas notes the "difficulties in trying to tie down any notion of a 'national character'" and moves on.

And yet, as everyone knows, the French really are different from the Germans. Canadians are different from Americans, and Australians are different from the Brits and even the New Zealanders. Imprinted, as they are, with their national cultures, they tend to exhibit distinctive habits of mind, emotion, and behaving, instantly noticeable to most outsiders. That many nationals do not exhibit their "national qualities," and that there may be contradictions in the national character or even vying national characters, is neither here nor there; in human affairs, the only surprise should be if it were otherwise. As the Austro-Marxist Otto Bauer (2000 [1907]: 22) put it, "The nation is a *relative community of character;* it is a community of character because, in any given era, a range of corresponding characteristics can be observed among the great majority of the nation's members." Bauer rightly emphasizes the dynamic and historically variable nature of national character. No educated person could deny, he says, that "the Germans of today have much more in common with the other civilized nations of their own time than with the Germanic tribes of Tacitus's time" (Bauer 2000: 20). The point applies with equal force to Anglo-Australians' relation to "ethnic" Australians today compared to Anglo-Australians of generations ago.

I suspect that liberal nationalists—who tend to travel a lot—might grant this much at a cultural level but insist that issues of national character should be separated from the state and quarantined from the business of liberal-democratic government. However, national character will perforce find expression through a society's governing institutions; how could it not do so? All three schools of thought tend to misunderstand the place of national character. The crucial point about national character is not that it doesn't exist (postnationalism) or that it should be quarantined from government (liberal nationalism) or that it should be politically promoted (cultural nationalism). Rather, the point is that while national character shapes government, government cannot legislate national character; it cannot be the *object* or intention of political administration without doing it violence. This is because national character is constantly evolving, and any *deliberate* attempt to represent it will wrench out particular aspects, ensuring that the accounts offered can, at best, bear a passing relation to it. The resultant image is bound to be "absurdly romanticized and exaggerated" (Ward 1958: 1)—indeed, a grotesque.

If national character is not to become national caricature, then it must be left to its own devices. It will find its own expression. Consider, for example, the extraordinary building that is the Parliament House in Canberra. That ordinary Australians and visitors can walk up grassy banks and literally stand over their political representatives not only exemplifies a characteristic Australian attitude to authority and an egalitarian temper; it springs from this attitude and temper. Or, still at Parliament House, take the public uproar in 2005 that followed a regulation requiring security guards to cease using the expression "mate" when addressing politicians and the public. An MP taking umbrage at the informality had prompted the move. The public's sense that acceptable norms had been breached came only when the guards were told to be more formal. National character, because it is character, expresses itself just in and through what we do and find "natural" or acceptable.

The second dimension of national identity that liberal nationalists tend to underplay concerns what may be called the crucible of civil society. Because they seek to render nationalism compatible with liberal democracy, liberal nationalists focus mainly on the legitimate boundaries of state action and on access to the public sphere. At the same time, the question of the place of cultural minorities tends to be viewed dichotomously in terms of the national culture, on the one hand, and discrete "minority cultures," on the other. Thus, Kymlicka (2001b) presents us with two domains culture-wise: a national culture embodied in societal institutions and overseen by the state, and ethnocultures that are the province of immigrant groups and individuals.[14] National cultures, as we have seen, are "thinned" out in terms of which aspects—typically, a shared language, societal and political institutions, the nation's history, and national symbols—are deemed to be appropriate for government involvement. Other cultural aspects—regarding food, dress, speech, surnames, leisure activities, and family size—some of which were once pursued by states in their more assimilationist days, are deemed to be the prerogative of ethnic groups or their individual members. As Kymlicka (2001b: 33) writes: "The 'melting pot' image was never accurate. Immigrants do indeed integrate into common institutions and learn the dominant language, but they remain, visibly, and proudly, distinctive in their ethnic identities and attachments."

But this picture of integration is as inaccurate as the assimilation model. A liberal-national culture is usually constructed and forged also among people's relations in civil society. In Australia, as in other liberal democracies, there are myriads of interactions among immigrant groups and between them and the dominant cultural majority that occur beyond societal institutions, and which result in cultural absorption and integration of one form or another. For obvious reasons, this absorption is mostly in the direction of the patterns of the dominant culture. John Hirst (2001: 30–31) cites the stories of a Greek husband rejecting his wife's request for the family to acquire a goat as un-Australian, and of a proud Sri Lankan, Bekaboru Kiyanahati Balapan Koyako, coming to the realization, in meeting other Australians, that he badly needed a shorter name (he chose Kojak). These are great examples of how national cultural integration is mediated also through interpersonal relations. There are many other examples of the inductive power of Anglo-Australian culture at work in everyday life, including the norms governing queue-forming, social space, voice-raising, speech turn-taking, spitting and belching, and the polite reluctance to use the car horn on anything but the most urgent occasions.[15] As Kalantzis (2000: 108) observes (albeit critically), although designating a "set of cultural characteristics" as "Anglo-Australian," "Anglo-Celtic Australian," or "mainstream Australian" is problematic in that it "masks real internal differences, it alludes to certain ways of speaking, thinking, working and being in the world."

In Australia, "Anglo-Australian" culture remains dominant, and one cannot begin to make sense of Australian institutions and life without understanding this much.[16] The mistake, of course, is to think that the integration is *always* in the direction of the cultural majority. The impact of Aboriginal culture on Anglo-Australian life—including vocabulary, motifs, art, and even the sense of emplacement and connection to the land—is clear, if too little appreciated (Mulcock 2002; Read 2000; Trigger 2006). Anglo-Australian culture also has been changed in various ways by successive waves of immigrants, from the rise of soccer to a popular sport, to so-called new Australian cuisine (incorporating Asian and Continental influences), to the now general preference for coffee over tea and wine over beer (Dale 2007). Judging by the entries in metropolitan telephone directories, the conventions regarding the complexity of surnames have also been greatly extended. So a national culture is also forged in the hurly-burly of civil society, as well as via common societal institutions. In subtle ways, the Anglo-Celtic Australian culture of old is becoming an "Anglo-meltic" one. That is, Anglo-Australian culture, while still dominant, is being modified.

Australian national identity, then, is multifaceted and occupies different domains. There are aspects of national identity having to do with Australian character that will naturally affect the way we govern ourselves, but which we can scarcely do anything about without warping them. There are aspects of national identity that are duly the province of government, such as the inculcation and transmission of a national language, the teaching of the nation's history, and the establishment of national institutions, holidays, and memorials. And there are aspects of national identity that properly belong in the realm of civil society and beyond the business of government, such as how people dress, call themselves, or spend their leisure, what languages they speak to each other, and even in what accent they speak their English. Here, among the myriad relations of Australians, will also be forged the habits and sentiments and character of the Australian people.

I do not mean to suggest that this account of the sites of Australian identity amounts to a radically new or fourth model. On the contrary, in differentiating domains of national identity and delimiting those that are and are not the province of government, it is indelibly a version of *liberal* nationalism. It is a version, however, that accepts that Australian character has a place in national identity and an implicit impact on government, and which recognizes that Australian national identity and character will be forged in the relations among *all* people in civil society, and not only by state policy, societal institutions, or the dominant Anglo-Australian majority. Protagonists of a "thick" conception of Australian identity such as Hirst are right to note that there is more to Australian culture and identity than merely civic values or a multicultural mélange. However, the question is *which* aspects of Australian culture and *which* of its values, if any, should define the conditions of membership and govern access to opportunities in the polity. Postnationalists such as Kalantzis (2000: 108) are rightly concerned that Anglo-Celtic ways of "being in the world" are "explicitly and implicitly valued and rewarded" across the board in Australian society. However, the answer to inappropriate cultural privileging is not to be found in expunging or denying a place for Australian culture and identity, as if this were even possible, and installing a "new civic compact" in its stead. Rather, the answer lies in delimiting the domains of national culture and checking the privileging.

In terms of Australian policy, the 1989 *National Agenda for a Multicultural Australia* presents a very similar approach to Australian identity. It acknowledges the importance of "our British heritage" in helping "to define us as

Australian." It emphasizes that "multiculturalism does not entail a rejection of Australian values, customs and beliefs." As part of this "common core," it highlights the "basic institutional framework of Australian society," including English as the national language, rule of law, democracy, freedom and tolerance of expression, equality of the sexes, and an "overriding and unifying commitment to Australia." It expressly *excludes* from the public definition of Australian identity ethnocultural aspects such as skin color, style of dress, mode of worship, or other languages spoken. And it recognizes that the "Australian way of life" will evolve and change over time with the "changing face of the Australian population," among other influences (OMA 1989: 50–52). The *National Agenda* has some weaknesses. For example, it does not explain what is meant by an "overriding commitment" to Australia's interests "first and foremost," which, as I noted in chapter 1, seems overreaching (Kymlicka 2001a: 173; Levey 2001a: 877–78).

Nevertheless, the *National Agenda* outshines the subsequent national multicultural policies on the matter of national identity. Both the *New Agenda* and *Multicultural Australia* (Commonwealth of Australia 1999, 2003) tie multiculturalism to Australian national identity in a much less differentiated fashion. While they also promote the same core civic values, they emphasize the idea of Australians' "multicultural identity" and treat the country's British heritage and predominant "Anglo-Australian" culture as if they were of minor significance, if not antiquarian interest. And, of course, prior to the 1970s, government policy was to do the very reverse and emphasize "thick" conceptions of national identity in the form of Anglo-conformity above all else. It is to the credit of the architects of Australia's first national statement of multiculturalism that they fashioned such a subtle and sophisticated version of liberal nationalism, in key respects superior to prevailing models in multicultural political theory. But as we will now see, a policy statement, even a finely crafted one, does not a country remake.

CULTURAL RESISTANCE AND BORDER CROSSINGS

To return to our question—what has Australia changed to?—the answer is to a much more open, tolerant, culturally diverse society than it once was. Still, it is far from clear that Australia is best likened to the immigrant and pluralistic model of the United States, or even the multicultural experience of Canada. In some ways, Australia never has practiced multiculturalism in the manner of its policy aims and commitments. To this extent, I agree with Brian Galligan and Winsome Roberts's argument in this volume that multiculturalism misdescribes the Australian reality, but would add to their account of why it does. It is not only that Australia is wonderfully integration-ist. The flipside of an "integration" that welcomes immigrants on condition that they "be like us" and no longer themselves is, after all, not altogether welcoming. As Malcolm Fraser (1981) put it in his day as prime minister, "We cannot demand of people that they renounce the heritage they value, and yet expect them to feel welcome as full members of our society." Yet there is a strong strain in "Anglo-Australian" thinking and culture that is exclusivist and culturally nationalistic in exactly this way.[17] Consider two instructive social facts, what may be called "warped melting pot" and "no hyphen."

The nature of the continued and overwhelming dominance of "Anglo-Australia" on the country's institutions and norms reveals itself in the curi-ous way in which the metaphor or even the idea behind the melting pot has been deployed in Australia. In its traditional meaning, as made popular in the United States by the English-Jewish playwright Israel Zangwill (1975 [1909]), the melting pot stood for a kind of democratic assimilation in which all the various immigrant cultures would combine to produce a "new Amer-ican" identity. A less "democratic" formulation of the image would have immigrant cultures melt and disappear into the dominant culture—assimila-tionism. Zangwill's notion of the melting pot is generally how the metaphor has been understood and deployed in Australia, but its suitability has always been stretched in a context where Anglo-Australian norms loom so large. During the heyday of postwar assimilationism, for example, Department of Immigration officers drew on the melting pot image in portraying Aus-tralia by pointing to how the British were an amalgamation of "Celts, Ro-mans, Angles, Saxons, Jutes, Normans and the rest" (Australian Citizenship Convention *Digest* quoted in Lopez 2000: 47, and n. 7, 473). The analogy sim-ply begs the question of why the department was then insisting on Anglo-conformity in a new society.

Hirst (2001: 35) also appeals to the melting pot in concluding his essay:

> The marrying and partnering of people of all sorts across all boundaries is the great unifying force in Australia. The United States of America never saw such a rapidly melting melting pot. It will produce before too long a new people, who will have darker skins, much better suited to this place and our sun.

Hirst certainly suggests Zangwill's idea by his vision of a "new [Australian] people." Yet it is significant that while he entertains a changed skin color, all but one of his examples of immigrant cultural absorption involve im-migrants accepting the established Anglo-Australian way of life. The one exception concerns a Vietnamese busker in downtown Sydney playing the didgeridoo. Unimagined, and perhaps unimaginable, are true-blue Austra-lians playing the sitar. As Hirst himself notes, "new Australian" was the standard term bestowed on recent immigrants in the postwar period, and it presumed their acceptance of the Australian way of life as they found it. For Zangwill and the American "melting pot," the notion of a "new American" involved a genuinely new identity; Down Under, being a "new Australian" meant that one was on route to becoming an "old Australian."

Even more oddly, in recent years the melting pot idea has tended to be associated, if anything, with multiculturalism. For example, in a speech on Australia's national identity in the twenty-first century, former prime minister Bob Hawke suggested that the success of Australia's multicultural society is evidenced by the high intermarriage rate across the different ethnic communities: "a new and richer character is emerging from the extent of intermarriage between different ethnic groups within the Australian community" (Hawke 1999).[18] If this seems a strange way of trumpeting multiculturalism—a policy ostensibly about celebrating cultural difference—the melting pot also is often associated with multiculturalism as cultural maintenance (e.g., Burn 2002). These associations arise and get their traction in the Australian context because both multiculturalism and the melting pot are seen as opposing the old but still popular cultural nationalist model of Anglo-conformity and monoculturalism.

A related social fact is that, unlike in the United States and even Canada, the rubric of hyphenated identities is scarcely used in Australia.[19] We have indigenous Australians and Greek Australians and Vietnamese Australians, and so on—all without a hyphen. There are exceptions, and they, too, are significant: Anglo-Australians or Anglo-Celtic Australians.[20] The hyphen is reserved for the dominant groupings that first defined the core culture of the nation. As I suggested above, some hybridization or mutual cultural borrowing and absorption perforce occurs between cultural minorities and the Anglo-Australian majority. On the one side, the core culture has broadened over time with the changing face of the population; on the other side, most "ethnic" Australians find, on visiting their mother countries after some years, that they are no longer the same as their former countrymen—their Australianness makes a difference. For all that, and with the possible exception of gastronomy, the hybridization or integration of one's minority and Australian identities remains widely discouraged. The expectation, rather, is that one relinquishes one's minority identity and assimilate or else bracket that identity when participating in mainstream Australian life. Multiculturalism, in practice, has done little to dislodge this expectation.

Peter Medding has remarked on the political implications of this compartmentalization of identity in multicultural Australia in relation to the Jews, comparing it to the very different situation in the United States, with its long tradition of cultural pluralism. For Australian Jews, their "two sets of

identities and commitments"—their Australianness and their Jewishness—
"are compatible," says Medding (2004: 238–39), in

> that both can be maintained fully and simultaneously, but that essentially they
> are on separate planes and address different aspects of individual and group
> existence.... [In contrast,] American Jews operate in the public arena on the
> premise that it is their *right and duty* as citizens and as members of a culturally
> distinct group to contribute their vision of what is good for American society
> to the ongoing debate in the public square, and in the belief that they may have
> something unique or of value to add to the whole society.... Multiculturalism in
> Australia does not beckon groups to participate in the public square in anything
> like this way.

Studies of ethnic participation in Australian politics have tended to focus
on the questions of their vote choice, political influence, and political representation (Anthony 2006; Jupp, York, and McRobbie 1989; McAllister
1988; Zappalà 1998). The *National Agenda* (OMA 1989: 9–10) similarly drew
attention to the underrepresentation of ethnic minorities in government,
the public service, and other institutions. Medding's critical observation
of Australian multiculturalism highlights another dimension and complements Philip Pettit's argument in this volume that having minorities politically engaged and "urging the case" for their own interests and insights can
well serve the democratic process and the citizenry in general. To borrow
from James Jupp's (2003) valuable inquiry, *How Well Does Australian Democracy Serve Immigrant Australians?* we need also to ask: "How well does Australia allow immigrants to serve Australian democracy?"

Despite thirty years of official multiculturalism, cultural difference is still
commonly perceived as a mark of separating oneself from the broader community. The current public disquiet over the *hijab* and *burka* worn by some
Muslim women is a good example, with coalition MPs Sophie Panapoulos
(now Sophie Mirabella) and Bronwyn Bishop, *The Australian* newspaper, and
conservative commentators such as Janet Albrechtsen leading the charge
against allowing forms of dress that "ordinary Australians" find "confronting" (e.g., *The Australian* 2006).[21] While the concern over Islamic headwear
is sometimes framed in terms of women's rights, often it turns on the cloth-
ing simply being seen as a rejection of integration and an "iconic item of
defiance," as Bronwyn Bishop put it (*Sydney Morning Herald* 2005b). Such
perceptions might be compared with the specially made *hijab* that allowed
Constable Maha Sukkar to graduate from the Victorian Police Academy,
and so become Australia's first Muslim police officer to wear the traditional
headpiece (*The Australian* 2004). Few career choices better illustrate a woman's independence and integration in society.

Part of the Australian ambivalence toward cultural diversity and multiculturalism has a long and honorable pedigree in a new, faraway, and egalitarian society not wanting to replicate the ethnonationalist divisions and conflicts that have plagued other parts of the world. Some of it has to do with the deep assumption embedded in the concept of the modern nation-state that sovereignty and political integrity simply require cultural homogeneity. But much of it emerges also from conventional tendencies of cultural nationalism and ethnic hierarchy (Anthony Smith 1986). Even allowing for its overstatement in the American context, one can scarcely say of Australia what Michael Walzer (2001: 151) has opined about the United States: "What has always struck me as the most remarkable feature of American history, impossible to imagine in any 'old world' nation-state, is that the Anglo-Americans allowed themselves to become a minority in—what they must have imagined to be—*their* country."

Of course, to many of its critics, the adoption of multiculturalism marks the moment when Anglo-Australians began allowing themselves to be a minority in "their" country (e.g., Windschuttle 2004: 333). John Kane (in this volume) is right to note the postnationalist echoes of this position in some of the multicultural advisory and policy statements during the Howard years. Anglo-Australians' sense of their privileged status is, however, revealed by the resentment and contempt such policies, statements, and challenges arouse. Consider the visceral reaction to suggestions that the public celebration of Christmas be modified in some ways to include minorities who do not observe the festival. "The statistical evidence is that there will probably come a time when the celebrations of other faiths will loom larger in Australian life," Brisbane's *Sunday Mail* newspaper (2005) editorialized. "In the meantime, Christians will continue joyously to observe their important celebrations in a manner that will reflect their historical dominance." Unguarded remarks tell the same story. Witness former federal health minister Tony Abbott's jibe in Parliament in connection with what he viewed as ethnic "branch stacking" in a Labor Party preselection battle: "Are there any Australians left in the so-called Australian Labor Party today?" he asked rhetorically.[22] Such examples of cultural exclusiveness and exclusion can easily be multiplied (see Hage 1998; Johnson 2002; Stratton 1998).

For all its changes over recent decades, then, Australia is still, in the manner of its majority-minority relations, more akin to the Old World "nation-states" of Europe than it is to the other great immigrant societies of the United States and Canada. To be sure, there also are important differences. Not least is that "Anglo-Australian" dominance and nationalism are remarkably relaxed, forgiving, and nonmurderous compared to many European versions. The cultural exclusions in Australia tend to be much more subtle, although they are no less powerful for that (Levey and Moses 2008).

If there are deep resistances in Australian culture and society to "difference" that always made multiculturalism cut against the grain, there also are dangerous propensities in nationalist sentiment that make some form of liberal multiculturalism advisable. As with religion, when the state aligns too closely with ethnonational identity, liberty is the first casualty. The liberal nationalist account of the various sites of national identity and character that I sketched in the previous section depends on the boundaries of these sites being respected by government and society. Government has carriage over some aspects of national identity; others are best left to the people. National character has a place in both but again should not be the aim of legislation. Respecting these borders allows, at once, for a unifying national identity, space for cultural difference and liberty, and thus the opportunity for everyone, including cultural minorities, to contribute to the ongoing process of national identity formation. It bears emphasizing that the problem, on this account, is not ethnic hierarchy *per se;* few, if any, states eschew privileging particular cultures. History and demography have political consequences.[23] Liberal nationalists recognize the inevitability and legitimacy of some cultural privileging and thus of ethnic hierarchy. They insist, however, that such privileging be appropriately limited or redressed where—and here they vary—it adversely affects citizens' common citizenship rights, sense of belonging to the political community, or corresponding rights to cultural expression.

As John Kane shows in this book, there are inherent tensions between liberalism and nationalism, which multiculturalism refashions rather than overcomes. Border skirmishes and incursions across the respective domains of national identity are probably inevitable. But this is why multiculturalism is all the more valuable to a liberal democracy. Understood as a set of policies integrating a culturally diverse society around a shared national identity and liberal democratic values, multiculturalism helps check the oppressive tendencies of nationalist sentiment, whether of the nation writ large or of its constituent ethnic groups. In other words, multiculturalism grants national identity its place by dint of liberalism's "art of separation" (Walzer 1984).

CONCLUSION

Whether Australia jettisons multiculturalism in word or even in policy, it will have to come to terms with its cultural diversity as a liberal democracy. In this, it faces two defining challenges.

First, while Australia has a legitimate interest in integrating its minorities as Australians—which governments now seek to achieve more than ever—its dominant norms and expectations press heavily in the opposite direction. As discussed, Anglo-Australian culture tends to resist integration and hybridization with minority cultures and identities, even as it absorbs aspects of them. Compartmentalized identities mean that one's two (or more) identities are less readily bridged; one's Australianness remains estranged from one's "otherness" and vice versa. Multicultural policy sought to address this problem by "celebrating" cultural diversity and creating a space in which cultural identity and difference could be seen as legitimate and a part of one's Australian identity. Critics assert that such policies simply gave a green light to cultural separatism, and a shared Australian identity was eroded. Even if there is some truth to this claim, multiculturalism, in practice, never succeeded in overcoming the deep suspicion of cultural difference in Australian culture and society, which itself promotes cultural alienation and separatism. Australia has thus oscillated between two counterproductive approaches: one that construes Australian national identity narrowly in Anglo-Australian terms but is applied widely as the standard of acceptability; and one that, in recent years, has perhaps underemphasized the importance of an Australian national identity, or which has come to define such an identity almost in opposition to Anglo-Australian heritage.

In this chapter, I have sought to clarify and defend a particular liberal nationalist conception—or perhaps better, map—of national identity for Australian conditions that avoids these equally problematic alternatives. Understood multidimensionally and as operating across several domains, national identity and character have a legitimate and vital place in Australian politics and society. On this account, Anglo-Australian culture is duly recognized both inside and beyond the sphere of government, but so is the input of non–Anglo-Australians and the evolving nature of Australian identity and character. Suggested, to some extent, in the *National Agenda* multicultural policy of 1989, something like this multifaceted map of the domains of national identity is also *implicitly* respected by many Australian political leaders, institutions, and practices today. The trouble and controversies arise when it is not. At the same time, encouraging multiple, hybridized Australian identities in the manner of "Anglo-Australians" themselves would help facilitate the sought-after integration under a shared *Australian* national identity. Again, such a move does not devalue Anglo-Australian culture and institutions since these already largely shape Australian identity and culture. Rather, it simply allows the latter to be more readily wed to minority identities, and so be broadened in the process. A little hyphen can go a long way.

The second challenge relates to the importance attached to respecting "core Australian values." Australian governments today define these values mainly in terms of liberal democratic norms. This should be unproblematic as long as two additional and opposing political tendencies are checked. One is the postnationalist inclination to present these values as if these were all there is or should be to Australian culture and identity rather than simply as a statement of the political ground rules of Australian society. The other and more enduring tendency is to allow dominant Australian cultural norms—captured in the sentiment "this is what we do around here"—automatically to define the meaning of liberty and equality and toleration and democracy, and so on. Honoring these values warrants a more critical engagement with them than that.

Cultural diversity poses many challenges for Australian liberal democracy. But chief among them is the need for Australians to come to terms with the multiple and respective domains of their national identity and their own proclaimed core values. The significance of the Australian case for multicultural political theory may lie as much in how these twin challenges are negotiated in the Australian polity as in the innovative liberal formulation of multiculturalism that Australian policymakers once developed on the drawing board.

NOTES

1. In his influential book advancing the "clash of civilizations" thesis, Samuel Huntington (1996: 151–54) refers to Australia's efforts under Labor prime minister Paul Keating to "redefine itself as an Asian society, and cultivate close ties with its geographical neighbors." Keating—who fancied Italian suits, German music, and French clocks—sought to reposition Australia economically and strategically, not culturally. Huntington doubted this could be achieved precisely because "culture and values are the basic obstacle to Australia's joining Asia."

2. "Religion by Year of Arrival 1982–2001," unpublished commissioned data set, Australian Bureau of Statistics 2006.

3. An abbreviated and somewhat different version of this section appeared as Levey 2007c.

4. "Ethnic nationalism" is commonly contrasted with "civic nationalism," where the latter is usually taken to designate a shared identity based on the acceptance of a political creed and set of political institutions and values (e.g., Ignatieff 1994). It thus resembles civic republicanism and constitutional patriotism. Some writers, however, equate civic nationalism with the kind of national-cultural identity and sense of belonging here attributed to liberal nationalism (e.g., Abizadeh 2002). Further complicating matters, some critics argue that civic nationalism differs from constitutional patriotism in that civic nationalists appeal to

pre-political or national-cultural forms of identity and belonging, despite their ostensible ethnocultural neutrality (Keitner 1999). Others criticize civic nationalism and constitutional patriotism alike for presenting an unrealistic model of and for shared identity in the modern nation-state system (Kymlicka 2001b: 16–17; Nielsen 1996–97). I return to these criticisms in discussing the postnationalist approach below.

5. Keith Windschuttle (2004) has idiosyncratically defended the "white Australia" policy by denying that it was premised on racist or ethnically exclusivist assumptions. Rather, he sees it as a progressive policy designed to protect the dignity of labor.

6. Similar observations have been made in relation to criticisms of multiculturalism in Britain. See Modood 2000.

7. The same claim is made today by the conservative commentators Janet Albrechtsen, Piers Ackerman, and Andrew Bolt—albeit, ironically, with the shrill rider that multiculturalism has succeeded in making "distinct ethnic groups" a reality.

8. Kallen's famous essay "Democracy Versus the Melting-Pot" was originally published in *The Nation* in 1915. Stephen Whitfield (1998: xxix–xxx) notes that Kallen later "softened" his national ideal for the United States to a "fellowship of freedom and cooperation," which amounted to "voluntary pluralism."

9. As Kane notes (in this volume), the Australian Citizenship Council seemed to take this postnationalist position in recommending that "it might be better to proclaim not a 'national identity', but a national civic 'compact'" (Australian Citizenship Council 2000: 10–11).

10. Stephen Castles (2001: 811) astutely observes that the NMAC's recommendation that multicultural policy be henceforth called "*Australian* multiculturalism" also seemed to be an attempt to generate nationalist sentiment around multiculturalism.

11. Along the same lines, Andrew Mason (1999: 272–73) has suggested that "Charles Taylor's [1993] proposal that Canada might become a polity held together by the acceptance of a 'deep diversity' in which a plurality of ways of belonging were acknowledged" might serve as a basis for a shared identity tied to "belonging to the polity."

12. Survey research also suggests sociodemographic variations in the level and kind of support for "multiculturalism," with university graduates being particularly strong supporters compared to the less educated. Too much can be made of this so-called "great divide" between the "intellectual class" and other Australians (Betts 1999; Windschuttle 2004: 333–40). For one thing, most prominent opponents of multiculturalism are recipients of higher education, have fashionable cosmopolitan addresses, and are known to imbibe café lattes and Chardonnay—popular images for disparaging the urban, educated "elites." More fundamentally, survey research misses the way cultural attitudes are institutionalized and are provoked at particular moments. I return to these latter issues below.

13. David Miller (1995: 25–26) refers to national character but equates it with national identity and the "public culture" more generally. I see national character

as referring more specifically to the personality characteristics of the members of a nation.

14. Kymlicka (1995) allows that states may harbor more than one societal culture where indigenous and national minorities are present.

15. David Miller (1995: 26, chap. 5) does include these kinds of cultural dimensions under his notion of a national "public culture" (he expressly mentions religious beliefs and how people queue at a bus stop). Nevertheless, his account does not, in my view, sufficiently differentiate between those aspects of the public culture that rightly fall within *and* outside the sphere of government and law. Neither religious beliefs nor queuing at a bus stop, for example, would seem to be a proper concern of liberal democratic government.

16. Given the effects today of globalization and the U.S. hegemon, the American influence on Anglo-Australian culture must also be reckoned with. For a subtle analysis, see Altman 2006.

17. The pollster "[Irving] Saulwick found that migrants from non-English-speaking backgrounds are accepted, but that acceptance is qualified. The more these people are like 'us', or become like 'us', the more readily they are accepted" (NMAC 1999: 96).

18. Unfortunately, Hawke chose exactly the wrong venue and audience to air this view: a Melbourne Orthodox synagogue, whose congregants were instantly upset (*Australian Jewish News* 1999).

19. To be sure, the hyphenation tends to have a different emphasis in each country: in the United States the stress is on fusion and "Americanization"; in Canada the hyphen signifies more a "demarcation-line" and cultural pluralism (Verhoeven 1996: 97). Australia is different again.

20. The English in Australia are also a minority (see Jupp 2004), although the term "English Australians" is not much used. The preferred, albeit colloquial, term for them is "poms."

21. *The Australian* (2005b) initially dismissed Panapoulos's and Bishop's calls to ban the wearing of headscarves as a "distraction," but a year later, following former British foreign secretary Jack Straw's intervention on the subject, declared strongly against the practice. Panapoulos's involvement in the "campaign" highlights the fact that anxieties about difference and separation are not the preserve of Anglo-Australians alone. In a pattern observed the world over, many immigrants strongly identify with—and share the anxieties and even xenophobia of—the host culture. As Andrew Lattas (2008) notes regarding Panapoulos's stance, that "Greek culture and identity ... closely mirror Middle East cultures"—with many Greek women wearing headscarves for modesty purposes—is "conveniently forgotten" as the assimilated members revel in "their new found regard in the dominant culture."

22. House of Representatives, Official Hansard, No. 3 (28 February 2006): 10: www. aph.gov.au/hansard/reps/dailys/dr280206.pdf.

23. As Connor Cruise O'Brien (1984: 11) wryly put it, "sometimes the only right a minority seems to want is the right to become a majority."

Contributors

George Crowder is Professor in the Department of Politics and Public Policy, Flinders University, Adelaide. He is the author of *Classical Anarchism* (1991), *Liberalism and Value Pluralism* (2002), and *Isaiah Berlin: Liberty and Pluralism* (2004), and coeditor (with Henry Hardy) of *The One and the Many: Reading Isaiah Berlin* (2007). He is currently completing a book (with Ian Haddock), *Theories of Multiculturalism.*

Brian Galligan is Professor of Political Science at the University of Melbourne. He researches and teaches mainly in Australian and comparative politics and political economy. His books include *Australian Citizenship* (with Winsome Roberts, 2004), *Australians and Globalisation* (with Winsome Roberts and Gabriella Trifiletti, 2001), *Citizens Without Rights: Aborigines and Australian Citizenship* (with John Chesterman, 1997), and *A Federal Republic* (1995). He is coeditor (with Winsome Roberts) of *The Oxford Companion to Australian Politics*. His current research is focused on the politics of rights protection and on comparative federalism.

Moira Gatens is Professor of Philosophy at the University of Sydney. She is the author of *Imaginary Bodies: Ethics, Power and Corporeality* (1996) and *Collective Imaginings: Spinoza Past and Present* (with Genevieve Lloyd, 1999). She currently holds an Australian Research Council Professorial Fellowship.

Arthur Glass is Senior Visiting Fellow in the Law Faculty at the University of New South Wales, where he taught for many years. He is editor of the journal *Australian Immigration Law*. His publications include *Federal Constitutional Law: An Introduction* (with Keven Booker and Robert Watt, 1998); and many contributions to edited works, including *Australian Constitutional Landmarks* (2003); *Proof and Truth: The Humanist as Expert* (2003); and *Legal Interpretation in Democratic States* (2002).

Barry Hindess is Professor of Political Science in the Research School of Social Sciences at the Australian National University. His publications include *Discourses of Power: From Hobbes to Foucault* (1996), *Governing Australia: Studies in Contemporary Rationalities of Government* (with Mitchell Dean, 1998), *Corruption and Democracy in Australia* (2004), *US and Them: Anti-elitism in Australia* (with Marian Sawer, 2004), and numerous papers on democracy, liberalism and empire, and neoliberalism.

Duncan Ivison is Dean of the Faculty of Arts and Social Sciences and Professor of Political Philosophy at the University of Sydney. His research interests include contemporary political theory and the history of political thought, especially the early modern period. He is the author of *The Self at Liberty* (1997), *Postcolonial Liberalism* (2002), and *Rights* (2008), and coeditor of *Political Theory and the Rights of Indigenous Peoples* (2000).

James Jupp has been Director of the Centre for Immigration and Multicultural Studies at the Australian National University since 1988. He was a member of the Commonwealth Advisory Council on Multicultural Affairs (1988–89) and was chairman of the Review of Migrant and Multicultural Programs and Services, which presented its report *Don't Settle for Less* to the Minister for Immigration in August 1986. His publications include *From White Australia to Woomera* (2001), *The English in Australia* (2004), and, as editor, the encyclopedia *The Australian People* (1988 and 2001).

John Kane is Professor in the School of Government and International Relations, and Deputy Director of the Centre for Governance and Public Policy at Griffith University, Brisbane. He has published extensively in the areas of political theory, political history, and political leadership. He is coeditor of *Rethinking Australian Citizenship* (2000) and author of *The Politics of Moral Capital* (2001), and *Between Virtue and Power: The Persistent Moral Dilemma of US Foreign Policy* (2008).

Martin Krygier is Gordon Samuels Professor of Law and Social Theory at the University of New South Wales, and since 2005 he has also been recurrent visiting professor at the Centre for Social Studies, Academy of Sciences, Warsaw. His work spans legal, political, and social philosophy; communist and postcommunist studies; sociology of law; and the history of ideas. His publications include a book of his selected writings, *Civil Passions* (2005), and two coedited books, *Rethinking the Rule of Law After Communism* (2005) and *Spreading Democracy and the Rule of Law?* (2006).

Chandran Kukathas is Professor of Political Theory, London School of Economics and Political Science. He is the author of *Hayek and Modern Liberalism* (1989) and *The Liberal Archipelago: A Theory of Diversity and Freedom* (2003). He also coedited *The Sage Handbook of Political Theory* (with Gerald F. Gaus, 2004) and *Pierre Bayle's Philosophical Commentary* (with John Kilcullen, 2005).

Geoffrey Brahm Levey is an Australian Research Council Future Fellow in political science at the University of New South Wales, where he was founding director of the Program in Jewish Studies. He is co-editor of *Secularism, Religion and Multicultural Citizenship* (with Tariq Modood, 2008) and *Jews and Australian Politics* (with Philip Mendes, 2004).

Maria R. Markus was born in Poland and educated at the Lomonosov University in Moscow. She began her career as a researcher in Hungary, where she belonged to the so-called Budapest School of oppositional sociologists and philosophers. After losing her job in 1973 for political-ideological reasons, she moved to Australia in 1978. Since then she has been teaching sociology at the University of New South Wales. She is author and coauthor of several books and has published more than forty scholarly papers in sociological journals in the fields of political sociology, sociology of economics, and feminist theory.

Philip Pettit teaches political theory and philosophy at Princeton University, where he is L. S. Rockefeller University Professor of Politics and Human Values. Previously, he was for many years with the Research School of Social Sciences, Australian National University. His recent books include *Republicanism* (1997), *A Theory of Freedom* (2001), and *The Economy of Esteem* (with Geoffrey Brennan, 2004). He has also published a selection of his papers, *Rules, Reasons and Norms* (2002), and with Frank Jackson and Michael Smith, a selection of coauthored papers, *Mind, Morality and Explanation* (2004).

Winsome Roberts completed her doctorate at the University of Melbourne's Centre for Public Policy in 1998, and thereafter took up a research fellowship in the Department of Political Science. She is coauthor (with Brian Galligan and Gabriella Trifiletti) of *Australians and Globalisation* (2001) and (with Brian Galligan) of *Australian Citizenship* (2004). Since 2005, she has been a Lecturer in the School of Social Work at the University of Melbourne, where she teaches critical social policy. Her fields of research include immigration, multiculturalism, and racism.

Kim Rubenstein is Professor and Director of the Centre for International and Public Law (CIPL) in the ANU College of Law, Australian National University. Her research analyzes the legal status of citizenship alongside less formal and more normative understandings of citizenship as membership of a community. Her book *Australian Citizenship Law in Context* (2002) represents some of this core work. She has appeared three times in the High Court of Australia on citizenship matters, and her research work was cited in the judgment *Singh v. Commonwealth* (2004).

References

Abizadeh, Arash. 2002. "Does Liberal Democracy Presuppose a Liberal Nation? Four Arguments." *American Political Science Review* 96: 495–509.

Adler, Daniel, and Kim Rubenstein. 2000. "International Citizenship: The Future of Nationality in a Globalized World." *Indiana Journal of Global Legal Studies* 7: 519–48.

Aleinikoff, T. Alexander, and Douglas Klusmeyer. 2002. *Citizenship Policies for an Age of Migration.* Washington, D.C.: Carnegie Endowment for International Peace.

Allen, Danielle S. 2004. *Talking to Strangers: Anxieties of Citizenship since Brown v. Board of Education.* Chicago: University of Chicago Press.

Altman, Dennis. 2006. *51st State?* Carlton, Melbourne: Scribe.

Anderson, Benedict. 1983. *Imagined Communities: Reflections on the Origin and Spread of Nationalism.* London: Verso.

Anthony, Karina. 2006. *The Political Representation of Ethnic and Racial Minorities.* Briefing Paper 3/06. Sydney: NSW Parliamentary Library Research Service.

Arendt, Hannah. 1958. *The Human Condition.* Chicago: University of Chicago Press.

——. 1964. *Eichmann in Jerusalem: A Report on the Banality of Evil.* New York: Viking Press.

Arthur, Evan. 1991. "The Impact of Administrative Law on Humanitarian Decision-making." *Canberra Bulletin of Public Administration* 66: 90–96.

Attwood, Bain. 2003. *Rights for Aborigines.* Sydney: Allen & Unwin.

Austin, John. 1869. *Lectures on Jurisprudence, or the Philosophy of Positive Law.* London: John Murray.

Australia, House of Representatives Standing Committee on Community Affairs. 1996. *A Fair Go for All: Report on Migrant Access and Equity.* Canberra: AGPS.

The Australian. 2004. "New recruit's headpiece sets her apart." 27 November.

——. 2005a. "Most still enjoy a culture cocktail." 22 December.

——. 2005b. "What not to wear." 1 September.

——. 2006. "The veiled conceit of multiculturalism." 24 October.

Australian Bureau of Statistics (ABS). 2001. *Australian Demographic Statistics,* Cat. No. 3101.0 (December).

——. 2004–5. *Migration, Australia,* Cat. No. 3412.0.

———. 2006. *Year Book Australia,* Cat. No. 1301.0.

Australian Citizenship Council. 2000. *Australian Citizenship for a New Century.* Canberra: Ausinfo.

Australian Council on Population and Ethnic Affairs (ACPEA). 1982. *Multiculturalism for All Australians: Our Developing Nationhood.* Canberra: AGPS.

Australian Ethnic Affairs Council. 1977. *Australia as a Multicultural Society.* Canberra: AGPS.

Australian Jewish News. 1999. "Hawke stuns Jews, praises intermarriage." 16 July.

———. 2000. "Concern voiced, but eruv approved." 9 June.

Australian Law Reform Commission. 1992. *Multiculturalism and the Law,* Report no. 57.

Bader, Veit. 2007. *Democracy or Secularism? Associational Governance of Religious Diversity.* Amsterdam: Amsterdam University Press.

Banting, Keith, and Will Kymlicka. 2003a. "Do Multiculturalism Policies Erode the Welfare State?" Working Paper no. 33, School of Policy Studies, Queens University, Canada.

———. 2003b. "Multiculturalism and Welfare." *Dissent* 50, no. 4: 59–66.

———. eds. 2006a. *Multiculturalism and the Welfare State: Recognition and Redistribution in Contemporary Democracies.* Oxford: Oxford University Press.

———. 2006b. "Multiculturalism and the Welfare State: Setting the Context." In *Multiculturalism and the Welfare State: Recognition and Redistribution in Contemporary Democracies,* ed. Keith Banting and Will Kymlicka. Oxford: Oxford University Press.

Barker, Ernest. 1950. "Introduction." In *Gierke, Natural Law, and the Theory of Society,* ed. Ernest Barker. Cambridge: Cambridge University Press.

Barnett, David. 1986. "How the Bloated Ethnic Industry Is Dividing Australia." *The Bulletin* (18 February): 58–62.

Barry, Brian. 1995. *Justice as Impartiality.* Oxford: Oxford University Press.

———. 1999. "Statism and Nationalism: A Cosmopolitan Critique." In *Nomos 41, Global Justice,* ed. Lea Brilmayer and Ian Shapiro. New York: New York University Press.

———. 2001. *Culture and Equality: An Egalitarian Critique of Multiculturalism.* Cambridge: Polity Press.

Bar-Yaacov, Nissim. 1961. *Dual Nationality.* London: Stevens.

Bauer, Otto. 2000 [1907]. *The Question of Nationalities and Social Democracy.* Minneapolis: University of Minnesota Press.

Baumann, Gerd. 1996. *Contesting Culture: Discourses of Identity in Multi-Ethnic London.* Cambridge: Cambridge University Press.

———. 1999. *The Multicultural Riddle. Rethinking National, Ethnic, and Religious Identities.* London: Routledge.

BBC News. 2010. "Merkel says German multicultural society has failed," 17 October. www.bbc.co.uk/news/world-europe-11559451 [accessed 10 February 2012].

BBC News. 2011. "State multiculturalism has failed, says David Cameron," 5 February. www.bbc.co.uk/news/uk-politics-12371994 [accessed 10 February 2012].

Behrendt, Larissa. 2003. *Achieving Social Justice: Indigenous Rights and Australia's Future*. Sydney: Federation Press.

Beitz, Charles R. 1979. *Political Theory and International Relations*. Princeton, N.J.: Princeton University Press.

Bellah, Robert. 1996. *Habits of the Heart: Individualism and Commitment in American Life*. Rev. ed. Berkeley: University of California Press.

Bellamy, Richard. 1999. *Liberalism and Pluralism: Towards a Politics of Compromise*. London: Routledge.

Benhabib, Seyla. 2002. *The Claims of Culture: Equality and Diversity in the Global Era*. Princeton, N.J.: Princeton University Press.

Berlin, Isaiah. 1969. *Four Essays on Liberty*. Oxford: Oxford University Press.

——. 1978. *Russian Thinkers*, ed. Henry Hardy and Aileen Kelly. London: Hogarth.

——. 1979. *Against the Current: Essays in the History of Ideas*, ed. Henry Hardy. London: Hogarth.

——. 1990. *The Crooked Timber of Humanity: Chapters in the History of Ideas*, ed. Henry Hardy. London: John Murray.

——. 1997. *The Proper Study of Mankind: An Anthology of Essays*, ed. Henry Hardy and R. Hausheer. London: Chatto & Windus.

——. 2000a. *The Power of Ideas*, ed. Henry Hardy. London: Chatto & Windus.

——. 2000b. *Three Critics of the Enlightenment: Vico, Hamann, Herder*, ed. Henry Hardy. London: Pimlico.

——. 2002. *Liberty*, ed. Henry Hardy. Oxford: Oxford University Press.

Berlin, Isaiah, and Bernard Williams. 1994. "Pluralism and Liberalism: A Reply." *Political Studies* 42: 306–9.

Betts, Katharine. 1988. *Ideology and Immigration: Australia 1976 to 1987*. Melbourne: Melbourne University Press.

——. 1999. *The Great Divide: Immigration Politics in Australia*. Sydney: Duffy and Snellgrove.

Birrell, Robert. 1995. *A Nation of Our Own: Citizenship and Nation-building in Federation Australia*. Melbourne: Longman.

Bittner, Rudiger. 1994. "Ressentiment." In *Nietzsche, Genealogy, Morality: Essays on Nietzsche's Genealogy of Morals*, ed. Richard Schacht. Berkeley: University of California Press.

Blackstone, Sir William. 1979 [1765]. *Commentaries on the Laws of England. A Facsimile of the First Edition of 1765–1769*, introduction by Stanley N. Katz. Vol. 1. Chicago: University of Chicago Press.

Blainey, Geoffrey. 1984. *All for Australia*. North Ryde, Australia: Methuen Haynes.

Borradori, Giovanna. 2003. *Philosophy in a Time of Terror: Dialogues with Jürgen Habermas and Jacques Derrida*. Chicago: University of Chicago Press.

Bosniak, Linda. 2000. "Citizenship Denationalized." *Indiana Journal of Global Legal Studies* 7: 447–509.

Bowen, Chris. 2011. "The Genius of Australian Multiculturalism," Address to the Sydney Institute, 17 February. www.minister.immi.gov.au/media/cb/2011/cb159251.htm [accessed 10 February 2012].

Bratman, Michael E. 1999. *Faces of Intention: Selected Essays on Intention and Agency.* Cambridge: Cambridge University Press.

Brighouse, Harry. 1998. "Civic Education and Liberal Legitimacy." *Ethics* 108: 719–45.

———. 2000. *School Choice and Social Justice.* New York: Oxford University Press.

Brown, Wendy. 1995. *States of Injury: Power and Freedom in Late Modernity.* Princeton, N.J.: Princeton University Press.

———. 2003. "Neo-liberalism and the End of Liberal Democracy." *Theory & Event* 7, no. 1. http://muse.jhu.edu/journals/theory_and_event/v007/7.1brown.html [accessed March 2005].

Brubaker, Rogers. 2001. "The Return of Assimilation? Changing Perspectives on Immigration and Its Sequels in France, Germany, and the United States." *Ethnic and Racial Studies* 24, no. 4: 531–48.

Bryant, Gerald. 2003. "Promised Marriages—The Jackie Pascoe Case." *Indigenous Law Bulletin* 5, no. 23: 20.

Buchanan, James M., and Gordon Tullock. 1962. *The Calculus of Consent.* Ann Arbor: University of Michigan Press.

Burn, Margy. 2002. "Melting Pot or Monoculture: Archives and Cultural Diversity in Australia." Paper presented to the Australian Society of Archivists Annual Conference, *Past Caring? What Does Society Expect of Archivists?* www.nla.gov.au/nla/staffpaper/2002/burn.html.

Cahill, Desmond, Gary Bouma, Hass Dellal, and Michael Leahy. 2004. *Religion, Cultural Diversity, and Safeguarding Australia.* Melbourne: Australian Multicultural Foundation; Canberra: Department of Immigration and Multicultural and Indigenous Affairs.

Canning, Joseph P. 1980. "The Corporation in the Political Thought of the Italian Jurists of the Thirteenth and Fourteenth Century." *History of Political Thought* 1: 9–32.

———. 1983. "Ideas of the State in Thirteenth and Fourteenth-Century Commentators on the Roman Law." *Transactions of the Royal Historical Society* 33: 1–27.

———. 1996. *A History of Medieval Political Thought, 300–1450.* London: Routledge.

Canovan, Margaret. 1996. *Nationhood and Political Theory.* Cheltenham, UK: Edward Elgar.

Carens, Joseph H. 2003. "Who Should Get In? The Ethics of Immigration Admissions." *Ethics and International Affairs* 17, no. 1: 95–110.

Castles, Stephen. 2001. "Multiculturalism in Australia." In *The Australian People: An Encyclopedia of the Nation, Its People and Their Origins,* ed. James Jupp. Cambridge: Cambridge University Press.

Castles, Stephen, Mary Kalantzis, Bill Cope, and Michael Morrissey. 1992. *Mistaken Identity: Multiculturalism and the Demise of Nationalism in Australia.* 3rd ed. Sydney: Pluto Press.

Chambers, Simone. 2004. "Behind Closed Doors: Publicity, Secrecy, and the Quality of Deliberation." *Journal of Political Philosophy* 12, no. 4: 403–4.

Chang, Ruth. 1997. "Introduction." In *Incommensurability, Incomparability, and Practical Reason,* ed. Ruth Chang. Cambridge, Mass.: Harvard University Press.

Charlesworth, Hilary. 1997. "Taking the Gender of Rights Seriously." In *Rethinking Human Rights,* ed. Brian Galligan and Charles Sampford. Sydney: Federation Press.

Chesterman, John, and Brian Galligan. 1997. *Citizens Without Rights: Aborigines and Australian Citizenship.* Cambridge: Cambridge University Press.

Chipman, Lauchlan. 1980. "The Menace of Multiculturalism." *Quadrant* 24 (October): 3–6.

Christiano, Thomas. 1996. *The Rule of the Many: Fundamental Issues in Democratic Theory.* Boulder, Co.: Westview Press.

Civic Experts Group. 1994. *Whereas the People.* Canberra: AGPS.

Cocks, Joan. 2002. *Passion and Paradox: Intellectuals Confront the National Question.* Princeton, N.J.: Princeton University Press.

Cole, Douglas. 1971. "'The Crimson Thread of Kinship': Ethnic Ideas in Australia, 1870–1914." *Historical Studies* 14, no. 56: 511–25.

Coleman, James S. 1974. *Power and the Structure of Society.* New York: Norton.

———. 1990. *Foundations of Social Theory.* Cambridge, Mass.: Harvard University Press.

Commission for Racial Equality. 2004. *Press Release of 26 April.* London.

Committee to Advise on Australia's Immigration Policies. 1988. *Immigration: A Commitment to Australia.* [Fitzgerald report.] Canberra: AGPS.

Commonwealth of Australia. 1999. *A New Agenda for Multicultural Australia.* Canberra: AGPS.

———. 2003. *Multicultural Australia: United in Diversity.* Canberra: AGPS.

Constant, Benjamin. 1988. *Constant: Political Writings,* ed. and trans. Biancamaria Fontana. Cambridge: Cambridge University Press.

Convention on the Reduction of Cases of Multiple Nationality and Military Obligations in Cases of Multiple Nationality. 6 May 1963, Dur. TS No. 4.

Cope, Bill, and Mary Kalantzis. 2000. *A Place in the Sun.* Sydney: Harper Collins.

Council for Aboriginal Reconciliation. 2000. *National Strategy to Promote Recognition of Aboriginal and Torres Strait Islander Rights.* Canberra: CBR. http://138.25.65.50/au/orgs/car/docrec/policy/natstrat/4rights.htm.

Crotty, Martin. 2001. *Making the Australian Male: Middle-class Masculinity, 1870–1920.* Melbourne: Melbourne University Press.

Crowder, George. 1994. "Pluralism and Liberalism." *Political Studies* 42: 293–305.

———. 2002a. *Liberalism and Value Pluralism.* London and New York: Continuum.

———. 2002b. "Two Value-pluralist Arguments for Liberalism." *Australian Journal of Political Science* 37: 457–73.

———. 2004a. "Galston's Liberal Pluralism." In *Isaiah Berlin Virtual Library,* ed. Henry Hardy. http://berlin.wolf.ox.ac.uk/lists/onib/onib.htm [accessed 24 November 2004].

———. 2004b. *Isaiah Berlin: Liberty and Pluralism.* Oxford: Polity Press.

Cunneen, Chris, and Terry Libesman. 1995. *Indigenous People and the Law in Australia.* Sydney: Butterworths.

Dale, David. 2007. "Who we are: A column about Australia." *Sydney Morning Herald,* 19 August.

Davis, Megan, and Hannah McGlade. 2005. "International Human Rights Law and the Recognition of Aboriginal Customary Law." Law Reform Commission of Western Australia, Project no. 94, Background Paper no. 10 (March).

Demetriou, Andrew (Chair, AMAC). 2009. Letter to author. 4 August.

Department of Immigration and Citizenship [DIAC]. 2007. Background, Fact Sheet No. 1.: www.immi.gov.au/media/fact-sheets/01backgd_01.htm [accessed 6 November 2007].

———. 2011. *The People of Australia: Australia's Multicultural Policy.* Canberra: Author.

Department of Immigration and Ethnic Affairs. 1982. *National Consultation on Multiculturalism and Citizenship.* Canberra: AGPS.

Department of Immigration and Multicultural Affairs (DIMA). 1998. *A Good Practice Guide for Culturally Responsive Government Services: Charter of Public Service in a Culturally Diverse Society.* Canberra: AGPS.

———. 2006a. *The Abolition of the "White Australia" Policy,* Fact Sheet No. 8. www.immi.gov.au/media/fact-sheets/08abolition.htm [accessed 20 March 2006].

———. 2006b. *The Evolution of Australia's Multicultural Policies,* Fact Sheet No. 6. www.immi.gov.au/media/fact-sheets/06evolution.htm [accessed 20 March 2006].

de Schoutheete, Philippe. 2000. *The Case for Europe: Unity, Diversity, and Democracy in the European Union,* trans. Andrew Butler. Boulder, Co.: Lynne Rienner.

Deveaux, Monique. 2000. *Cultural Pluralism and Dilemmas of Justice.* Ithaca, N.Y.: Cornell University Press.

Dietrich, Franz. 2006. "Judgment Aggregation: (Im)possibility Theorems." *Journal of Economic Theory* 126, no. 1: 286–98.

Dixson, Miriam. 1999. *The Imaginary Australian: Anglo-Celts and Identity, 1788 to the Present.* Sydney: UNSW Press.

Dodson, Michael. 1995. *Indigenous Social Justice.* 3 vols. Sydney: Human Rights and Equal Opportunity Commission.

Dunn, Kevin, James Forrest, Ian Burnley, and Amy McDonald. 2004. "Constructing Racism in Australia." *Australian Journal of Social Issues* 39, no. 4: 409–30.

Dworkin, Ronald. 1978. *Taking Rights Seriously.* Cambridge, Mass.: Harvard University Press.

———. 2000. *Sovereign Virtue: The Theory and Practice of Equality.* Cambridge, Mass.: Harvard University Press.

Elster, Jon. 1986. "The Market and the Forum: Three Varieties of Political Theory." In *Foundations of Social Choice Theory,* ed. Jon Elster and Aanund Hillard. Cambridge: Cambridge University Press.

Entzinger, Han. 2003. "The Rise and Fall of Multiculturalism in the Netherlands." In *Toward Assimilation and Citizenship: Immigrants in Liberal Nation-States,* ed. Christian Joppke and Ewa Morawska. London: Palgrave.

Etzioni, Amitai. 1996. *The New Golden Rule: Community and Morality in a Democratic Society.* New York: Basic Books.

Fish, Stanley. 1999. "Mutual Respect as a Device for Exclusion." In *Deliberative Politics: Essays on Democracy and Disagreement,* ed. Stephen Macedo. Oxford: Oxford University Press.

Forbes, Hugh Donald. 1997. *Ethnic Conflict: Commerce, Culture, and the Contact Hypothesis.* New Haven, Conn.: Yale University Press.

Forst, Rainer. 1999. "The Basic Right to Justification: Toward a Constructivist Conception of Human Rights." *Constellations* 6: 35–60.

Foucault, Michel. 1997. *Ethics: The Essential Works of Foucault 1954–1984.* Vol. 1, ed. P. Rabinow. Harmondsworth, UK: Penguin.

Franck, Thomas. 1996. "Clan and Superclan: Loyalty, Identity, and Community in Law and Practice." *American Journal of International Law* 90: 359–83.

Fraser, J. Malcolm. 1981. "Multiculturalism: Australia's Unique Achievement." Inaugural Address to the Australian Institute of Multicultural Affairs, Melbourne. 30 November.

Fraser, Nancy. 2002. "Recognition without Ethics." In *Recognition and Difference: Politics, Identity, Multiculture,* ed. Scott Lash and Mike Featherstone. London: Sage Publications.

Gaita, Raimond. 1999. *A Common Humanity.* Melbourne: Text Publishing.

Galbally, Frank (chair). 1978. *Migrant Services and Programs: Report of the Review of Post-arrival Programs and Services for Migrants.* Canberra: AGPS.

Galligan, Brian, and Winsome Roberts. 2004. *Australian Citizenship.* Melbourne: Melbourne University Press.

Galston, William A. 2002. *Liberal Pluralism: The Implications of Value Pluralism for Political Theory and Practice.* Cambridge: Cambridge University Press.

Gambaro, Teresa. 2007. "What's in a Name?" *Australian Mosaic* 16 (April): 28–30.

Gardiner-Garden, John. 1993. *The Multiculturalism and Immigration Debate, 1973–1993.* Canberra: Parliamentary Research Service.

Garnett, George, ed. 1994. *Vindiciae contra Tyrannos.* Cambridge: Cambridge University Press.

Garton, Stephen. 1990. *Out of Luck: Poor Australians and Social Welfare, 1788–1988.* Sydney: Allen & Unwin.

Gatens, Moira. 1996. *Imaginary Bodies.* London: Routledge.

———. 2004. "Can Human Rights Accommodate Women's Rights? Towards an Embodied Account of Social Norms, Social Meaning, and Cultural Change." *Contemporary Political Theory* 3, no. 3: 275–99.

Gatens, Moira, and Genevieve Lloyd. 1999. *Collective Imaginings.* London: Routledge.

Geertz, Clifford V. 1973. *The Interpretation of Cultures.* New York: Basic Books.

Gellner, Ernest. 1971. *Thought and Change.* London: Wiedenfeld & Nicolson.

———. 1983. *Nations and Nationalism.* Oxford: Blackwell.

Gilbert, Margaret. 1989. *On Social Facts.* Princeton, N.J.: Princeton University Press.

———. 2001. "Collective Preferences, Obligations, and Rational Choice." *Economics and Philosophy* 17: 109–20.

Gill, Emily R. 2001. *Becoming Free: Autonomy and Diversity in the Liberal Polity.* Lawrence: University Press of Kansas.

Ginsberg, Morris. 1963. *Nationalism: A Reappraisal.* Leeds: Leeds University Press.

Glazer, Nathan. 1997. *We Are All Multiculturalists Now.* Cambridge, Mass.: Harvard University Press.

——. 1999. "Multiculturalism and American Exceptionalism." In *Multicultural Questions*, ed. Christian Joppke and Steven Lukes. Oxford and New York: Oxford University Press.

Glazer, Nathan, and Daniel Patrick Moynihan. 1963. *Beyond the Melting Pot: The Negroes, Puerto Ricans, Jews, Italians, and Irish of New York City*. Boston: Beacon Press.

Gobbo, James. 1995. "Criticisms of Multiculturalism." Paper presented to the 1995 Global Diversity Conference, Sydney.

Goodhart, David. 2004. "Too Diverse?" *Prospect Magazine* 95 (February).

Goodin, Robert. 2006. "Liberal Multiculturalism: Protective and Polyglot." *Political Theory* 34, no. 3: 289–303.

Goodin, Robert, Bruce Headey, Ruud Muffels, and Henk-Jan Dirven. 1999. *The Real Worlds of Welfare Capitalism*. Cambridge: Cambridge University Press.

Goot, Murray, and Ian Watson. 2005. "Immigration, Multiculturalism, and National Identity." In *Australian Social Attitudes: The First Report*, ed. Shaun Wilson, Gabrielle Meagher, Rachel Gibson, David Denemark, and Mark Western. Sydney: UNSW Press.

Gordon, Milton. 1964. *Assimilation in American Life*. New York: Oxford University Press.

Grassby, Albert J. 1973. "A Multi-cultural Society for the Future." Presentation to the Cairnmiller Institute's symposium *Strategy 2000: Australia for Tomorrow*. Canberra: AGPS.

Gray, John. 1993. *Post-Liberalism: Studies in Political Thought*. New York and London: Routledge.

——. 1995a. *Isaiah Berlin*. London: Harper Collins.

——. 1995b. *Enlightenment's Wake: Politics and Culture at the Close of the Modern Age*. London and New York: Routledge.

——. 2000. *Two Faces of Liberalism*. Cambridge: Polity Press.

Gupta, Dipankar. 1999. "Survivors or Survivals: Reconciling Citizenship and Cultural Particularisms." *Economic and Political Weekly*, 14 August: 2313–23.

Gutmann, Amy. 2003. *Identity in Democracy*. Princeton, N.J.: Princeton University Press.

Gutmann, Amy, and Dennis Thompson. 1996. *Democracy and Disagreement*. Cambridge, Mass.: Belknap Press.

Habermas, Jürgen. 1984, 1989. *A Theory of Communicative Action*, Vols. 1 and 2. Cambridge: Polity Press.

——. 1992a. *Autonomy and Solidarity*, rev. ed., ed. Peter Dews. London: Verso.

——. 1992b. "Citizenship and National Identity." *Praxis International* 12, no. 1: 1–19.

——. 1994. "Struggles for Recognition in the Democratic Constitutional State." In *Multiculturalism: Examining the Politics of Recognition*, ed. Amy Gutmann. Princeton, N.J.: Princeton University Press

——. 1995. *Between Facts and Norms: Contributions to a Discourse Theory of Law and Democracy*. Cambridge, Mass.: MIT Press.

——. 1998. *The Inclusion of the Other: Studies in Political Theory*. Cambridge, Mass.: MIT Press.

Habermas, Jürgen, and Jacques Derrida. 2003. "February 15, or What Binds Europeans Together: A Plea for a Common Foreign Policy, Beginning in the Core of Europe." *Constellations* 10, no. 3: 291–97.

Hage, Ghassan. 1998. *White Nation: Fantasies of White Supremacy in a Multicultural Society.* Sydney: Pluto Press.

Hager, Mark M. 1989. "Bodies Politic: The Progressive History of Organizational 'Real Entity' Theory." *University of Pittsburgh Law Review* 50: 575–654.

Hague Convention on Certain Questions Relating to the Conflict of Nationality Laws, 12 April 1930, 179 LNTS 101.

Hale, Matthew (Sir). 1971 [1713]. *The History of the Common Law of England,* ed. Charles M. Gray. Chicago: University of Chicago Press.

——. 1971 [1736]. *Historica Plactorum Coronea.* London: Professional Books.

——. 1982 [1787]. "Considerations Touching the Amendment or Alteration of Laws." In *A Collection of Tracts Relative to the Law of England.* Vol. 1, ed. Francis Hargrave. Abingdon, England: Professional Books.

Hancock, W. K. 1961 [1930]. *Australia.* Brisbane: Jacaranda.

Hartwich, Oliver Marc. 2011. *Selection, Migration and Integration: Why Multiculturalism Works in Australia (and Fails in Europe).* St Leonards, N.S.W.: Centre for Independent Studies.

Hawke, Robert J. 1999. "Australia's 21st Century Identity: Confidence at Home and Abroad." B'nai B'rith Anti-Defamation Human Rights Oration, St. Kilda Synagogue, 11 July.

Helliwell, Christine, and Barry Hindess. 2002. "The 'Empire of Uniformity' and the Government of Subject Peoples." *Cultural Values* 6, no. 1: 137–50.

Herder, Johann Gottfried. 1968 [1784–91]. *Reflections on the Philosophy of the History of Mankind.* Abridged and with an introduction by Frank E. Manuel. Chicago: University of Chicago Press.

Hindess, Barry. 2000. "Divide and Govern: Governmental Aspects of the Modern States System." In *Governing Modern Societies,* ed. R. Ericson and N. Stehr. Toronto: University of Toronto Press.

——. 2001. "Citizenship in the International Management of Populations." In *Citizenship and Cultural Policy,* ed. Denise Meredyth and Jeffrey Minson. London: Sage.

Hirschl, Ran. 2004. *Towards Juristocracy: The Origins and Consequences of the New Constitutionalism.* Cambridge, Mass.: Harvard University Press.

Hirst, John. 2001. "Aborigines and Migrants: Diversity and Unity in Multicultural Australia." *Australian Book Review* 228: 30–35.

Hirst, P., and G. Thompson. 1995. "Globalisation and the Future of the Nation State." *Economy and Society* 24: 408–22.

Hobbes, Thomas. 1994a [1650]. *Human Nature and De Corpore Politico: The Elements of Law, Natural and Politic.* Oxford: Oxford University Press.

——. 1994b [1651]. *Leviathan.* Indianapolis: Hackett.

Hobsbawm, Eric. 1990. *Nations and Nationalism Since 1780: Programme, Myth, Reality.* Cambridge: Cambridge University Press.

Hobsbawm, Eric, and Terence Ranger, eds. 1983. *The Invention of Tradition.* Cambridge: Cambridge University Press.

Holmes, Stephen. 1995. *Passions and Constraint: On the Theory of Liberal Democracy.* Chicago: University of Chicago Press.

Horne, Donald. 1997. *The Avenue of the Fair Go: A Group Tour of Australian Political Thought.* Pymble, N.S.W.: Harper Collins.

Hudson, Wayne, and John Kane, eds. 2000. *Rethinking Australian Citizenship.* Cambridge: Cambridge University Press.

Human Rights and Equal Opportunity Commission Report. 2004. *Isma–Listen: National Consultations on Eliminating Prejudice Against Arab and Muslim Australians.* Sydney: HREOC.

Huntington, Samuel P. 1996. *The Clash of Civilizations and the Remaking of World Order.* New York: Simon & Schuster.

———. 2004. *Who Are We? The Challenges to America's National Identity.* New York: Simon & Schuster.

Hurka, Thomas. 1996. "Monism, Pluralism, and Rational Regret." *Ethics* 106: 555–75.

Huxley, Julian S., and A. C. Haddon. 1940. *We Europeans.* London: Cape.

Ignatieff, Michael. 1994. *Blood and Belonging: Journeys into the New Nationalism.* New York: Farrar, Straus and Giroux.

Ingram, Attracta. 1996. "Constitutional Patriotism." *Philosophy and Social Criticism* 22, no. 6: 1–18.

Ireldale, R., and I. Nivison-Smith. 1995. *Immigrants' Experiences of Qualifications Recognition and Employment.* Canberra: Bureau of Immigration, Multicultural and Population Research, AGPS.

Irving, Helen. 2000. "Citizenship Before 1949." In *Individual, Community, Nation: Fifty Years of Australian Citizenship,* ed. Kim Rubenstein. Melbourne: Australian Scholarly Publishing.

Ivison, Duncan. 1997. *The Self at Liberty: Political Argument and the Arts of Government.* Ithaca, N.Y.: Cornell University Press.

———. 2002. *Postcolonial Liberalism.* Cambridge: Cambridge University Press.

———. 2003. "The Logic of Aboriginal Rights." *Ethnicities* 3, no. 3: 321–44.

Ivison, Duncan, Paul Patton, and Will Sanders, eds. 2000. *Political Theory and the Rights of Indigenous Peoples.* Cambridge: Cambridge University Press.

Jahanbegloo, Ramin. 1992. *Conversations with Isaiah Berlin.* New York: Charles Scribner's Sons.

James, Susan. 2002. "Freedom and the Imaginary." In *Visible Women: Essays on Feminist Legal Theory and Political Philosophy,* ed. Susan James and Stephanie Palmer. Oxford: Hart Publishing.

Jayasuriya, Laksiri. 1994. "Citizens." In *Australian Civilisation,* ed. Richard Nile. Melbourne: Oxford University Press.

———. 2005. "Australian Multiculturalism and the Politics of a New Pluralism." *Dialogue* 24, no. 1: 75–84.

Johnson, Carol. 2002. "The Dilemmas of Ethnic Privilege." *Ethnicities* 2, no. 2: 163–88.

———. 2007. "Howard's Values and Australian Identity," *Australian Journal of Political Science*, 2: 195-210.

Joint Committee on Foreign Affairs and Defence. 1976. *Dual Nationality.* Canberra: AGPS.

Joint Standing Committee on Migration. 1994. *Australians All: Enhancing Australian Citizenship.* Canberra: AGPS.

Jones, Peter. 1999a. "Human Rights, Group Rights, and Peoples' Rights." *Human Rights Quarterly* 21, no. 1: 80–107.

———. 1999b. "Group Rights and Group Oppression." *Journal of Political Philosophy* 7, no. 4: 353–77.

Joppke, Christian. 2004. "The Retreat of Multiculturalism in the Liberal State: Theory and Policy." *British Journal of Sociology* 55, no. 2: 237–57.

———. 2010. "How Liberal are Citizenship Tests?" In *How Liberal are Citizenship Tests?* ed. Rainer Bauböck and Christian Joppke. EUI Working Papers 41. Florence: RSCAS.

Jordens, Ann-Mari. 1997. *Alien to Citizen: Settling Migrants in Australia, 1945–1975.* St. Leonards, N.S.W.: Allen & Unwin.

Jupp, James. 1996. *Understanding Australian Multiculturalism.* Canberra: AGPS.

———. 1998. *Immigration.* 2nd ed. Melbourne: Oxford University Press.

———. 2000/2001. "Multiculturalism: Maturing or Dying?" *Dissent* [Melbourne] (Summer): 30–31.

———. 2002. *From White Australia to Woomera.* Melbourne: Cambridge University Press.

———. 2003. *How Well Does Australian Democracy Serve Immigrant Australians?* Democratic Audit of Australia Report No. 1. Canberra: Australian National University.

———. 2004. *The English in Australia.* Cambridge: Cambridge University Press.

Jupp, James, and John Nieuwenhuysen, eds. 2007. *Social Cohesion in Australia.* Cambridge: Cambridge University Press.

Jupp, James, Barry York, and Andrea McRobbie. 1989. *The Political Participation of Ethnic Minorities in Australia.* Canberra: AGPS.

Kalantzis, Mary. 2000. "Multicultural Citizenship." In *Rethinking Australian Citizenship,* ed. Wayne Hudson and John Kane. Cambridge: Cambridge University Press.

Kallen, Horace. 1998. *Culture and Democracy in the United States.* New Brunswick, N.J.: Transaction Books.

Kane, John. 1997a. "From Ethnic Exclusion to Ethnic Diversity: The Australian Path to Multiculturalism." *Ethnicity and Group Rights: Nomos* 39: 540–71.

———. 1997b. "Racialism, Democracy, and National Identity: The Legacies of White Australia." In *The Politics of Identity in Australia,* ed. Geoffrey Stokes. Melbourne: Cambridge University Press.

———. 2004. "Comparative Government-Business Relations: Europe and America." In *Government, Business, and Globalisation,* ed. E. van Acker and G. Curran. Melbourne: Pearson Education.

Keating, Paul J. 1995. "Opening Address." Global Cultural Diversity Conference Proceedings, Sydney, 26 April: www.immi.gov.au/media/publications/multicultural/confer/speech2a.htm

Keitner, Chimène I. 1999. "The 'False Promise' of Civic Nationalism." *Millenium* 28, no. 2: 341–51.

Kekes, John. 1993. *The Morality of Pluralism*. Princeton, N.J.: Princeton University Press.

Kellas, James G. 1991. *The Politics of Nationalism and Ethnicity*. London: Macmillan.

Kelly, Paul. 1997. "The Curse of the M-word." *The Weekend Australian*, 30–31 August.

——. 2011. "Weighed down by the M-word," *The Australian*, 23 February.

Kennedy, Paul M. 1994. *Preparing for the Twenty-first Century*. New York: Vintage Books.

Khoo, Siew-Ean. 2004. "Intermarriage in Australia: Patterns by Ancestry, Gender, and Generation." *People and Place* 12, no. 2: 34–43.

Khoo, Siew-Ean, Peter McDonald, Dimi Giorgas, and Bob Birrell. 2002. *Second Generation Australians: Report for the Department of Immigration and Multicultural and Indigenous Affairs*. Canberra: Australian Centre for Population Research and the Department of Immigration and Multicultural and Indigenous Affairs.

Knopfelmacher, Frank. 1982. "The Case Against Multi-culturalism." In *The New Conservatism in Australia*, ed. Robert Manne. Oxford: Oxford University Press.

Kohn, Hans. 1966. *The Idea of Nationalism*. New York: Collier Books.

Krygier, Martin. 1986. "Law as Tradition." *Law and Philosophy* 5: 237–62.

——. 1998. "Common Law." In *Routledge Encyclopedia of Philosophy*, Vol. 1, ed. Edward Craig. London: Routledge.

——. 1999. "Institutional Optimism, Cultural Pessimism, and the Rule of Law." In *The Rule of Law After Communism*, ed. Martin Krygier and Adam Czarnota. Aldershot, U.K.: Ashgate.

——. 2005. *Civil Passions*. Melbourne: Black Inc.

Kukathas, Chandran. 1992. "Are There Any Cultural Rights?" *Political Theory* 20, no. 1: 105–39.

——. 1993a. "The Idea of a Multicultural Society." In *Multicultural Citizens: The Philosophy and Politics of Identity*, ed. Chandran Kukathas. Sydney: Centre for Independent Studies.

——. 1993b. "Multiculturalism and the Idea of an Australian Identity." In *Multicultural Citizens: The Philosophy and Politics of Identity*, ed. Chandran Kukathas. Sydney: Centre for Independent Studies.

——. 1997a. "Liberalism, Multiculturalism, and Oppression." In *Political Theory: Tradition and Diversity*, ed. Andrew Vincent. Cambridge: Cambridge University Press.

——. 1997b. "Multiculturalism as Fairness." *Journal of Political Philosophy* 5, no. 4: 406–27.

——. 1997c. "Cultural Toleration." In *Nomos 39, Ethnicity and Group Rights*, ed. Ian Shapiro and Will Kymlicka. New York: New York University Press.

——. 1999. "Tolerating the Intolerable." *Papers on Parliament* 33 (March): 67–82.

——. 2001. "Is Feminism Bad for Multiculturalism?" *Public Affairs Quarterly* 15, no. 2: 83–98.

——. 2002. "The Life of Brian, or, Now for Something Completely Difference-Blind." In *Multiculturalism Reconsidered,* ed. Paul Kelly. Cambridge: Polity Press.

——. 2003. *The Liberal Archipelago: A Theory of Diversity and Freedom.* Oxford: Clarendon Press.

Kumar, Krishan. 2003. *The Making of the English National Identity.* Cambridge: Cambridge University Press.

Kymlicka, Will. 1989. *Liberalism, Community, and Culture.* Oxford: Clarendon Press.

——. 1995. *Multicultural Citizenship: A Liberal Theory of Minority Rights.* Oxford: Clarendon Press.

——. 1998. *Finding Our Way: Rethinking Ethnocultural Relations in Canada.* Toronto and New York: Oxford University Press.

——. 2001a. *Politics in the Vernacular: Nationalism, Multiculturalism, and Citizenship.* Oxford: Oxford University Press.

——. 2001b. "Western Political Theory and Ethnic Relations in Eastern Europe." In *Can Liberal Pluralism Be Exported?* ed. Will Kymlicka and Magda Opalski. Oxford: Oxford University Press.

——. 2002. *Contemporary Political Philosophy: An Introduction.* 2nd ed. Oxford: Oxford University Press.

——. 2005. "Liberal Multiculturalism: Western Models, Global Trends, and Asian Debates." In *Multiculturalism in Asia,* ed. Will Kymlicka and Baogang He. Oxford: Oxford University Press.

Kymlicka, Will, and Baogang He, eds. 2005. *Multiculturalism in Asia.* Oxford: Oxford University Press.

Kymlicka, Will, and Wayne Norman. 1994. "Return of the Citizen: A Survey of Recent Work on Citizenship Theory." *Ethics* 104: 352–81.

Kymlicka, Will, and Magda Opalski, eds. 2001. *Can Liberal Pluralism be Exported?* Oxford: Oxford University Press.

Laden, Anthony S. 2001. *Reasonably Radical: Deliberative Democracy and the Politics of Identity.* Ithaca, N.Y.: Cornell University Press.

Lake, Marilyn. 1986. "The Politics of Respectability: Identifying the Masculinist Context." *Historical Studies* 22, no. 86: 116–31.

——. 1997. "Stirring Tales: Australian Feminism, 1900–1940." In *The Politics of Identity in Australia,* ed. Geoffrey Stokes. Cambridge: Cambridge University Press.

Langton, Marcia, Maureen Tehan, Lisa Palmer, and Kathryn Shain. 2004. *Honour Among Nations? Treaties and Agreements with Indigenous People.* Melbourne: Melbourne University Publishing.

Larmore, Charles. 1996. *The Morals of Modernity.* Cambridge: Cambridge University Press.

——. 2003. "Public Reason." In *The Cambridge Companion to Rawls,* ed. Samuel Freeman. Cambridge: Cambridge University Press.

Laster, K., and V. Taylor. 1995. "Law of Our Multicultural Society? No Worries." In *Tomorrow's Law,* ed. Hugh Selby. Sydney: Federation Press.

Latham, Mark. 2004. "A Big Country: Australia's National Identity." ALP press release, 20 April.

Lattas, Andrew. 2008. "The Etiquette of Nationalism: The Cronulla Riot and the Politics of Greekness." In *Lines in the Sand: The Cronulla Riots and the Limits of Australian Multiculturalism,* ed. Greg Noble. Sydney: Institute of Criminology.

Lefort, Claude. 1988. *Democracy and Political Theory.* Cambridge: Polity Press.

Leigh, Andrew. 2006. "Trust, Inequality and Ethnic Hetrogeneity." The economic record 82, no. 258: 268–80.

Leiter, Brian. 2002. *Nietzsche on Morality.* London: Routledge.

Levey, Geoffrey Brahm. 1997. "Equality, Autonomy, and Cultural Rights." *Political Theory* 25, no. 2: 215–48.

———. 2001a. "The Political Theories of Australian Multiculturalism." *University of New South Wales Law Journal* 24, no. 3: 869–81.

———. 2001b. "Liberal Nationalism and Cultural Rights." *Political Studies* 49, no. 4: 670–91.

———. 2005. "National-Cultural Autonomy and Liberal Nationalism." In *National-Cultural Autonomy and Its Contemporary Critics,* ed. Ephraim Nimni. Routledge: London.

———. 2006a. "Symbolic Recognition, Multicultural Citizens, and Acknowledgement: Negotiating the Christmas Wars." *Australian Journal of Political Science* 40, no. 4: 355–70.

———. 2006b. "Judaism and the Obligation to Die for the State." In *Law, Politics, and Morality in Judaism,* ed. Michael Walzer. Princeton, N.J.: Princeton University Press.

———. 2007a. "Cultural Diversity and its Recognition in Public Universities: Fairness, Utility, and Inclusion." *Political Crossroads* 15, no. 2.

———. 2007b. "Multiculturalism *is* Integration." *Australian Mosaic* 16 (January): 28-30.

———. 2007c. "The Antidote of Multiculturalism." *Griffith Review* 15 (Summer): 199–208.

———. 2008. "Multiculturalism and Terror." In *Multiculturalism and Terrorism,* ed. Raimond Gaita and Robert Manne. Melbourne: Text Publishing.

Levey, Geoffrey Brahm, and Tariq Modood. 2008. "Liberal Democracy, Multicultural Citizenship, and the Danish Cartoon Affair." In *Secularism, Religion, and Multicultural Citizenship,* ed. Geoffrey Brahm Levey and Tariq Modood. Cambridge: Cambridge University Press.

Levey, Geoffrey Brahm, and A. Dirk Moses. 2008. "'The Muslims are our misfortune!'" In *Lines in the Sand: The Cronulla Riots and the Limits of Australian Multiculturalism,* ed. Greg Noble. Sydney: Institute of Criminology.

Levy, Jacob T. 1997. "Classifying Cultural Rights." In *Nomos 39, Ethnicity and Group Rights,* ed. Ian Shapiro and Will Kymlicka. New York: New York University Press.

———. 2000a. *The Multiculturalism of Fear.* Oxford: Oxford University Press.

———. 2000b. "Three Modes of Incorporating Indigenous Law." In *Citizenship in Diverse Societies,* ed. Will Kymlicka and Wayne Norman. Oxford: Oxford University Press.

Lijphart, Arend. 1999. *Patterns of Democracy: Government Formation and Performance in 36 Countries.* New Haven, Conn.: Yale University Press.

Lind, Michael. 1995. *The Next American Nation.* New York: Free Press.

———. 2000. "National Good." *Prospect Magazine* 56 (October). www.prospect-magazine .co.uk/highlights/essay_oct/index.html.

List, Christian, and Philip Pettit. 2002. "The Aggregation of Sets of Judgments: An Impossibility Result." *Economics and Philosophy* 18: 89–110.

———. 2004. "Aggregating Sets of Judgments: Two Impossibility Results Compared." *Synthese* 140: 207–35.

Lopez, Mark. 2000. *The Origins of Multiculturalism in Australian Politics, 1945–75*. Melbourne: Melbourne University Press.

Lukes, Steven. 1991. *Moral Conflict and Politics*. Oxford: Clarendon Press.

MacIntyre, Alasdair. 1984. *After Virtue*. 2nd ed. Notre Dame, IN: University of Notre Dame Press.

MacKenzie, Iain. 1999. "Berlin's Defence of Value-pluralism: Clarifications and Criticisms." *Contemporary Politics* 5, no. 4: 325–37.

MacKinnon, Catharine A. 1987. *Feminism Unmodified: Discourse on Life and Law*. Cambridge, Mass.: Harvard University Press.

Mahmood, Saba. 2005. *Politics of Piety: The Islamic Revival and the Feminist Subject*. Princeton, N.J.: Princeton University Press.

Malouf, David. 1994. "Identity as Lived Experience: Uniquely Australian." *The Sydney Papers* (Spring): 147–56.

Mamdani, Mahmood. 1996. *Citizen and Subject: Contemporary Africa and the Legacy of Late Colonialism*. Princeton, N.J.: Princeton University Press.

———. 2001. *When Victims Become Killers: Colonialism, Nativism, and the Genocide in Rwanda*. Princeton, N.J.: Princeton University Press

Mann, Michael. 1993. *The Sources of Social Power*. Vol. 2. Cambridge: Cambridge University Press.

Manne, Robert. 2005. *Left, Right, Left: Political Essays, 1977–2005*. Melbourne: Black Inc.

Margalit, Avishai. 1996. *The Decent Society*. Cambridge, Mass.: Harvard University Press.

Markell, Patchen. 2003. *Bound by Recognition*. Princeton, N.J.: Princeton University Press.

Markus, Andrew. 2011. "Attitudes to Multiculturalism and Cultural Diversity." In *Multiculturalism and Integration: A Harmonious Relationship* ed. James Jupp and Michael Clyne. Canberra: ANU E Press.

Markus, Maria R. 1998. "Cultural Pluralism and the Subversion of the 'Taken-for-Granted' World." In *Blurred Boundaries: Migration, Ethnicity, Citizenship*, ed. Rainer Baubök and John Rundel. Aldershot, U.K.: Ashgate.

Marshall, T. H. 1950. *Citizenship and Social Class and Other Essays*. Cambridge: Cambridge University Press.

Martin, Ben L. 1991. "From Negro to Black to African American: The Power of Names and Naming." *Political Science Quarterly* 106, no. 1: 83–107.

Martin, Jean. 1981. *The Ethnic Dimension: Papers on Ethnicity and Pluralism by Jean Martin*, ed. S. Encel. Sydney: George Allen & Unwin.

Martiniello, Marco. 1995. *Migration, Citizenship, and Ethno-national Identities in the European Union.* Aldershot, U.K.: Avebury Press.

———, ed. 1998. *Multicultural Policies and the State: A Comparison of Two European Societies.* Utrecht: European Research Centre on Migration and Ethnic Relations.

Mason, Andrew. 1999. "Political Community, Liberal-Nationalism, and the Ethics of Assimilation." *Ethics* 109: 261–86.

Mathew, Penelope. 2000. "Conformity or Persecution: China's One Child Policy and Refugee Status." *University of New South Wales Law Journal* 23, no. 3: 103–34.

McAllister, Ian. 1988. "Ethnic Issues and Voting in the 1987 Election." *Politics* 23, no. 2: 219–47.

McCormick, John P. 2001. "Machiavellian Democracy: Controlling Elites with Ferocious Populism." *American Political Science Review* 95, no. 2: 297–313.

McGregor, Russell. 2006. "The Necessity of Britishness: Ethno-cultural Roots of Australian Nationalism." *Nations and Nationalism* 12, no. 3: 493–511.

McLean, Janet. 1999. "Personality and Public Law Doctrine." *University of Toronto Law Journal* 49: 123–49.

Medding, Peter Y. 2004. "Australian Jewish Politics in Comparative Perspective." In *Jews and Australian Politics*, ed. Geoffrey Brahm Levey and Philip Mendes. Brighton, UK: Sussex Academic Press.

Meyer, William J. 1998. "The Politics of Differentiated Citizenship." In *Citizenship After Liberalism*, ed. Karen Slawner and Mark E. Denham. New York: Peter Lang.

Mill, John Stuart. 1972 [1859]. *Utilitarianism, On Liberty, and Considerations on Representative Government*, ed. H. B. Acton. London: J. M. Dent & Sons.

Miller, David. 1995. *On Nationality.* Oxford: Clarendon Press.

———. 1998. "The Left, the Nation-State, and European Citizenship." *Dissent* (Summer): 47–51.

———. 2000. *Citizenship and National Identity.* Cambridge: Polity Press.

Miller, Seumas. 2001. *Social Action: A Teleological Account.* Cambridge: Cambridge University Press.

Modood, Tariq. 2000. "Anti-Essentialism, Multiculturalism, and the 'Recognition' of Religious Groups." In *Citizenship in Diverse Societies*, ed. Will Kymlicka and Wayne Norman. Oxford: Oxford University Press.

———. 2007. *Multiculturalism: A Civic Idea.* Oxford: Polity.

Modood, Tariq, Anna Triandafyllidou, and Richard Zapata-Barrero. 2006. "European Approaches to Multicultural Citizenship: Muslims, Secularism and Beyond." In *Multiculturalism, Muslims and Citizenship: A European Approach*, ed. Tariq Modood, Anna Triandafyllidou and Richard Zapata-Barrero. London: Routledge.

Momigliano, Arnaldo. 1976. "On the Pioneer Trail." *New York Review of Books*, 11 November.

Mulcock, Jane. 2002. *Searching for Our Indigenous Selves: Belonging and Spirituality in Anglo-Celtic Australia.* Ph.D. Thesis, University of Western Australia.

Nagel, Thomas. 1991. *Mortal Questions.* Cambridge: Canto.

National Commission for Minorities (India). N.d. "Minority Population." http://ncm.nic.in/ [accessed 13 November 2005].

National Multicultural Advisory Council (NMAC). 1997. *Multicultural Australia: The Way Forward.* Canberra: AGPS.

———. 1999. *Australian Multiculturalism for a New Century: Towards Inclusiveness.* Canberra: AGPS.

New South Wales, Parliament, Legislative Council, Standing Committee on Social Issues. 1998. *Enhancing Aboriginal Political Representation: Inquiry into Dedicated Seats in the New South Wales Parliament.* Sydney: The Committee.

Nielsen, Kai. 1996–97. "Cultural Nationalism, Neither Ethnic Nor Civic." *Philosophical Forum* 28, nos. 1-2: 42–52.

Nietzsche, Friedrich. 1969. *Thus Spoke Zarathrustra.* Harmondsworth, U.K.: Penguin.

———. 1998. *On the Genealogy of Morality,* ed. M. Clark and A. Swenson. Indianapolis: Hackett.

Nimni, Ephraim. 2005. "Introduction: The National-Cultural Autonomy Model Revisited." In *National-Cultural Autonomy and Its Contemporary Critics,* ed. Ephraim Nimni. Routledge: London.

Nonet, Philippe, and Philip Selznick. 2001. *Law and Society in Transition: Toward Responsive Law.* 2nd ed. New Brunswick, N.J.: Transaction Publishers.

Norman, Wayne, and Will Kymlicka. 2003. "Citizenship." In *Blackwell Companion to Applied Ethics,* ed. R. G. Frey and Christopher Wellman. Oxford: Blackwell.

Novak, Michael. 1993. *The Catholic Ethic and the Spirit of Capitalism.* New York: Free Press.

Nozick, Robert. 1974. *Anarchy, State, and Utopia.* Oxford: Blackwell.

Nussbaum, Martha C. 1986. *The Fragility of Goodness: Luck and Ethics in Greek Tragedy and Philosophy.* Cambridge: Cambridge University Press.

———. 1992. *Love's Knowledge: Essays on Philosophy and Literature.* Oxford: Oxford University Press.

———. 2000a. "The Costs of Tragedy: Some Moral Limits of Cost-Benefit Analysis." *Journal of Legal Studies* 29: 1005–36.

———. 2000b. *Women and Human Development: The Capabilities Approach.* Cambridge: Cambridge University Press.

O'Brien, Connor Cruise. 1984. "What Rights Should Minorities Have?" In *Minorities: A Question of Human Rights?* ed. Ben Whitaker. Oxford and New York: Pergamon Press.

Office of Multicultural Affairs (OMA). 1989. *National Agenda for a Multicultural Australia.* Canberra: AGPS.

Okin, Susan Moller. 1999. "Is Multiculturalism Bad for Women?" In *Is Multiculturalism Bad for Women? Susan Moller Okin with Respondents,* ed. Joshua Cohen, Matthew Howard, and Martha C. Nussbaum. Princeton, N.J.: Princeton University Press.

———. 2002. "'Mistresses of Their Own Destiny': Group Rights, Gender, and Realistic Rights of Exit." *Ethics* 112, no. 2: 205–30.

O'Neill, Michael, and Dennis Austin, eds. 2000. *Democracy and Cultural Diversity.* Oxford: Oxford University Press.

O'Neill, Onora. 1996. *Towards Justice and Virtue.* Cambridge: Cambridge University Press.

Orgad, Liav. 2010. "Illiberal Liberalism Cultural Restrictions on Migration and Access to Citizenship in Europe," *American Journal of Comparative Law,* 58: 53-106.

Organisation for Economic Co-operation and Development (OECD). 2006. "Population and Migration: Country Statistical Profiles." http://stats.oecd.org/WBOS/Default.aspx?QueryName=245&QueryType=View.

Owen, David. 2002. "Criticism and Captivity: On Genealogy and Critical Theory." *European Journal of Philosophy* 10, no. 2: 216–30.

Palmer, Mick J. 2005. *Inquiry into the Circumstances of the Immigration Detention of Cornelia Rau: A Report.* Canberra: Department of Immigration and Multicultural and Indigenous Affairs.

Parekh, Bhikhu. 1999. "Political Theory and the Multicultural Society." *Radical Philosophy* 95 (May/June): 27–32.

———. 2000. *Rethinking Multiculturalism: Cultural Diversity and Political Theory.* Basingstoke, U.K.: Macmillan.

Parkin, Andrew, and Leonie Hardcastle. 1997. "Immigration and Ethnic Affairs Policy." In *Government, Politics, Power, and Policy in Australia,* ed. Andrew Parkin, John Summers, and Dennis Woodward. 6th ed. Melbourne: Longman.

Partington, Geoffrey. 2000. "'Empowered' but Impoverished: Multiculturalism and Aboriginal Education." *Quadrant* 44: 33–43.

Pauly, Marc, and Martin Van Hees. 2006. "Logical Constraints on Judgment Aggregation." *Journal of Philosophical Logic* 35, no. 6: 569–85.

Pearson, Noel. 2000. *Our Right to Take Responsibility.* Cairns: Noel Pearson & Associates.

———. 2001. "On the Human Right to Misery, Mass Incarceration, and Early Death." Charles Perkins Memorial Address, University of Sydney, 25th October.

Peterson, Nicolas, and Will Sanders, eds. 1998. *Citizenship and Indigenous Australians: Changing Conceptions and Possibilities.* Cambridge: Cambridge University Press.

Pettit, Philip. 1997. *Republicanism: A Theory of Freedom and Government.* Oxford: Oxford University Press.

———. 2000a. "Democracy, Electoral and Contestatory." *Nomos* 42: 105–44.

———. 2000b. "Minority Claims Under Two Conceptions of Democracy." In *Political Theory and the Rights of Indigenous Peoples,* ed. Duncan Ivison, Paul Patton, and Will Sanders. Cambridge: Cambridge University Press.

———. 2001. *A Theory of Freedom: From the Psychology to the Politics of Agency.* Cambridge and New York: Polity Press and Oxford University Press.

———. 2003. "Groups with Minds of Their Own." In *Socializing Metaphysics,* ed. Frederick F. Schmitt. New York: Rowman and Littlefield.

Pettit, Philip, and David Schweikard. 2006. "Joint Action and Group Agency." *Philosophy of the Social Sciences* 36, no. 1: 18–39.

Phillips, Anne. 1995. *The Politics of Presence.* Oxford: Oxford Clarendon Press.

———. 1999. *Which Equalities Matter?* Cambridge: Polity Press.

Pickus, Noah M. J. 1998. "Creating Citizens for the 21st Century." In *Immigration and Citizenship in the 21st Century,* ed. Noah M. J. Pickus. Lanham: Rowman and Littlefield.

Plattner, Mark F. 1997. "Rousseau and the Origins of Nationalism." In *The Legacy of Rousseau,* ed. Clifford Orwin and Nathan Tarcov. Chicago: University of Chicago Press.

Pocock, J. G. A. 1987. *The Ancient Constitution and the Feudal Law: A Study of English Historical Thought in the Seventeenth Century. A Reissue with a Retrospect.* Cambridge: Cambridge University Press.

Pogge, Thomas. 1993. "An Egalitarian Law of Peoples." *Philosophy and Public Affairs* 23: 195–224.

Poole, Ross. 1999. *Nation and Identity.* London: Routledge.

Popper, Karl. R. 1960. *The Poverty of Historicism.* London: Routledge & Kegan Paul.

Post, Robert. 1999. "Between Norms and Choices." In *Is Multiculturalism Bad for Women? Susan Moller Okin with Respondents,* ed. Joshua Cohen, Matthew Howard, and Martha C. Nussbaum. Princeton, N.J.: Princeton University Press.

Povinelli, Elizabeth A. 1999. "Settler Modernity and the Quest for an Indigenous Tradition." *Public Culture* 11, no. 1: 19–48.

——. 2002. *The Cunning of Recognition: Indigenous Alterities and the Making of Australian Multiculturalism.* Chapel Hill, N.C.: Duke University Press.

Price, Charles A. 2001. "The Ethnic Character of the Australian Population." In *The Australian People,* ed. James Jupp. Cambridge: Cambridge University Press.

Pryles, Michael. 1981. *Australian Citizenship Law.* Sydney: Lawbook.

Pye, Lucien W., and Sidney Verba. 1966. *Political Culture and Political Development.* Princeton, N.J.: Princeton University Press.

Queensland, Parliament, Legislative Assembly, Legal, Constitutional and Administrative Review Committee. 2003. *Hands on Parliament: A Parliamentary Committee Inquiry into Aboriginal and Torres Strait Islander Peoples' Participation in Queensland's Democratic Process.* Brisbane: The Committee.

Quinton, Anthony. 1975/76. "Social Objects." *Proceedings of the Aristotelian Society* 75: 1–27.

Racial Discrimination Act 1975 (Cth).

Rawls, John. 1971. *A Theory of Justice.* Oxford: Oxford University Press.

——. 1993. *Political Liberalism.* New York: Columbia University Press.

——. 1999. *The Law of Peoples.* Cambridge, Mass.: Harvard University Press.

——. 2001. *Justice as Fairness: A Restatement.* Cambridge, Mass: Harvard University Press.

Raz, Joseph. 1986. *The Morality of Freedom.* Oxford: Clarendon Press.

——. 1994. *Ethics in the Public Domain: Essays in the Morality of Law and Politics.* Oxford: Clarendon Press.

Read, Peter. 2000. *Belonging: Australians, Place, and Aboriginal Ownership.* Cambridge: Cambridge University Press.

Reich, Rob. 2002. *Bridging Liberalism and Multiculturalism in American Education.* Chicago: University of Chicago Press.

Report of the International Law Commission to the General Assembly on Multiple Nationality. 1954. ILC at 6 UN Doc. A/CN.4/83.

Reuters. 2011. "Sarkozy joins allies burying multiculturalism," 11 February. www.reuters.com/article/2011/02/11/us-france-sarkozy-multiculturalism-idUSTRE71A4UP20110211 [accessed 10 February 2012].

Richardson, Henry S. 2000. "The Stupidity of Cost-Benefit Analysis." *Journal of Legal Studies* 29: 971–1003.

Rickard, John. 1996. *Australia: A Cultural History.* 2nd ed. London: Longman.

Rimmer, Stephen J. 1988. *Fiscal Anarchy: The Public Funding of Multiculturalism.* Perth: Australian Institute for Public Policy.

——. 1991. *The Cost of Multiculturalism.* Bedford Park, Australia: Flinders Press.

Robb, Andrew. 2006a. "The Importance of a Shared National Identity." Address to the Transformations Conference, Australian National University, Canberra, 27 November.

——. 2006b. "Australia to Introduce Citizenship Test." Media Release, 11 December.

Roberts, J. M. 1996. *The Penguin History of Europe.* Harmondsworth, U.K.: Penguin.

Rothwell, Nicolas. 2001. "Wholly holier than thou." *Weekend Australian,* 14 July.

Rousseau, Jean-Jacques. 1973. *The Social Contract and Discourses.* London: J. M. Dent & Sons.

Rovane, Carol A. 1997. *The Bounds of Agency: An Essay in Revisionary Metaphysics.* Princeton, N.J.: Princeton University Press.

Rowse, Tim. 2002. *Indigenous Futures: Choice and Development for Aboriginal and Islander Australia.* Sydney: UNSW Press.

Rubenfeld, Jed. 2001. *Freedom and Time: A Theory of Constitutional Self-Government.* New Haven, Conn.: Yale University Press.

Rubenstein, Kim. 1995. "Citizenship in Australia: Unscrambling Its Meaning." *Melbourne University Law Review* 20: 503–27.

——. 2002. *Australian Citizenship Law in Context.* Sydney: Lawbook.

——. 2003. "Globalisation and Citizenship and Nationality." In *Jurisprudence for an Interconnected Globe,* ed. Catherine Dauvergne. Aldershot, U.K.: Ashgate.

——. 2006. "Shifting Membership: Rethinking Nationality in International Humanitarian Law." In *The Challenge of Conflict: International Law Responds,* ed. Ustinia Dolgopol and Judith Gardam. Leiden: Martinus Nijhoff.

Rubio-Marin, R. 2000. *Immigration as a Democratic Challenge: Citizenship and Inclusion in Germany and the United States.* Cambridge: Cambridge University Press.

Runciman, David. 1997. *Pluralism and the Personality of the State.* Cambridge: Cambridge University Press.

Sandall, Roger. 2001. *The Culture Cult: Designer Tribalism and Other Essays.* Boulder, Co.: Westview.

Sandel, Michael. 1982. *Liberalism and the Limits of Justice.* Cambridge: Cambridge University Press.

——. 1996. *Democracy's Discontent: America in Search of a Public Philosophy.* Cambridge, Mass.: Harvard University Press.

Scholte, Jan Aart. 2002. "Civil Society and Democracy in Global Governance." *Global Governance* 8, no. 3: 281–304.

Schuck, Peter H. 2003. *Diversity in America: Keeping Government at a Safe Distance.* Cambridge, Mass.: Harvard University Press.

Scott, Evelyn. 2000. "The Importance of Reconciliation for Multiculturalism." Speech at the Multicultural Extravaganza Dinner, Logan Diggers Club, 7 October. www.austlii.edu.au/au/other/IndigLRes/car/2000/0710.html.

Shachar, Ayelet. 1998. "Group Identity and Women's Rights in Family Law: The Perils of Multicultural Accommodation." *Journal of Political Philosophy* 6, no. 3: 285–305.

———. 2001. *Multicultural Jurisdictions: Cultural Differences and Women's Rights.* Cambridge: Cambridge University Press.

Shafer, Byron E., ed. 1991. *Is America Different? A New Look at American Exceptionalism.* Oxford: Clarendon Press.

Shapiro, Ian. 2001. "Enough of Deliberation: Politics Is About Interests and Power." In *Deliberative Politics: Essays on Democracy and Disagreement,* ed. Stephen Macedo. Oxford: Oxford University Press.

Shergold, Peter. 1994/95. "A National Multicultural Agenda for All Australians." In *Making Multicultural Australia.* www.multiculturalaustralia.edu.au/history/timeline.php?myOption=Transforming+Multiculturalism&currentRecord=7 [accessed 5 June 2006].

Shumpeter, Joseph A. 1984. *Capitalism, Socialism, and Democracy.* New York: Harper Torchbooks.

Shweder, Richard, Martha Minow, and Hazel Rose Markus, eds. 2002. *Engaging Cultural Differences: The Multicultural Challenge in Liberal Democracies.* New York: Russell Sage Foundation.

Simms, Marian, and John Warhurst. 2000. *Howard's Agenda: The 1998 Australian Election.* Brisbane: University of Queensland Press.

Skinner, Quentin. 1989. "The State." In *Political Innovation and Conceptual Change,* ed. Terence Ball, James Farr, and Russell L. Hansen. Cambridge: Cambridge University Press.

———. 2002. *Visions of Politics. Vol. 2, Renaissance Virtues.* Cambridge: Cambridge University Press.

Slawner, Karen. 1998. *"Uncivil Society: Liberalism, Hermeneutics, and 'Good Citizenship'."* In *Citizenship After Liberalism,* ed. Karen Slawner and Mark Denham. New York: Peter Lang.

Smith, Anthony D. 1986. *The Ethnic Origin of Nations.* Oxford: Blackwell.

———. 1991. *National Identity.* London: Penguin.

Smith, Rogers M. 1997. *Civic Ideals: Conflicting Visions of Citizenship in U.S. History.* New Haven, Conn.: Yale University Press.

Spiro, Peter J. 1997. "Dual Nationality and the Meaning of Citizenship." *Emory Law Journal* 46, no. 4: 1411–85.

Standing Committee on Legal and Constitutional Affairs. 1997. *Aspects of Section 44 of the Australian Constitution.* Canberra: AGPS.

Stocker, Michael. 1990. *Plural and Conflicting Values.* Oxford: Clarendon Press.

Stoetzler, Marcel, and Nira Yuval-Davis. 2002. "Standpoint Theory, Situated Knowledge, and the Situated Imagination." *Feminist Theory* 3, no. 3: 315–34.

Stokes, Geoffrey, ed. 1997. *The Politics of Identity in Australia.* Melbourne: Cambridge University Press.

Stratton, Jon. 1998. *Race Daze: Australia in Identity Crisis.* Sydney: Pluto Press.

Sunder, Madhavi. 2001. "Cultural Dissent." *Stanford Law Review* 54 (December): 495–567.

Sunstein, Cass. 2001. *Designing Democracy: What Constitutions Do.* Oxford: Oxford University Press.

Swaine, Lucas. 2006. *The Liberal Conscience: Politics and Principle in a World of Religious Pluralism.* New York: Columbia University Press.

Sydney Morning Herald. 2005a. "Voters disagree with PM on racism." 20 December.

———. 2005b. "Push to ban headscarves divisive: Dems." 28 August.

———. 2006. "A glue that keeps Australian society together." 16 December.

Tamir, Yael. 1993. *Liberal Nationalism.* Princeton, N.J.: Princeton University Press.

Tate, John. 2009. "John Howard's 'Nation' and Citizenship Test: Multiculturalism, Citizenship, and Identity," *Australian journal of Politics and History,* 55,1: 97-120.

Tavan, Gwenda. 2007. "John Howard's Multicultural Paradox," paper presented to *John Howard's Decade* conference, School of Social Sciences, Australian National University, 3-4 March.

Taylor, Charles. 1977. "What Is Human Agency?" In *The Self: Psychological and Philosophical Issues,* ed. Theodore Mischel. London: Blackwell.

———. 1989. "Cross Purposes: The Liberal–Communitarian Debate." In *Liberalism and the Moral Life,* ed. Nancy L. Rosenblum. Cambridge, Mass. Harvard University Press.

———. 1993. *Reconciling the Solitudes: Essays on Canadian Federalism and Nationalism,* ed. Guy Laforest. Montreal: McGill-Queen's University Press.

———. 1994. "The Politics of Recognition." In *Multiculturalism: Examining the Politics of Recognition,* ed. Amy Gutmann. Princeton, N.J.: Princeton University Press.

———. 2004. *Modern Social Imaginaries.* Durham, N.C.: Duke University Press.

The Age. 2011. "Bolt loses high-profile race case," 28 September.

The Australian. 2011. "Canberra cool on state push for cultural law." 19 November.

The Australian. 2012. "Hygiene lessons will help migrants integrate: Coalition," 10 January.

Theophanous, Andrew. 1995. *Understanding Multiculturalism and Australian Identity.* Melbourne: Elikia Books.

Thomas, J. 1993. "Citizenship and Historical Sensibility." *Australian Historical Studies* 25: 383–93.

Toohey, Paul. 2005. "The Age of Contempt." *The Bulletin,* 17 August.

Trigger, David. 2006. "Place, Belonging, and Nativeness in Australia." Unpublished paper.

Tully, James. 1995. *Strange Multiplicity: Constitutionalism in an Age of Diversity.* Cambridge: Cambridge University Press.

———. 1999. "To Think and Act Differently." In *Foucault Contra Habermas,* ed. Samantha Ashenden and David Owen. London: Sage.

———. 2000a. "Struggles Over Recognition and Distribution." *Constellations* 7, no. 4: 469–82.

———. 2000b. "The Challenges of Reimagining Citizenship and Belonging in Multicultural and Multinational Societies." In *The Demands of Citizenship,* eds. Catriona Mackinnon and Iain Hampsher-Monk. London: Continuum.

———. 2001. "Introduction." In *Multinational Democracies,* ed. Alain G. Gagnon and James Tully. Cambridge: Cambridge University Press.

———. 2003. "Identity Politics." In *The Cambridge History of Twentieth-Century Political Thought,* ed. Terrence Ball and Richard Bellamy. Cambridge: Cambridge University Press.

———. 2005. "Exclusion and Assimilation: Two Forms of Domination in Relation to Freedom." In *Political Exclusion and Domination,* ed. Stephen Macedo and Melissa S. Williams. New York: New York University Press.

Tuomela, Raimo. 1995. *The Importance of Us: A Philosophical Study of Basic Social Notions.* Stanford, Calif.: Stanford University Press.

United States v. Rossler, 144 F.2d 463, 465 (2d Cir. 1944).

Velleman, J. David. 2000. *The Possibility of Practical Reason.* Oxford: Oxford University Press.

Verhoeven, W.M. 1996. "How Hyphenated Can You Get?" *Mosaic* 29, no. 3: 97–116.

Victorian Office of Multicultural Affairs (VOMA). 2004. *Multicultural Victoria Act: Many Cultures–One Future, A Discussion Paper.* Melbourne: VOMA.

Viroli, Maurizio. 1995. *For Love of Country: An Essay on Patriotism and Nationalism.* Oxford: Oxford University Press.

Vrachnas, John, Kim Boyd, Mirko Bagaric, and Penny Dimopoulos. 2005. *Migration and Refugee Law: Principles and Practice in Australia.* Melbourne: Cambridge University Press.

Waldron, Jeremy. 1995. "Minority Cultures and the Cosmopolitan Alternative." In *The Rights of Minority Cultures,* ed. Will Kymlicka. Oxford: Oxford University Press.

———. 1999a. *Law and Disagreement.* New York: Cambridge University Press.

———. 1999b. *The Dignity of Legislation.* Cambridge: Cambridge University Press.

Wallace, R. Jay. 2003. *Responsibility and the Moral Sentiments.* Cambridge, Mass.: Harvard University Press.

Walters, William. 2004. "Secure Borders, Safe Haven, Domopolitics." *Citizenship Studies* 8, no. 3: 237–60.

Walzer, Michael. 1983. *Spheres of Justice: A Defense of Pluralism and Equality.* New York: Basic Books.

———. 1984. "Liberalism and the Art of Separation." *Political Theory* 12, no. 3: 315–33.

———. 1992a. "Comment." In *Multiculturalism and "The Politics of Recognition": An Essay by Charles Taylor,* ed. Amy Gutmann. Princeton, N.J.: Princeton University Press.

———. 1992b. *What It Means to Be an American: Essays on the American Experience*. New York: Marsilio.

———. 2001. "Nation-States and Immigrant Societies." In *Can Liberal Pluralism Be Exported?* ed. Will Kymlicka and Magda Opalski. Oxford: Oxford University Press.

———. 2004. *Politics and Passion: Toward a More Egalitarian Liberalism*. New Haven, Conn.: Yale University Press.

Ward, Russel. 1958. *The Australian Legend*. Melbourne: Oxford University Press.

The Weekend Australian. 2004. "Latham lifted my ideas, says academic." 24–25 April.

Weil, Patrick. 2001. "Access to Citizenship: A Comparison of Twenty-five Nationality Laws." In *Citizenship Today: Global Perspectives and Practices,* ed. T. Alexander Aleinikoff and Douglas Klusmeyer. Washington, D.C.: Carnegie Endowment for International Peace.

Wentworth, William Charles. 1853. "Debate on the Second Reading." *Constitution Bill: The Speeches in the Legislative Council of New South Wales, on the Second Reading of the Bill for Framing a New Constitution for the Colony,* ed. Edward Kennedy Silvester. Sydney: Thomas Daniel.

White, Stuart. 2000. "Should Talent Be Taxed?" In *The Demands of Citizenship,* ed. Catriona Mackinnon and Iain Hampsher-Monk. London: Continuum.

Whitfield, Stephen J. 1998. "Introduction to the Transaction Edition." In Horace Kallen, *Culture and Democracy in the United States*. New Brunswick, N.J.: Transaction Books.

Wiebe, Robert H. 1975. *The Segmented Society: An Introduction to the Meaning of America*. New York: Oxford University Press.

Williams, Bernard. 1978. "Introduction" to Isaiah Berlin, *Concepts and Categories: Philosophical Essays*. London: Hogarth.

———. 2002. *Truth and Truthfulness: An Essay in Genealogy*. Princeton, N.J.: Princeton University Press.

———. 2005. *In the Beginning Was the Deed: Realism and Moralism in Political Argument*. Princeton, N.J.: Princeton University Press.

Windschuttle, Keith. 2002. *The Fabrication of Aboriginal History*. Sydney: Macleay Press.

———. 2004. *The White Australia Policy*. Sydney: Macleay Press.

Wingo, Ajume. 2003. *Veil Politics in Liberal Democratic States*. Cambridge: Cambridge University Press.

Wishart, David A. 1986. "Allegiance and Citizenship as Concepts in Constitutional Law." *Melbourne University Law Review* 15: 662–707.

Wohlan, Catherine. 2005. "Aboriginal Women's Interests in Customary Law Recognition." Law Reform Commission of Western Australia, Project No. 94, Background Paper No. 13.

Wood, Alan. 2007. "Multiculturalism becomes poison for social capital." *The Australian,* 26 September.

Young, Iris Marion. 1990. *Justice and the Politics of Difference*. Princeton, N.J.: Princeton University Press.

———. 1996. "Communication and the Other: Beyond Deliberative Democracy." In *Democracy and Difference: Contesting the Boundaries of the Political,* ed. Seyla Benhabib. Princeton, N.J.: Princeton University Press.

———. 2000. *Inclusion and Democracy.* Oxford: Oxford University Press.

Zamoyski, Adam. 1999. *Holy Madness: Romantics, Patriots, and Revolutionaries, 1776–1871.* London: Wiedenfeld and Nicolson.

Zangwill, Israel. 1975 [1909]. *The Melting-Pot: Drama in Four Acts.* New York: Arno Press.

Zappalà, Gianni. 1998. "The Influence of the Ethnic Composition of Australian Federal Electorates on the Parliamentary Responsiveness of MPs to Their Ethnic Sub-constitutencies." *Australian Journal of Political Science* 33, no. 2: 187–209.

Zappalà, Gianni, and Stephen Castles. 2000. "Citizenship and Immigration in Australia." In *From Migrants to Citizens: Membership in a Changing World,* ed. T. Alexander Aleinikoff and Douglas Klusmeyer. Washington, D.C.: Carnegie Endowment for International Peace.

Zubrzycki, Jerzy. 1995. "The Evolution of the Policy of Multiculturalism in Australia, 1968–1995." Paper presented to the 1995 Global Diversity Conference, Sydney.

———. 1996. "Cynics Woo the Ethnic Vote." *The Australian,* 15 October.

Index

Index note: page references with an *f* indicate a figure on the designated page.

Abbott, Tony, 271
Aboriginal and Torres Strait Islander Commission (ATSIC), 11, 60, 61, 169n18, 228
Aboriginal and Torres Strait Islander peoples, 4
Aboriginal populations
  arranged marriage practices, 11, 152–60, 162, 164–65, 166, 260
  assimilation of, 15, 32, 43n4, 95
  breakdown of traditional communities and law, 163–67
  customary law, 8, 21, 134, 156, 163–67
  land rights of, 60, 95, 131
  political and legal recognition of, 3–4, 7–8, 123–24, 210, 232
  self-government, 10, 21, 134
affirmative multiculturalism, 9
Afghanistan, 3, 67
Albrechtsen, Janet, 270
Aleinikoff, T. Alexander, 174
Al Qaida, 127
Amin, Idi, 36
anarcho-multiculturalism, 29–35, 35*f*, 36–43

Anderson, Benedict, 81n11, 81n15, 170n22, 239
apartheid, 30, 34, 35*f*, 36
Applicant A, case of, 197, 198, 201
Applicant S v *Minister,* case of, 197
Arendt, Hannah, 108
Argonauts Ship, 123
Aristotle, 46
arranged marriages, 11, 152–60, 162, 164–65, 166, 250
Asian immigrant populations, 31, 43n3, 256, 274n1
assimilation
  Australian immigration policy of, 5, 79, 80, 213–14, 234, 237, 247–48, 265
  return of, 18–19
assimilationism, 5, 11, 30, 32–33, 35*f*, 36, 43n4, 60, 268
Attwood, Bain, 90
Austin, John, 108
Australia
  Asian immigrant populations in, 31, 43n3, 256, 274n1
  citizenship law, 4, 25n3, 171–87
  core values, 19, 180–81, 274
  crisis of multiculturalism, 242–52
  dominant Anglo-Australian culture, 265, 266, 267, 273, 276n16
  ethnic uniformity, 227

www.ingramcontent.com/pod-product-compliance
Lightning Source LLC
Chambersburg PA
CBHW060025030426
42334CB00019B/2188